D1319650

That unique character—
the G. I.

"It is about time someone devoted an entire, big, three-dimensional book to this complex and purely American character. . . .

"Anecdotes of cowardice and courage are interspersed with those celebrating the everlasting ingenuity of G.I.'s . . . And then there are unforgettable ones of pure terror—of death by flame thrower or phosphorous grenade or tank tread.

"Ex-G.I.'s as well as civilians who lived through those endless days will find many rewarding, nostalgic moments in its pages."

The New York Times

THE
1941–1945
GI
WAR

**Ralph G.
Martin**

AN AVON BOOK

AVON BOOKS
A division of
The Hearst Corporation
959 Eighth Avenue
New York, New York 10019

First Avon Printing, December, 1968

Cover design by Dick Smith

AVON TRADEMARK REG. U.S. PAT. OFF. AND
FOREIGN COUNTRIES, REGISTERED TRADEMARK—
MARCA REGISTRADA, HECHO EN CHICAGO, U.S.A.

Printed in Canada

Author's Note

The focus of this book is sharp and deep. It concerns itself completely with the American enlisted man in World War II.

GI meant "Government Issue"—shoes, guns, garbage cans, toilet paper. Bill Mauldin rightly felt it was "faintly offensive" to tag the phrase onto the American enlisted man. And yet, in a strange way, the phrase fit. Our government had taken civilians and issued them forth as soldiers. It *was* a GI war.

Most of the material comes from my own experience and reportage as a combat correspondent for *The Stars and Stripes* and *Yank, The Army Weekly*. For the rest, I relied on extensive interviews, combat reports, diaries, letters and personal histories. Among these were some excerpts from essays—later compiled in *The Purple Testament*—by a group of disabled veterans in an English class at American University, taught by a remarkable teacher named Dr. Don Wolfe. All of the material in the Epilogue was based on a year's travel throughout the country shortly after the war.

This book deliberately does not mention units by name or number. Nor does it pretend to deal with every battle of every campaign, or every branch of every service. Nor does it involve itself with overall strategy, except as a kind of counterpoint to the main theme.

The reach, however, is for the whole war—not just the combat men, who were few, but the men in the rear, who were many; not just the war of jungle and mud and mountains, but the war of sea and air; not just the war of quiet courage and warm women and cold beer, but the war of loud fear and stinking misery and unutterable loneliness and high excitement and incredible horror.

This is not just a memory book of a war that was.

Acknowledgments

My deep thanks to Shirley Green, who has a greater knowledge of where to find pictures in Washington, D.C., than anybody I know.

My personal appreciation to the reporters on *The Stars and Stripes* and *Yank, The Army Weekly,* as well as other Marine, Navy, Army, Air Corps and Coast Guard combat correspondents, particularly to Sgts. Jack Foisie, Milton Lehman, Andrew Rooney, Ed Cunningham, Debs Myers, Mack Morriss, Robert Leckie, Marion Hargrove, Dave Richardson, Bill Hogan, Ernest Leiser and Bill Brinkley, USNR.

The photographs in this book are the work of unidentified and unknown combat photographers of the Armed Forces, with such exceptions as that magnificent picture of the tired soldier by Sgt. Pat Coffey (frontispiece). The cartoons by Bill Mauldin, George Baker, Dick Wingert and Tom Flannery are more easily identifiable, as is the great drawing by Howard Brodie.

For a vast variety of information and help, my thanks to Col. W. Morris and Sgt. J. Glover, U.S. Marine Information Service; Maj. Joseph McCaffrey, Sgt. Robert Puchicki and S/Sgt. Paul A. Berger of the Photographic Unit of the U.S. Marine Corps; Norwood Biggs and Virginia Lee of the U.S. Navy Still Pictures Section of the National Archives; A. J. Wilde of the News Photo Branch of the Department of the Navy; Robert Higdon, chief of the Chart and Pictorial Unit of the U.S. Air Force, and Ruth Smith; Elizabeth Segedi, Photo Editor of the Public Information Division of the U.S. Coast Guard, and Capt. W. K. Thompson, Jr., and Lt. Comm. A. L. Honsdale; Col. Klein and his staff of the Office of the Chief of Information of the U.S. Army; Mrs. Donna Traxler and Mrs. Annie Seely of the U.S.A.P.A. Reference Branch; Lt. Comm. David Cooney, Lt. F. X. Steele, Ens. Claude E. Erbsen and Anthony Metro of the Magazine and Book Branch of the Office of Navy Information and Lt. Col. C. V. Glines of the Office of the Assistant Secretary of Defense.

My appreciation also to Ruth P. Greene and her excellent staff at the Oyster Bay Public Library. My special thanks to Mrs. Christine Lane, who is always so patient with me, and to Mrs. Annette S. Macedonio, Helen Baldwin and Ellen Coshignano, Gene McGrath, Patricia Stirrat, and Rosemary Burlew. Similar thanks to Romana Javitz and her staff at the New York Public Library Picture Collection. I am also indebted to Joseph Bennett, Sam Feldman, Ruth Hall, Richard Walker, Ed Plaut, John Byrne, Clifford Pastel, and to Mari Walker, who transcribed my tape recordings and typed my manuscript, Isabel Kurzon, who copyedited it, Mr. Lee Fischer, who proofread it, and Peter Carr, who designed it.

For other help, my thanks to my bosses and friends of *The Stars and Stripes* and *Yank, the Army Weekly,* Col. Egbert White and Col. Franklin S. Forsberg; my special gratitude to my GI editors: on *The Stars and Stripes,* Sgts. Bud Hutton in England, Robert Neville in North Africa; Herbert Lyons in Sicily, and David Golding in Italy; and on *Yank,* Merle Miller in France and Germany, and Joe McCarthy in New York.

But, most of all, my warmest appreciation and thanks to my good friend and editor, Harry Sions, who believed in this book from the beginning and helped it grow and change into the book it is.

Contents

The
Western Mediterranean
Theater

0   100   500
MILES

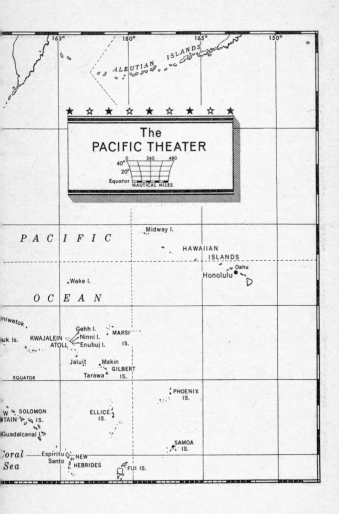

ALEUTIAN ISLANDS

★ ☆ ★ ☆ ★ ☆ ★ ☆ ★

The
PACIFIC THEATER

40° 0 240 480
20°
Equator
NAUTICAL MILES

P A C I F I C

Midway I.

HAWAIIAN
ISLANDS

Oahu
Honolulu

Wake I.

O C E A N

niwetok
uk Is.
KWAJALEIN   Gehh I.   MARSH
ATOLL   Ninni I.
Enubuj I.   IS.

Jaluit   Makin
GILBERT
EQUATOR   Tarawa   IS.

PHOENIX
IS.

W SOLOMON   ELLICE
TAIN IS.   IS.

Guadalcanal I.

SAMOA
IS.

Coral Espíritu   NEW
Sea   Santo   HEBRIDES   FIJI IS.

The
Western European
Theater

0   50   100   300
MILES

HOME FRONT

Greetings. You are hereby ordered for induction into the Armed Forces of the United States and to report . . ."

"The civilian went before the Army doctors," wrote Sgt. Debs Myers, "took off his clothes, feeling silly; jigged, stooped, squatted, wet into a bottle; became a soldier.

"He learned how to sleep in the mud, tie a knot, kill a man.

"He learned the ache of loneliness, the ache of exhaustion, the kinship of misery. He learned that men make the same queasy noises in the morning, feel the same longings at night; that every man is alike and that each man is different."

The typical draftee was slightly taller than his World War I father, but no healthier. Almost one out of every three were rejected for physical, moral or mental reasons. More 1-A men came out of the Northwest, referred to by draft boards as "the health triangle," but 4-F rejections in the South averaged one out of every two. The time would come when local boards so eased their health requirements that the running gag would be that they no longer examined eyes—they just counted them.

Fighting the draft was a publicized mountaineer family in Izard, Ark., who used shotguns and double-bladed axes in a battle with G-men to keep their kin at home. They were just as unsuccessful as the man in Ohio who gave his fourteen-year-old brother six dollars to register in place of him.

19

There was also Edward Sheridan of Los Angeles who listed a Mary Anne Sheridan as his dependent. Investigation revealed that Mary Anne was a horse. "Whether Mary Anne is a daughter or a horse is beside the point," said Sheridan. "The way she eats oats, she certainly is a dependent."

It had to happen. We had 6,443 local draft boards and they were not the most popular places in town. Chief Clerk of Local Draft Board No. 25 in Chicago, Joseph Salak, found himself in the strange position of drafting himself. Then, one day, Salak found himself face to face with another soldier who stared at him, then yelled, "Hey, you're the sonofabitch who drafted me!"

Some of the earliest, most popular advice to draftees came from Pvt. Edward Thomas Marion Lawton Hargrove, ASN 34116620:

"If I were giving advice to the boys who have already been called into the Army and will go away in the next few days, I'd sum it all up in this: Paint the town red for the rest of your civilian week. Pay no attention to the advice that is being poured into your defenseless ears for twenty-four hours a day. Form no idea of what Army life is going to be like. Leave your mind open.

"Two weeks from now, you will be thoroughly disgusted with your new job. You will have been herded from place to place, you will have wandered in nakedness and bewilderment through miles of physical examination, you will look upon privacy and individuality as things you left behind you in a golden civilian society.

"Probably you will have developed a murderous hatred for at least one sergeant and two corporals. You will writhe and fume under what you consider brutality and sadism, and you will wonder how an enlightened nation can permit such atrocity in its Army. Take it easy, brother; take it easy.

"Keep this one beam of radiant hope constantly before you: the first three weeks are the hardest."

Hargrove then told the story of a friend of his, whose brother was inducted in Alabama:

"There was a tough old sergeant who was having an awful time keeping the men quiet. 'Gentlemen,' he would beseech them, 'Quiet, please!' They were quiet during the administration of the Oath, after which they burst forth again.

"The old sergeant, his face beaming sweetly, purred: 'You are now members of the Army of the United States. Now, goddammit, SHUT UP!' "

Not everybody was drafted. Some enlisted. One of them was Leonard Neely of Altus, Okla. When Neely went to draw his clothes, he discovered that his Army pants were only twenty-nine inches long but his legs were thirty-five inches long.

"I told the sergeant either my legs were too long or the pants were too short. He informed me, with the usual amount of sarcasm, that in his nineteen years in the Army, he had seen only two sizes—too large or too small, and that I was unfortunate to get mine too small. My shirt turned out to be too large, so I tried to get my shirt and pants both of the too-small size. But luck wasn't with me. I was so mad I could have shot the sergeant, but as yet, I was a soldier without a gun. My conviction was confirmed when he threw at me an old campaign hat that had seen too many wars. It had been soaked in sugar and water, to restore its original stiffness. But it became too stiff, and every time it was bent, it would break. It, too, was of the too-small size, so I had to use my chin-strap to keep the Oklahoma wind from carrying it off toward the south. I left the quartermaster, my spirits ebbing low, only to cross the drill floor to be informed by the sergeant of the guard that I was to go on guard at ten o'clock. When I told him I didn't have a rifle, he informed me, in no uncertain terms, that I could draw one from the quartermaster.

" 'Instead of going to the quartermaster, I should be going to the doctor to have my brain examined for volunteering for this damn outfit anyway,' I thought. But it was too late. So I went on, and drew my rifle. Cosmoline covered it, and I had only one hour to get it clean before going on guard. I appeared ready for guard at the correct time, the major part of the Cosmoline still on the rifle and the rest of it on my high-water trousers. I was placed on the last relief, and was told to spend my spare time on my rifle. Two o'clock came much too soon. My luck, as it was, still failed me, for I was given the post walking up and down the highway in front of the armory, parading in my too-small pants and hat, and too-large shirt, with white shoes and dirty rifle. To complicate the situation, my parents came out to see me. I was reluctant to see them in this ill-fitting uniform. But I was relieved from guard for fifteen minutes to visit with them. As they started to leave, my father said, 'You look nice in your uniform, son.' It was the first and last time I ever had reason to doubt my father's word. I finished my daylight hours in mortal fear that my girl would come to see me also, but she didn't, and that was the only good luck I had, that first day in the Army."

Everything by the numbers: March in step by the numbers; snap your rifle by the numbers; make your bed by the numbers.

Learn how to clean a latrine, scrub a garbage can until you can see your face in it, break up your cigarette butt, make your bed so tight a coin can bounce on it, keep your barrack windowsill so clean a white glove would wipe it and stay white, force your eyes to stay open during lectures on venereal disease, and never, never, never, never volunteer.

"The day I enlisted, they shipped me out to Fort Jay and practically nobody was there. They gave me my clothes and I didn't have anything to do. Everybody was on the rifle range shooting for record. Anyway, there was a truck going out and the sergeant said that as long as I was there, I might as well go out on the range with the outfit and I might learn something. Well, when I got there, a corporal said I might as well learn how to fire a rifle, so he told me how to spread out on the ground and hold the rifle and squeeze. Of course I never hit anything—they were waving Maggie's red drawers over my target all the time. I guess I was doing everything wrong, and I heard somebody yell and finally this corporal nudges me to turn around. Well, I swung around, but I was still holding the rifle. There was this colonel and a captain and a sergeant and when they saw me with this rifle pointed at them, they all flattened out. Then this corporal came up behind me and grabbed the rifle.

"When he got up, this colonel was absolutely white. He said a lot of unprintable things and then asked me how long I had been in the Army. I told him that this was my first day. Then he chewed out the captain and the captain chewed out the sergeant and the sergeant chewed out the corporal.

"Naturally, I was on KP for a long, long time."

Said Pvt. Orlie Alden Kennerly, Jr., of Roseburg, Tex.:

"At 5:01, I opened my bloodshot eyes and gazed wistfully at the row of bunks around me. They were single-decker bunks, and I could see the length of the barracks. The rows of grim-looking gas masks were forever gazing at me. Then I could smell the sweaty socks that were thrown under the bed next to me. The straight rows of green fatigues and the uniform tan of our shirts as they hung at attention on the wire hangers beside each bunk. I eyed the other men, trying to catch that precious extra moment's sleep, and with a shout of disgust, I thundered out, 'Hit the deck, you goldbricks. If I can't sleep, then you sure as hell can't.' A shower of GI shoes rained down on me, and I heard glorious words and wonderful news: 'Go back to sleep, you fool. This is Sunday.' "

"You wanna go home?" said the sergeant, not too lovingly. "Hell, you never had it so good. You found a home in the Army. You're living a clean, healthy outdoor life and you're even getting paid for it, seventy cents a day."

The sergeant was not exactly the father figure.

This poem by Pvt. Joe Sims is called "The Sergeant":

> *I do not like the sergeant's face,*
> *I do not like his chatter.*
> *And what I think about his brain*
> *Is censorable matter.*

>> *He sits in a tent*
>> *At the end of the street*
>> *And clutters the desk*
>> *With his oversized feet.*

> *I do not like the sergeant's nose.*
> *It would look better broken.*
> *I do not like his tone of voice*
> *When drill-commands are spoken.*

>> *He walks in the rear*
>> *When we're out on march,*
>> *And never relaxes*
>> *To "Route step Harch!"*

23

> *I do not like the sergeant's views*
> *On Army life and such,*
> *But what I think about the sarge*
> *Don't seem to matter much.*

> *He can still pull his rank*
> *When I enter my pleas*
> *And when I find myself stuck*
> *With the chronic KP's.*

The food was also not to everybody's taste. One of the lesser delights for breakfast was creamed beef on toast, more popularly known as SOS—shit on a shingle.

Somebody found this instruction in Training Manual 10-405, *The Army Cook:*

"There is no limit to what can be done to improve a mess by thought and care and seasoning, attractive serving, and inventing new combinations and mixtures of foods. The pleasant task of cooking becomes doubly interesting to the cook who is not satisfied with merely cooking well, but takes advantage of every opportunity of finding new and pleasing ways to prepare food. To him, cooking is not just a task—it is a pleasure.

"Good cooking is recognized the world over as a fine art, and a good cook commands respect. Cooks who perfect themselves in their art are always in demand, and many have acquired wealth and fame."

Everybody thought this was as funny as Bob Hope.

All our early equipment was strictly World War I stuff —campaign hats, leggings, ancient tanks. In fact, we had so few tanks for training that we often had trucks with big cardboard signs on them that said TANK.

Training toughened by the fourth week. Fourteen-mile hikes, where the one-two-three-four cadence count now sounded like Hut-Tup-Thrup-Frup. And there was always at least one guy who hiked all day, then walked six miles to town, danced all night, then walked back to camp and was fresher than any of us the next morning.

We hated him.

"All right now," said the bayonet instructor. "Kill me! Come and get me! Cut my throat!"

We were also taught to gouge eyes, twist arms, kick groins.

"Put the weight of your body on one leg, bend the knee

24

of the other by drawing your heel back and drive your knee as hard as hell into his testicles. . . . Crack at the sides or back of his neck or below his Adam's apple. Get at his kidneys or the base of his spine. Use your boot on him, always kicking sideways, so that you can put more force behind the kick and make it reach farther. Kick at his leg, just below the kneecap. Follow through by scraping down his shin with the edge of your boot, from the knee to the instep. Finish the job by stamping with all your weight on his foot to smash its small and delicate bones."

With the finish of eight weeks of Basic Training, the GI was ready to specialize.

For George Veach at Fort Benning, Ga., it was the paratroopers: "The sergeant called for us to sing. Those who could open their mouths were trying to sing, and the rest of us were too scared and paralyzed to open our mouths.

"We circled the field, and the order to stand up was given. I began to feel nauseous. My hands turned white, and I felt weak all over. The devil himself seemed to have released a monster inside of me. It seemed like weeks, but it was only a matter of minutes before I wanted to heave up my guts. I looked around and saw my green-faced buddy, who was vomiting into the bucket. By the time he had made way for me, it was too late. Up it came, over my legs and the floor.

" 'Stand up and hook up,' was the sergeant's command. 'Stand in the door and prepare to jump.' It seemed years before the final order, 'Jump!' Now the minutes changed to seconds, then to split seconds; then it was my turn. Everything seemed to pass before me. All the paddlings over my dad's knee, my mother giving me money to buy candy, the fights I'd had, and little incidents throughout my boyhood, as I stood for a fraction of a second in the doorway.

"There it was, the tap on my leg which meant I was airborne. My head snapped, and I felt myself being slowed down in the air; then I looked above me, and there was Old Man Fate himself, holding my pure-white silk chute aloft in the air, many feet above the ground. My mind was at rest now. Everything was going to be all right."

"Don't you like to jump?" a new trooper was asked.

"I love to jump," he said. "I just don't like these damned airplanes."

Air Force training had its own hazards. Sgt. William Gontcharuk of New York City had this reaction to an early flight on a bomber crew:

"Suddenly the vibration ceased. The rackety-sounding engines stopped. We were thrown against the side of the fuselage as the ship slipped and lost altitude. Quickly, the pilot trimmed the ship and held it to its planned course. Thoughts raced through my head. Would we make it? Of all the places to be flying over. Swampland! Why did I ever pick the Air Corps? It should have been called the Air Corpse! I saw a sickly paleness shine through the sun-tanned face of the navigator. I knew what he was thinking. My stomach began to gnaw and twist. I tasted something flat and sour. I swallowed again and again. My mind and body concentrated on keeping that fermented hash down. Noticing me, the flight engineer said, 'It ain't that tough, kid.' I prayed not to puke in front of the crew.

"The roar of the right engine sounded more powerful than ever. We were going in fast. The tension grew in ever-leaping bounds. I felt as if I must vomit.

"Suddenly, I heard the shrill shriek of burning rubber, felt the lurch of the ship as we sped down the runway like a bat out of hell. We had made it! Then the harsh, sopranic squeals of brakes being applied. Coming to a stop at the apron, we tumbled out of the escape hatch, pounded each other's backs, and were joyously proud that no one 'broke down'—outwardly."

The hit song on the forty-five million radios in the United States in December 1941 was, "I Don't Want to Set the World on Fire." It might also have been the title of the nation's mood.

British soldiers were fighting the Germans at some place called Tobruk and Nazi troops had pushed into the outskirts of Moscow but most Americans saw the whole thing as somebody else's war. We did have the Committee to Defend America by Aiding the Allies, as well as Bundles for Britain, but we also had the America First Committee, a strong isolationist group with such fervid spokesmen as Charles Lindbergh.

Minnesota was voted the top college football team for the fifth year in a row; heavyweight champion Joe Louis successfully defended his title for the nineteenth time; *Hellzapoppin'* was closing on Broadway after fourteen hundred performances; and New York City was having its worst whooping-cough epidemic in years—309 cases in a single week.

The fourteen-month-old draft had caught some 800,000 men, and the Carolina maneuvers had dramatized the favorite GI phrase, "SNAFU"—Situation Normal, All Fucked Up.

In the Navy, a more sophisticated version of SNAFU was FUBAR—which applied to more critical conditions. FUBAR translated into "Fucked Up Beyond All Recognition."

One of the quoted GI comments on being a citizen-soldier—"I guess I wouldn't mind all this too much, if it wasn't for the Army."

And then, one day, it was December 7, 1941.

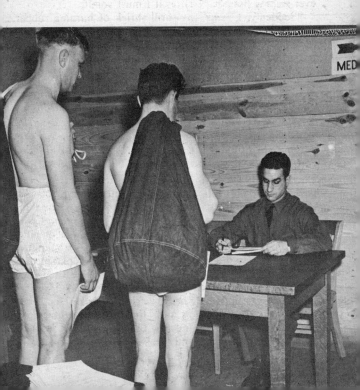

THE BEGINNING

We're the battling bastards of Bataan,
No Mama, no Papa, no Uncle Sam,
No aunts, no uncles, no cousins, no nieces,
No pills, no planes, no artillery pieces,
. . . and nobody gives a damn

—anonymous

Pearl Harbor

We knew war was coming and we almost knew when, but we didn't know where.

War was coming because we refused to pay the Japanese price for peace. Their price: our renewed trade in oil, our consent that they control China and Indochina.

We knew about the war because of MAGIC. MAGIC meant that a small group of anonymous American brains had broken the most secret Japanese code. We now learned the Japanese government had informed its Washington envoys to complete negotiations with the United States by November 29, 1941. "The deadline cannot be changed," they said. "After that, things are automatically going to happen."

Based on this, we sent an alert to all our Pacific bases on November 27: "Japanese future action unpredictable but hostile action possible at any moment."

Not everybody in Japan wanted the war. Even Admiral Isoroku Yamamoto expressed public doubt. "It is a mistake to regard the Americans as luxury-loving and weak. I can tell you Americans are full of the spirit of justice, fight and adventure. . . . Do not forget American industry is much more developed than ours—and unlike us, they have all the oil they want. Japan cannot beat America. Therefore, she should not fight America."

But when the Tojo government convinced Emperor Hirohito that this war must happen, it was Yamamoto who planned the perfection of the Pearl Harbor attack.

And it was perfection. Almost a year-long study of the harbor, with plastic models, silhouettes of all the ships; development of aerial torpedoes fitted with a special stabilizing device for Pearl's shallow water, and a full-time spy attached to the Japanese Embassy in Honolulu.

You could see him almost every day at one of the cafés facing the harbor at Pearl. His name was Takeo Yoshikawa and he wore the uniform of a Japanese naval ensign. Yoshikawa later wrote that the one thing that puzzled him was the people. Here on the Islands were 180,000 citizens of Japanese ancestry and yet all of them were fanatically loyal to the United States. Yoshikawa could not understand it. Their skin was yellow, their origin Japanese, but their hearts and their loyalty were pure American. What kind of thing was this democracy anyway?

Our Intelligence had moved slowly.

Back in 1924, General Billy Mitchell not only predicted war with Japan, in a 325-page secret report, but even foresaw "air operations for the destruction of Pearl Harbor."

And, on January 27, 1941, American Ambassador Joseph Grew in Japan notified Washington of repeated rumors that the Japanese planned "a surprise mass attack on Pearl Harbor." Our Naval Intelligence, however, expected the attack everywhere else: on the Philippines, on the Soviet Union, on Guam, and even on Peru.

Meanwhile, the Japanese were plotting the exact position of each ship parked at Pearl. For final confirmation of all this, another Japanese naval officer, disguised as a merchant-ship steward, called on the Japanese consul in Hawaii, handed him a tiny ball of rice paper on which were written ninety-seven questions. The most important was: "What day will most ships be in Pearl Harbor?"

The answer: "Sunday—Kimmel brings his fleet into Pearl Harbor every weekend."

We had eighty-six ships in the harbor that weekend, set up for disaster. Despite the strong war warning of a week before, eight of the nine battleships of our Pacific fleet were berthed alongside each other. Clustered with them were twenty of our destroyers, nine cruisers, five submarines and a fleet of auxiliary ships. Fortunately, our aircraft carriers had slipped off to sea earlier.

Our ships were all on Condition Three. That meant only one-fourth of our antiaircraft batteries were manned, and a large part of the crews were ashore on leave.

Saturday night at Pearl always found loud crowds of GI's and sailors at the Two Jacks or the Mint or the New Emma Café. Considering, though, how much of the Fleet was in, the night noise seemed comparatively quiet. "Tantalizing Tootsies" was showing at the Princess Theater to the usual packed crowd, the new Navy Recreation Center had its share of bowlers and beer drinkers, but, somehow there seemed to be a minimum of hell-raising. Here's how proper Pearl was that Saturday night: out of 42,952 available soldiers and sailors, the MP's picked up only 25 enlisted men who had passed out.

Cagily, the Japanese kept out any mention of objectives, even in their secret code.

By they did make a strange slip. They ordered their Washington envoys to deliver a message breaking off diplomatic relations—specifically at 1300 hours Sunday, December 7.

The specific time puzzled our Intelligence people. Consulting a time chart, they saw that this Sunday afternoon hour in Washington was nighttime in the Philippines but it was 7:30 Sunday morning in Pearl Harbor. This was slightly more than an hour away.

We sent an urgent wire to Pearl Harbor: "Just what significance the hour set may have we do not know, but be on the alert, accordingly."

That morning our Army communications had some mechanical trouble and the message went off by Western Union. The message arrived several hours after the attack was over. It was delivered by a boy on a bicycle.

The Japanese had prepared well. Six of their newest, largest aircraft carriers, crammed with 423 combat planes, formed the core of their striking force of 32 ships. This included a support force of battleships and cruisers, an advance screen of nine destroyers, and a patrolling flank of submarines, including some new midget subs.

Patrolling the mouth of the harbor at Pearl, the overage decrepit destroyer U.S.S. *Ward* was on the watch. Hours earlier, a minesweeper had reported sighting a sub in the area. Orders were clear: sink all unidentified subs.

Seaman Second Class H. E. Raenbig spotted it first—a curiously small, cigar-shaped silhouette unlike any submarine he had ever seen, but its squat, moss-covered conning tower was two feet out of the water and its periscope was so clear that Raenbig could see the gleam of glass in it.

He passed in word and the young captain came rushing out in a kimono. It was the first day of his first command and he quickly ordered, "Commence firing."

And Raenbig had the sinking feeling, "What if it's ours?"

Our first shot was a near miss, our second hit the conning tower at the waterline. And then we rolled down the ash cans, the depth charges going off at each blast of the ship's whistle, each set to explode at a different stage of the sub's estimated descent. The pattern was perfect. "I think the sub waded directly into our first charge," said Chief Torpedoman W. C. Maskzawitz.

Running through the heads of men all over the *Ward*: "What if it's one of ours . . . what if it's one of ours . . . ?"

But it was a midget Japanese sub, a two-man type, one of five released from their mother subs in advance of the planes. And since there was no hatch between the conning tower and the hull, a hit meant a kill.

The young captain sent off his message: "WE HAVE ATTACKED FIRED UPON AND DROPPED DEPTH CHARGES UPON SUBMARINE OPERATING IN DEFENSIVE AREA."

The time was 0651.

Liaison between Admiral Kimmel and General Short was haphazard at best. Neither knew that the other had not started any long-range air reconnaissance. Furthermore, neither felt the need of any antisubmarine nets and both made the major mistake of expecting their main trouble to come from local sabotage. That's why they parked their planes wing to wing on all Army and Navy airfields, many of the planes with their gas tanks emptied, their guns dismounted for cleaning, and many of the airfield's antiaircraft guns so unready as to need several hours' maintenance before they would work.

Throughout the entire war, the FBI failed to find a single instance of sabotage among any local citizens of Japanese ancestry. Not only that, but these Nisei formed the core of the famous 442nd Regiment in Europe, one of the most decorated outfits in the war.

"Nagata Yama Nabore" (Climb Mount Nagata). Nagata in Formosa was the highest mountain in Japanese territory. This cryptic code meant that Japan was now ready to climb the highest mountain, that the war was on.

Japan had its war song ready. It was called *"Umi Yukaba,"* which meant, "I shall never look back."

> *Across the sea,*
> *Corpses in the water;*
> *Across the mountains,*
> *Corpses heaped upon the field;*
> *I shall die only for the Emperor,*
> *I shall never look back.*

They were just a couple of privates. The two of them, Joseph Lockhard and George Elliott, were part of a six-man team operating an Army mobile radar station at Opana, a remote place thirty miles from Pearl Harbor. They had the early Sunday morning shift from four to seven.

Except for some quick blips of single planes, they had seen nothing on their screen. They were all set to shut up shop, but the breakfast truck was late and so they decided to keep the radar set open a while longer so that Elliott could practice. He was still new at it.

Then they saw it, a big blip, bigger than anything they had ever seen. No, the set wasn't broken—it must be a flight of planes. Quickly they called headquarters. The young duty officer, a lieutenant, listened impatiently to their excited report. Probably some Navy planes off the carriers or some friendly Flying Forts, he said. They again stressed the huge size of the flight, but the officer had the final word: Forget it, he said.

After all, they were just a couple of privates.

For the attacking Japanese, the scene and setting seemed almost perfect—just enough clouds to conceal their coming; the fat battleships parked alongside each other, peacefully unalert; the packed planes on all airfields inviting complete and quick destruction. The pilots of the 353 attacking planes had been steeped in silhouette recognition, each had his own carefully timetabled target.

Code name for the peel-off was, *"Tora . . . tora . . . tora,"* the Japanese word for tiger. It came from the saying, "The tiger goes out two thousand miles and returns without fail."

At 0758 hours, a naval air commander of Patrol Wing Two broadcast the message to all ships: "AIR RAID PEARL HARBOR, THIS IS NOT A DRILL. . . . THIS IS NOT A DRILL!!!"

It all technically took one hundred and ten minutes, but most of the damage was done in the first fifteen.

First came waves of dive-bombers and torpedo planes, then a forty-five-minute lull, followed by a high-altitude bomber attack, then more dive-bombers for another half hour.

"I lay flat on the floor to watch the fall of the bombs through a peephole," later wrote Japanese pilot Fuchida Mitsuo. "Four bombs in perfect pattern, plummeted like the devils of doom. The target was so far away that I wondered for a moment if they would reach it. The bombs grew smaller and smaller until I was holding my breath for fear of losing sight of them. I forgot everything in the thrill of watching them fall toward the target. They became small as poppy seeds, and finally disappeared from my view, just as tiny white spurts of smoke appeared on or near the ship. I shouted, "Two hits' . . ."

Never volunteer.

Standard GI joke of the Draft Days was the sergeant saying, "I want three volunteers, you, you and you . . ." But somehow that joke never really fitted the real war.

The war was real for Sgt. Thomas Edgar Hailey of St. Joseph, Mo., when he heard the call to General Quarters. He was part of a Marine Corps gunnery detail assigned to the U.S.S. *Oklahoma*. He was in charge of the Number 10 broadside five-inch gun. When the first torpedo hit the hull and the ship began to turn over, he was in his summer underwear, jumping out of his bunk. Thirty feet away was the U.S.S. *Maryland* and Hailey swam over, climbed up, saw an antiaircraft gun not fully manned and moved in on it with some of his oil-covered shipmates. A bomb soon blasted them out of there, too, and Hailey was again in the water, this time swimming through flaming oil. He found a suction pipe four feet under the water and walked it tightrope-style to Ford Island, reported at once to the air station there, still in his oil-soaked underwear.

A small unarmed observation plane was taking off and the pilot needed an expert rifleman to sit in the rear seat to give him some cover. Any volunteers?

Still in his summer underwear, still dripping from oil, Sgt. Thomas Edgar Hailey stepped forward.

A bomb had landed smack down the smokestack of the U.S.S. *Oklahoma,* blowing her forward magazines and boilers sky-high. The *Arizona* was an inferno, its oily smoke so dense that it covered the harbor like funereal fog. The *Maryland* had a huge hole in its forecastle. The *Pennsylvania,* resting in its moorings for repair, had an armor-piercing bomb explode in its casements. The *California* had its heavy list to portside while the smoke poured out of her. The *Nevada* had run hard ashore, seemed to be sinking quickly. And the *West Virginia* took eight torpedoes at the waterline. Heroes were everywhere.

How can you be a hero when you're a Negro mess attendant and your first name is Doris?

His full name was Doris Miller, and he was big and powerfully built. He was on deck of the U.S.S. *West Virginia* when the first wave of dive-bombers swept in on the ship. Doris Miller had never been trained to work a machine gun but he had watched them do it and so he took over an empty one and started firing. There is no record that he downed any planes, but the hard fact is that he stayed and tried, and that they gave him a Navy Cross for it—although he never lived long enough to wear it.

Still, he was one of the lucky ones. When they raised the sunken hulk of the *West Virginia,* known more intimately to its men as "Weevie," they found sailors who had been buried alive in an airtight chamber. Markings on the wall indicated they had survived until shortly before Christmas.

The constant question of the Navy men was, "Where the hell is our Air Force?"

The Japanese, in simultaneous sweeps of our airfields, had destroyed 140 planes on the ground, damaged eighty others. Only a handful managed to get into the air. Caught in the melée were some incoming planes from the aircraft carrier *Enterprise,* just 175 miles out at sea.

So great was the hysteria that we shot down several of our own planes.

"Please don't shoot! Don't shoot!!!! This is an American plane," yelled one *Enterprise* pilot over the radio. His last heard words were to his enlisted-man gunner in the rear seat. "We're on fire . . . Bail out . . ." But they didn't have time.

One American pilot, forced down by the enemy, managed a safe landing and tried hitchhiking back to base. An elderly couple stopped their car but were reluctant to take him, despite his story. "Our friends are waiting for us," they explained. "We are bringing the potato salad and they have the chicken . . ."

If you can't save planes, save lives.

There were 34 planes at Kaneohe Airport, but the first Japanese fighter attack put them all out of commission.

But what do you do when a thirty-two-year-old Aviation Chief Ordnanceman, John Finn, gets mad and grabs a loaded machine gun, mounts it in a wide-open exposed ramp and starts firing. Japanese planes came back at him again and again, wounded him a few times but he kept on firing. Finn hit several planes, helped destroy two of them. It took a direct order to force him to leave and get medical attention. By that time he was hit so bad he could hardly move.

The Kaneohe Station Commander called it "reckless resistance." There was a shorter word for it: guts.

Two waves of planes in less than two hours sank five of our battleships, severely damaged another and hit two more, sank two destroyers and either sank or seriously damaged nine others. Our Navy lost 2,008 men, five times as many as it had lost in all of World War I. Others killed included 218 soldiers, 109 Marines and 68 civilians.

Japanese casualties: one large submarine, five midget submarines and 29 planes.

A naval historian later called the attack "a strategic imbecility" because the Japanese had concentrated on ships instead of permanent installations and oil tanks. "On a strategic level, it was idiotic," he wrote. "On the political level, it was disastrous."

It was a day of many medals, a day of national shock and shame, a day that "will live in infamy."

36

Guam

Beer cost a dime and the best bourbon only $1.50 a bottle and the copper-skinned Chomorro full-bosomed girls couldn't be more friendly. That was Guam for the 365 Marines. As one of them put it, "Guam duty beats the hell out of Iceland."

But not for long. After the Pearl attack, the Guam Marines knew they were next. Only Sgt. Tim Shannon seemed optimistic. "Boys, don't sweat a thing," he told them. "All we've got to do is sit tight, kiss the babes goodbye and fight this one out in the Philippines. Keep a tight line on the broads, you guys, and leave them a little dough because we'll be right back in the sack with them in a couple of months."

The Japanese, however, sent in an armada with 5,000 invading soldiers. And how can 365 Marines fight off an army like that when their heaviest weapon is a machine gun?

Wake

Shaped like a wishbone, the four-square-mile Wake Island was much smaller and much lonelier than Guam, but tougher.

It had a half-dozen five-inch naval guns, a dozen ack-ack, some fifty machine guns, eight flyable planes and 452 Marines. The three islets also had scrub trees, coral beaches, a flourishing breed of big rats and a large lagoon full of vicious eels. Our government officially had designated Wake as a bird sanctuary.

But a sanctuary was the one thing it was not.

So confident were the Japanese of simply walking in on Wake that they had printed plans for the island's administration long before their landing.

Our Marines, however, caused a slight postponement of those plans.

The Japanese sent in 36 twin-tailed bombers flying in three V-formations at two thousand feet and they left the tiny airfield a shambles. There was no time to bury our dead and so we simply put them in the freeze room of a contractor's storehouse. One of our planes was still flyable and it went up and sank a sub. But we waited with all our guns until the Japanese put their men in landing boats and then our guns opened up. We not only wiped out hundreds of their troops but we sank two of their destroyers and made them withdraw.

The breather was short. They came back again, this time with aircraft carriers and thousands of troops and overwhelmed Wake by sheer mass of men.

Consoling one of the captured Marines, a Japanese soldier said, "Pretty soon, war over. Everybody shakes hands."

That would take a long, long time.

The Philippines

It just didn't make any sense. The Japanese attack on Pearl Harbor had happened ten hours before. And yet when the Japanese came in over Clark Airfield in the Philippines, they found a whole fleet of Flying Fortresses parked neatly in rows, awaiting ready destruction. Not a single American fighter plane was flying cover over the field.

We were, in fact, so sure that the incoming planes were friendly that somebody said, "Here comes the Navy," and Sgt. Dwaine Davis of Carlsbad, N. M., grabbed a movie camera to take pictures of the perfect V-formations. Finally somebody saw the rising-sun emblem and the radio operator sent his message, "Tally-Ho! Bandits over Clark!"

But it was too late. Down came the incendiaries, the bombs, the bullets. Racing for the latrine slit trenches, already filled with camp cooks, Cpl. Durwood Brooks saw one of his friends who had been hit by an explosive bullet —he was blown up so big that he looked almost transparent. Half of our 123 combat planes were completely destroyed on the ground. Most of the others so badly hit they were unflyable.

In a single raid, the Japanese had knocked out half of General MacArthur's Far East Air Force.

It was Christmas and there was a plush party at the Manila Hotel. Men were wearing their formal jackets and the women their dressiest evening gowns while the band played "Joy to the World." These were people of pride and you had to look hard to find the war in their faces. Some hands, however, did tremble when they lit their cigarettes with their golden lighters. Pvt. Sidney Stewart had stumbled in on the party and he couldn't believe it when he found himself dancing with a lovely lady in a low-cut dress who seemed particularly anxious to please him. Everything seemed even more unreal when they went out on the balcony, and saw our ships still burning in the harbor. And then Pvt. Stewart remembered the stinking unburied bodies still lying out in the street.

Have faith, said the local radio to the Filipinos—Help is coming.

But there was no help.

Counting Army, Navy and Marines, we had some 12,000 GI's, plus 8,000 Filipino Scouts and 60,000 poorly trained and equipped troops of the Philippine Army.

The Japanese landed invasion forces at Luzon, and then unloaded eighty transports of troops at Lingayen Gulf.

We declared Manila an open undefended city and our troops started to pull out.

"Hi Marine!" said a smiling Filipino boy, still making his V-sign along the highway.

"Hello there, sonny," said Pvt. William Martin Camp.

"Say, Marine," said the little boy, "you're not leaving us here alone, are you? You're not running away, are you?"

But we were, we were . . .

What was left of our Air Force had already flown off to Australia. Air Corps ground crew stayed behind to fight alongside our infantry. But the superior Japanese force slowly pushed us back toward the dead end of Bataan and Corregidor.

Bataan

Our troops squeezed into Bataan like a cat slipping into a closed bag. The bag was a peninsula bounded by Manila

Bay and the South China Sea, and our front was a thin line across the mouth of it. The war was soon packed into an area of twelve square miles, and there was no rear echelon. Japanese planes could bomb and strafe anywhere because our ack-ack were so ancient and unreliable that they were dangerous to fire.

We had no planes. Many of our native troops had no shoes. We had nowhere to move our wounded. We were surrounded by impenetrable jungle, creeping bamboo, pythons and masses of malarial mosquitoes. And facing us were 65,000 crack Japanese troops, fully equipped, with their artillery so positioned that they could kill at will wherever they fired.

Pfc. John Lemke remembered quoting from Oliver Goldsmith's "Deserted Village": *"Even now the devastation has began and half the business of destruction done."* But there was another GI there who broke the tension even better by saying, "I'll bet if my mother knew this, she'd sure raise hell."

Counting the civilian refugees, we had almost a hundred thousand people to feed. The carabao disappeared first, then the 250 horses, then the 48 pack mules followed by the local iguana lizards and monkeys.

"I can recommend mule," wrote a GI. "It is tasty, succulent and tender. There is little to choose between Calesa pony and carabao. Iguana is fair. Monkey I do not recommend."

President Roosevelt ordered General MacArthur to leave for Australia. It was a direct order but the Marines were bitter about it. They sang a song to the tune of "Battle Hymn of the Republic":

Dug-out Doug's not timid, he's just cautious, not afraid.
He's protecting carefully the stars that Franklin made.
Four-star generals are rare as good food on Bataan,
And his troops go starving on.

Dug-out Doug is ready for his Chris-Craft for the Flee,
Over bounding billows and the wildly-raging sea.
For the Japs are pounding on the gates of old Bataan.
And his troops go starving on.

One Bataan regiment paraphrased MacArthur's statement "I shall return," by saying, "I am going to the latrine, but I shall return."

40

"Dear friends, lay down your arms," Tokyo Rose told them over Japanese radio. "It is useless to resist. . . . You are completely encircled. . . . You will get no assistance."

To heighten the surrendering mood, the Japanese broadcast over a loudspeaker near the front lines such tunes as "Home Sweet Home." At night they also played recorded screaming that seemed to come from every direction. Their planes dropped long strings of firecrackers behind our lines so that GI's would think themselves surrounded and fire back at the blackness in panic. And the Japanese infiltrated everywhere. An American soldier was found with his hands and feet cut off, bayonets driven into his stomach.

But the most devastating thing of all was the dysentery.

There were two kinds of dysentery—the so-called Yangtze Rapids, and the other kind, the nameless kind that could kill you.

First your teeth chattered until you bloodied your tongue and they had to put a bayonet between your teeth. Then your body started twitching and your eyeballs seemed to turn inward into your head and then came the violent uncontrollable hemorrhaging from your rear.

What do you do when you're stuck in a hole up front under artillery observation and you can't get out and your buddy starts hemorrhaging?

"We rolled him over on his stomach and parted his legs," a soldier wrote. "I placed my hand over him to try to stop the blood but it came through my fingers. I tried stopping him up with slimy dirt, but it was useless. The blood forced the mud poultice away. He died a few minutes later, without opening his eyes again. Since we couldn't move out of the hole, we dug the sides in until his body was covered with the fresh earth."

Our troops on Bataan surrendered on April 9. Some, however, managed to pull back onto the rock of Corregidor.

Corregidor

Corregidor once had been a garden place of vivid green foliage covered with an enormous variety of flowers. Incessant bombing and shelling had transformed it into a black mass of scorched rock.

When you walked inside the labyrinth of tunnels, the stink hit you like a blow in the face. It was a graveyard smell of sweat and wet rock and disinfectant and blood. There was no room to stretch out, no air to breathe deep, no radio contact with the world, and no hope. But even toward the end of that extra month before surrender, somebody there still had the strength of will to play a violin.

Meanwhile, out of Bataan, the Death March already had begun.

Bataan Death March

The hate was black.

If a Japanese soldier wanted a GI's ring, and the soldier objected, he simply chopped off the GI's finger, ring and all.

If a GI crawled out of line to drink the slimy carabao wallow from a stagnant pool filled with bloated bodies, the guard might smash his rifle butt into the boy's head—making a dull splattering sound as the head split open.

If a GI with dysentery stopped by the roadside to relieve himself, the guard might order him to eat his own excrement—and kill him if he didn't.

If a prisoner dropped from exhaustion during the sixty miles of march, you might soon see his head sticking on the end of a guard's bayonet—the blood still running from the neck and the open lips, the eyes protruded, the teeth clenched in a ghastly smile.

Some guards in some parts of the march let their prisoners have regular rest breaks, permitted them to forage for food, even distributed fresh water and cigarettes. One American soldier could afterwards truly write of his treatment on that march. "The Japanese were kind and helpful to us." Cpl. L. Arhutick told how his guards gave his group all the rice they could eat, and how he traded his six cans of condensed milk for everything from chickens to pork chops.

But they were the few. Some ten thousand soldiers died on the march, or soon afterwards. And, for the many thousands more who watched them die, the hate was black.

"A big Japanese officer instantly threw the American to his knees, pulled his sword from his scabbard, and raised it with both hands high above his head. It glistened there for a moment, brightly in the sun, and then while the other prisoners watched incredulously, the Japanese brought it down swiftly. It struck the back of the neck with a heavy thud, like a butcher's cleaver chopping into a large piece of meat. As the sword went through the neck and struck the ground, the head seemed to leap forward as if it had a life of its own. It hit the earth, bounced, rolled forward crazily among the men, while the body tumbled forward, the arms jerking, and the hands opening and closing jerkily while blood spurted in great gushes from the gaping wound turning the dusty white earth into dark red mud."

ENGLAND

Ballad of the Bombardier

At night a white-faced nineteen-year-old bombardier
Sits writing.
The wonder of his crew tonight,
Before the flight.
Sits writing.
Behold the stern precision of time and plan:
Regard one sudden man
In a given hour.
The hand, the eye, the deliberate brow—
This veteran now
Sits writing a letter home.
"I take my pen in hand, Emily,
To make you understand
What you are to me.
I write as far as 'Dear Emily'—
And cannot make it clear
What you are to me.
You are my heart's one cry.
Foolish words that I
Wish to say, and try,
So terribly.
The words are like a wall, Emily.
I cannot write at all
What you are to me.
You are my heart's one cry.
If you were nearby,
You could tell me why,

So easily.
Write me you will be true, Emily.
Write me I am to you
What you are to me."
At night a white-faced nineteen-year-old bombardier
Sits writing.
The wonder of his crew tonight,
Before the flight,
Sits writing.

—Cpl. Marc Blitzstein

Greenock came out of the misty dawn like a fuzzy painting in some museum, green and calm and lovely. The snugness of this Scottish port and the homes around its rim, all had the soft and settled look of complete peace. And, for a second, the silence was almost overwhelming.

We had made it; we were here. We had crossed the ocean without being sunk by a U-boat or bombed by an enemy plane. We were alive; we were safe.

But where was the war?

And, then, suddenly we saw it. Barrage balloons hanging ugly in the sky, spoiling the picture postcard.

The war was here, too.

The first American ship to arrive in England as part of the war was the U.S.S. *Albatross,* a fishing schooner converted into a minesweeper. That was in the middle of January 1942. A week later, our first troop convoy came to northern Ireland. Soon afterwards, all over England, our GI's were moving into everything from Nissen huts to a former racetrack in Cheltenham. These were advance headquarter units setting up the ETO, the European Theater of Operations, under a commanding general named Dwight D. Eisenhower.

" 'This,' you say to yourself, when you look out of the train window, 'is England,' " wrote Pfc. William Hogan, San Francisco. "And you find yourself repeating the fact all during the long train ride through the Midlands from a west coast port, and later, too, when you bivouac temporarily in a grove of tall trees in an immense meadow with thatched-roof farmhouses nearby, and quiet peaceful people in the small village below you.

". . . and you keep saying to yourself: 'Look, this is England.' . . .

48

"You're on top of a bus coming back to your camp late at night. Outside, the hills and the land are black, and there are no people on the roads, but far down on the horizon sharp antiaircraft searchlights intertwine together, making an eerie background, like something out of a spectacular motion picture. The important thing now is that it is not a motion picture anymore.

"Around you on the bus are soldiers, British and American, all of them singing. The Welshmen sing loudly and beautifully, and the Americans keep quiet for a minute after shouting their own Tin Pan Alley tunes to listen to those Welshmen, and then to the answering Scots, and then all of them sing out together, 'Keep the home fires burning!' "

The pamphlet began, "You are going to Great Britain as part of an Allied offensive—to meet Hitler and beat him on his own ground. For the time being, you will be Britain's guest. . . ."

It then went on to say that Great Britain was no bigger than Iowa, that its forty-five million people had learned to guard their privacy and were "equally careful not to invade another man's privacy."

It had some hints about words, too. "Bloody," it warned, was one of the worst British swear words. "To say, 'I look like a bum' is offensive to their ears," the pamphlet added, "for to the British this means that you look like your own backside."

The pamphlet then recommended, "If you want someone's friendship, don't snatch it; wait for it."

For a final suggestion, the pamphlet urged, "Get acquainted."

British NAAFI girls got their own pamphlet, telling them about Americans:

"The first time that an American soldier approaches the counter and says, 'Hiya baby,' you will probably think he is being impudent. By the time several dozen men have said it, you may have come to the conclusion that all Americans are 'fresh.' Yet, to them it will be merely the normal conversational opening, just as you might say, 'Lovely day, isn't it?' Remember that most Americans think that English people are 'standoffish.' If you snub them you will merely confirm this impression."

There was no snubbing in England in 1942. The British

had been through the Blitz, the bombing which had killed 44,000 civilians, seriously wounded another 50,000, and had left 375,000 people homeless in London alone. The worst of it was in September 1940, when the Blitz destroyed some 50,000 homes a week in London and there had not been a single bomb-free night.

But Hitler had badly misjudged this people.

"What kind of people do they think we are?" Prime Minister Winston Churchill asked. "Do they not realize we shall never cease to persevere against them until we have taught them a lesson which they and the world will never forget?"

Men and women worked all night searching for bodies of their neighbors in the rubble, and then went to work as usual the next morning. Some children never knew any other home but the bunks in the underground shelters. There were few families unmarked by some death of a close kin. The Blitz was a shared horror and a shared courage.

And now, as the British put it, we had come to help them give Hitler "a bit of his own back." And so they opened their homes and their hearts to us, gladly divided their tiny rations of food and tea, accepted us as their own.

On July 4, a fit day for the purpose, we released our first American war communiqué from the ETO:

"In a joint operation with RAF light bombers, six American air crews attacked targets in German-occupied territory today. Two American planes are missing. The Americans flew A–20 type aircraft [Bostons] in a daylight minimum altitude attack." The A–20 was a two-engine bomber that carried a crew of three. The targets were German airports in Holland.

"I drew the floor position, firing from the belly of the plane," said Sgt. Robert L. Golay. "I lay flat on my stomach, the monkey chain fastened to my chute. The planes flew about thirty feet above the water when they crossed the Channel and I got a fine faceful of spray.

"Those babies on the coast started firing even before we came into range and we could see the flak coming right at us . . . The flak got the other American plane just as we reached the coast. We could see it go all to pieces . . .

"All of a sudden I saw part of a propeller fly past and I said to myself, 'We've got a Messerschmitt.'"

"I don't know why I thought that but then I took another look and nearly fell out of the plane. 'God,' I said, 'that's *our* propeller.'

"Then things got really confused. We saw the right engine burst into flames. The ground was a dizzy blur, so close we could almost touch it.

"Then all of a sudden there was a terrible crash and I could see the whole floor of the plane buckle up. I went bang against the ceiling and my legs went all numb. I was afraid to look at them because I thought they were shot off. But they were all right.

"I didn't know what the hell was going on. All I could see was a pair of legs of another crew member up front. The captain says I kept yelling, 'Give 'em hell, Captain, give 'em hell.'

"I don't remember. Maybe I did. Nobody knows to this day how the captain managed to right the plane after we jolted against the ground like we did, and nobody knows how we managed to keep flying all the time, or how we managed to beat out the fire in the engine.

"But we did and pretty soon we were around on the other side of the airdrome, streaking for home. We dropped one load and got two more flak towers.

"Then we were over the Channel again. It was the funniest thing in the world. I mean, no one said a word; I don't know how long it was like that, but it was the funniest thing in the world. Then Captain Kegelman called back to ask if we were all right and everybody started talking at once.

"We were forty-five minutes overdue at the base and everyone had almost stopped looking for us. We only had one engine and a big hole in the fuselage. Part of a wing was gone.

"The thing I remember most was when I got out of the plane. They had a whole bottle of Scotch waiting for us. You don't know what that means . . . Why, you have to walk twenty miles just for a glass of beer . . ."

Two GI's on the loose in London at a time when the GI uniform was still rare enough to stare at. They were AWOL for a weekend but the hell with it. The price was right.

If the beer was warm, so were the women.

They saw their first sign of war in the bleak mass of rubble behind Fleet Street, and it hit them hard.

They joined the unquenchable merry mood of men in a pub, and never forgot it.

They walked into the awesome Westminster Abbey and the Houses of Parliament and London Bridge as if they were small boys turning the pages of a history book.

They admired the English accent of a Chinese waiter, the perfect cocktails in a posh club, the lovely lilt of a Gilbert and Sullivan operetta, the tucked-away scatter of pocket parks lined with ancient walls, the odd-shaped houses on tiny intertwining streets, the long queues of patient people, and the calm courage in their faces.

And when it was all over, they returned quietly to their camp in the Midlands, prepared to spend the next year on KP—only to discover that, in the confusion of their still-disorganized camp, nobody had even missed them. Long after everything else that would happen to them, this was a special smiling piece of memory to share for the rest of their lives.

GI's in England soon had a stream of visitors: Al Jolson, Eleanor Roosevelt, the King of England.

Jolson sang the songs they liked to hear.

Eleanor Roosevelt collected GI names so she could call their mothers back home; decided their GI socks were not warm enough for the weather; and toured one hospital after another. When a colonel complained that they were already behind schedule, the First Lady said firmly, "Just one more ward, Colonel." And Cpl. Vincent Strianse of Brooklyn summed up the GI reaction when he said of her, "Ain't she a honey?"

The King of England visited the newly arrived Flying Fortresses and their crews, talked to the men about jeeps, weather and cheese. He asked T/Sgt. Norman Tussey, State College, Pa., how he liked English weather.

"Don't like it, sir," said Tussey. "It's too damp."

Asked later how he could say such a thing to King George, Tussey answered, "You wouldn't want me to lie to the King, wouldja?"

King George lunched with the men, spotted a cook grating cheese. He nibbled at it.

"Good cheese," he said.

"It should be," said the cook, "it comes from Wisconsin."

The King smiled, but only slightly.

Just before he left the airfield, the King asked a crew,

"Are those your names on different parts of the plane?" When they said yes, the King laughed and said, "Good, now those Nazi planes will know your names when they go down."

The King's car was leaving when a rich southern drawl yelled out of the watching GI crowd, "Y'all hurry back, y'Majesty."

The dramatic news out of England in August was a hit-and-run Commando raid on six beaches near the French coastal town of Dieppe. We used a mixed force of Canadians, British, French and Americans, sent in tanks as mobile artillery, supported them with a constant air umbrella of fighter planes.

Object of the nine-hour battle was to destroy some key installations, kill Germans and bring back some prisoners.

We did all those things and we did them well.

It was just a military pinprick into the rear end of the enemy, but it boosted our morale.

One of the American Rangers on the raid, Cpl. Bill Brady, Grand Forks, N.D., celebrated his twenty-third birthday on French soil, and one of the little things he remembered was lying in a ditch counting the money in his pocket—a nickel, a dime and a penny—brought along for good luck. He remembered thinking, "Hell, I can't spend that stuff here."

And he remembered the British Commandos picking apples in an orchard on the way back to the boats, the bullets still flying. And he also remembered running across a garden plot and wondering whether the Frenchman who owned that house would be angry. (A French housewife did bawl out Sgt. Alex Szima for trampling on her vegetable garden.)

Another American on the raid, who got the British Military Medal, was Cpl. Franklin M. Koons, a twenty-three-year-old former livestock auctioneer from Swea City, Ia. "Our bunch had to wade ashore, through thirty yards of water up to our waist," said Koons, "and then get across forty yards of beach and up and over a cliff along a small and winding footpath. Then we were supposed to clear away a crew of Nazi snipers from some farmhouses so that another Commando gang could knock out a battery of six-inchers, situated near there in a strategic spot.

"There's an old Army saying," said Koons, "that soldiers are no good until they see their own men drop. Well, that's the truth. I was scared to death until a Britisher right near me got hit. Then a bullet damned near took my hand off.

"Suddenly I wasn't scared anymore, I was just hopping mad.

"I managed to get through the farmyard . . . found myself behind a stone wall with a nice opening between the stones for my rifle. So I started shooting at the gunners in that six-inch battery two hundred yards away. I don't know if I killed any of them. But I know that some of them disappeared."

Another Commando unit made a bayonet rush on the battery, blew up the guns and ammunition. On the way back to the ships, Koons saw a French family alongside the road staring at them as if they were a traveling circus.

"They didn't speak English," said Koons, "so I got a Canadian to translate for me and make them a little speech.

" 'We're only the first of many thousands of Americans who are coming over here,' I told them. 'We sympathize with you and we're working hard to liberate you.

" 'We're going back now but someday we'll land and we won't go back.' "

Our first all-American air raid on Europe in this war featured a dozen bombers in a daylight attack on a railroad terminus at Rouen toward the end of August 1942. Soon our raids increased in size and scope, deep into Germany, up to a thousand planes at a time.

Wahoo. The Avenger. Eight Ball. Dry Martini. Flaming Mamie. Holey Joe. Teggie Ann. The Goon. Playboy. Hellzadroppin'.

The crews sit on hard seats in a big room to look at a map, listen to the weather report, hear a flat voice describe the probable amount of flak over target.

Check oxygen, bomb fuses, radio, a hundred other things: don't forget electrically heated boots or your feet will freeze; remind new radio operator to turn on detonator to destroy secret equipment in case of crash; crawl forty feet inside bomber wing to replace gas tank.

Airborne. Test-fire the guns over the Channel. Guns O.K. No rank inside of a bomber. Every man has an equal chance to die.

"Enemy fighter coming in from three o'clock . . . Here comes another sonofabitch from six o'clock . . . Watch him . . . get him . . . I got the sonofabitch! . . . I got the sonofabitch! ! ! !"

Bomb doors open over target. Cold blast of air rushes in. Press camera button for two minutes.

"Let's get the hell out of here . . ."

Pilot to tail gunner: "How is the formation?"

No reply.

"Hey Jerry, was that gal in town too much for you last night?"

No reply. There never would be. There was a hole in the plane and a hole in the tail gunner.

Come in with a gaping flak hole, a shot-up engine, torn-up controls; come in on a pancake landing, the plane slithering on its belly.

Tomorrow is another map, another weather report, another day when you must not forget your electrically heated boots.

Our troops and planes kept pouring into England but now some of them started moving out. There were ships waiting to catch a convoy to make an invasion.

Most of the GI's couldn't kiss their girls goodbye, but one GI got a note, months later, which said, "God bless you, Yank, but please come back . . ."

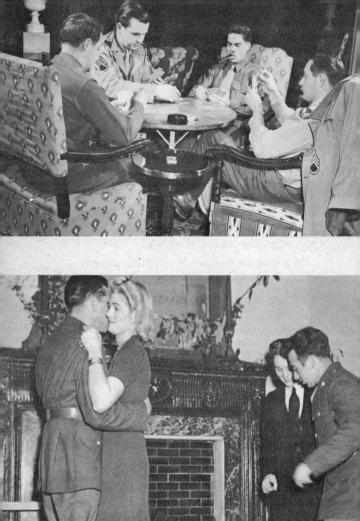

NORTH AFRICA

Cpl. Doyle to Africa Come!

Oh sound the trumpet and beat the drum!
Cpl. Doyle to Africa come!
To Africa come in enormous force
To alter the global battle's course.
Already the dastard foeman fly;
We'll all be home by the Fourth of July.
Oh, smite the zither, rattle the gourd!
Cpl. Doyle in Afrique du Nord!
Now for a speedy end to the war;
Summon a hearse for the Afrika Korps,
For here comes the guy the enemy fears—
The paragon of the Engineers,
So, smite the zither, rattle the gourd!
Cpl. Doyle's in Afrique du Nord!

Cpl. John Doyle's poem fitted the spirit but not the facts. True, we had come to North Africa in enormous force, but the foeman wasn't flying and the war's end was still some heavy years away.

Operation Torch presented question marks. Would the Vichy French manning the port guns fight us or embrace us? Could we really bottle up the German Afrika Korps? How many Nazi divisions would we divert from the fighting Russian front? In fact, was this North African trip really necessary?

We had sent secret agents in submarines in advance of TORCH trying to firm up a deal with the Vichy leaders so that we could walk in without worry—but the French wouldn't say yes and wouldn't say no.

On TORCH D-Day, November 8, 1942, Marshal Henri Petain, the Nazi puppet in Vichy France, broadcast the official word to French troops in North Africa:

"FRANCE AND HER HONOR ARE AT STAKE. WE ARE ATTACKED AND WE WILL DEFEND OURSELVES. THAT IS THE ORDER I GIVE."

The landing net swings clear and the climb down comes easy, with the outboard roll of the ship. But with the ship's inboard roll, the net flattens tight against the ship's side and you find no gripping room for your fingers and feet and the sixty-five pounds of equipment on your back feels like a ton and everything is suddenly slippery and you hold on with a frenzy and everybody is saying hurry, hurry, goddammit, hurry . . .

The information booklet on North Africa told our troops, "Our welcome by the inhabitants is not known at this time."

We landed near Casablanca, Oran, and Algiers. Our troops were green; our reception varied. Coming into Casablanca, straight from the States, we ran into heavy shellfire from the 15-inch guns of the new French battleship, the *Jean Bart*—until we silenced it.

Heading this Casablanca task force, General George Patton sent this directive to all troops: "There is not the least doubt that we are better in all respects than our enemies, but to win, the men must KNOW this. It must be their absolute belief. WE MUST HAVE A SUPERIORITY COMPLEX."

The password on the beaches was "GEORGE," and the answering password was, "PATTON."

"Men wandered about aimlessly, hopelessly lost, calling to each other and for their units, swearing at each other and at nothing," later wrote one of the generals, L. K. Truscott.

". . . I was sitting there with my cigarette half-smoked wondering what I was going to do next and how, when out of the gloom from the shore appeared a strange-looking figure . . . He stopped in front of me and in alien accents addressed me: 'Heyyuh, gimme a cigarette.' I handed him one from the package I held. He spoke again: 'Goddam. All wet. Gimme a light, too.' I extended the lighted end of my cigarette."

As he put the cigarette to his face, two of the general's

aides arrived and shoved tommy guns into the man's midriff, and challenged him with the first part of the password, "GEORGE."

"George? George, hell. Me no George. My name Lee, Cook, Company C. 540th Engineers."

General Patton's advice on the way to fight the war was, "Grab the enemy by the nose and kick him in the pants."

But where was the enemy? Some fire came from French military barracks, a few light tanks, assorted machine-gun positions.

What kind of war was this anyway? A GI would belly his way through some rubble, carefully set up his gun, aim it toward some set-in snipers, and then would look up and around and there he'd see himself surrounded by a dozen curious natives. If a GI opened a map to see where he was, he would suddenly have an audience of Arabs staring over his shoulder. If a GI was wounded, they would cluster around him, occasionally poking him to see if he was still alive. It was almost as if this were a game and they were the audience.

Once they had made their fierce gesture of defiance, the French surrendered the city. Casablanca had the million-watt sunshine, the white look of California, plus bicycle taxis, outdoor egg stands and the only two automats in North Africa. A two-franc slug bought a glass of *bière blonde*.

As for the native women, an anonymous GI wrote a limerick:

> *Now every young Yank who was in Casablanca*
> *Knows Stella the belle of Fedala.*
> *A can of C-ration will whip up a passion*
> *In this little gal of Fedala.*

Fighting near Oran had been heavier. French coastal guns blasted the troops who tried to come straight into Oran harbor, and a French motor launch gunned down our wounded. But, at the same time, more friendly Frenchmen in rowboats were circling the harbor picking up our survivors, and a French captain greeted an American boarding party with a bottle of gin in his hand, a smile on his face, saying, "What's the matter? We expected you last night."

For three days, men died on both sides as we swept our tanks through the airfields, into the city. Once inside Oran, though, the Zouaves, who had fought us fiercely only hours before, were now pleased to parade alongside our GI's through the streets.

"This is what I call a *belle guerre*," said a French soldier to a correspondent.

The first American tank in town found itself surrounded, swarmed over, its gun barrels covered with flowers, its crew covered with kisses, filled with wine and cheered as heroes.

The source of some of the cheers was not only the fresh sense of freedom but the real promise of food. Behind the colorful café lights in this beautiful harbor were gaunt faces and empty bellies. The Germans and Italians had systematically stripped them of all their produce, left them only wine, rationed horsemeat and surplus oranges. For those GI's coming from England, oranges had been almost invisible and they pleasurably gorged themselves into a state of diarrhea. As for the wine, it was cheap, plentiful and had 13 percent alcohol. To make the matter complete, the French women were eager and adoring, and GI's everywhere soon had a French-English dictionary in one hand, a smiling girl on the other.

As for the Arab women, the GI Guide made its warning loud and clear: "Never stare at one. Never jostle her in a crowd. Never speak to her in public. Never try to remove the veil."

A few GI's, more curious than others, were found with their testicles sewn in their mouths—the Arab men had done the killing and cutting, and their women had done the sewing.

Algiers was the easiest. We landed almost unopposed, took over the airport and the city by noon of the first day.

The campaign's Commanding General, Dwight D. Eisenhower, set up his headquarters there, a mixed headquarters of American, English and French. It was Eisenhower's job to keep the mix smooth, and he was good at it. He had to be. Most of the hundred thousand invading troops were American, but a British force landed at Bône, closer to the front, and a conglomerate French force also moved in on our side.

The front was five hundred miles away, a country bare and brown with steeply walled eroded wadis and sharply ridged djebels. It was a country of knee-high bunch grass, olive groves, and cactus cultivated for camel feed. The cactus had thorny stickers, an inch long and tough as steel, but the camels somehow thrived on them.

Camels were everywhere and so were the Arabs. Arabs would pop up in the middle of a battle to sell eggs, dates, even, sometimes, their daughters. We felt sorry for some of them: the children, asking for "chawklit" and "shoongum," who shined our shoes, aped our ways and became our mascots; the old man who cut two holes in a barrack bag for his legs and tightened the drawstring around his middle; the mothers who ate our garbage and tried to suckle their babies with dry breasts.

But we also knew that Arabs spied on our positions and sold the information to the enemy; that they helped us unload our cargo at the ports but stole an immense amount of it—from insulated wire (which they used as clothesline) to latrine screens (which they cut up into cloaks); that they led an escaped Allied prisoner back to the Germans for eleven pounds of tea; that they attacked our isolated soldiers with stones, killed them, stripped their bodies.

We knew that most of them favored the Germans.

The Germans had some 12,000 troops in Tunisia (plus a large force of Italians) at the start of the war, and Hitler rapidly reinforced them by ship and plane. The British force from Bône had pushed within a dozen miles of Tunis, within sight of the city, before they were stopped. They only had a brigade of old tanks and some infantry, but they were stopped by the weather as well as the enemy. The winter rains had started. The mud deepened daily, disintegrated long stretches of road. The reinforced Axis troops pushed our line back to the eucalyptus trees and battle-scarred buildings of Medjez-el-Bab, near the Mediterranean. By the time American reinforcements arrived, the supply question had become critical.

The quartermaster trucking outfit had started driving from the time they first got off the ship, and they were still driving four million miles later. Trackless desert, total blackout, the long drive through Messerschmitt Lane. If you spotted a plane, you slowed down, kept your door open, and drove with one hand. And if it was a German plane, you signaled the rest of the convoy by lifting and lowering your helmet. That meant break formation and get the hell out of the way.

Two Stukas dropped four bombs uncomfortably close to the ammunition-loaded truck of T/5 John "Jeep" Jones. The officer told Jeep to stop the truck, stay put and see what would happen.

"Sir," said Jeep, "I can put on them brakes and stop this truck from moving, but I sure can't stop my feet from traveling."

When there were fewer than fifteen trucks in a convoy, a noncom was in charge; more than that, and an officer went along. Sgt. Exerzene Dotson, of Augusta, Ga., was driving in the Sbeitla sector with his captain when some artillery opened up all around them. The sergeant suggested that perhaps they turn back.

The captain said sternly, "Sgt. Dotson, you don't want to turn back now. Why, you and I have been through thick and thin together."

"Yes, sir, Captain," said Dotson. "I know that. But when it starts getting too thick, I figure we oughta start thinning out."

Just then a gas dump blew up at the left of the road and the captain agreed with the sergeant.

But, mostly they just drove, day and night, feeling lucky to get a cup of hot coffee when they got back, but often settling for a can of cold C-rations. Their day room had three records which they played over and over again: "One Dozen Roses," "President's Birthday Ball" and "All I Need Is You."

They were one of the few integrated units of Negroes and white soldiers. "It doesn't make any difference," said their CO. "There's no time now for differences."

The front was thinly held and highly fluid on both sides, mostly a series of probing patrols and sharp, local attacks and counterattacks. Some of our early raiders were the Rangers, our American version of the tough British Commandos. We flew them to the front in a fleet of C–47's. Their first raid was set for Sened station.

Sened had been won and lost by our side twice. But the purpose of the raid was to "terrorize and demoralize."

Between the French outpost and Sened were twenty

miles of desert and mountains, an area crawling with enemy patrols. Their faces blackened, the Rangers were supposed to move out at dark, hide in the mountains during the day, then attack the next night.

They were supposed to advance silently until they were on top of the outpost, and then open fire, annihilate the garrison, destroy the cannon and supplies and take only ten prisoners.

"I could tell by the flashes of our own gunfire and the roaring cursing shouts of Rangers that our entire company was sweeping up the slopes in an unbroken unremitting line," said Sgt. James Altieri. "Suddenly a blast from a 47-mm cannon directly overhead illuminated a patch of hill just long enough for me to recognize Garrison firing on his knees toward the cannon. It was two feet to his right when another horrifying blast swooshed by me, followed by a brilliant bluish flash that revealed Garrison still on his knees—but without his head.

"A booming explosion from one of our grenades silenced the gun as I continued upward, stepping on squashy bodies, slithering on squirming entrails. A blast from a concussion grenade picked me up, lifted me through the air and hurled me down with a crash flat on my back."

He found himself in a deep slit trench, wedged in face to face with an Italian soldier.

"He was as surprised as I was. He just stood there for a long moment transfixed. My rifle was still in my hand but the trench was too narrow for me to bring it to my hip and fire. In the flashing second of indecision I nearly panicked. Then I remembered my commando knife . . . with a lightning thrust brought it up with all my strength into his stomach. 'Mamma mia,' he cried. 'Mamma mia.' I felt the hot blood spurt all over my right arm as I pulled the knife out, then rammed it home again and again. As the body sagged and slid to the ground, I reeled and vomited."

Out of the distance a Ranger voice yelled, "Don't kill 'em all—we need some prisoners."

One of the letters waiting for the Rangers on their return to base was from the president of the Boy Rangers of America. It read:

I am very anxious to make the acquaintance of our Big Brother Rangers overseas. Upon receipt of this letter, please write and tell us your experiences and we will assign one of your little Ranger brothers to tell you of our doings.

Yours for Victory,
Trusty Tommy

What could they tell "Trusty Tommy"?

We waited for the weather to improve to make our major move, but it only worsened. We joined the British in an unsuccessful attack on a djebel called Longstop Hill, and the casualty cost was heavy. The Germans had brought in crack troops to reinforce the wavering Italians. We had more tanks and more guns, but their individual tanks were better than ours, and so were some of their guns, particularly the 88-mm.

"The 88," said the artillery officer, "is merely a dual-purpose gun, with a jacketed barrel, an easily detachable set of breech rings, a supported interchangeable A-tube, a carriage consisting of an upper carriage with a protective armor shield, a buffer fitted into the barrel cradle, a hydropneumatic recuperator fitted above the barrel and a special trailer (No. 201) which is fitted with pneumatic tires and drawn by a half-track vehicle."

For the average GI, though, "88 fever" was the worst kind you could get. All they knew was that the 88 had a rate of fire running up to twenty rounds a minute, that it could tear apart a low-flying plane or a tank or a troop concentration. Aimed in your direction, it had the horror of hell.

Our hate of the 88 was matched only by our fear of Messerschmitt Lane and Stuka Alley where the German planes strafed and bombed anywhere, almost at will. Our own airstrips were few and soggy, but the Germans operated their planes out of all-weather airports in nearby Sicily.

Camouflage meant life. Hide a jeep under a tree, on the shady side of a wall, or at least slip a canvas hood over the folded windshield so that the glint of glass doesn't catch a pilot's eye. Dig your hole as deep as you can because when the bomb hits close, you may still find yourself scratching even deeper with your nails.

In a single day, our outfit was dive-bombed by Stukas twenty-three times.

"I hear there's one man who says he was not scared last night," said Sgt. Claude Coffey, Richmond, Va., an airplane mechanic with a fighter squadron. "I want to meet that man and shake his hand. Then I'll knock him down for being a damned liar."

Eisenhower called off our planned offensive because of

70

winter weather and the Germans put some of their bombing on a more methodical basis.

Flying from makeshift airstrips, our outnumbered Air Force often flew more than three missions a day. At 30,000 feet without pressurized cabins or electrically heated suits, cockpits were cramped and cold, but you still sweated enough to wet your underwear during combat. Some Americans flew the British Spitfire, which could twist inside of any German fighter, and the American twin-tailed P–38, so highly respected that the German planes stayed away from them unless one of them dropped out of formation.

At first, their conversation was all garbled, everybody talking at once. Somebody told how he blew up a truck convoy and how the men inside "flew out like firecrackers." Another laughed out loud about how long it took for a German soldier on a motorbike to skid to a stop after he had been hit. And Sgt. James Edward Butler, a telephone lineman from Grass Valley, Calif., who became an enlisted-man pilot flying a Spitfire, told how he was chasing this Stuka so close to the ground that when the Stuka took a sharp angle trying to escape, the Stuka's wing clipped the ground and took three cartwheels.

"You oughta see this ME–109 going straight down and crashing and it wasn't even smoking. No, I don't know who got it. Hey, who got the ME?" . . . "All I heard him say was there were three Messerschmitts on his tail. You can't horse around and leave a formation at a time like that and expect to get away with it." . . . "Is that new kid missing too? He was a nice kid . . ."

The garble gradually grew quieter and the Intelligence officer, who had been waiting patiently, started to piece together the different parts of the picture. One squadron leader helped out by marking a map with a crayon pencil showing just where they passed over the enemy airfields, at which points flak was most intense and accurate, how many ships were in what harbor, how many destroyed, probables and damaged Axis planes they got. Soon they were grouped around the map, correcting, amplifying. Fifteen minutes later the Intelligence officer walked away with his report.

Our American Commander in Chief, President Franklin Delano Roosevelt, came to Casablanca in January for a conference with Prime Minister Winston Churchill and the leaders of Free France, Charles de Gaulle and Henri Giraud. Mess Sgt. Joseph Baer, Shearns, Wis., handed the President a clean mess kit and Sgt. J. H. Osborne, Twin Bridges, Mont., dished out some ham and beans and both men beamed when the President afterwards said, "This is really good ham."

There were some who thought that a great opportunity had been lost here: had those GI chefs served the powdered eggs or powdered lemonade, or a can of K-ration cheese or C-ration stew, our Commander in Chief might have ordered a full investigation of the questionable quality and poor variety of GI food.

Also on the arrival list in Algiers was the first group of WAAC's (soon changed to WAC). The girls were promptly installed in an Algiers convent, and the only men officially allowed within perfume-smelling distance were two MP's. The girls got up at 0630, cut their cosmetic routine short because they bussed to headquarters at 0700 to work as typists, drivers and even mechanics. The only girls who came to breakfast in their bathrobes were the ones on late duty.

Somebody wrote a poem about them, part of which read:

> *Once her mummy made her bed*
> *Cleaned her clothes*
> *And buttered her bread.*
> *Once her favorite dress was red.*
> *Oh me, oh my—*
> *That ain't GI.*

They played bridge instead of craps, made their own fudge, were permitted to date only enlisted men—and the looming question in every GI mind was: Do they, or do they not really want to earn the Good Conduct Ribbon?

The Army set up a local radio station in Algiers and a Cpl. George McCoy, the "Real McCoy," ran an interview program with GI's on the Rue Michelet and his opener was, "Is there anybody here from out of town?"

A Red Cross club opened with flourish, offered doughnuts and coffee and conversation with French girls. One of the first things GI's on leave learned to say was, *"Où est le W.C.?"* (Where is the water closet?)

72

Sgt. Rodney Russell noted in *The Stars and Stripes* that the pleasant part of his job in a QM laundry unit was that it enabled him to correspond with a nurse by attaching a note to her panties.

Up front, the war was going nowhere.

Then came the critical battle of Kasserine Pass.

We were expecting a Nazi breakthrough somewhere, but not at Kasserine.

Looking at it from the air, Kasserine Pass has the shape of a crude X. It almost seems impregnable. A strong force dug in on the mountain heights on both sides of the pass automatically dominates the triangular area of approach. Since the area lacks cover, any attacking force comes under immediate observation and faces flanking fire from both heights. At its narrowest point, the pass is only a mile wide.

The German attack started on February 14 in the dips and folds of the plain near Sidi-bou-Zid. Their panzer tanks pushed in full force past Faïd Pass, past Sbeitla, past the ancient Roman triumphal arch at Kasserine down the throat of the Kasserine Pass itself.

Talking to a correspondent, while drinking cold coffee made from collected rainwater, S/Sgt. Melvin Blackburn, of Huddy, Ky., said, "You tell the folks back home not to worry about us. We feel bad because we've got only one life to give Uncle Sam if he needs it."

But if Blackburn wasn't worrying, his colonel was. He told corps headquarters:

"I am holding a lot of mountain passes against armor with three and one half battalions of infantry. If they get together anyplace a couple of infantry battalions, they might smoke me out . . . I haven't got a damn bit of reserve. I need a combat team of infantry worse than hell. All I have got are three and one half battalions of infantry. They are not enough."

The night of February 19 was a night of fog and rain, the mist so thick that one of our main mine-laying groups got lost. The engineer officer in charge had never seen the terrain in daylight, and couldn't find anyone to tell him where it was. When his unit finally got there, it was so close to daylight and their digging tools were so inadequate for the rocky soil that they simply strewed the mines

73

unburied over an area a hundred yards wide.

Our troops were too few and too scattered—and in the wrong places—and so the Germans arrived under cover of darkness, infiltrating easily around them, carefully avoiding the marked-off minefields. The pass was soon theirs, wide open for seventy German tanks to rush through, followed by infantry, fanning out in two columns, one toward our supply base at Tebessa and the other northwards toward Thala.

Our panic was real. If we couldn't hold the almost impregnable Kasserine Pass, how could we hold anything else?

Retreat is a nightmare. Destroy, burn, leave nothing. Speed, frenzy, horror. Every thirty seconds all night long, another vehicle passed a turn in the road: first the kitchen trucks and engineers, then the artillery with some protective infantry, then the long trail of supply trucks, then the infantry, and finally the tanks. Everything motorized. No passing, no waiting, no jamming. One vehicle every thirty seconds.

An evacuating French hospital gave away everything it couldn't carry and Sgt. Donald Schiavone found himself with an alarm clock, a silver letter opener, a basket of eggs, three dozen olives and a bottle of peach brandy. A passing truckload of soldiers saw the bottle and started yelling. Schiavone hesitated, then ran toward the truck, gave them the bottle and waved.

The ones who didn't wave were the natives of small towns and villages. We had evacuated most of the French, but not the natives. Most of the Moslems were pro-German, but what of those who made themselves our friends, what of the native Jews, what would happen to them when the Germans came back?

Some stared at us with hate, some with horror, some with tears. And the Arab kids who had shined our shoes, worn our cut-down uniforms, learned our language, warmed our hearts—these Arab kids watched us leave, a blank unbelieving look on their faces, almost as if they were pleading, "Say it isn't so, Joe . . . ."

The Germans pushed us back sixty miles in seven days. We even pulled out of Thelepte, the best airfield we had in the area. The only thing we left there was a big map of the Russian front, the pins still in to show the battle line, to remind the Germans that they still weren't winning everywhere.

Our main concern was Tebessa, our central supply depot, whose loss would have been catastrophic. We threw in all our planes to stall the Nazi tank thrust.

Sometimes a formation of our bombers passed within ten miles of a formation of JU–88's, each heading in opposite directions on the way to bomb each other's territory and each ignoring the other. Not all of our planes were well briefed. A group of Flying Fortresses, scheduled to bomb Kasserine Pass, instead dropped their full loads a hundred miles *within* our lines, killing a sizable number of Arabs before they had time to be surprised.

But our planes plus artillery and tanks finally stopped the German panzers on the plains of the Hatab Valley on the murky day of February 22. To plug the gap, we not only brought up every gun we had, but we raced two American divisions into the area on a forced march, borrowed a British brigade to cover our flank. Faced with this fresh strength, the Nazis withdrew to regroup, only eight miles from Tebessa.

You never saw eight more surprised soldiers in your life. Here they were all dressed up, shoes shined, driving along in their two reconnaissance cars toward Tebessa, when this 37-mm starts blasting at them, forcing them to stop and surrender. The big surprise came when the American Intelligence officer told these German Afrika Korps MP's that there was really no need for them to go to Tebessa to direct traffic because the American MP's there didn't need any help.

After some futile probing, the Nazis decided to pull back. Within five days, we had regained all our lost ground.

But, in that week of war, we had lost 112 medium tanks and a vast amount of vehicles including eighty half-tracks, and we had two thousand casualties.

Kasserine had taught us many combat lessons.

We learned that you don't gallop tanks into combat like cavalry. Speed and thick armor mean nothing when you get into gun range of the 88's. Nazis not only carefully reconnoitered their routes of advance, but often crept forward so slowly that you sometimes couldn't even tell they had moved unless you checked them against a prominent terrain feature.

Tank for tank, our Grants and Shermans were no match for the heavier armor and the better guns of the Nazi panzers. While our Sherman was more powerful, more dependable, it was also a firetrap—its high-octane fuel going up like a torch often after a first hit.

"In a second, the whole upper part of the tank was white hot, covering us with a blanket of unbearable heat," said Pvt. Francis Sternberg. "My hair and uniform caught on fire instantly. I leaped up, disregarding my wounded leg, dove through the turret hatch which had been blown open. Pulling myself out, I had to grab the metal with my hands. The hot iron ate into them as if they were made of butter. I struck the ground face first, blazing. . . . I sat up in the smoke and tore the jacket off my back. It came off in flaming shreds . . .

". . . I got onto my elbows and found that by digging them into the ground and pulling, while I shoved with my good leg. I could move about ten feet every five minutes . . . I kept on crawling . . .

"I wasn't ready to die . . ."

Hitler was highly unhappy at the way of the war in North Africa. Field Marshal Rommel was recalled to Germany for an explanation. Later, Rommel would write, "The mismanagement, the operational blunders, the prejudices, the everlasting search for scapegoats, those were to reach the acute stage. And the man who paid the price was the ordinary German and Italian soldier."

Rommel said of the GI determined stand: *"Die Amerikaner hatten sich verzueglich geschlagen."* (The Americans were good fighters.)

But, back in America, we had the same search for a scapegoat, blamed our Kasserine defeat on "a green and inexperienced Army." Eisenhower then decided to give II Corps a new general, the brash George Patton, with his pearl-handled pistols and his special sense of push.

Patton's first effort was to get his troops into "a fighting pitch." He ordered the wearing of leggings and neckties and helmets (with chin straps fastened) at all times in the corps sector. Even frontline troops had to wear neckties. No more helmet-liner "beanies" could be worn alone. Enlisted men disobeying regulations were fined twenty-five dollars. "When you hit their pocket books, you get a quick response," Patton said.

Mechanics too? "You're goddam right," said Patton. "They're soldiers, aren't they?"

Back in Algiers, the morale problem was also pushed to a new crisis by a GI named T/5 Archibald MacGonigle. A series of letters he wrote to *The Stars and Stripes* Mail Bag almost caused a revolt in the ranks.

Wrote MacGonigle:

Dear Editor:
From the look of all the hundreds of mailbags floating around, you'd never think there was a war on. It looks like the soldiers just sit back all day and write letters. All I have to say is that it's a fine way to win the war. To win a war, fellows, we all must pitch in and give it everything we've got. Writing letters all the time is just like this absenteeism thing back home. We'll never get anywhere that way. Besides, by the time your letter gets home, it's old news anyway.
I think we'd do a lot better for our home and country and further the war effort if we adopted this slogan: "Don't write, fight!"

Unfazed, MacGonigle soon followed up with other letters saying such things as, "It seems to me that the boys at the front are getting all the breaks and that we poor guys in the rear have to drink all this crummy vino. It isn't fair that's all." He added that he strongly felt that "the rear-echelon typist was just as important to the war effort as the front-line rifleman."

Before he was through MacGonigle also defended the tough spit-and-polish rear-echelon MP. "Sure, some MP's get a little tough sometimes, but usually it's for a man's own good. It makes him a lot better soldier, I always say. Believe me, fellows, I know what I'm talking about. Some of my best friends are MP's."

Overnight, Algiers seemed to become a combat zone. Frontline troops on leave dropped into *The Stars and Stripes* office demanding to know, "Where the hell is this MacGonigle?" *Life* magazine made a special offer for more of MacGonigle's views. And Axis Sally devoted a whole program to detailing how her hero MacGonigle and his MP friends were starting a revolution in Algiers against the American Army.

Faced with this furor, T/5 Archibald MacGonigle quietly went back into the woodwork and *The Stars and*

Stripes decided not to print his last letter saying that the American Army should provide the Arabs with cars, refrigerators and tuxedos, to make them a showcase of the good life of democracy.

Spring seemed to come slowly to Tunisia that year and the heavy spring rains blunted our hope for a fresh tank attack. Meanwhile, the British Eighth Army had arrived in our area. Supplied by 1,00,000 trucks, General Montgomery's troops had chased the Afrika Korps some fourteen hundred miles across the desert to Tunisia's Mareth Line. This was a twenty-mile-long border fortification that the French had built to protect themselves from the Italians.

The Axis force of some 250,000 men was now bottled up in a rectangular bridgehead the size of Pennsylvania. Back in Berlin, Goebbels reported to his Fuehrer that this Axis force "lacks weapons, fuel and in some places, food. Only sixty percent of the supplies reach Tunis; forty percent must be written off as lost. What is being sent to the bottom of the ocean in the way of equipment almost baffles description."

Our plan was to alternate our attacks on the II Corps front and the Eighth Army front, hoping to keep the enemy armor skidding back and forth between us until we could force a breakthrough to Bizerte and Tunis.

To dramatize the problems of Nazi General Jurgen von Arnim, T/5 Wallace Irwin wrote the poem for *The Stars and Stripes* which began:

> *Oh, Jurgen J. von Arnim wore an armor-plated*
> * monocle,*
> *But he could not see behind him—now wasn't that*
> * ironocle?*
> *He fought a rear-guard action and he did it very*
> * bitterly*
> *With booby traps and Tellermines and gallant sons of*
> * Iterly.*

II Corps' planned attack was to retake Gafsa, drive past El Guettar, then down the coastal road toward Gabes. That Gafsa-Gabes road was the most sensitive Axis artery since it cut directly into the rear of the Nazi defenses on the Mareth Line.

Gafsa was an unattractive town of 10,000 people, one of the oldest continuously inhabited places on earth, an oasis for ancient caravan routes that still had an outdoor swimming pool of sulphur springs where Roman emperors once bathed. An Englishman once described it by saying, "Gafsa is miserable; it's water is blood."

There had been blood in its water when we abandoned the town a month before.

The same Arabs who smiled at us with friendly V-signs, now put German signs in their windows saying *Araber Geschäft* (Arab business), told their returning German soldier friends which Gafsa citizens were Jews or Allied sympathizers, and helped to loot their homes and stores. Otherwise the bordello with its dozen girls and clean sheets continued their thriving business, and the cows and camels still walked the streets.

Nobody, however, seemed to have any explanation for the fact that the Arabs smashed every toilet, every window, every mirror in the town's only hotel, and uprooted every private garden they could find.

Our troops detrucked just outside Gafsa just before daylight. We carefully bypassed a big crater in the road where an Arab and his donkey had touched off a mine, and disappeared. You could still see pieces of the Arab's carpet bags and scattered corn. It reminded somebody of the Arab who stole a grenade, thinking it was a coconut, and was last seen pounding it on a rock, trying to open it.

Our planes and artillery already had blasted Gafsa in preparation, and we moved in slowly, carefully, ready for combat. But the Nazis and Italians had left with their loot, including most of the town's cattle and camels. What once had been a living town with a noise and smell to it now was only a graveyard full of ghosts and rubbled buildings with roofless walls and a little old lady on a broken balcony wailing as if the world had ended.

Slowly, some of the people started coming out of the cellars, some Arabs again making tentative V-signs; the kids staring with their hard, questioning look; and an old native Jew with haunted eyes and torn pants, whose family had lived here for a thousand years. "They took everything I had," he said slowly in French, as if he still didn't believe it.

Three GI's returned to Gafsa to find their girl friends happy to see them. The girls had feared their GI friends

79

were long since killed. In fact, they said they had found three American graves and had covered them with flowers in mourning. When the GI's heard about this, they asked to see the graves. The girls took them to this place and sure enough there were three mounds of earth with a sign over each of them, "LATRINE CLOSED."

El Guettar was another date-palm oasis area, where steep rocky hills covered our route of advance—the Germans parked on the ridges. Everywhere on the valley floor were sharp-sided impassable wadis and formidable areas filled with mines—the pie-shaped Teller mines and the variety of anti-personnel mines; Schu mines that blew off your foot; three-pronged Bouncing Betties that exploded a canister of marble-sized steel pellets, covering a fifty-foot area; and a special, smaller, sinister, pencil-shaped mine that headed straight for the genital area.

In the fog before dawn, Sgt. Sidney Alexander, Columbia, Tenn., sitting in an OP on Djebel Mcheltat reported to regimental headquarters, "Whenever I listen out there, I hear trucks. I hear tanks warming up. I hear lots of tanks."

Communiqué 138, March 24, read:
IN THE GAFSA AREA, EAST OF EL GUETTAR, AN ENEMY ARMORED DIVISION LAUNCHED SEVERAL ATTACKS FROM THE SOUTHEAST WHICH WERE REPULSED BY AMERICAN TROOPS WHO HELD THEIR POSITION FIRMLY. A NUMBER OF ENEMY TANKS WERE DESTROYED AND OVER 200 GERMAN PRISONERS WERE CAPTURED.

"The thing I remember most on that day," S/Sgt. Andrew Kukucka, North Tonawanda, N.Y., battalion headquarters operations sergeant, told Sgt. Milton Lehman, "was that business in the afternoon, when G-2 Intelligence told us that the attack would come at 4 o'clock. How they knew that God only knows. But it didn't come at 4 o'clock. Jerry had changed his plans—and G-2 knew about that, too, and they told us the attack would come at 4:40.

"At 4:35, I was talking to Capt. Donald Fogg, CO of Co. L, on the field phone. I called him up and told him that we got word from Regimental that the attack would

80

open up at 4:40.

" 'We ain't gonna budge an inch,' said the captain.

" 'Neither am I,' I tell him.

" 'They gotta make me know it,' says the captain.

" 'They gotta make me know it, too,' Kukucka said.

"All the time," Kukucka later continued, "them Stukas and JU–88's were bombing around and then the ME's come over and we hear the siren—the loudest siren I ever heard."

" 'What was that?' the captain asks me.

" 'That was a siren,' I tell him.

" 'I think I see something moving,' says the captain. 'Pardon me while I hang up.' "

We were all set. A thousand tons of supply moved from Tebessa to our front every day. Our artillery was waiting, big guns of every size dug in all along the line.

Coupled with their tank attack, the Germans threw in all the planes they had.

G-3 sitrep (situation report) for April 1:

FORWARD TROOPS HAVE BEEN CONTINUOUSLY BOMBED ALL MORNING. TOTAL LACK OF AIR COVER FOR OUR UNITS HAS ALLOWED GERMAN AIR FORCE TO OPERATE ALMOST AT WILL. ENEMY AIRCRAFT HAVE BOMBED ALL DIVISION CP'S AND CONCENTRATED ON UNITS SUPPORTING THE MAIN EFFORT.

The British air marshal caused some bitter stir when he answered, "It can only be assumed that II Corps personnel concerned are not battleworthy in terms of present operations."

However, on the day the skeptical British air marshal arrived in Gafsa to investigate air-support conditions, four FW-190's strafed the streets and stampeded a camel caravan, and then dropped bombs. It almost seemed as if it had been staged just for him, and the Americans couldn't have been more pleased.

"Come on, you bastards, earn a day's pay!"

It was a GI in an artillery outfit, yelling at some disappearing American fighter planes who had come to their call for air support to fight off a group of attacking Messerschmitts. The ME-109's had done their strafing and disappeared by the time our fighters arrived, and so our planes started heading home, too. Just then, a flight of Junker 88's arrived to drop their bombs on this same artillery outfit, and it was then that this frustrated GI yelled at our own planes to come back and fight.

Almost as if they had heard him, our fighter planes suddenly zoomed back—they had seen the heavy flak of our antiaircraft. The JU–88's tried to make a run for it, but our fighters shot down two of them, then waggled their wings to the cheering GI's below, and, again, headed home.

The Nazis sent their prize panzers in two separate attacks. Some sixty German tanks even got within 3,000 yards of one of our division command posts before we finally stopped them. Before we blunted their second attack, they had left behind a litter of thirty-two burned-out tanks on the valley floor. Then our own tanks started smashing back.

It was a German gun position our troops had bypassed, and now it opened up on our rear. A tank simply lumbered straight up to it, ground into it, then moved on.

"With the curiosity of the human and for security's sake, I decided to take a look at the damage done," said Cpl. Melvin Linton of Denver, Colo. "I gazed on the most ungodly sight . . . There in the hole were the bodies of men whose nerves were still twitching. Little parts of the human anatomy were strewn from one end to the other. These maimed and cut-up bodies poured blood and guts over the earth so that in spots where the blood had touched the ground it first turned purple and then the very earth beneath it seemed to be black. Extremities seemed to wriggle trying to get back to the other part of the body. One Jerry's eyes bulged out of his head and seemed to be asking, 'Why?' "

But the German retreat was far from a rout. We still had to clear the enemy from the ridge lines. This was a job for troops, not tanks.

From an artillery OP, you could see the thin path winding into the hill like a ribbon, up a hill, down a slope, up another hill, and all along it were the GI's, spaced fifty feet apart carrying boxes of ammo, machine-gun barrels, heavy steel tripods, reels of telephone wire; their walk slow, deliberate, weary.

82

That night in those hills, they would find the ground rough, full of holes and creeks and gullies, covered with waist-high shrubs. But GI guides had gone before them, memorized much, marked trails with white tape or toilet paper.

They would sleep on their raincoats. If the days were hot, the nights were cold, but there would be no blankets, no extra clothes. The jeeps would come cross-country after dark with cans of water and C-rations. The GI's would eat their cold C-rations in the cold dark, without seeing what they were eating. They would make coffee with cold water. Everything cold, cold, cold.

No fire. And you could only smoke a cigarette if you got deep down in your hole and covered your head with a raincoat.

"Some of the fellows had old hometown papers with them, sometimes as much as six momths old, which they had been carrying around since leaving the States. In the early evening, these papers would be carefully unfolded and passed from one to the other. We had all read them before, but it made no difference. They were from America, and we couldn't get enough of them. I remember reading one paper from a small town in Tennessee over and over. It sounded so small and safe, some place a million miles away, where the fact that some little girl had a birthday party was reported carefully and in full, with the names of all her guests listed and the party itself described in detail. It was strange, exotic stuff to be reading out there in the desert, waiting for the sundown Stuka raid to start."

A GI going into combat would take three bars of D-ration chocolate—enough to last one day—and two canteens of water instead of one. No other food. Tight excitement of combat usually canceled out hunger. The hunger came afterwards.

By the beginning of April, the enemy's defense in southern Tunisia had collapsed. His forces were gathered in a compact sector in northeastern Tunisia behind a great arc. His forward positions extended over mountains and valleys, plains and marshes, at a distance of some thirty miles from Bizerte and Tunis. Both sides regrouped.

The British went on the offensive at the end of March,

and by April 7 our two armies finally joined together.

The five American armored cars and the three British scout cars, gingerly inspected each other from a distance before closing in with a rush.

"Hello, you bloody Limey," shouted Sgt. Joseph Randall, State Center, Ia.

"Very glad to see you," said Sgt. A. W. Acland, a freckle-faced, red-haired soldier in a blue beret, from London.

For a short while again, it became a war of artillery. We had much of it and we used it liberally, and with great effect. We had learned the art of the "serenade"—a prolonged concentration of slow fire proving more effective than a heavier mass of fire for a shorter period.

The foot soldier had an interval of hot meals and a few even had hot showers.

Six soldiers were luxuriating in a homemade shower unit right off the side of the road when nurses from a nearby evacuation hospital tramped by. The soldiers were so surprised at seeing American women that they just stood out near the road and waved and yelled and whistled, completely forgetting that they were stark naked. The nurses just smiled, waved back, kept walking.

A soldier summed up the wadis and the djebels by telling a correspondent, "You fight all day here in the desert and what's the end of it all? Night just closes down over you and chokes you."

But the time had come to move out of the desert into the hills. By the middle of April, II Corps had moved 110,000 men in 30,000 vehicles two hundred miles across the British supply lines up to the most northern part of the front, near the Mediterranean. It was an intricate maneuver of the most complex logistics, a timetable of crisscrossing routes that also involved the moving of our main supply base from Tebessa to Beja. To maintain as much secrecy as possible, our MP's directing traffic even wore Arab burnooses.

The move had been pressured by the new II Corps Commanding General, Omar Bradley, a soft-spoken Missouri man whom Ernie Pyle later called the GI General. Bradley felt the British were pinching the American corps out of the final drive for Bizerte and Tunis and he persuaded Eisenhower to let the GI's prove themselves in an area of their own.

It was an area of hills and valleys covered with small, wild, purple flowers, narrow black gorges, growing fields of grain, a lovely, gentle, peaceful-looking country.

Dominating the scene was a hill that looked like a crude arrowhead with deep notches bounded by precipitous slopes, the Germans snugly dug into all the crevices. It was listed on the French maps as Hill 609 (the number representing the altitude in meters). Also known as Djebel Tahent, Hill 609 sat serenely atop a fifteen-mile wedge of lesser djebels, a massive area of interlocking defense. Hill 609 was a pivotal place, vital to both sides.

From Hill 609, the Germans could see Bizerte thirty miles away and they could pinpoint their artillery fire into the narrow draws between the hills which looked like our only approach. Bradley's answer was to send our soldiers straight up the sides of the hills, like "hunting wild goats."

There are all kinds of officers.

A small infantry unit had a visitor who brought with him a precious bottle of whiskey. The visitor offered the captain a drink, but the captain didn't even stir. He simply asked, "Have you got enough for my men, too?"

The pattern seemed always the same. We would take a hill, dig in for expected enemy artillery fire, then get set for the expected counterattack. In the final phase, we found a surprise use for tanks as mobile artillery—seventeen Sherman tanks firing on enemy strongpoints from the flank and rear.

A German prisoner later protested: "We could have held out against your infantry for another week, but we didn't expect to see tanks. As a matter of fact, you had no right to use them. We had been told that was not tank country and as a result we had few defenses."

Through the narrow neck of Green and Bald Hills, we soon moved into Mousetrap Valley, the brink of the salt plain that led into Bizerte. Now the tanks could be cut loose onto this coastal flatlands.

Should they kill him or shouldn't they? He was a member of a German tank crew who had been heading straight for their machine-gun position when one of our shells smacked it squarely and stopped it. This German had managed to crawl out of his tank, into their gun position. Some of the boys wanted to finish him off, but the sergeant said no. Just then, in came another shell, this time a German 88, this time aimed at them.

When the sergeant awoke hours later, he was in a field hospital. Several beds away, in the same ward, was the German whose life he had saved.

Bizerte was set aside for the American troops; Tunis for the British Tommies. Pvt. William L. Russell wrote a poem about Bizerte which was later set to music. It never did catch on.

> *Dirty Gertie from Bizerte*
> *Had a mousetrap 'neath her skirtie*
> *Strapped it on her kneecap purty*
> *Baited it with Fleur de Flirte*
> *Made her boy friends most alerty*
> *She was voted in Bizerte*
> *"Miss Latrine" for nineteen-thirty.*

Inside Bizerte itself, the Germans had trained their guns from across the channel firing straight up the waterfront streets. They also had machine-gun nests in the church belfry and inside the clumps of trees near the water's edge. The last one hundred yards of road leading into the town itself were completely exposed to enemy fire.

Our jeep raced around the lake's rim into the straight flat stretch that rushed into Bizerte. Against the backdrop of the city's outline we could see parts of eight ships jutting out of the gutted harbor.

The MP told us there had been a recon patrol in and out of the town but that it was still full of German snipers and machine-gun nests, and our own tanks and troops hadn't moved in yet.

As we got close, we saw something that the MP had forgotten to tell us. The Germans were now shelling the town from firmly entrenched positions on the opposite end of the lake. We could see the thick black smoke spurting from sections near the docks.

By the time we passed under the archway entrance of Bizerte, our jeep was doing a slow crawl.

Bizerte looked like the back end of Fleet Street in London—busted brick walls, single sections of houses standing lonely, grotesque wooden gargoyles shaped by shells and bombs where people used to live. And there were no people.

And then, suddenly, out of this nowhere and nothing, out of all this death and destruction, came the crazy noise of live music. Outside a little hole in the wall, flanked by rubble, were a jeep, a British station wagon and some French bicycles. Inside was the Café de la Paix—and the only life left in town.

The Café de la Paix was a single room with a few tables and a bar and an old-style, out-of-tune piano. Clumped together around the piano were two pretty French girls dressed in blue corduroy slacks, some British soldiers and a few civilians. In the corner of the room sat a crumpled-looking little old lady with a wonderfully happy smile on her face. Banging away on the piano was a British soldier from Glasgow named Martin Wilson, and while he played, the barmaid scurried around the room, setting up drinks for everybody. Then all of a sudden two American officers rushed in. "One of those snipers just took a potshot at me," said the American major excitedly.

Everybody else just smiled. "Have a drink," one of them said.

Then, in rapid succession, the British Tommy played "It's a Long Way to Tipperary," "The Marseillaise" and "Stars and Stripes Forever." Everybody was standing up straight at attention, partly humming, partly singing because nobody knew all the words. Even the little old lady in the corner joined in.

Outside, some shells had broomphed by, tearing the top off of another house several blocks away. Almost at the same time one of our Sherman tanks, which had just moved in, let loose with its big gun at a machine-gun nest parked down the street. Intermittently we could hear the splatter of the machine gun and the zinging sound of an individual rifle.

But this café was part of another planet. The British soldier kept playing the piano, good and loud. For a few minutes, there was no war. It was the craziest thing in the world.

Then, just as suddenly, quiet came. The war noises had stopped. And then the British soldier played a hushed rendition of "Stardust" and everybody in the room was quiet, listening hard, and you could hear the tinkling of the wine glasses.

It was getting late and the ride ahead of us was long and dusty, so we sneaked out of the place, disturbing nobody, and drove our jeep slowly up to the tank at the corner. There we waved furiously until we attracted the attention of the tank gunner. Several times, in clear simple sign language, we explained that we wanted to drive past and would he please, for the love of heaven, hold his fire until we went through.

And then we headed for Tunis.

Almost overnight the well-trained Axis Army of 250,000 men became a disorganized mob, drained of the will to fight, surrendering en masse. There was one German platoon, though, which waved its white flag for surrender, marched toward our waiting troops, then suddenly dropped to the ground and started firing. We wiped them out.

War soon dissolved into a series of small actions with isolated and confused German pockets.

Typical of the mood of victory was our reception in Ferryville.

If Bizerte was death, Ferryville was life. Somehow both sides had left the town alone.

No sooner had we entered the town square, when our jeep was surrounded by all kinds of people, clapping and cheering, "Vive la France! Vive l'Amerique!" and throwing flowers and confetti all over us. A grayish-haired, proud-looking old man pushed himself forward with a huge jug of wine, pouring it out for us in big glasses. Then some impulsive, cute French girls came up and kissed us, French-style, on each cheek. Then we kissed them American style. And we got an encore of that, everybody approving.

They were just standing around, staring at us, smiling. One dark-haired guy, obviously their spokesman, came up, shook our hands, then said, without stopping, "You Americans, oui? Clark Gobble, American, oui? Goodbye." It was obviously the sum total of his English vocabulary and when he finished, he just stood there, with a big grin on his face and everybody looked at us expectantly as if we were supposed to say something. So we just stood up in our jeep and yelled, "Vive la France!" and everybody started yelling and kissing us all over again. It was wonderful.

At the crossroads there was an MP who looked like a walking flower garden, so we stopped to talk with him. And just before we left, he said, "Hell, today isn't May eighth, it's Independence Day."

On May 9, 182 days after the North African invasion, 518 days after Pearl Harbor, the American Army secured its first unconditional surrender of Axis forces.

German officers arrived in full dress in Mercedes Benz cars and an American soldier commented, "You would have thought the bastards were going to a wedding."

Asked by a correspondent how he felt to be making history, Sgt. William Benson answered, "History, hell! I wish to hell I was back in Iowa running my butcher shop."

And, in Tunis, an MP, breaking up a traffic jam of American and British trucks, said, "We're going to keep in a bloody straight line from here to Sicily."

SICILY

The indigent Sicilian,
With freedom in his belly,
Who once cheered Garibaldi,
Now yells for caramelli.
                        —an anonymous GI

We put a phony, official-looking letter in a briefcase indicating that we planned in invade Sardinia. We then chained the briefcase to the wrist of a dead body whose lungs indicated death by drowning. We gave this body a name and military rank and dropped it off the coast of Spain.

It worked. The body was found, the letter accepted as genuine, and the Germans promptly started reinforcing Sardinia.

It was the old Army game of "Hurry up and wait," but this time, nobody griped; everybody understood. The boys knew how many ears and eyes the enemy had. That's why our LST (landing ship, tanks) had been sailing from one African port to another, sometimes staying in one place for a week, sometimes only for a day.

Except for the missing women in chaise longues, it had really been a Mediterranean cruise—a lot of sunbathing, reading, record concerts, some hot poker games, and swimming off the starboard side several times a day.

But then things changed. One morning, as far as we could see and wherever we looked—there were ships, all kinds—ships from Tripoli, Benghazi, Port Said, Beirut, Alexandria, Haifa, Oran, Algiers and Bizerte. With a strong skirt of sub-chasers and destroyers in an outer fringe of larger ships, most of the boys stopped worrying about torpedoes.

The strong westerly winds turned into heavy gales with forty-mile-an-hour gusts. But, suddenly the storm stopped and the tossing sea turned gentle with long, rolling swells. . . .

We were briefed today. They told us where we were going, what we expected to find lined up against us.

We were going into Sicily, a stepping-stone to Italy, but a big stepping-stone. A triangular island the size of Vermont, it had a population of four million. Scattered throughout the island were some ten Italian divisions and three German divisions. Our G-2 described the Italian troops there as third-rate: "Stick them in the belly and sawdust will run out." Of the Germans, though, he said, "Strictly hot mustard."

Our convoy headed south to give the Axis the idea that we might be moving in on Greece. We had some 600 big ships and 2,100 small landing craft carrying some 600 tanks, 1,800 big guns, and two armies: the American Seventh Army, under Lt. Gen. Patton, had four divisions; the British Eighth Army, under General Montgomery, had five divisions.

We were going in on the southwestern coast opposite the Gulf of Gela, the British moving in on our right.

D-Day for Operation Husky was July 10. H-Hour: 0245.

The sea had turned rough again and the men in the LCI (landing craft, infantry) started vomiting, one by one, all of them moaning softly as if it were a secret shame. One GI clambered to the side of the boat, moving out to a narrow ledge, fumbling with his pants.

With the rocky sea and the swaying boat, it seemed as if the GI would fall overboard, and an ensign ordered him to come back into the boat.

"I have to move my bowels, sir," said the GI in a pain-filled voice.

Somebody inside the boat laughed nervously.

"Jesus! What's so funny about that?" said another soldier. Then he got up, went over to the GI on the ledge, and said, "Here, Joe, hold on to me."

Before anybody else, the Rangers went in to knock out

two batteries of big coastal guns, and clean out the town of Gela.

It wasn't simple. They landed in these small LCI's, with a half-dozen Italian searchlights focused right on them, and a flock of big guns shelling their boats. Some boats didn't make it.

At the beaches, they found minefields, barbed wire and some concentrated gunfire all ready and waiting. One first sergeant got hit in the guts with a blast that killed his captain and temporarily blinded his lieutenant. With one hand covering his wound, the sergeant led his men past the beaches into cover. Then, as soon as the lieutenant recovered from the concussion, he and the sergeant each took one-half the outfit and did their next clean-up job.

After that, the lieutenant finally persuaded the sergeant to quit and fall back to some first-aid station. "Hell," said the sergeant, "I'm not helpless yet. Give me some prisoners to guard or something."

Rangers spread out at the town's perimeter and went through every house in every street in Gela. It was all very systematic and scientific, with one section covering each side of the street, watching the buildings on the other side, so that there would be no surprise sniping. There wasn't.

But there were all kinds of incidents. A small group of eighteen Rangers barged into a hotel packed with fifty-two Italian officers. There was a lot of noise, a lot of shooting, a lot of grenades going off. It all lasted about five minutes, and then the Rangers walked out with what was left of the fifty-two officers.

From somewhere, the Italians sent several tanks into town to do a little street fighting. They had little chance to do much. One ranger got within fifteen feet of one tank and let loose. He stopped the tank cold, killing one of the crew. The other two of the Italian crew refused to come out until they were persuaded by an incendiary grenade. Sgt. Shirley ("Call Me Jake") Jacob and his captain spotted another tank, but they were all out of ammunition except a 15-pound "pole" charge of TNT. So they both ran to the top of a nearby building, waited until the tank was directly beneath them, and then dropped the TNT. "It was a neat, simple job," said the captain.

Shortly after dawn, Gela was as peaceful and safe as a small New Hampshire town.

It was a long stretch of beach, high sand dunes with scrubby vegetation, then a broad open plain sloping gradually into the foothills. Bulldozers were busy cutting a path toward the good coastal roads. But the most valuable vehicles were the 700 ugly DUKW's which made their debut here. This DUKW was an amphibious truck that could carry twenty-five men or more than two tons of cargo, driving right out of the sea to an inland area—rather than unload on the congested beach. So bad was the beach congestion that some other supply craft had to return to their mother ships, still fully loaded.

But while we were firmly planted on the ground, the Axis still controlled the air. They had nineteen airfields all over Sicily, only minutes away from the invasion areas, and they concentrated on both the boats and the beaches.

One of the favorite Axis tricks—something they did dozens of times that first day—was to send a single plane tearing out from inland, sweeping across the beaches on a fast strafing job. Or else they sent out a couple of dive-bombers, barely skimming above the docked ships. Sometimes, when our Spitfires were around, we would see a fast movie-thriller chase, several Messerschmitts flaming to the ground.

Finally, like everything else, our nerves got dulled to it. Still, when a flock of fifty Nazi bombers were passing immediately overhead, not too high, in a tight formation, and it was light enough for them to see you very plainly —it was tough for anybody to appear disinterested. You never saw such a flak-freckled sky. Every ship in the harbor threw up everything it had. But the bombers weren't interested. They had already dropped their load.

We had two paratroop drops scheduled for the first two nights of the invasion. The first was unsuccessful: high winds, bad navigation and ack-ack so dispersed the troop carriers that 3,400 paratroopers found themselves scattered some sixty miles from the coast. But if they were disorganized and confused, so was the enemy.

The second drop seemed to be going according to plan. The leading flight unloaded its troopers close to the drop zone. Then, out of the silence of the night came the sound of a single machine gun. Within minutes, every antiaircraft gun on the beach and on the ships all opened up on our own planes.

"Why did I have to go on deck?" asked Machinist's Mate First Class Herbert Bair, Los Angeles. "Sure I needed a cup of jo; sure I needed a breath of fresh air. . . . Hadn't I spent the whole day in this hold, magnifying the concussions and explosions of bombs, the muffled roar of exploding tankers, the incessant staccato of the ack-ack, until I felt that the seams of my skull must certainly burst? . . .

"Above the roar and crashing of the five-inchers, I hear the talker on the fantail shout into his phone, 'Aircraft approaching off port bow. Elevation, twenty thousand. Bearing one-six-zero. Range, five miles.' Instinctively I train my eyes in this direction. Finally I see them—a dozen at least, big green birds of death they seemed to be. Too late now to return for my Mae West and helmet . . .

"Now the AA's and 40-mm's are training their sights on the approaching craft. Slowly but surely they elevate their guns. Comes the order, 'Commence firing!' and trajectories of tracer shells ascend in flaming parabolic arcs to encircle the entire flight. . . . Hit after hit we score until ship after ship bursts into flames or falls spiraling into the sea.

"But something is wrong. From the wounded ships, parachutes come fluttering, some to fall in flames into the sea . . . others to billow out in slow descent. Then some trigger-happy gunner aboard another ship decides to pick off the supposed helpless Jerries. Soon every gunner is firing away at the helpless troopers who dangle limply beneath the umbrellas of their chutes . . .

" 'Cease firing! Cease firing! Cease firing! Stand by to pick up survivors! Stand by to pick up survivors!'

"Only then does the dreadful realization descend like a sledgehammer upon us. We have wantonly, though inadvertently, slaughtered our own gallant buddies . . .

". . . I feel sick in body and soul."

Our own antiaircraft shot down 23 of our own troop carriers with 229 casualties. One returning plane had more than a thousand shrapnel holes.

Why?

Few planes were more easily identifiable than our C-47's.

They had been flashing their amber belly lights continuously as a recognition signal.

Word of the proposed drop had been sent to all headquarters.

Then, why?

There had been 24 German air attacks on our beachheads and ships that day involving some 400 planes. At
2150 hours, just before our troop carriers arrived, German
planes had hovered over us for almost an hour.

One military critic called attention to the fact that the
planes had to fly over thirty-five miles of active battle-
front, and he said, "Even if it was physically possible for
all the ships and troops to be warned, which is doubtful,
any fire opened, either by mistake or against any enemy
aircraft, would automatically certainly be supported by all
troops within range . . . Antiaircraft at night is infectious
and control almost impossible."

Or as a troop-carrier pilot put it, "Evidently the safest
place for us over Sicily that night would have been over
enemy territory."

We took the two hilly knobs six miles north of Gela
that controlled the nearby roads, and then managed to
beat back a German counterattack of some sixty tanks—
with the key help of our big guns. Some Mark IV's had
come within 2,000 yards of the sea before our naval guns
pinpointed on them. The nearby wheatfields were littered
with more than thirty burned-out Axis tanks.

Back in Gela, there was now a more highly schemed
order of things.

Gela itself didn't look like much—a slightly overgrown
Gafsa without the Arabs. Some of the streets were skinnier than any in the Medina. The jetty was blown up in
the middle, the wires were down, but none of the roads
were busted, and only a few of the houses had been badly
hit by bombs and shells.

All the people looked at us as we drove in, but there
was no cheering. These people had relatives and friends
fighting us only a few miles away. Still, some were glad to
see us. "We have starved too much," one of them said.
Everywhere, you saw soldiers handing out their rations
and cigarettes to poorly dressed, skinny little kids and
ragged men.

Lines of prisoners were marched through town, all day
long. They were dark, wiry-looking guys, showing up
small against our big MP's. The prisoners walked past
buildings marked with encouraging printed words, signed
by their Duce. Some of the women on the sidelines were
bawling, but one of them yelled out in Italian to one of
the prisoners she recognized, "You're all right now, you're

100

all right now."

The Italian-speaking GI's (and there were plenty of them) were telling the people that we were going to help them, not hurt them. One of them, S/Sgt. Frank Sclafani, of the Bronx, N.Y., went around quoting Tom Paine in Italian. Something about, "We fight not to enslave, but to set a country free and make room upon the earth for honest men to live in."

We overran Camiso Airfield on our second afternoon ashore, caught 25 intact enemy planes on the ground, and the wreckage of a hundred more on the field. Shortly after our arrival there, a JU–88 lowered its landing gear to come in. Our antiaircraft opened up on him, and missed. The JU–88 completed its landing and the angry German pilot shook his fist at the ack-ack crew. Only then did he suddenly realize that they were Americans, not Italians.

We weren't supposed to be there. Ragusa was supposed to be in the British Eighth Army sector but the British were stalled on the eastern slopes of Mount Etna. Anyway, there was Ragusa, open and available, and so we moved in. Not only did we capture the police and the mayor, but the main telephone switchboard was still working when we took it over.

All afternoon the calls came in from Italian military posts and authorities all over the island asking where the Americans were and what was happening anyway. Some Italian-speaking GI's who took over the switchboard assured everybody that everything was just fine and dandy, that it couldn't be better, and that the Americans had probably gone back to America. They had a ball.

While the British were pinned down in their sector, the American Seventh Army was freewheeling all over the western end of the island, with little opposition. Within five days, we had split the island in two. So anxious were the people of Palermo to surrender that they sent a delegation of prominent citizens to seek out our military commander and offer us the keys to an open city. Palermo was a prime prize because it was the biggest city and the best available port.

"There was this gal, see, and she was really stacked. I mean, lovely. And we didn't have to find her—she came to us. Her English wasn't too good, but we got the message. She was staying at this hotel in town, and we could come in, one at a time. She didn't want money, she said; she just wanted food.

"There were eight of us, and we were ready!

"But you know what, she was a great piece of ass and all that, but it was all spoiled for me. You see, she had her kid asleep in the other room. Just a little baby.

"I've got a kid of my own back home."

We had cut up our end of the island in broad, sweeping strokes but there was still much assorted real estate that needed the final mop-up. One of those areas was at the extreme western end of the island, a city called Trapani.

I was going to Palermo. In four hours I had hitched only two short rides. . . . In my last half hour of cubstone-sitting. I had had a very interesting sign-language discussion with a kid who gave us the stiff-arm fascist salute. I carefully explained to him that he was definitely out of tune with the times. Just as he was getting the Boy Scout salute down pat, a truck loaded with paratroopers came up and stopped.

"Going to Palermo?" I asked.

"No, we're going to Trapani," one of them said.

"Have we got Trapani already?" I asked.

"We're gonna take it now," they said. "Wanna come?"

It's a twisting road to Trapani. We kept picking up troop road guides at the outskirts of every town we passed. The crisis came when we picked up the last guy. He had four prisoners with him. Everybody had all kinds of pleasant suggestions as to what to do with the prisoners. But finally, somehow, they squeezed in. All four sad-sacks stared at the troopers with scared looks in their eyes until someone handed them some cigarettes. Then they all broke into smiles, and the tension was broken.

From the receptions we got at the different towns, it seemed as if the word had been flashing ahead of us all over the Sicilian grapevine: The Americani are winning this war. Be good to the Americani and they will be good to you.

All along the streets, they lined up to cheer us, to hand us apples and pears and melons and almonds. Instead of sullen suspicion peering from balconies (which we got during the first few days), the people waved homemade, crudely drawn American flags. In one town, Vita, they

102

even threw Italian chocolate bars at us. It was probably ransacked from some Italian barracks, and most of it was tasteless stuff. But the important thing was—for the first time since we hit this part of the world—people were giving *us* candy.

After a short exchange of artillery fire outside of Trapani, the town commander drove up with a white flag. He was an Italian admiral, all dressed up in a gold-braided zoot suit, quite ready to surrender the town, his sword and his field-glasses on our unconditional terms. But that night, except for a few roving patrols, Trapani was declared Off Limits.

It was getting late, and I was hungry, so I squatted down near the road and started to open some C-rations. Within a few minutes, I was surrounded by smiling people, who lived in the nearby farmhouses. They started handing me things, shyly, like little children. One woman gave me five tomatoes. A girl gave me a little salt and a small, freshly made Italian brown bread, still warm. Another woman gave me a ripe watermelon. In exchange, I emptied my pockets of all the candy and cigarettes I had.

As I was eating, an old farmer pushed his way through the crowd. Sticking out his chest, in a loud voice he said, "Gooda morning. I gotta two sons in America. I gotta one son in da United States Army, and I gotta son who gotta da best barbershop inna da Brookalyn."

He stopped for breath, and I stopped eating.

We had a long talk after that, over a bottle of Chianti. The old man had been to the States himself, for a few years, and was going back again, after the war. When he found out that I was going to sleep in a foxhole that night, he said, "You gotta come sleep in my house. It willa make me verra happy . . . like my son come home." So I went with him.

It was a crumbling little farmhouse, maybe a hundred years old, probably more. Two families lived in the house and they all came up to shake hands with me, and then they kept staring until I felt like both halves of the Siamese twins.

That night, I slept in the only bed of the only bedroom. I slept with my clothes on, dive bombed and strafed by several million flies and mosquitoes. For breakfast, I had walnuts and wine, no side dishes. And then I went to Trapani.

Trapani itself had been hit hard, whole blocks plastered,

the rubble still in the streets. The only stores open were the barbershops.

People still hadn't come back to town yet, but there were lots of Italian soldiers walking down the streets. Whenever they saw us, they stopped, saluted smartly and then said, *Buon giorno*. A few of them had guards, most of them didn't. All of them were heading for the prison stockade to give themselves up. One MP told me of Italian soldiers coming into town with their own trucks, with their own drivers, with no guards, hunting for somebody to surrender to. At the end of the day, we had taken 5,000 prisoners.

The weather couldn't have been nicer—soft springy air with warm days and cool nights and no rain. But the mosquitoes liked it as much as we did and there was soon a considerable number of cases of malaria among our men. Battle casualties at this stage were small, but men were still getting hit.

The kid sipped his bottle of Coke with an unbelieving look in his right eye. His left eye had been knocked out by a piece of shrapnel, just twenty-four hours ago. "From hell to heaven in less than a day . . . That's pretty damn good, isn't it, bud?" asked the kid. He was only twenty. His face still had that beardless fuzz to it. Only a few hours ago, he'd been brought on the ship, dirty and bloody, brooding. Now he was washed clean, carefully propped up in between white sheets, and he was smiling.

"Did you ever see such beautiful white sheets in your life?" he asked. "I told the nurse here to give me one sheet at a time, so I can get used to it gradually."

The young, pretty nurse standing next to his bed, smiled a wide, sweet smile for the kid.

"And you know what I had for supper?" he continued. "I had roast beef and all kinds of vegetables and apple pie and orange juice and real honest-to-goodness milk. And now they gave me this Coke . . . the first Coke I've had in eight months . . . The Army is really taking care of us."

This hospital ship, first American ship to carry back the wounded from Sicily, had been furnished with the best of everything—the best food, the best equipment, the best facilities. "And the best is none too good," said the ship's commanding officer, a colonel from Bay City, Tex.

We now controlled the air, and enemy planes were few.

All Axis planes had moved out of Sicily to Italy. So swift was our race that we even felt it unnecessary to call on our Air Force for close-support missions. Most of our planes kept themselves busy with targets of opportunity deep in the enemy rear.

"When the going gets rough," our G-2 wisely predicted, "the Boche will pull the plug on the Eyeties and wash them down the drain." And that's just what happened. Within a week after the landing, the Seventh Army had captured more than 20,000 prisoners, most of them Italians. The Germans sacrificed Italian troops ruthlessly to screen their own retreat.

A great percentage of our prisoners were native Sicilians conscripted into the Army. We soon paroled most of them to their homes and farms. We now had something called AMG (Allied Military Government) to help these people help themselves back to freedom. This was much more than just scrubbing the Fascist slogans from their town walls or chasing the Mussolini men out of town and burning their rifles.

It's a slow job, the rebirth of a dead town.

The story of Marsala is the story of villages and towns and cities all over Sicily. It's the story of AMG.

Unofficially, Marsala died on Garibaldi Day, May 11, at noon. That's when several hundred of our big bombers swept in low from the sea, flying through the flak in tight formations, taking two hours to empty their bomb bays. When they left, Marsala looked like a squashed tomato.

There had been ample warning to the 30,000 people in this wine-heart city, fronting the sea on Sicily's west coast. Allied planes had dropped thousands of leaflets, yelled it over the radio, telling the people to get out of town, to head for the hills and the suburbs. Those who listened, lived. Those who didn't, died.

It was two months later, on July 24, 1943, that GI's marched into Marsala after some short, bitter fighting in the outskirts. Marching with them were some AMG men.

The AMG job was doubly tough here because the people were spread out as far as fifteen miles in a semicircle around the city. But as soon as they heard that the Americani had taken over, they began to dribble back.

"They all acted like a bunch of spoiled brats," said the AMG men. "From somewhere, they got the idea that the American troops would come marching in, loaded down with clothes and food and money. Some were expecting new donkey carts, cigarettes, new homes. It took a while before they understood."

But the Sicilians did understand, finally. And under our direction, they started clearing away the rotting dead, filling in the road craters, tying together the broken bridges, pulling down the tottering lonely walls of blasted buildings.

Still, the hungry had to be fed, the homeless had to be housed.

Then there was the pregnant girl who wanted the AMG to release her boy-friend from one of our prison camps so that he could come home and marry her. And the family who brought in an old, dead body which they found somewhere . . . "What are we supposed to do with it?" they asked.

There were five hundred people who lined up outside the AMG office every day with their problems. Some wanted passes to go to a different city, some wanted simple things, such as mailing a letter for them back to the States, a lot of them wanted to be sent to the States themselves, and there were still plenty of men who waited in line to tell the AMG, "I am a prisoner . . . I want to surrender."

For Marsala, AMG was a big word that meant peace, food and freedom.

Four roads led to Messina and one of them went through Troina.

At first, we thought Troina was lightly defended. Our G-2 reported, "Germans very tired, little ammo, many casualties, morale low." But then we discovered that Germans had made Troina the hinge of their first strong defense line. Six fortified hills controlled the approaching highway as well as the whole bowl-shaped valley.

Built on a dominating ridge, Troina itself was a natural strongpoint. A town of some 12,000 people, it had narrow streets with right-angle turns, a round, feudal tower overlooking the cliff, a rugged approach of steep slopes coming from canyons, all of it a demolition engineer's dream.

It took a reinforced division a full week to reduce Troina's defenses and beat back two dozen German counterattacks, a week that made this the bloodiest battle of the Sicilian campaign.

In the final intensified attack, we used eighteen battalions of artillery and a bombardment by seventy-two A–36's. But by then we were mostly killing civilians because the Germans had pulled out.

"Keep on throwing that high explosive at them, boys," said Pfc. Melvin Hollowell of Coloran, N.C. "I don't care if I'm paying taxes the rest of my life just so they throw that stuff at them, instead of throwing me at them."

One big gun found a target of opportunity, two figures zigzagging across a field. Asked how he could justify shooting big shells at such a small target, a GI said, "It's so seldom that an artilleryman gets a chance to shoot at live meat, he can't resist the opportunity."

It couldn't even happen in Hollywood, but it happened in a grayish-looking villa in Sicily, two miles behind the German lines.

It all started when a lieutenant walked into a frontline first-aid station and told S/Sgt. Earl Wills: "There are two wounded American soldiers and one badly hurt Jerry in a house a couple of miles behind the German lines. But I can take you right where they are. Can you come with me?"

Twenty-two-year-old Sgt. Wills, Cohoes, N.Y., with four years of Regular Army behind him, looked up at the looey for a long minute. "Yeah, sure I'll come," he said.

He came with three other medics piled into two jeeps: T/4 John Packard, Highland Falls, N.Y.; T/5 William Larson, Story City, Ia.; and Pvt. Robert Holden, Rochester, N.Y.

They raced along the road, far in front of our advance troops, their Red Cross flags flying, and finally the looey said, "This is the place."

Turning left off the highway, they came into a courtyard of a big old house, and when they approached the open door, the four medics stared, blinked, stared again. Inside the big front room, there were eighteen American paratroopers and two Germans, all of them armed, drinking wine and eating chow served by some Italian civilians, laughing, having a wonderful time.

When the four open-mouthed medics looked at the looey, he smiled, and then motioned them into a back room. In the back room, there were three wounded soldiers, two GI's, one Jerry. Still slightly bewildered by the whole thing, the medics dressed one GI's shattered arm, another's bullet wounds, and also fixed up the Jerry, who

107

had shrapnel wounds in his arms, legs and stomach. They were loading the patients onto the litters when the looey came up to Wills again. "Wait a minute," he said. "You guys are in a pretty hot spot."

The looey smiled again. "There are two German Mark VI tanks parked in the orchard right in front of the house, with their 88's covering the exit. I have to get their O.K. before you can leave."

Before Wills could close his mouth, the lieutenant had gone outside.

In the other room, the Jerries and Yanks were still drinking vino, still smiling at each other, and kidding the Italian civilians.

But a few minutes later, the party was over and the German soldiers trooped into the back room to say good-bye to their comrade. They made sure he was comfortable, reassured him that everything would be all right, and then motioned to the lieutenant.

"It's O.K. now," said the looey to Sgt. Wills. "You can put them into the jeep. And in case you're stopped by any German patrol, the password is 'German—Lisso.' "

With a wild look in his eye, Sgt. Wills walked up to the looey. "What the hell goes on here, sir?" he asked. "Who's crazy?"

And so the looey explained.

That afternoon, the paratroopers had brought their two wounded soldiers to this Italian villa, and they were chowing up and figuring out their next move. Suddenly, without knocking, a German soldier opened the door, walked in and politely informed them that there were two Mark VI's hidden in the brush outside, with their guns focused on the door, so would nobody please try to take a walk that afternoon. Then he proposed a "gentleman's agreement."

It seems that the two tank crews were one of the last few Nazi patrols in that sector, and everybody was pulling out that afternoon. Both tanks were out of order (except their guns, which worked perfectly), so the German crews had planned to blow up their tanks and leave on foot. But one of their comrades was wounded and needed immediate attention, and their own first-aid station had moved way back earlier that morning. If the Americans would send someone to bring back transportation to take their wounded comrade to an American hospital, the Germans would go their way and let the Americans go theirs.

There must be no funny business, the German added.

108

Everybody must give his word of honor, as a soldier and gentleman. Just to make sure, of course, the Germans would hold the seventeen paratroopers as forfeit.

And that's just what happened.

A much more publicized, more important incident concerned a general and a GI. The general was the commanding general of the Seventh Army, Lt. Gen. George S. Patton; the GI was a Regular Army man from a field artillery outfit, who had served with a good record throughout the Tunisian campaign.

The GI was shivering, huddled in his bunk, when Patton stopped by, in his tour of the hospital, and asked what was wrong with him. "It's my nerves," said the GI, and started to cry.

"What did you say?" said Patton, angry.

"It's my nerves," said the GI again. "I can hear the shells come over, but I can't hear them burst."

"Your nerves, hell!" said Patton. "You're just a goddamned coward, you yellow sonofabitch. You're a disgrace to the Army, and you're going right back to the front to fight, although that's too good for you. You ought to be lined up against the wall and shot. In fact, I ought to shoot you myself right now, goddamn you!"

Patton pulled one of his pearl-handled pistols from its holster, waved it in the face of the quivering GI, then struck him across the face with his free hand, still shouting at him.

Patton then started to leave, and the GI started to cry openly. Patton came back, hit him again so hard that it knocked off his helmet liner. The colonel in charge of the hospital then put himself between Patton and the GI, and Patton told the colonel, "I won't have these cowardly bastards hanging around our hospital. We'll probably have to shoot them sometimes anyway, or we'll raise a breed of morons."

After the general left, the GI, still crying, kept saying, "Don't tell my wife . . . don't tell my wife."

The doctors then confirmed the GI's shellshock, called it "Psychoneurosis Anxiety State—Moderate-Severe."

It was not a story you could smother for too long. It soon broke in a Drew Pearson broadcast and General Eisenhower sent Patton a severe reprimand.

"I clearly understand that firm and drastic measures are at times necessary in order to secure desired objectives," wrote Eisenhower. "But this does not excuse brutality, abuse of the sick, nor exhibition of uncontrollable temper in front of subordinates."

Patton promptly apologized to everybody involved.

But the smell of the story lingered for a long time.

To speed up our stalled push along the northern coastal road to Messina, we tried something new—an end run, an unopposed amphibious landing some seven miles behind the enemy lines. But we landed at the wrong beaches and the German panzer division already had retired from the area before we moved in.

We tried a second amphibious landing soon afterwards, and this one ran into more trouble. The beachhead area was heavily booby-trapped and mined and the Germans counterattacked quickly with tanks and planes.

If we had come in with more force, we might have trapped the Germans there, but again most of them made their getaway, even managing to withdraw the bulk of their heavy equipment.

The limited roadnet made it easy for Nazi engineers to slow us down with blown bridges and manufactured landslides and extensive minefields. For a while, it was almost a battle of engineers. Before it was over, the Germans had blown 138 highway bridges and cratered forty road areas. One of the worst was a 150-foot section of a cliff road blown right into the sea at Cape Calava. Our engineers took only eighteen hours to "hang a wooden bridge in the sky."

Cpl. John Peters of Edgar, Wis., created nine bypasses in a stretch of five miles with his 13-ton bulldozer. And, when we ran out of TNT, we used Italian TNT and even used the explosives we found in the German Teller mines. "That's one way of getting back at them," said a GI engineer.

The Germans already had started their evacuation of troops from Messina, across the narrow straits to the toe of Italy—and the blown bridges just gave them more time. Theirs was a most successful Dunkirk: they pulled out some 60,000 troops, 10,000 vehicles, a hundred guns, more than a thousand tons of ammunition and another thousand tons of fuel. They even managed to take almost 5,000 wounded with them. And they left behind the Italian troops as the rear-guard sacrifice.

We had built up a force of almost half a million men in the combined Seventh and Eighth Armies and our pincer pressure was now unstoppable.

"We could hear the shells shriek—our shells—and we could see the Jerry ammunition train still burning, the fast-growing forest fire on the nearby hill, the bumper-to-bumper convoy of trucks filled with waiting troops, the sweat-soaked GI's catching a short sleep on the side of the road— You could see all this under the floodlight of a full, fat moon as our jeep raced along in a midnight ride to Messina.

"The sound of an explosion woke us up. We didn't know it then, but the racket came from the Italian shore. Our bombers were giving their shore batteries a good going-over before we moved into Messina. They were met by plenty of flak. You could see the tracer, dazzling bits of light curving up into the blackness, silvered by a full moon. Then came the big white flash as a bomb struck, then the thunder of the detonation. We thought the flak was being sent up from the Messina beaches. 'Hell, plenty of stuff to fight yet,' muttered Pfc. Roger Hall, of Los Angeles, a reconnaissance scout. So he climbed on his cycle, 'Eva,' and moved on up the road toward Messina. The infantry, in two silent files, also resumed their march; and the vehicles followed as fast as the engineers could find a way for them.

"Dawn came quickly. Together with the first signs of life, the bombers were back again, to soften any enemy setup that might still be waiting for us. We could see the flak puffs more clearly now, but they were still wide of the mark.

"As we pushed ahead, we passed two more blown-up bridges. The first was a thorough job, would delay us almost an hour. The second was a sloppy demolition, would hardly slow us down more than fifteen minutes. There was another patrol going toward town, and we tagged along. Walking with them, we saw the litter of vehicles, ammunition, papers. Then, rounding a curve, we saw Italy."

The Battle of Italy began at twenty-six minutes before noon on a Monday late in August when the first American artillery shell landed in Villa San Giovanni, an important railway and ferry terminus on the Italian coast. It came from the Number One "Long Tom" of D Battery that had pushed itself into an advance position, its 155-mm nose pointed over Messina toward its Italian target.

You stood on your toes, your mouth hanging open, your fingers in your ears to relieve the concussion as the soldier pulled the lanyard which released the hammer, hit the primer, shot the flame through the vent into the powder and high-pressured the shell about fifteen miles onto the soft shoe of Italy.

"That's it," said Gunner Cpl. Peter Volpe, Cambridge, Mass. But Volpe and everybody else were too busy for further comment. They had to shove in more shells, pull more lanyards. There were 99 more rounds, all marked special delivery, waiting to hit roads and bridges up and down the Italian coastline, before the day was over.

"We walked slowly around the ribbon of a road, feeling a little uneasy, knowing that a Nazi OP [observation post] on the high ground across the thin stream of water could easily spot us. But nothing happened, and, four miles later, we were on the edge of town saying hello to Joe Guiseppe who had lived in Buffalo, Niagara Falls and Altoona, Pa. And when we asked him about Brooklyn, Joe said, in his chopped-up English. 'Me never live in Brookalyn.' There was something about the way he said it that annoyed some of the Brooklyn boys in the crowd."

Messina no longer had anything left worth bombing. It was just a pile of rubble where people used to live. But, as we came in, life had come back to the rubble. The people were streaming out of their caves, marching through the streets, yelling and cheering, drowning out their small bands whose members were fiercely playing on their battered instruments. In the back streets, we could see old people and kids and pregnant women loaded down with sacks of flour and boxes of canned goods. Too long starved, they had broken into an Italian warehouse, almost rioting, grabbing as much as they could carry. The slow-moving human convoy was a picture of the worst of war.

Lt. Gen. George S. Patton, Jr., commanding the American Seventh Army, entered Messina at 1045. So did shells from the Italian mainland.

And so it was all over in thirty-eight days. Our Allied casualties: some 30,000 men, dead and wounded and missing. The Axis loss: some 160,000 casualties, most of them prisoners, most of them Italians.

The end might have come sooner if the Americans had not been given a subordinate position in the overall plan. As it was, we still beat the British into Messina by a few hours. The British general told Patton, "It was a jolly good race. I congratulate you."

The few miles across the Strait of Messina to Italy looked deceptive in the mist when a recon sergeant, John Begovich, Plymouth, Calif., said, "Hell, we might just as well go over right now."

It would soon be soon enough.

ITALY

Mine Layers

Through nights of slanting rain
Marchers are planting pain;
Gardeners in boots
Plant tender seeds of mines
Where the dimmed flashlight shines,
Nursing the wire-vines,
Hiding the roots.
Boys in green raincoats scamper
Where grass will soon be damper
With sudden red.
Ripe, ripe the pain grows high
Sudden into the sky . . .
New-mown the new crops lie,
Earth's new-mown dead.

            —Sgt. Peter Viereck

"It is going to be one of the great marches of all military history," said a man in a Cairo bar to Sgt. Irwin Shaw. "A long, narrow, green country, full of handsome people who have been enslaved for twenty years and are now being liberated and know it. You will be greeted like water in the desert, like a circus on the Fourth of July, like Clark Gable at Vassar . . . The chianti will flow like water, and can you imagine," he speculated, narrowing his eyes dreamily, "what it will be like to an American of Italian descent?"

"I can imagine," said the other in a low, pensive voice. "He would never reach Florence. He would be worn to

118

the bone with hospitality. And would have to be invalided back to the States."

"A-a-a-h . . ." they both sighed.

All those pear-shaped Italian women, irritated at the Italians, full of gratitude at being delivered from Il Duce and Der Fuehrer . . . "Do you know any Italian?" "A little," said the man who was heading west. "I patronized an Italian restaurant in Greenwich Village for seven years. Lobster Neopolitan style with garlic sauce . . ."

"Can you say, 'What are you doing tonight, Signorina?' "

"Yes."

"Roses, roses all the way," sighed the other man.

But our Italian campaign was not one of the great marches of military history, and the roses were seldom and scattered. For us, Italy was mud, mules and mountains.

Before our invasion, our hopes were higher. The Italians had kicked out Mussolini and were secretly negotiating with us for their surrender. We planned a paratroop landing to capture Rome's airfields, a seaborne invasion near Naples and a quick crossing of the Strait of Messina from Sicily up the Italian boot. We changed our plans only because the Italian government kept stalling us on the surrender.

The new invasion plan eliminated the drop on Rome, the only element of dramatic surprise.

The logistics couldn't be clearer. Note the fuel capacity of a fighter plane. Note the distance from the closest Sicily-based airfield to Rome and Naples. Note how much mileage a fighter plane gets out of a gallon of gas.

Any GI with any pencil in any headquarters had the quick answer. Rome was too far away for our fighter planes to provide any air cover for any invasion. Our outer limit was the crescent-shaped, sloping beach of Salerno, about forty miles south of Naples. Even there, one of our fighters could only stay around for twenty-two minutes before lack of fuel forced his return.

If we could figure this out, so could the Germans.

They did.

They were waiting for us.

Our convoy collected troop-loaded ships with four full

divisions and extra units adding up to 100,000 British and 69,000 GI's. The night of the rendezvous, the night before the invasion, on September 9, 1943, General Eisenhower broadcast an announcement over all the loudspeakers of all the ships: "HOSTILITIES BETWEEN THE ARMED FORCES OF THE UNITED NATIONS AND ITALY HAVE TERMINATED, EFFECTIVE AT ONCE."

What did it mean? Did it mean that this was going to be a pleasure cruise? But weren't there Germans still all over the place? Would the Germans pull out now or stay?

There was this leaflet waiting for Allied troops, which few of them had time to read:

Brothers,
    After thirtynine months of war, pains and grieves; after twenty years of tiranny and inhumanity, after have the innocent victims of the most perverce gang at the Government; today, September 8, 1943, we can cry at full voice our joys our enthusiasm for your coming.
    We can't express with words our pleasure, but only we kneel ourself to the ground to thank Good, who have permit us to see this day.
    With you we have divided the sorrow of the war, with you we wish to divide the day of the big victory. We wish to march with you, until the last days again the enemy N. 1.
    We will be worth of your expectation, we will be your alied of twentyfive years ago.
    Hurra the allied
    Hurra the free Italy

The committee of antifascist
exfighters of the big war

If the Eisenhower announcement was a minor mistake of morale, we made a more major military mistake in our invasion which cost many lives.

Despite the fact that we knew the Germans were waiting for us at Salerno, despite the fact that we knew there was no hope of any strategic surprise, we still decided to try to sneak in quietly, without any preparatory naval bombardment. It was a pipe dream that became a nightmare. Just as GI's started climbing into the snub-nosed invasion craft in the silent darkness, a strident voice blared out of a giant loudspeaker from the beach, "Come on in

120

and give up. We have you covered."

Flares lit up the sky, German guns started to fire and men died who might have lived.

Flares or no flares, guns or no guns, our seasick assault waves arrived almost on schedule, every eight minutes. Some scattered scrub growth and shallow irrigation ditches provided the only available cover, but German guns sprayed straight through the scrub and deep down into the ditches.

Mines were thick and everywhere.

He was a Seabee named W. J. Burke who had come in on an early assault wave to help clear the beach. It was in the British sector and, sure enough, there were some eight Tommies building a fire and boiling some water. One of them yelled at Burke, "Say, chappie, come and have a spot of tea."

"I started toward them," said Burke, "and was within fifty feet of them when a land mine went off, right under that fire. The explosion knocked me flat, and when I got up, every one of them was dead and mangled."

A boat sent in for the early wounded was sunk by mortar fire, and two others turned back. On the sixth assault wave, just before dawn, the amphibious DUKW's came in with the first tanks and big guns. Each DUKW could carry a 105-mm howitzer complete with seven-man crew and twenty-one rounds of ammo. The DUKW would drive straight up to the dune line, unload the gun and crew, which often went into immediate action, right out in the open with absolutely no cover. One 105-mm knocked out five tanks, chased away eight others.

Their arrival was critical. A half hour later, the Germans launched a strong tank attack, coming from behind stone walls and farm buildings, trying to break through to the beach.

The combat was so close that Pfc. Alfredo Ruiz was caught by the brush camouflage of an enemy tank which dragged him for ten yards before he was able to break loose.

Two GI's, both named Manuel Gonzales, one a tech sergeant, the other a private. The T/Sgt. Gonzales had the pack on his back set on fire from machine-gun tracers, wriggled out of it, crawled toward the gun with grenades exploding all around him, lobbed a grenade of his own to destroy the gun, noticed an 88-mm gun firing at our men from behind a dune, crawled toward it, threw in some more grenades to kill the gun crew, set fire to their ammo.

The other Gonzales was working his way toward a tank when he was shot in both legs. As he lay there helpless, the enemy tank moved in and ran over him.

When dawn came, our planes came, too. But despite our heavy air umbrella, German planes still slipped through to strafe and bomb the beaches. The Nazis had boasted that they would turn Salerno into another Dunkirk, but by the end of D-Day we had occupied the high ground five miles from the beaches along a forty-mile stretch. Our bulldozers had opened up exit roads, our antiaircraft batteries were in position, our supply dumps in good working order, and we had pushed past Paestum.

Paestum was an objective of the American VI Corps, while the British were to take Salerno, the airfield, and head north for Naples. Paestum sat just below the foothills of the 3,000-foot Mount Soprano, which dominated an area of olive orchards, orange groves, cultivated fields. But Paestum also had a fifty-foot-high medieval watchtower with a circular stone balcony (which the Germans used as a machine-gun and sniper position) and an ancient Greek Temple of Neptune (which we used as a medical clearing station).

We had to push past Paestum into the passes of this great wall of surrounding mountain or else the survival of the whole beachhead would be in serious question.

One of the early GI arrivals, Sgt. John Leonard of Jefferson, O., found himself in the barnyard of a deserted farmhouse. His tank wedged in a deep gully, he and his crew were waiting for another tank to come and haul them out. While waiting, Leonard wandered around the farm and fed the chickens and cows and pigs. Back home in Jefferson, he had his own farm with chickens and cows and pigs.

In the pressure of war, the human mind moves in mysterious ways. A GI at Salerno, after almost drowning in an irrigation ditch, worried only whether the water had ruined the pictures in his wallet. Despite the shells and bullets around him, he took out the pictures, tried to wipe them on the grass, then waved them back and forth in the air to dry them.

Another GI stopped shooting just long enough to crawl over to eat some grapes. Still another soldier stopped suddenly in the middle of combat to bathe his feet in a creek, then wash his socks to get the salt out of them.

And many soldiers insisted they heard this one GI, right on the beach of Salerno, just after the landing, suddenly yell, "Where is the pro station?"

The Germans threw in counterattack after counterattack to drive a wedge to the sea between the American and British positions in its center, along the Sele River. Forty Nazi tanks broke into that gap, surrounded one of our battalions and chopped it up. We had no reserves to throw in and so we drafted mechanics, truck drivers and headquarters clerks to dig in with rifles to protect our big guns from being overrun. To stop the most serious breakthrough, two of our artillery battalions fired 3,650 rounds and were joined by the steady support fire from the big British and American warships in the harbor.

One of the fiercest fights was for the five large buildings of the tobacco factory set on three sides of a square crowning a high flat top of ground with excellent observation of a corridor of critical highways.

But the major Nazi effort was in the area of the village of Altavilla.

The mayor's house was on the slope of a hill on the square overlooking most of the town and the road below. Inside the mayor's house, a group of our soldiers was soon surrounded, a small GI island in an ocean of Germans.

The sergeant's name was Kelly and his buddies called him "Commando," because he had received some Ranger training in North Africa. They would later call him "a one-man Army." And so he was. This was his story:

"I'd worked my BAR so steadily that when I put the next magazine-load of cartridges in it, it wouldn't work any more. I laid it against the bed and went back to get another BAR, but when I came back, the bed was on fire. That first gun was so hot that it touched off the sheets and blankets. I worked the new BAR until the steel of the barrel turned reddish-purple with heat, and it became warped. I couldn't find another BAR, so I went upstairs and scouted around until I found a tommy gun with a full magazine. Then I went to the window and gunned for some more Germans. But that Thompson was too fast for me. It spat out thirty rounds almost as fast as I could pull the trigger, and it kept riding up, so I had to bear down on it to hold it on the target. After I had used up the tommy gun's magazine. I remembered I had seen a bazooka somewhere, but in order to fetch shells for it, I had to go to the third floor, and to get to the third floor, I had to crawl over our dead and wounded.

"Those bazooka shells weighed several pounds each. When I'd found them, I'd brought down six of them and put one of them in the gun, but it wouldn't go off. I worked on it for a while, then poked it out of the window again, and pulled the trigger. The men in the house with me thought a German 88-mm shell had hit the place. All the pressure came out of the back end of that tin pipe, along with a lot of red flame, and the house trembled and shook. I had shot it four times, when my eye lit on a box of dynamite sitting on the floor, but it was no soap—we had dynamite caps, but no fuses.

"Lying beside the dynamite was an incendiary grenade. Picking it up, I threw it on the roof of a nearby building the Germans were holding. It exploded there, and the house burst into flames.

"What with all the equipment and ammo we had brought inside with us, the place was like an Army Ordnance showroom. Now I picked up a 60-mm mortar shell and pulled out the pin or safety lock that controlled the cap which set off the propulsion charge. There was still another pin, or secondary safety lock, inside of it, which I didn't know how to get out. I started to tap it on the window ledge, and the safety dropped out, making it a live shell, or, the way I planned to use it, a live bomb. For, if I tossed it out of the window and it landed on its nose, the weight of its fall would give it the twelve pounds of percussion needed to explode it.

"As I looked out of the window, a handful of Germans came up a small ravine in the rear of the house, so I whirled that shell around and let it drop among them. I did the same thing with another shell. When I let go of each of them, there was a cracking roar, and the next time I looked out, five of the Germans were dead.

"Next, I found a carbine. But there were only a few clips of cartridges for it, and every time I fired fifteen rounds, I had to reload the clips. I didn't know much about the proper care and feeding of carbines, and presently it got too hot.

"Your mind gets single-tracked in a fight like that; and all I could think of was the problem of finding another weapon as fast as I used one up, so I could keep on blazing way. Propped in a corner was an '03 Springfield, like the one the AEF used in the last war. There were a few rounds of ammunition for it lying on the floor, and I picked them up and shoved them into the gun. It was a very accurate gun. Looking out of the window and down into the courtyard, I saw a 37-mm antitank gun, and seeing it there gave me an idea. I ran down, opened its breech and threw in a shell. A church steeple, which the enemy was using as a fortress, had been giving us trouble, and we hadn't been able to cool off the Germans in it with our small arms. I set the sights of that antitank gun right on the building. Then I ran into a snag. I didn't know how to fire it, but I kept on fumbling around, pulling this and jerking that, until I got hold of a handle and it went off. Not knowing anything about it, I had my chin too close to it, and the recoil knocked me kicking.

"In that courtyard, I was fairly safe from the fire of nearby Germans, for the wall protected me and their bullets went over my head. When I saw some Germans coming down a hillside, I threw in one of the shells with a tin hat over its ears, and fired point-blank. It hit one of them squarely, and put holes in the others. The Krauts who hadn't gotten it, turned and ran.

"I went back into the house, where I found a third BAR in the hands of a dead man on the third floor. He had been killed firing it. His ammunition was lying in a belt beside him, but there wasn't much of it left. So I collected machine-gun bullets of the same caliber and put them in the BAR magazines. Then I took it down in the front room and fired away. I worked that BAR until it began to smoke as if somebody had baked it in a hot oven. A Heinie shell hit the side of the building, and made a big hole in it, burying two men under the rubble. Snipers were touching them up down in the kitchen, and someone sent for me to go down there and help.

"I started down the hallway, but when I got there, a group of dizzy GI's were cooking spaghetti, just as if they were chefs in a ravioli joint back home, and all they had to think about was food. They had spread tablecloths, laid out knives and forks, sliced bread, opened watermelon and honeydews, and put grapes and tomatoes on the table. I don't mind people doing screwy things—it helps to let off the steam when things are so tight that otherwise you'd go off your rocker—but to see them readying that meal made me mad, and I got off a few overheated remarks. Then I thought, 'The hell with it, maybe they've got a good idea, at that.' I found a box of champagne, broke the neck off a bottle and wet my whistle. Then I took the straw off a basket, got out three or four eggs, broke them in an empty C-ration can and drank them raw. Nobody had time to give those snipers much attention. They had been having things pretty much their own way, and had grown careless about concealment. I saw one of them in a tree, and drew a bead on him. His rifle dropped from the tree first, and after a few seconds, he toppled to the ground after it. After working the BAR for a while, it began to heat up. I put it down, and went over to lap up some more champagne. To me, it tasted like soda pop or 7-Up."

There were still some thirty GI's alive in the mayor's house at the end of the day, and they broke down into groups of six to make a break for it that night. Kelly offered to stay behind as part of the rear guard.

He was still alive when they gave him his Congressional Medal of Honor.

After ten days of touch-and-go fighting, our bridgehead was finally safe and secure—from the toe of Italy to the hills within twenty-three miles of Naples. The single exception was the bridge above Salerno, still under harassing fire from a single 88-mm, which we couldn't seem to pinpoint.

She spoke only Italian and said her name was Alma, and that she would show us where to find the German gun. Some GI's went with her, crawling up the hill. Alma's young legs were bare and the underbrush scratched them until they bled and the GI's were breathing hard when she finally stopped, and pointed. Down below, in a cavern, was the 88-mm, in firing position, complete with crew.

The GI's had brought a field telephone with them and the artillery observer softly gave his fire command. The first round was short and almost blew Alma and the GI's off their hill. The next two came closer. The fourth shot was a direct hit.

126

And then Alma disappeared.
They didn't even have a chance to thank her.

As our troops turned toward Naples, we got a foretaste of our future. Roads so steep and sinuous that a hilly machine-gun position could cover the twists of a dozen curves, canyons so deep that they almost never saw the sun, and enemy observation so complete that a single 88-mm parked on the bare nose of a hill could deliver direct fire on almost the entire length of the valley floor.

To stall us still further, the Germans blew up all the mountain bridges—five of them on a stretch of road only 2,200 yards long. One of them crossed a sixty-foot gorge, but our engineers took only two days to build a two-story trestle bridge, eighty feet long, capable of carrying eighteen tons.

We entered Naples at the beginning of October, twenty-seven days after our invasion. We entered without opposition and found a city more terrified than destroyed.

"Snipers in Naples that first day were thicker than flies," paratrooper Cpl. Joseph Toporski, of Milwaukee, Wis., told Sgt. Jack Foisie. "And you know how thick flies are around here.

"If there is something I don't like, it's snipers," continued Toporski. "So me and my pal, finding ourselves all alone, just went down the street shooting. We got quite a few, and then they got my pal.

"I had no more carbine ammunition, so I took his. I got a few more. Then it got too hot, and I ducked inside a door. That's where I met my pal here." He indicated a British Tommy, Sam Wagne, of Leeds, Yorkshire.

Tanker Wagne took up the story. "It was very hot indeed. Inside the building, it was very cool. Two girls came down, and we got to talking. One was named Joan and one Marisa. We went upstairs, and they had a phonograph and American records, too. All old-fashioned, but American music. So we danced. We had a good time."

"And when it had quieted down outside, we went out and worked our way back to our units," said Cpl. Toporski. "I got one more sniper on the way."

Immediately after the Italian surrender, Nazi soldiers in Naples stripped women of their watches and jewelry, looted homes and shops, raped at will, killed on whim.

The Germans destroyed the flour mills, drained the reservoirs, blew up the main aqueduct, opened the doors of all prisons, smashed the sewage-disposal system, planted time bombs in public buildings that later killed hundreds of civilians.

But the most mindless desecration was at the University of Naples, founded in 1224 by Emperor Frederick II. Nazi soldiers went from room to room pouring gasoline on floors and furniture, soaking priceless books and archives, the accumulated wisdom of centuries—and then threw in hand grenades to set it all on fire. It was barbarism.

All this Nazi terror made our welcome that much warmer. The majority of Italians were surviving on potatoes, chestnuts and figs, and so GI food could buy anything, and did. Instead of shining shoes, many kids found it more profitable to pimp for their sisters.

Black market became the watchword and the GI courtroom at the Tribunale soon had a crowded calendar.

It included the acquisitive soul who "borrowed" nine gas masks; the timid little man who was preparing for the future with 29,000 pounds of GI flour stored away in his cellar; the pink-cheeked pleasant lady who always put sodium bicarbonate in vino bottles so that the cork-popping sounded like champagne; the three sad sacks who looked like refugees from a cross-country freight train who were just curious about what was in all those interesting-looking cans; and the skinny-shadow edition of Eddie Cantor, pop eyes and all, who kept bawling, "Yes, I did it . . . I did walk off with those 273 boxes of condensed milk. But please be lenient, please be merciful with me, because I have five women and nineteen children to support . . ."

As we moved north out of Naples, the question became overwhelming: how far do we go?

The Italian peninsula is almost eight hundred miles long and more than a hundred miles wide, with a central backbone of mountains as high as 6,000 feet. Out of this backbone branched a never-ending series of mountainous ribs and rivers. Roads were few, and the few were narrow, winding, and almost useless in the winter. The scattered plains were too small for tanks to maneuver. As a G-2 officer put it, "Every five hundred yards, there is a new defensive position for a company; every five miles, a new line for a division."

128

It would be a war of always one more mountain, one more river. German engineers had been ordered to destroy bridges, stations, water works, factories, power plants and to mine roads, houses, entrances to villages. Besides this, the German Tenth Army was busy building a winter line in the mountains behind Venafro, deeply dug-in gun positions blasted out of rock.

The soft underbelly had a steel corset.

But the decision was firm: keep moving. Our first major obstacle was a river, the Volturno.

A typical river patrol. You walk blind in the black night. A wrong step and you sink suddenly into a swirling stream. A lucky bullet and you crumple quickly and disappear. You watch the white tape on the man's back in front of you, but if you're the point of your patrol, you have nothing in front of you but fear.

Noise means death but water splashes, feet stumble, rocks fall. The current is too swift to get a rope across. The bank is too steep to climb without stumbling.

Every second you expect the ready bullets, the waiting grenades, the quiet mines.

So tight is the tenseness that it even wipes out the icy wetness; so deep is the fear that it almost wipes out hope.

You want only to be back again, and then you want to be dry, and then you want to be warm, and then you want to be fed, and then you want to sleep—without dreams.

The Volturno in mid-October was a raging, rain-swollen river, three hundred feet wide. Together with the Calore, it formed a continuous sixty-mile barrier directly blocking our road to Rome. And the longer the Nazis could stall us at this river crossing, the stronger they could make their mountain defenses.

Time meant lives. Meanwhile, many of our GI's were still wearing summer uniforms because their barrack bags were back in Sicily, due to insufficient shipping space.

Trench foot became the prime casualty-causer of the winter war. Too many GI's never took off their shoes for days, even weeks. Tissues gradually die, sores break out, and then gangrene may set in. Shoes were cut off the feet, and sometimes even the feet were cut off.

To keep dry, the ingenious GI mind had a variety of routines. For a short fire, they dug a hole about the size of a man's hand, poured gasoline into it, put some dirt over the gasoline and lit a match. The dirt kept the gas from burning too quickly. On a small fire like that they could heat a canteen or a cup of coffee. For a bigger fire, they filled a small can with gasoline and buried it even with the surface of the ground. They piled rocks around to set their cooking utensils on and then tossed a match at the gas.

T/4 Eugene Caton, Sturgis, S.D., sealed the open end of a brass casing of a 105-mm shell, plugged a hole in the top to which he welded a stovepipe made of empty grapefruit-juice cans. Then he ran a thin pipe from one end of the shell case to a small container of diesel oil. Five gallons of diesel oil lasted fifty hours, meant almost a week of comfortable nights. Pvt. Joe Carney, Philadelphia, took some white engineering tape, a burlap sack and blankets and made an airtight sleeping bag. Pfc. George Malloy, Vt., and Pvts. Rooks Glyne, Calif., and George Swan, N. Y., pooled their shelter halves, salvaged three others, cut some saplings, found some rope and made a tent.

To waterproof a tent, the GI formula was: "Melt eight candles (after carefully removing the wicks), add a pint of linseed oil, and a pint of paint. Mix well and add eight quarts of gasoline, and again mix well. Apply solution with either vertical or horizontal strokes."

But one of the prize GI homes belonged to S/Sgt. Wallace Odd, Kaysville, Utah.

"They laughed when we started digging a deep ditch," said Sgt. Odd. "They didn't know how beautiful it was going to be." It was four feet deep, seven feet wide, ten feet long, and it had a lot of gadgets inside. It was the gadgets that made it so wonderful.

"Home was never like this," said the sergeant, as he stretched out on a long, wide bed, pulling a book off the shelf, adjusting the convertible tarpaulin to let the sun in, and then reaching for a big orange.

It all started when Sgt. Odd stumbled across some strong, long logs, and used them as the side walls of the foundation. Then he dug out a small hallway leading to the door, and then he fixed up the bed.

"That was the most important thing of all," said Odd. "There's nothing like a soft, warm bed to come home to at night." To make it soft, he made a mattress of straw, six inches thick, under the blankets. To make it warm, he built a fireplace. At first, he used a tin German shell box, but the heat started the tin corners smoldering. Then he got an old 20-gallon German oil drum, and that worked beautifully, except for the smoke and fire hazard. Odd fixed that by adding an underground stovepipe section, which brought the smoke out several yards away.

"It's wonderful," he said. "Not only because it warms up the room and lets me dry my wet, muddy shoes at night, but because I can make some midnight snacks, whenever I get another package of Spam from home . . . I got four already."

Odd used to be a cook at the Blue Bird Café in Salina, Utah, and made midnight snacks all the time. "That's where I got the habit," he said. "We were all set to make a little sign saying, 'God Bless Our Little Home,' but the topkick just confirmed the rumor that we're moving up to-morrow," lamented Odd.

"That's the trouble with war," he said. "It breaks up a guy's home life."

We waterproofed our tanks, collected rope, assembled bridging equipment, borrowed rubber boats from the Navy, improvised rafts of canvas covers for our weapons, and liberated a thousand Italian kapok life-preserver jackets from a local warehouse.

We knew at what points we could ford the river—where the water was only chest-high; we knew the dire need of guideline ropes because of the swift current; we knew that enemy guns were registered on all likely crossing points; we knew that we had to break down the steep banks on the other side with bulldozers to ease the climb of our tanks.

We knew how rough it would be.

To keep our plans quiet, we made most of our troop movements at night, ordered our artillery to fire their usual morning rounds to avert suspicion—and we maintained our probing patrols.

Then came the crossing. Six divisions on a forty-mile front, the whole river area covered with our smoke shells. Guide ropes unhinged, rafts broke up, rubber boats kept drifting downstream.

"It looked like somebody zipped the whole sky wide open, because there was just a regular deluge. It turned everything into slippery slush. Then, on top of that, we had to climb an almost straight-up ledge. It was like going backwards up a ski runway.

"Well, my platoon sergeant, Vogel, got up there and somehow braced himself and used his rifle butt to help everybody else up. It took an hour and a half before the whole platoon and all the weapons were up.

"Later, I found out from one of the boys that the rifle barrel had cut deep into Vogel's hand. But he never told me about it."

The short, chunky lieutenant was silent again, then got up to leave. "Yes, he's a great man, my sergeant. . . . Never mind about *my* name . . . Just say that Platoon Sgt. 'Bugs' Vogel is a great man, that he's the best goddam mortarman I ever saw, and that he's a better man than I am."

The jumble of hills on the enemy side of the river looked like a clenched fist, and soon began to act like one. But our GI engineers built three bridges for tanks. They moved so fast that we captured two German 150-mm guns in perfect condition, intact with full crew. Our speed had cut them off, they said, and they were waiting to surrender.

After a full day and night of continuous fighting, we controlled the whole hill dominating the valley immediately north of the river.

But the Nazi Tenth Army had mostly retired in good order to their prepared positions behind their Winter Line.

And now the wounded were waiting.

Upstairs, eight Jerry planes were kept busy twisting inside the thick flak, circling the area, picking their spot to come in on a dive-bombing–strafing job.

Downstairs directly beneath them, in the Medical Clearing Station, the ambulance drivers were eating corned beef. Pfc. Paul "Santa Claus" Harvey looked up at the planes and cursed. The boys called him "Santa Claus" because he had a beautiful red beard with three-inch sideburns.

Harvey was bitter because of what had happened the week before. He was driving an ambulance full of patients to an evac hospital, crawling slowly through the slushy, slippery road, when suddenly he thought he was seeing things.

"I thought I was seeing little land mines bursting out of the road," he said.

Actually, the exploding spurts of red were 20-mm shells

spitting out of two German planes that had appeared out of nowhere.

There were only two cars on the long stretch of straight road. One of them was the ambulance.

The Jerry plane headed straight for the ambulance, firing his 20-mm cannons.

"It was a clear day, perfect visibility," said Harvey. "The red cross was all polished up and almost glaring. I hope it burned his eyes when he came down."

The Winter Line war, or the *Winterstellungen*, as the Germans called it, lasted from the middle of November to the middle of January. The Nazis had prepared their positions months before, using forced civilian labor as well as soldiers. Dug into five feet of solid rock, many of their gun positions were invulnerable even from our most intense artillery fire. The villages of tightly crowded gray stone houses clinging to the steep slopes had been converted into fortresses. Above all, the Germans had reinforced their troops.

But we lacked reserves, and so the war stayed static for a while. We issued wool underwear, extra blankets, shelter halves, overshoes and the lucky ones even got weather-proof combat suits and extra dry socks. Whenever possible, men got a double coffee allowance and a hot meal to replace the K-rations. But the greatest morale factor of all was a rotation system to guarantee every frontline soldier at least five days away from the war in a Naples rest camp.

The eight hundred soldiers jumped off the trucks, their clothing mud-caked, their faces dirty and bearded, their grenades still dangling from their belts. For about ten minutes, they mulled around in the courtyard, grumbling and suspicious, wondering what the score was.

And then a tough-looking soldier, with two stars on his field jacket, got up on a stand and told them:

"We went so far forward to get you guys that I wouldn't be surprised if we had some Jerries down there among you."

The boys laughed at that. The tension was broken.

"These five days are absolutely, completely yours," a Special Service officer then told them. "You're your own boss; nobody will tell you what to do or where to go. You want to sleep for five days, you can sleep; you want to go sightseeing at Capri or spend all your time at some bar or sit around and write letters, that's your business," the major told them.

For most of the soldiers coming from thick, gooey mud, this was their first hot shower in three months. For Pvt. Harold Josephson, Bristol, R.I., this was his first hot shower since he had left England, more than a year before. "I was under that shower for more than an hour," Pvt. Josephson said. "I felt so good that, if General Clark came around, I woulda kissed him on both cheeks."

Sgt. John Paul Jones scratched the head of the little brown puppy who was busy chewing on his socks.

"Her name's Volturno," said the sergeant. "She was just a shivering pup, only four inches long, when she wandered into the bivouac area one day. She was so cold, she couldn't even squeal."

The sergeant smiled a sad smile. "I was fast asleep when she hopped into bed with me last night and started yanking on my hair. I guess we're both lonely."

There was no brassard on the sergeant's arm, but he was an MP, a frontline MP, attached to a recon patrol, which hunted for supply roads where there were no roads. The sergeant had been up front for a long while; this was his first pass.

"My buddy Andy was supposed to meet me here. He got his pass the same day I did. We had all kinds of plans to tear up the town, just as we did in Honolulu, three years ago . . . ."

The sergeant was quiet for a while, and then he continued.

"Andy isn't coming here. He's dead."

More quiet. Even the puppy stopped jumping around and lay still in the sergeant's lap.

"I didn't know Andy was dead until I got here yesterday," he said.

"One of the boys told me how he got it. He had his pass, and he was leaving his gun position to get back to the CP, and he told the boys in his squad, 'Well, I beat this one.' Then he forgot himself and stood up. A sharpshooting sniper with a machine-gun pistol got him right here."

The sergeant made a motion across his forehead.

The puppy tried to get the sergeant's attention, and then impatiently jumped off his lap and scampered away.

134

"I tried to sit down yesterday and write a letter to his folks, but I just couldn't. I don't know what the hell to say. Did you ever write a letter like that?" he asked.

Nothing was said for a few minutes, and then Sgt. John Paul Jones looked at his watch. "Hell, it's getting late," he said. "I better get going . . . I've got to have enough fun for the two of us now."

Then he added quietly, "That's the way Andy would have wanted it . . . He was that kind of a guy."

South of Naples were dozens of scattered GI units, mostly supply setups, remote from the war and isolated from each other. Their way of life was so rear-echelon, it was almost unreal.

It was a warehouse, not too far from the railroad station, where the doorways were marked by the signs, "Engineers' Spare Parts." In this particular warehouse, thousands and thousands of carefully cleaned C-ration cans, all of them labeled and indexed, lined several hundred long shelves. Each can was the home of some small, important spare part, which some engineer outfit, somewhere in Italy, would soon cry for.

The Army even handed a Legion of Merit to a Bronx boy, T/4 Joseph Canzoniero, who devised a super-simple index system, whereby anybody could find any particular spare part, out of all the thousands that were there, within a few moments.

Probably the most interesting isolated outfit of all consisted of a single man, Sgt. Delbert Darnell, Boonsville, Tex., and thirty not-so-bad-looking Italian signorinas. It was the sergeant's job to keep the girls busy, all day long, testing spark plugs. Sgt. Darnell's girls put out at least 4,300 tried-and-true spark plugs every single day. Darnell was really proud of his girls, who worked for him without the slightest fuss or bother.

Working with women is nothing new to the sergeant. Back at the Sunshine Curtain Company in Los Angeles, he was shop foreman, and had 169 girls working under him at one time.

Sgt. Darnell's biggest difficulty was in the initial organization of the section, because he was told to go out and rustle up his own womanpower. Since there were no employment agents in town at the time, the embarrassed sergeant had to stand at street corners, waiting for a likely looking girl to pass by so he could ask her, "Will you come with me and test my spark plugs?"

James Thurber once wrote: "The men of Italian towns and villages do not seem to do anything except stand in the street. Many of them stand quite still, others move around slightly."

But in one village, one wandering GI found fantasy:

"How would you feel, if you were walking down the cobblestoned street of a peaceful fishing village, where nothing ever happens, and you suddenly saw some clowns, gypsies, Spanish dancers, bullfighters and Arabian dancing-girls, all coming toward you?

"Well, that's the way I felt.

"To make matters worse, as soon as they spotted me, they all started racing after me, as if I was the last potato in a potato race.

"The first one to grab me (I was paralyzed) was the gypsy with the Greta Garbo mask and Betty Grable legs.

"But the mystery cleared up in a minute when Greta Garbo looked at me with her expressionless masked face and said, 'Carnivale . . . Carnivale.'

"Now, I could have done several things. I could have called the MP's and had them all arrested; or I could have silently stolen away in the night with my two blankets and shelter-half.

"Instead, I followed Miss Garbo.

"We didn't walk very far before we heard music, and everybody walked up a narrow stairway, Indian-file, until we came to an enormous room. The room had been stripped clean of all the furniture, except straight-backed chairs which lined the walls. In the corner, a five-piece band was playing desperately, trying to dish out sweet and hot music at the same time, and almost succeeding. As for the floor space, all of it was taken up by more people in costumes and masks, hopping around furiously, trying to keep in time with the music as if their lives depended upon it.

"In the straight-backed chairs on the sidelines, mothers and fathers, and their mothers and fathers, watched the proceedings, beaming and gabbing at one another, and giggling.

"In Manfredonia, this was the Italian version of Halloween. It always lasts three days and nights, and ends in a dusk-to-dawn carnival. This was the final night of the carnival.

136

"When Miss Garbo and I were on the dance floor, doing a modified Lindy-Hop, I inquired further into the original history of the carnival. Miss Garbo merely looked at me queerly through the slits in her mask and asked, 'What's the difference?'

"All the people had politely ignored me, as if my uniform was just my costume for the evening. Single exception was a little old man, who must have lived there, because he didn't wear a costume. He kept trailing me with a trayful of molasses-covered almonds and glasses of vino until I had to push him away, gently.

"Somebody else borrowed Miss Garbo from me, for some folkdance which greatly resembled the Russian *Kizatzke*. Meanwhile, some more clowns came up, with another 'captured' Americano, who turned out to be Sgt. Cornelius Hook, of Clifton, N.J., an MP who happened to be off duty at the time. The sergeant soon got into the swing of things, showing the curious Italians the fifty-seven varieties of American jitterbugging.

"It was getting quite close to midnight when Miss Garbo took her mask off, looking very pretty indeed. I was patting myself on the back when I saw her dragging in an Italian sailor. The sailor was obviously very reluctant about the whole thing. Miss Garbo pointed to the sailor proudly and said, 'She is my husband.' I shook hands with Mr. Garbo, and told him how happy I was to see him, and then I said Happy Halloween to everybody, put on a clown's mask, and went home."

The umbilical cord in southern Italy was the GI-operated railroad. It was a lonely job, a dirty job, a vital job.

He spoke in a flat voice, almost as though he were talking in his sleep. "The train got stuck in a four-mile tunnel, and he couldn't make the steep grade. We must have waited at least two hours for a diesel engine to come along and give us a push, and the Italian brakeman passed out from the gas fumes and I had to take over his job. It took fourteen hours to get here."

It was almost midnight, and the blackness was so thick I could almost feel it pressing down on him, slowing up his speech to keep in time with his dragging steps. The two of us had bumped into each other when I hopped off the troop train. He was a railway MP, but he looked more like a frontline infantryman who had just come back from

137

months of fighting at Cassino. His clothes were dirty, his unshaved beard was covered with soot, his sunken eyes had deep rings beneath them.

"The first sergeant will fix you up with a place to sleep," he said. "He's a good Joe."

Walking carefully along the tracks, we passed a crowd of crying women near one of the freight trains. Another MP was trying to shoo them away. The MP with me started walking a little faster, without looking back at them. "Wherever I go, I see them," he said in a strained voice. "Wherever I go, I can hear them crying . . .

"Those women want to get a ride to the next city, but we're not supposed to let them get on any freight trains unless they got an AMGOT pass," he said. "The Army's afraid of stealing and sabotage and things like that.

"But sometimes it's so goddam tough to kick them out," he said. "I've seen them, old women and little kids, falling down on their knees in the mud, begging for a ride. I've got two kids of my own," he said. "Sometimes, when I have to turn them down, I feel like a Fascist."

Inside the warm, brilliantly lit Orderly Room, the tall first sergeant with the fine, friendly face took a good look at the tired MP and said, "You better knock off tomorrow, sleep all day if you want to . . ."

He didn't sound like a first sergeant at all, much less the first sergeant of an MP outfit.

After the MP left, Sgt. Ed Matthews pointed at the door. "They come in like that all night long," he said. "Sometimes one of them stumbles in, ready to drop, because a freight car's wheels start smoking and he has to stay with it on a siding until they send up another car to pile the freight into. Sometimes they stay there and freeze and starve for three or four days.

"When I think of those good old days when I had my own little saloon in New Hope, Pa., when I only had a few drunks to take care of . . ." said the sergeant wistfully.

The road back to war from the rest camp was the road to Rome, better known to GI's as Highway 6. It was a road of straight stretches and twisting turns cutting through unpronounceable tiny Italian towns and spread-out bivouac areas, past the 1,200-room palace at Caserta where the Fifth Army headquartered.

Every day, the holes in the road to Rome were filled with broken bathtubs and statues and sinks and hairbrushes and fancy fedora hats.

All these things were part of the indiscriminate rubble of Italian houses, which were air-conditioned by shells, sliced open by bombs, then flattened by TNT or bulldozers and piled onto waiting trucks to be distributed to different engineering outfits along the road.

"You know, I've heard a lot about the road to Rome, but I never thought we'd have to build it," said the soldier, "and it's tough going."

He was thinking about the mud—slushy mud that reaches almost up to your knees, sticky mud that grips onto jeep wheels like quicksand, squashy mud that splashes all over everybody and everything, making the roads dangerously slippery.

Long before dawn, the boys of Company A were out of bed, eating their breakfast in the moonlight, cursing the rain-filled clouds, putting on their still-wet shoes.

"If it would only stop raining," the young captain said wistfully. "My boys never get to see a single stretch of finished road. They knock off only when it's too dark to see anymore. By that time, the road is almost cleared of mud and then that night the rains come, and the next morning, the boys have to start all over again."

"The trouble with this mud," said Pvt. Elmer Ponks, Gladwin, Mich., "is that it's too thick to drink, and too thin to plow."

You found everything on Highway 6: a shepherd shooing his sheep out of the way of oncoming tanks; two GI's getting their hair cut, watching the war go by; slow-moving horse carts piled high with people and furniture, going in both directions. *"Io vado casa,"* they say smilingly, without knowing whether the house will still be there when they get there; a jeep driver cursing a flock of turkeys who refuse to be ruffled off the road; and, at chowtime, a long line of scrawny kids and old people, all carrying small pails, heading for the nearest GI chowline to fill their pails with the slop from our garbage cans.

"These people are dressed in rags," wrote T/Sgt. Leonard Neely, Altus, Okla. "Their faces have the look of hungry dogs who are tormented with bowls of food just beyond the reach of their chains. Each one has from one to two dirty pails in his hands. . . .

"It is hard to eat with hungry people looking on, staring like hungry wolves. I picture my little brother and sister begging for food, or my mother! I can hardly swallow."

It's an Army rule: no GI can give his food to civilians. But there is no rule that you have to eat everything they give you, or that you can't take seconds and throw most of it away.

"They stand there and gulp it down from their filthy pails—like hogs feeding from a trough," said Neely. "When they have feasted, they will try to fill the pails to take home for the next meal, or to a sick relative."

In one of his great cartoons, Bill Mauldin in *The Stars and Stripes* showed his GI Joe, tired and battered and covered with mud, holding a mess kit, looking at a small Italian girl, holding her pail. Mauldin's caption was, "The Prince and the Pauper."

Up front, it was almost like a prehistoric war, a war of small hills, a war of caves, a war of single soldiers. Snaking around a mountain trail, a GI found himself face to face with a Nazi snaking around from the other side. The slope on the Nazi's side was so steep that he had to cling to a bush with his right hand, holding his machine pistol in his left. To fire his pistol, he would have had to let go of the bush, and would have rolled down the hill. So he surrendered.

It was the kind of war Eric Severeid described as the "slow spasmodic movement from one patch of silence to another."

Even in this kind of creeping war, there were occasional rare compensations, high moments for weary men.

On one side of the valley, a mountain loaded with German troops; on the other side, was a mountain loaded with American troops. In the center of the valley was a hill, which was completely bare, except for a single shell-shocked white house parked on the rear slope. Resting quietly in the cellar of the farmhouse, stored in big barrels, were no less than 150 gallons of wonderful wine.

That's what sixty tired, footsore GI's found when they got there, one night. Unanimously, they decided that the cellar would make an ideal CP.

Before the boys had their first housewarming party, of course, they had hard work to do. They had to dig deep holes for their machine guns and 81-mm mortars. There was a large-scale infantry push along the low, level valley scheduled for the next morning, and these two heavy-weapons platoons were supposed to provide supporting fire for the flank.

Pvt. John Raymond, Taunton, Mass., was smoothing out his hole, to make it more homelike, when his shovel glanced off a booby-trap, and it exploded. Luckily, Raymond fell flat just in time, and wasn't even scratched. When Raymond told his story at the CP, everybody was naturally jubilant, and that called for a round of wine.

Since the farmhouse was big and white, and the only house on the hill, it made an ideal shelling target for the neighboring Germans. The Germans scored three direct hits on the house, ripping away most of the upper story. Nobody in the deep-down cellar was hurt, but one of the wine barrels broke loose and rolled against the wall. That made Pvt. Carol Shaffer, Warsaw, Ill., very mad indeed. He stood up and shook his fist in the general direction of Berlin and yelled, "You almost hit our vino . . ."

Anyway, the incident called for another round of drinks, and everybody felt better.

That night, the Germans counterattacked the hill. The GI's had strategically spread out their machine-gun and mortar positions, and very soon the Nazis decided that the hill was too expensive a proposition, and called the whole thing off. After they left, the Americans treated their wounded, buried their few dead, and had another round of drinks.

They had only one vino-drinking casualty. He was a Kentucky boy, who suddenly got up and put on his overcoat, and tried to persuade the platoon sergeant that the two of them should immediately ride into Cassino and get a shave and haircut. He was the same guy who, once during Louisiana maneuvers, jumped on a mule and rode right through a practice battle formation, yelling, "Hi-Ho, Silver . . ."

The next morning, after long, hard fighting and heavy casualties, the Germans were finally driven out of their mountain and pushed back to another mountain. Just as the two platoons were having their last round of drinks before they moved out, looking lingeringly at the still-full barrels of wine, one of the boys got up and made a moving speech and ended up, "I hereby name this hill, 'Vino Hill.' "

"Amen," said the Kentucky boy.

Operation Raincoat was well named. It was the first assault on the Winter Line—against the Camino hill mass in early December—and the rain never seemed to stop. We started RAINCOAT with an artillery serenade of almost a thousand guns.

The front line's busiest field phone was ringing again. The sergeant answered it, jotted down some notes quickly, and then handed it to the major. "Here's the Shell Rep, sir."

The major read the notes carefully, walked over to the wall maps and made some calculations and then he yelled across the room, "Hey, Stoops, have you got anything at the XYZ position?"

Stoops was Pvt. Daniel E. Stoops, a former tobacco salesman from Chambersburg, Pa.

Stoops fingered swiftly through his complicated-looking files.

"Yes, sir, here are some Flash & Sound Reports and a couple of photographs."

The major busied himself over the detailed reports, checked over the photographs, then looked at the reports again. After that, he handed a slip of paper to the sergeant, T/4 Peyton Auxford, a former New York advertising man. Auxford picked up the phone, gave some terse, specific instructions to somebody at the other end, and reported to the major.

"They should be firing within three minutes," said the major. "You'll be able to hear them from here."

Three minutes later, the big guns started booming.

"I think we've got them this time," said the major to the small group. "I think we really got them."

The major was talking about a big concentration of German artillery, only a few miles away. The major, who used to be a pharmacist, headed a small section of seven enlisted men and four officers, who constituted the counterbattery nerve center of the American II Corps front.

"We've got a pretty intimate knowledge of all the enemy artillery in this area," said the major, pointing to the file cases and the wall maps. "And as soon as we can get a Shell Rep [shell report] from the soldiers themselves, then we can compare notes and photographs and double-check with our own observers in Piper Cubs and before long we've got a detailed picture of the enemy battery's exact position.

142

"The American soldier is our finger-man. He gives us the final information to make our picture complete," said the major.

"As soon as any outfit around here gets shelled, somebody there is supposed to call us up and tell us as much as possible where the shells landed, how many, when and from what direction. And sometimes they can also tell us how long it took from the muzzle flash to the sound of the gun firing, and maybe even tell us what type of gun it was.

"If we know all that, we can have our counterbattery shooting within a few minutes. Like this job right now," he said.

The front line's busiest phone was ringing again. This time the captain answered. When he finished, he was smiling and rubbing his hands.

"There's a long German convoy moving up down that road beyond the next hill . . . This is going to be fun," he said.

Then he looked at me. "Oh, I forgot to tell you, this is one of our sidelines."

For the artillery of both sides, often the only visible targets were the tiny villages, tucked in on the slopes of the heights along the front, the buildings serving as strongpoints with their thick masonry walls.

"There's a tiny village of about twenty houses, where every person in town thinks he's the luckiest person alive," said Pvt. Lawrence John Michael Francis O'Brien. "Joe told me about it," he said. "Joe lives there. Joe used to be one of those Brooklyn boys," he explained.

"Some drunken German soldiers had wandered into the village, broke into the houses, filled themselves up on vino and used wine barrels for target practice, laughing loudly when the old wine gushed onto the ground. One of the Germans tried to requisition Joe's fifteen-year-old son for the labor battalion, and when the kid would not come, the German shot him and took his younger brother.

"Finally, the American artillery started shelling nearby, and the Nazi drunks started petering out of the place. All except one German, who decided to see how his new tommy gun worked. So he lined up all the people he could find, was all set to start shooting, when a few shells hit the top of the building across the street, and the falling rubble killed a few people, including the German. The townspeo-

143

ple buried their own dead, but left the German where he lay. For a week, the body lay there, stinking in the sun, and nobody would bury it. Instead, every time the people passed the body, they would spit on it.

"When the American soldiers entered the town, they buried the body.

"Those Italians still haven't forgiven the American soldiers for doing that," said O'Brien.

One of the standard Allied communiqués out of that winter war said simply that the Americans had taken "certain high points" and "straightened their lines." That announcement did not mention that this "straightening" used up 3,000 hand grenades and 400,000 rounds of rifle and machine-gun fire and cost more than 400 casualties in a single regiment in six days of fighting in the fog and slimy mire for a small knob of a small hill.

That six days' fighting was in a two-mile sector in between "Prisoner's Knob" and "Graveyard Hill."

Most murderous was the Nazi *Nebelwerfer,* their six-barreled rocket mortar which we called "Screaming Meemie" or "Wailing Willie." The big need was to knock out their observation posts.

The cave was a perfect OP. It was blasted into the solid rock, just beneath the mountain peak. From either side of the cave, the Germans could see everything they wanted to see—troop concentrations, gun emplacements and convoy movements. Consequently, the entire American sector was under German artillery fire, all of it concentrated, blistering, deadly accurate. Before anything else, then, the Americans had to knock out that OP. It stuck out like a skinny finger, flanked on both sides by American troops. The problem was: "How?"

Direct artillery might do it, except that the target was almost insignificantly small. The GI's might storm the heights, but the casualty cost would be terrific. So the Combat Engineers got the job, a three-man patrol with a lot of TNT. To get onto the short, flat ledge above the cave, the three soldiers had to creep and crawl up the slope, with their faces on the ground, as if they were kids again, rolling peanuts across a room.

The three of them—Pvt. Woodrow W. Smouse, Farmington, N.M., S/Sgt. Charles Corella, Ajo, Ariz., and 1st Lt. Bernard Gordon, Jr., Larchmont, N.Y.—carefully ex-

144

amined the situation, finally decided that it could be done.

Only to do it, they needed at least 500 pounds of explosives. Five hundred pounds of TNT, planted on top of the ledge, would collapse most of the cave, make it completely unusable.

Making eleven separate trips, carrying fifty pounds of TNT each time, Pvt. Smouse sweated out the ammunition-passing, wondered when the Jerries on the neighboring hills would spot him and open up. Meanwhile, the sergeant and the lieutenant busied themselves on the three fuses—two time fuses and one electric fuse. Several yards of rock beneath them were the Germans, blissfully unaware of everything.

Finally, all done, the three got up and ran like hell, diving into a foxhole fifty yards away before turning the handle of the electric fuse.

Only several seconds after the explosion, came the full force of the German shelling, machine-gunning, mortaring, all focused on that single slope. But the three already were racing down the hill toward our positions, shells exploding all around them.

Miraculously, nobody was hurt. Sgt. Corella had the only souvenir—a piece of shrapnel that had pierced his combat suit, struck the rounded part of the spoon in his shirt pocket, deflected off, lodging in a candy bar.

But there was no more German OP. And that day, the American troops rushed forward from the front on both flanks, helping the Germans straighten out their line by completely cutting off the bulge of hills.

Next day, the three engineers were back to work on another hill, this time digging into thick mud, trying to spread a thin, winding donkey trail into a wide bypass for the advancing infantry.

"That's what I like about an engineer's job," said Pvt. Smouse. "We get so many different things to do."

San Pietro became the symbol of success for the next phase of the winter campaign. Set on the lower slopes of Mount Summucro, San Pietro had a clear look across a mile-wide valley which we soon called "Death Valley." We could only take the town by outflanking it, and dominating the heights above it, which we did. Some of the German-entrenched gun pits, deep in rocks, were covered by three layers of logs with an opening just large enough for a single man to crawl through. Before the Germans withdrew, they launched a strong counterattack to cover their withdrawal.

During December, our combat casualties came close to 5,000.

Somewhere in an evac hospital, close behind the front lines, there was a lieutenant colonel with a piece of shrapnel in his brain. He was the "Old Man" of an infantry outfit, who got hit while leading his troops in the fight for Mount Porchia.

Back in the bivouac, some of the boys were talking about him.

"I went down to see him today," said T/Sgt. Chester Wisniewski, Chicago. "His left arm is still slightly paralyzed and he talks so slowly, you'd think he was dragging out every word, one by one, and the first thing he asked me was, 'How's the Battalion? Are the boys getting plenty of rest?' "

"That's just like the Old Man," said the Co. Clerk. "He's always thinking of the Battalion first. I remember the time he was in the hospital with four slugs inside of him. But as soon as he heard that our outfit was going to pass through town in review, he got dressed and borrowed a jeep and went AWOL from the hospital, coming sixty miles just to see us."

"Yeah," said Wisniewski, "but he spent three extra weeks in the hospital for that."

There was a short stretch of quiet then, until the company clerk spoke up again. "And the Old Man's a regular fruit salad of ribbons and medals." He started counting on his fingers. "He's got the DSC, and the Silver Star, and the Purple Heart, and a lot of clusters, and the Croix de Guerre."

"I remember when he was just a looey in charge of the Service Company," said Cpl. Homer Timbale, Gothenburg, Neb. "He knew the name of every guy in his outfit, and everybody who had a legitimate bitch about something just went up to him and got it off his chest, and the funny thing was that the Old Man really went out and did something about it. He didn't give a damn about red tape."

"How old is the colonel, anyway?" asked the new looey in the corner.

"Why, the Old Man is almost twenty-eight," said Wisniewski.

146

As we started moving forward, we had more roads for vehicles. At the key crossroad of Venafro—high in the mountains above the Volturno—more than 4,000 vehicles moved through every twenty-four hours. The headache of control belonged to the Military Police.

Up front, nobody kidded or cursed the MP's. That's because a frontline MP's job was neither safe nor soft.

When the infantry moved in to take a town, the MP's moved right in with them, ready to direct traffic, keep the roads open, bring back prisoners. And no matter how thick the mud, how cold the wind or how hard the rain poured, they were standing there in the road, doing their job.

One MP was posted on a bypass which was shelled out of existence three times in one night. Another MP counted 150 shells that landed in his area in a single afternoon.

Of course, when the shelling got too heavy and too accurate, there was no longer any traffic to direct, and the MP, like everybody else, retired to his private foxhole.

Besides traffic control (their biggest headache), the MP's brought back all the prisoners. "Business has been a little slow lately, but it always picks up after a battle," said Sgt. Glenn Cook, Anderson, Ind.

They got all kinds of prisoners—the still, sullen young ones, the broken-spirited older ones, and occasionally they ran across some vino-happy Germans who barely staggered across the lines.

They had found their latest drunken Nazi almost breaking his neck trying to walk down the slippery slopes of Mount Maggiore, which is tough enough to do when you're cold sober. The German was singing and laughing and very good-natured and cooperative, but he couldn't be classified because he was too drunk to talk without garbling his words. He had no liquor on him, all of it was in him.

Still another MP job was to tell lost soldiers where their unit was, but they also answered such questions as "Do you think this road will be shelled while I'm on it?" and "Can you tell me where I can get some hay for this mule?"

Only mules made the winter war possible.

The *Encyclopaedia Britannica* (20th ed.) describes the mule as a cross between the horse and the ass, and adds:

"In its short, thick head, long ears, thin limbs, small

147

narrow hoofs, and tail destitute of hair at the root, the mule resembles the ass, while in height of body, shape of neck and croup, uniformity of coat and in teeth it resembles the horse. It has the voice neither of the ass nor the horse, but emits a feeble, hoarse noise. . . . It possesses the sobriety, patience, endurance and sure-footedness of the ass, and the vigor, strength and courage of the horse. As a beast of burden it is in many environments preferable to the horse, being less impatient under heavy weights, while the skin being harder and less sensitive renders it more capable of resisting sun and rain. . . ."

One division brought its own mules with it from Sicily, but the other divisions scrounged the area to find them. The few mules they had were literally worked to death— an average Italian mule could carry 220 pounds, but it took 250 mules to supply the basic needs of a regiment up front.

The mules took up food and water and ammo and brought back the dead. The dead were put belly-down across the wooden packsaddles, their heads hanging on one side, bobbing up and down with the mule's stride, while on the other side, the legs of the dead stuck out stiff and awkward.

Rule number one was never to let the mule know you were scared of him.

"The way to make a mule behave," said Pfc. Howard Potter, Kent, Conn., "is to get behind him and push. When that doesn't work, put a half-hitch on his nose and get in front and pull. And when that doesn't work either, and he begins to kick, bite his ears."

But there were places where even mules couldn't go. Then it was a GI's job, climbing a few inches at a time with a packboard on his back loaded with a case of rations or a can of water, sometimes hauling their packs up by rope. Coming back, it took one litter squad of eight men twelve hours to bring a single wounded GI to the nearest aid station. "We spent more time on our backs than on our feet," said Pvt. Anton Jeckich of Cleveland.

Back in bivouac after eleven days, Mess Sgt. Wilfred "Old Folks" Newton, of Carlsbad, N.M., scrounged the first hot food. "We had hot coffee and cereal and butter and jam and cream gravy and bacon," said 1st Sgt. Jefferson Adams, of Brownwood, Tex.

"And we had three fat slices of fresh white bread."

The field phone rang, and the captain answered. His face tightened up a little as he spoke and said, "Yes, sir," a few times and hung up.

"You better forget about the white bread, Sergeant," he said. "We've got some more hills to visit tomorrow morning."

Christmas only meant more mud and mountains to most GI's, but some of the lucky ones saw the inside of a church.

You could hear the ringing of the church bells and the booming of the big guns at the same time.

In the war-torn town of Venafro, the pouring rain slowed down to a drizzle as the soldiers jumped out of their six-by-sixes and walked to the top of the hill, up the narrow cobblestone street.

They were the frontline soldiers coming to Midnight Mass.

Only it wasn't midnight; it was late afternoon. That's because there was a war going on, 3,500 yards away, and they couldn't satisfactorily black out the church, and it was dangerous and difficult to replace troops and transport them in the pitch-dark.

The Mass wasn't all GI. Besides Chaplains Aloysius Carney, East Orange, N.J., and Joseph Barry, Notre Dame, Ind., there were five Italian priests. And besides the soldiers themselves, there were the townspeople.

The women wore their faded-colored skirts and dark veils; the men wore simple-cut black suits; the children wore their cleanest rags.

Everybody walked quietly and solemnly into church except the children, who kept running around and yelling and laughing. *"Buon Natale, Americano!"* The shrapnel-pockmarked Church of Annunziata was an old church which dated back to the seventeenth century, and once before had been partially destroyed by an earthquake. It looked dirty and crumbling from the outside. But inside, with the candlelight throwing shadows onto the intricate artwork, everything was impressively beautiful. A small church organ supplied the slow background for the sing-song chanting of the five priests at the altar.

With their helmets in their hands, the unwashed, bearded soldiers crowded into the already packed church.

They dipped their hands in the holy water, crossed and blessed themselves, then went down on their knees.

Their heads bared and bowed, they prayed.

"I prayed that there would be no more wars after this one," said Pvt. Jim Doyle, Denver, Colo.

"I guess I prayed for the same thing," said Pvt. Frank Ryan, a gunner on a 105-howitzer. "I prayed for the same thing at the Queen of Angels Church in Chicago last Christmas, but this time I really felt more deeply what I was praying for. You see, this is my first Christmas away from home."

Outside the church, the ragged kids were having a field day, getting filled up on *caramelli*. Some of the kids were getting the candy, even without asking for it.

Pvt. James J. Breslin, of Brooklyn, N.Y., who was passing out some Life Savers to the *"piccolo* babies," explained how he felt about it. "I'm married," he said, "and I don't have any kids of my own to give things to, and these kids don't look like they ever had a real Christmas party."

After Mass, there were three soldiers buttoning up their field jackets, getting ready to go back to the war. The three—Pvt. Frank Mazurkiewicz, St. Paul, Minn., Pvt. Edward Martas, Detroit, and Pvt. Francis Saumier, Saranac Lake, N.Y.—had been the first soldiers to enter Venafro more than a month ago. They were minesweepers.

"We were lucky to get the afternoon off to get here," one of them said. "Now we'll have something to think about when we go on the recon patrol tonight."

One of their buddies passed by and yelled, "Merry Christmas."

The three minesweepers waved at him.

"Merry Christmas," they said.

Pfc. Nicholas La Verghetta, Union City, N.J., pointed to a tiny spot on the large-scale Italian map on the wall. "That's where I used to live," he said. "It's called Istonia and I know every foot of the coastline over there, some sections where the fighting is going on right now. From my room, I could see the sea . . ."

Nicholas smiled. "But if I know every foot of it, then my grandfather knows every inch. My grandfather's been fishing up and down that coast for more than sixty years. He's an old man, my grandfather; he's eighty-seven now."

He took out an expensive-looking pipe. "This is for my

grandfather," he said. "When I left for America, five years and three days ago, he only asked me for one favor. He said that if I ever came back to Italy, and he was still alive, then he wanted me to bring him a good pipe."

He hesitated, then said slowly, ". . . if he's still alive . . ."

High on a hilltop near Foggia, far from the war, is the tiny town of Panni, where men still strut around in fancy blue capes and women wear bright-colored skirts, and everybody is everybody else's cousin. One of the cousins who came back was Sgt. Carl Longo. He had moved from Panni to Barrington, R.I., where he played third base and managed a New England semi-pro baseball team called the "Barrington Townies."

Longo told how he had parked his jeep on the bottom of the hill and walked along the cobbled streets, and how the crowd opened the way for him, and how they yelled, "Bravo . . . Bravo!"

"Everything was pretty much the same as it had been fourteen years before when I left it," he said.

"It's just a one-room house with a hole over the doorway to let air in and smoke out, and there's a picture over the bed and a small old fireplace, and peppers hanging down from the ceiling. The only thing different about the place was the pig who lived with us in the corner of the room . . . It was a different pig," said Longo, laughing again.

When the time came to kiss the cousins goodbye, they all crowded around again and filled his jeep with eggs and sausages and cheese and several gallons of wine.

"It was good to get home again," said Longo.

There was another reunion story that made a perfect Christmas story for *The Stars and Stripes*.

It concerned two soldiers:

Charlie was busy unloading Air Corps depot supplies when the first sergeant yelled at him, "Pvt. Talley, report to the Orderly Room immediately. Better wash up before you go in."

Slightly bewildered, Charlie washed the dirt off his hands, buttoned the top of his fatigues, and walked into the Orderly Room.

He was quiet for a long minute, his eyes staring, his mouth dropping open . . .

And then he yelled . . .

"Oh, baby doll . . . Oh, baby doll . . ."

For the next few minutes, the two privates were kissing and hugging each other, laughing a little hysterically, their eyes wet.

The two privates were Pvt. Charles Talley and Pvt. Maxine Talley, both from Crystal City, Tex. Before the war, they were known simply as Mr. and Mrs. Charles Talley.

To celebrate New Year's, the entire II Corps artillery had a "shoot," firing three rounds per gun on specific targets. The Germans answered the greeting, but in smaller volume.

By mid-January, we had reached the edge of the Liri River valley, the main corridor for our road to Rome, while the British had made a similar push on the Adriatic coast, past Foggia.

It had taken eight divisions six weeks to advance seven miles at a cost of 16,000 casualties.

The bitter winter war had helped make the human animal more animal than human.

The German was dead, his boots sticking out in the street, his head hidden in the doorway. Two GI's smoked their cigarettes a few feet away.

Asked about the dead German, one of the GI's said, "Oh him? Sonofabitch kept lagging behind the others when we brought them in. We got tired of hurrying him up all the time."

And Eric Severeid told of overhearing a pink-cheeked private hesitantly ask a lieutenant, "Sir, pardon me, I can't find my officer. We've got some civilians in a house back there. What shall we do with them, sir?"

The lieutenant snapped, "If you can spare a guard, send them back. If you can't, why shoot 'em in the back. That's what we always did in my outfit. Don't take no nonsense from 'em."

The pink-cheeked private saluted and left.

He had received a simple order for mass murder.

Back at Naples, everything was back to normal. The citizens had been powdered with DDT to prevent a typhus epidemic; the Funiculare Centrale was back in business, its Toonerville cable car hauling people up the hill; and USO visitor Humphrey Bogart competed with the San Carlo Opera.

Backstage, the San Carlo players were finishing their final primping as the old man tinkled the warning-bell. The tenor adjusted his wig, the soprano cleared her throat for the last time, and the baritone and the bass crossed themselves for luck and went onto the stage for the first act of *La Bohème*.

Pfc. Clarence Bennett, detailed to drive the opera stars home after the show, was watching everything very carefully.

"This is the first opery show I ever seen," he confided as he sat down on the steps next to me.

Onstage, Rudolfo and his two friends were worrying how to pay the landlord when Clarence nudged me to give me his solution. "I bet one of those guys is gonna pick the landlord's pocket and give him his own dough back as rent." Clarence went on to explain that back in Norwalk, O., he didn't have to pay any rent because he had his own farm, "where I raise a lot of corn and feed a lot of cattle." By the time he finished telling all about his cattle, the landlord had already gone, and Clarence never did find out whether his prediction was right or not.

Mimi came on the scene; and then she and Rudolfo were getting intimately acquainted. Clarence was very much interested, and kept quiet for a while. Then, when Rudolfo tried to kiss Mimi, and was gently, shyly repulsed, Clarence chuckled and winked at me. "Didn't quite make the grade, did he?" he said.

At the end of the first act, Clarence took a deep drag on his cigarette and made his criticisms. "I'll tellya," he said, "I like music with a lot more snap to it, with a lot more pep . . . like hillbilly songs and square dances . . . I just love that kind of stuff."

The second act was more to Clarence's taste. It was the café scene, where there's a lot of moving around and a lot of people. What Clarence liked most of all, was the part where the pretty flirt, Musetta, sends her old sugar-daddy on an errand out of the café, so that she can talk to her sweetheart, Marcello. Throughout the scene, Clarence kept slapping his knee and chuckling. "That's good," he said. "That's real good."

Latecomers drove up in their 18-ton tanks, which they

153

parked on the fringe of the crowd. The early-birds were already sitting on their gas-can seats in front of the open-back truck where the microphone was.

Some plumpish, funny man was dishing out a fast line of patter, in Bob Hope style, skillfully speeding over the corny jokes, stretching out the good ones, keeping everybody constantly belly-laughing.

A few soldiers spotted Humphrey Bogart, and walked over quickly. One of the guys kidded him about his movie, *Sahara*. "Where in the hell did you ever get a .45-caliber pistol that could fire sixteen shots without reloading, Mr. Bogart?" Or, "How come you crossed the whole desert without refilling your gas tank?"

Bogart smiled. "Hollywood is a wonderful place," he said. "They can do anything."

Bogart listened to the loud cheering being given to his second show of that day, and said, "There's nothing very fancy about our show . . . Just some singing and skits and gags, but the boys all seem to like it. Especially those guys in the hospital. I guess that's because it makes them forget for a few minutes those shrapnel holes or that missing leg. I've never heard any of those guys bitch or gripe about anything yet. If they have the strength to smile, they smile. It makes a guy proud."

Bogart was quiet for a while, and then he smiled faintly and rubbed a black welt over his right eye. "I was almost in the hospital myself," he said. "I celebrated my forty-fourth birthday a few weeks ago, and I had a bunch of the boys over for a few drinks. Well, we had bum cognac and worse vino, and before I knew it, I was on the table with a paratrooper, and we were yelling, 'Geronimo' and jumping off . . ."

Bogart rubbed his eye again. "I guess my chute failed to open," he said, laughing.

His wife was just finished singing "Stardust," and Bogart flicked away his cigarette and coughed again and said, "That's my cue again," and he hopped up the side of the truck, stepped in front of the mike and put on his movie-tough face and said, "I'm looking for a new mob . . . You guys look like a likely bunch of triggermen . . ."

Everybody laughed again.

The troop trains out of Naples got busier suddenly: the new men needed to fill the divisions full again to replace the men with frozen feet, torn bodies and broken minds.

Everything was bedlam in the Naples railroad station as the short, fat man in the funny red cap yelled something. Italians seemed to rush in all directions at the same time, jabbering instructions at each other, carrying huge bundles on top of their heads, all crowding toward the ticket entrance.

At one of the platforms, several hundred yards away, soldiers were loading onto a waiting troop train. You could tell how new they were from their unmuddied helmets and their clean duffel bags, and the way they pointed curiously to the twisted pieces of rusted steel that used to be railroad cars before the bombs came—our bombs, long ago.

One of the last soldiers to pile in, had a small, brown puppy poking his head out of his field jacket. "I brought her all the way from the States," said the soldier proudly.' "She was born in Hoboken."

It was dusk when the train pulled out of the station, chugging along slowly, almost at bicycle-speed. Most of the GI's were lined up in the narrow corridor on the side of the train car, half leaning out of the windows, staring at the scenery of torn-up tracks and busted buildings and large, unfilled crater holes at the edge of the city. Nobody said much, until somebody spotted a healthy looking signorina strutting alongside, and gave out with a low, long whistle, and a dozen others joined in the chorus. The signorina just looked up and yelled, "Whacha want, Joe?" and everybody laughed.

Later, they laughed even louder when the train was passing through a long tunnel and some soldier screamed in a feminine voice, "Help, help . . ."

But when dusk settled into darkness, and the war-torn Naples melted into a low, rolling countryside of small, peaceful farms, the loud talk and laughter quieted down. One of the boys started saying something about how this countryside reminded him of his farm back in Pennsylvania, and others soon chimed in how it brought back memories of New York, Minnesota, North Carolina, Ohio and Oregon.

Most of the soldiers soon dribbled back into their compartments, except for a lingering few who kept standing around and looking into the blackness, talking in a hushed voice as if they were in a hospital. Soon, there was no one except a young kid and his older buddy, who were sitting on their barracks bags at the back of the car.

The younger one was doing most of the talking. He was telling his buddy about his girl back home, and how much he missed her already. He said his folks had a dairy farm out in Wisconsin, and that he used to have so much fun there and that he felt homesick, even though he just came over.

His buddy mumbled something about, "You'll get used to it," but the younger one didn't seem to hear him. He just kept puffing on his cigarette, nervously, awkwardly, and then went into his compartment.

Soon afterwards, his buddy got up to follow him in. When he noticed that I had been standing there all the time, he said, apologetically, "He's only a kid. He's never been away from home before." Then he walked away quickly.

It was hours later that the train pulled into the station. Most of the soldiers were then fast asleep.

The worst of the war was yet to come: Rapido, Cassino, Anzio.

A Fifth Army Intelligence summary on January 16 assessed the situation in this way:

> Within the past few days, there have been increasing indications that enemy strength on the front of the Fifth Army is ebbing due to casualties, exhaustion, and possibly lowering of morale. One of the causes of this condition, no doubt, has been the recent continuous Allied attacks. From this, it can be deduced that he has no fresh reserves and very few tired ones. His entire strength will probably be needed to defend his organized defensive positions.
>
> In view of the weakening of enemy strength on the front, as indicated above, it would appear doubtful if the enemy can hold the organized defensive line through Cassino against a coordinated army Attack. Since this attack is to be launched before Shingle [the code name of the Anzio landing], it is considered likely that this additional threat will cause him to withdraw from his defensive position, once he has appreciated the magnitude of that operation.

Our G-2 summary was wrong.

An enemy is not weak when he is up in the mountains and you are down in the valley.

An enemy is not weak when his guns are parked deep

in rock.

An enemy is not weak when he sits behind a raging river and you must cross it.

"Weakening of enemy strength" is a phrase written in a quiet, warm room far from the sound and smell of war.

The Rapido River was the Volturno all over again, but worse, much, much worse. One military observer even called it "the biggest disaster to American arms since Pearl Harbor." Another called it "The Battle of Guts."

We were crossing at a place southeast of Cassino, above and below San Angelo, a village built on a bluff forty feet high, dominating the area of the river crossing. The river there was bent in a tight S-formation. We were supposed to converge from both sides of the village and pinch it out. Another divison would cross the flooded river north of Highway 6, where they would wade through two miles of quagmire.

Our problems were many and vital. Crossing any river at night is rough enough, but our defense line wasn't even at the river's edge—some of it was two miles behind the river, flat, open land under easy enemy observation. The Germans had planted these two miles thick with mines. At night, our engineers would remove enough of them to make a path, but the next night the Nazis were back to replant them.

Then there was the river itself.

During the dry season, the Rapido was a trickle of a stream. But, after three months of continuous rain, the Rapido was a torrent, often more than nine feet deep. To make it worse, the Germans had methodically dynamited the upstream dams adding to the flood and force of the water.

Then, too, it was a narrow river, only sixty feet wide. If it had been wider, we could have maintained an artillery barrage on the enemy side of the bank throughout our crossing. Since it was so narrow, our artillery had to quit during our crossing for fear of hitting our own men. This gave the German guns full leeway to fire on all the likely crossing points where their guns were long ago registered.

Our attack began in the foggy darkness of January 20.

Each GI carried one K-ration, one D-ration, overcoat, cigarettes, rifle and ammo, hand grenades and part of a cumbersome boat. The lucky guys carried the rubber pontoon boats, the others hauled the steel assault boats.

The enemy guns churned up the white tape guiding our men through the mines, and some of our men blew up before they even reached the river. Some of the shells hit some of the boats before we could launch them, and they sank without a gurgle.

Our GI's learned about boats the hard way. You can't launch a steel boat prow-first into a swift river down a steep bank and you can't launch it sideways. The fast flow of the river swept them downstream, out of reach. The ones who made it into the boats found themselves cut by withering crossfire from the entrenched German guns, high in the heights.

Waiting for the ones who crossed were 400 yards of minefields, barbed wire, interlocking fire from mortars and machine guns and the screeching sound of the "Screaming Meemies."

Our artillery put up a barrage of 30,000 shells to pulverize a small area on the other side of the river, but the Germans were dug-in too deep. Shortly before daybeak, we lit smoke pots on our side of the river, but the wind carried the smoke high and left a tunnel of clear air over the river, clearly outlining our few footbridges for German gunners. The busiest traffic on those bridges were the litter-bearers going for the wounded. And, soon, we were sending litter-bearers to bring back the wounded litter-bearers. One medic raced his way across a footbridge ten times.

"Everybody pitched in to help," said Pvt. Albert Pickett, Corinth, Ky. "The MP's, who were right up with the combat engineers, were carrying the wounded on home-made stretchers of shelter halves or blankets, but mostly carrying them on their backs."

"It was easy to dig foxholes in the marshland," said Pickett, "but then we had to stay there, and the water seeped through, and soon we had water up to our bellies, and we couldn't move or get out of there because the guns were shooting right on top of us. We could see the dead and wounded all around us, Americans and Germans."

There were some new replacements who had never been under shellfire before. One private, with a very young, intense face, blurted out how he had been completely terrified, and broken down and cried. "I don't know what happened," he said. "But it won't happen again."

"I guess my first sergeant was one of the last guys to

158

leave," said Pfc. Nicholas Carapelli, Millville, N.J. "He had been wounded twice, but refused to be evacuated. When he was finally ordered to leave, he insisted on walking across the broken, heavily shelled footbridge all by himself."

Bridges were the big thing. One of our bridging parties was found hours later two miles from the needed crossing site. But worst of all, the Germans knew where to expect our bridges.

"These German guns kept going all the time," said Pvt. James Matthies, Garfield, N.J. "They knocked out every pontoon bridge the engineers tried to put up. They knocked out the footbridges, and they knocked out a lot of the boats. It was a tough thing to look at. All of us kept praying and praying that some of the fog would lift, so that our planes could come down and dive-bomb the hell out of them, and our artillery could spot their flashes and blast their gun positions."

Ceiling zero canceled any air support that morning, and the fog put our artillery OP's out of business. Icy roads on our side of the river slowed down supply and reinforcements.

We filled the river with smoke again on Friday night, pushed over more reinforcements but the heavy cross fire forced them to dig in alongside the others. German snipers had a field day.

His combat suit was sodden with mud. He had just come back from across the river. "I've got men still over there," he said. Then he added slowly, "This is the worst I have ever seen . . . I'm not doing anybody any good over there . . . I'm tired . . . I haven't got anything in me anymore. . . . There's nothing else to do. I'm going back over there." And so he went.

We managed to keep a toehold of troops on the other side, but now the fog lifted at the wrong time, and our GI's found themselves surrounded by Nazi tanks and guns wheeling into position, prepared to annihilate them. And so they did, slowly and systematically. We could hear our American guns gradually diminishing in strength until the only sound was silence.

By the end of the second day, the Germans were in

complete possession of their side of the Rapido and we had more than 2,000 casualties.

It was a disaster.

His foot clung to his leg by a shred of skin. There was little blood because the heat of the blast had seared his arteries. He had crawled out of his foxhole, pushing with his one good leg, gripping with his nails, fainting several times before he reached the river some four hundred yards away. He rolled into the icy water, somehow swam across, somehow climbed the steep rocky bank, somehow crawled another four hundred yards until we found him.

At the aid station, they wrapped him up, gave him hot coffee.

"My foot's gone, Doc. I know that," the twenty-year-old GI said. And then he added quietly, "I'm all right. I made it. How about the other boys?"

The whole action had lasted less than forty-eight hours, and one division had been almost reduced to a regiment (which had been in reserve), with 1,681 men lost—of whom 875 were missing.

Military analysts afterwards decided that our major mistakes were in not having a firm base closer to the river, not planning a diversionary attack and not allowing infantry commanders more flexibility.

But a key fact was that most of our troops were exhausted. They had been fighting continuously without time for rest or reorganization or proper planning. And the reason for the rush was that the Rapido River crossing was to synchronize with a major amphibious landing at Anzio, sixty miles behind the German lines and just thirty-seven miles south of Rome. The Anzio landing was a pet project idea of Prime Minister Winston Churchill. Operation Shingle, as it was called, was supposed to panic the Germans into withdrawing from their prepared positions on the southern front. Our Fifth Army troops would then break through, join up with our troops at Anzio and sweep into Rome. It was all supposed to happen within seven days.

It was a major idea, but, unfortunately, we played it in a minor key.

"It's too quiet," said one soldier.
"It stinks with quiet," said another.
"I like it quiet," said a third.

A thin slice of moon took the edge off the darkness as our men moved onto the beaches. The only light came from our own boats, the only noise came from our own men, the only shelling came from our own guns.

The surprise was complete. The Germans only kept one company in that Anzio-Nettuno area, and we literally caught them with their pants down, pulled them out of their beds. This was a bathing-resort area before the war, noted as the birthplace of Nero, and the Germans used it as a rest area. The Germans had had another full division there, but they had withdrawn it just the day before our landings.

But we had underestimated our enemy. Field Marshal Kesselring did not panic at our amphibious force of only two British and American divisions. The day before, he had successfully beaten back our Rapido River crossing, and now he felt safe in diverting those troops quickly to the Anzio front.

The Anzio plain stretched inland some twenty miles across reclaimed marshes and drainage ditches which flowed into the Mussolini Canal—a man-made river, sixteen feet deep, which converted easily into a convenient tank trap. Within the plain area, there was a pine forest, thick-walled farmhouse, gullies often fifty feet deep. But, overlooking everything, were the Alban Hills, whose heights reached to 3,000 feet.

Before we could take that high ground, the Germans were there, with elements of eight divisions. And, without the reserve troops to blast them out, we were trapped.

Anzio had no rear echelon. Anybody could die anywhere—a clerk or a nurse as well as a frontline soldier. From their heights, the whole Anzio beachhead was a moving picture within a frame and German gunners only had to aim and fire.

It was a dogfight over Anzio between a single Spitfire and a German fighter plane. To gain altitude, the German pilot dropped his bombs, and they landed directly onto the surgery area of an evacuation hospital, killing 28, including three nurses, injuring 64 others.

The Spitfire shot down the German plane, but the pilot was still alive. They brought him for emergency treatment at the very same hospital he had bombed. Unfortunately, the surgical facilities were no longer as good as they had been less than an hour before. The pilot, however, survived. The doctor and nurses treated him like any other patient.

While they died like soldiers, the nurses were still women.

On an LST, coming from Naples to Anzio, a nurse asked Motor Machinist's Mate First Class Bill Nackovina, Cleveland, a question he had never been asked before, "Is the water soft? . . . I'd like to wash my hair."

The tall, blond Nackovina gulped, then answered, "Yes."

One nurse, Rose Craig, expressed the wish of many a GI when she wrote:

> *If a fairy, good, would grant one wish,*
> *And I could have no more,*
> *I'd have a bathroom built for one*
> *And I'd close and lock the door.*

And a GI, Cpl. G. M. Sperling, wrote his feeling about nurses:

> *God made a nurse.*
> *He made her heart brave, true and kind,*
> *And like the mountain streams her mind;*
> *As crystal clear, yet swift and deep*
> *As where its waters rush and sweep.*
> *He made her hands strong, tender, skilled,*
> *Their touch with His own pity filled*
> *And gave to make His nurse complete*
> *A sense of humor, wholesome, sweet.*
> *God made a nurse.*
> >   *Thank God.*

As a further proof that there were women in this war, there was this requisition to replace equipment lost aboard a torpedoed ship:

"Three (3) pair corsets, adjustable, pink." This item was starred, and at the bottom was a notation: "Requires immediate replacement."

Once settled firmly in the hills, the Germans decided to drive the Allied "abscess" into the sea, make it another Dunkirk. In such a situation, the attacker had all the advantage. He could bunch his strength anywhere on the thin line, punch his hole in depth, then fan out. To contain these punches, we relied on our big guns often firing at almost point-blank range.

The barbed wire was filled with bodies.

Stretched out on the barbed wire in front of our positions was a wounded German who cried out, at regular intervals, in English: "My name is Müller. I am wounded." Over and over again, "My name is Müller. I am wounded."

Neither side made a move to get him, and the battle went on and there were soon many more bodies crumpled around the barbed wire, but there was only that one voice, still crying out, "My name is Müller. I am wounded."

Our GI's there were surrounded, and our own wounded lay where they were hit. Their desperation was deep. And, from that barbed wire, the voice, still pleading, "My name is Müller. I am wounded."

It was too much for one of our GI's and he pulled a grenade pin, lobbed it at the barbed wire, and just after the explosion, a buddy heard him mutter, "What's your name now, you sonofabitch?"

The German radio referred to Anzio as "a prison camp where the inmates feed themselves."

Within a few days, the Anzio "prison" had some 70,000 men and 18,000 vehicles. The beachhead became so packed that an enemy shell could land almost anywhere and hit something of military value. To feed the "prison" and strengthen it for the eventual breakout called for a continual parade of LST's going back and forth to Naples, 120 miles, and it took a full day. At Anzio, the German guns waited impatiently for them to return because they were fat targets, 327 feet long. There were few LST's lucky to get away without some shrapnel, and some never got away. For those who did, there was soon a covey of enemy subs waiting along the way.

"The first torpedo was just like running into a stone wall at full speed," the men told Bill Brinkley, USNR. "It was not so bad. But the second torpedo, ten minutes later, broke the ship in half."

After the first torpedo, the engineering officer started below to set up the ballast pumps. He met John J.

163

O'Brien, Chief Motor Machinist's Mate, from New York.

"Where are you going, sir?"

"I'm going down to trim her," the engineering officer said.

"I'll go down," said O'Brien.

The officer looked at O'Brien. "No," he said. "I'm older. I'll go down." He was four years older. That was the last anybody saw of him until his body was picked up several hours later, stiff and swollen.

When the second torpedo hit, men were beating out the flames of their burning buddies with their bare hands, or else throwing the human torches into the sea. Among the wounded, there was moaning but no crying. "Mostly they got madder than hell," a seaman told Brinkley. "One man kept shouting into the wind, 'God damn those Jerries' over and over again, 'God damn those Jerries!'"

When they abandoned ship, not everybody could find boats or rafts. Three burned sailors were huddled together in the water. One of them soon died. The choppy waves calmed slightly and the moon came out. "Let's go swim to that ship," the eighteen-year-old sailor told the other man named Heistand.

"That isn't a ship," said Heistand quietly. "That's the moon. Just take it easy. Everything will be all right."

But the boy broke away, started swimming toward the moon with all his might. Heistand swam after him, caught him.

"I held him for a while," Heistand told Brinkley, "and then he began to stiffen up and I let him go. He was a good man. I hated to see him go. It was a hell of a thing to have one of those boys slip away, then the other. You know, I used to say when I was a kid that I would swim all day every day if I had the chance. I used to like swimming that much. Now I don't know. I don't think I will ever feel that way about swimming again."

The warships in the Anzio harbor had supplied vital support fire on enemy targets, particularly at crossroads and bridges during enemy attacks. Chief Gunner's Mate James Johnson has the memory of an enemy shell landing on his ship, the U.S.S. *Ludlow,* a dud that spun all over the deck, a hot projectile which was spilling its explosive charge all over the place until he picked it up and threw it overboard.

164

Besides the 280-mm German railroad gun, the Anzio Express, there was Popcorn Pete who flew over the beachhead every night to drop hundreds of tiny "butterfly bombs." The bombs would drop a short distance, explode in midair, scattering smaller delayed-action grenades which exploded before hitting the ground, sounding like popping corn. The Germans also had small remote-control tanks filled with high explosives. Much more important were their huge Tiger tanks used in mobile groups as artillery. By the time we threw counterbattery fire, these tanks had moved elsewhere. Our tank destroyers were not effective against the German Tiger tank, the TD shells just bouncing off its armor. Four TD's crossed the canal, concentrated their shells on a single Tiger tank without effect. The Tiger simply turned on them with its huge gun and demolished all four of them with five shells.

But the greatest gnawing fear was that wherever you were, you knew the Germans could see you, knew what you were doing. You even played softball near slit trenches. And every time you stood up in a clear area, you felt naked.

Some GI's used cardboard cartons from the field rations to waterproof their foxhole walls and keep out rats and sand. Even more valuable were the cardboard tubes that packed the big shells. These, the GI's filled with earth and lined crosswise over deep slit trenches.

The inventive GI mind found other uses for other items: a popular tooth powder was excellent for both scouring rifle barrels and substituting for baking powder in pancakes; the red circle on the pack of Lucky Strikes was just the right size to fit behind a flashlight lens to provide a properly dim light at night; howitzer recoil oil did very well as a shortening for French-fried potatoes, especially if you needed an added cathartic effect; the cellophane gas cape was great for wrapping bed rolls; copper wire from a shot-down German plane could be combined with an empty K-ration box and a razor blade to produce a workable crystal radio set.

From nearby Rome, Axis Sally's favorite song for her Anzio audience was, "Between the Devil and the Deep Blue Sea."

February was the month of the fierce battles. We wanted out and the Germans wanted in. The Germans had bigger guns and we had more ammunition. In that single month, our four artillery battalions of a single division fired almost 130,000 rounds. In that single month, one division suffered more than 5,000 casualties, almost one-third its overall strength.

One of the replacements, Pvt. George Carr, Watertown, N.Y., wrote his reaction on reaching the Anzio front:

"Where were the slick, unspotted 'fighting men' of the ads back home? Not here. Straggle-bearded, haggard-eyed, black-faced men—these weren't the garrison soldiers I always had known. Unmatched clothing and equipment—everyone wore and carried what he best liked. Dried brown mud from Anzio's creeks and mudholes clung to them and their weapons. These guys looked tough and unfriendly.

"When I saw these men at chow that morning I noticed their eyes. They were tired, bloodshot . . . Some eyes were continually blinking, some were continually shooting to right and left as though something would creep up on them unless they kept vigilance. I watched and it appeared that most of these fellows couldn't realize that they were away from the front, for a while at least.

"I wanted to talk to these men, learn what it was like 'up there.' But I felt that to speak to them would heighten the tenseness. It gave me the feeling of smallness, of not belonging. We had nothing in common. I was a rookie replacement among veterans."

Anonymity often created invisibility. Parked in an isolated position, his name known to nobody, a new GI sometimes felt that if he didn't fire his rifle, then even the enemy wouldn't know he was there, and then, maybe, he could stay alive a little longer.

To strip him of this, the platoon sergeant would crawl to the man's hole, take his rifle, fire a quick clip, return the rifle, say his name. Gone was the anonymity; gone was the invisibility; and another GI became part of the war.

For a handful of serious malingerers, there was the stockade; for the shirkers and the stragglers there were such jobs up front as collecting human excrement—scooped into empty K-ration boxes out of foxholes.

But there were more citations for courage than there were courts-martial for cowards.

Every man is a coward and every man has courage.

"I had hoped we were hurling a wildcat on the shore," Churchill later said of the Anzio invasion, "but all we got was a stranded whale."

He later qualified it to say, "The story of Anzio was a story of high opportunity and shattered hopes, of skillful inception on our part and swift recovery by the enemy, of valor shared by both."

Field Marshal Kesselring would describe the Anzio invasion as a failure because it was "a halfway measure" but he referred to the Allied troops on Anzio as *"ausgezeichnet"*—which meant "distinguished." And he would later say of it, "Anzio was the enemy's 'epic of bravery.' We felt we were opposed by equals. Our enemy was of the highest quality."

Whenever the war became quiet, the number of visiting VIP's increased proportionately. GI's referred to such VIP visits as "swanning." The term came from the swan's habit of taking short flights that created much commotion, without any serious purpose.

Fifth Army Commanding General Mark Clark made one of his PT-boat trips to the Anzio area, accompanied by his usual entourage of correspondents and photographers. Clark posed for one picture with a GI, both of them supposedly sharing a K-ration. After the photographer snapped his picture, General Clark handed the uneaten K-ration to the soldier and said, "Here, son, eat this."

In this single gesture, before a large audience, the general created the impression that while K-rations were good enough for the GI, they were not good enough for him.

Anzio was a small place. Before the week was out, every GI there had heard the story. It was not a morale-builder.

Our German prisoners indicated that they were not living the high life either.

The Germans were getting short of equipment. One of their captured documents read, "The problem of replacing material is growing more and more difficult and even unsolvable in some cases. This leads to insufferable weakness in our combat efficiency. I am not willing to allow the reputation of the Regiment [29th Panzer Grenadier Regiment] to be torn down by such losses in weapons."

Some of the surrendering Nazis came out of their lines "trembling and shaking," testifying to the effectiveness of our continuous artillery bombardment. One of them said that some Germans trying to surrender had been machine-gunned by other Germans.

But the Germans were not caving in—they had strong plans for a counterattack.

A GI, Cpl. Lloyd Greer, Lindsay, Okla., who had been captured and managed to escape, was told by a German colonel:

"For you, the war is finished. In three days, the others will be swimming in the sea."

"Schwerpunkt" was the German word for "point of attack." We had constructed a secondary defense line and even a final beachhead defense line to fall back on, all the while trying to maintain our frontline positions, wondering where the *schwerpunkt* would come.

When it did come, at the center of our line, we had four hundred pieces of artillery, throwing out an average of 25,000 rounds a day. One gun section of 155-mm under Sgt. William Hedges had a rate of fire of eight rounds each forty-five seconds.

Our Air Force flew a total of 468 sorties in a single day. Our big Navy guns added their force. But the *schwerpunkt* had still penetrated four miles on a four-mile front, their six divisions pressing against our depleted four. They were pounding against the final beachhead defense line at one point and a breakthrough seemed imminent.

The world headlines again started using the name "Dunkirk."

The Battle of the Caves was a battle of watery foxholes cut into the loamy slopes of a maze of ravines, a strategic point that controlled the use of a network of roads feeding south to the final beachhead defense line. A battalion of infantry was dug in, and soon cut off. Attacked by enemy tanks and troops on all sides, the battalion often directed our own artillery fire on their own positions, to smash the waves of Germans who were almost upon them.

We had machine guns set on top of the ridge where the caves were dug, and they slaughtered waves of Germans, but they, too, finally had to retreat into the caves. Armored patrols occasionally fought into the cut-off battalion, bringing supplies and taking out wounded. But, most of the time, the battalion was on its own.

Inside the caves, the echo of each rifle shot sounded like

a cannon. During any lull, the GI's stripped useless machine-gun belts to refill M-1 clips and listened to the garble of the German prisoners huddled in the corners of the caves.

Not only did the stubborn defense blunt the German attack but it gave our left flank an anchor.

When we were finally forced to pull out, we had to leave behind some of our wounded.

The sergeant lifted Pfc. William Johnston so that he could sit behind his machine gun. The medic knew he was dying and Johnston said he wanted to be with his gun. And then G Company pulled out.

All that afternoon, from their new position, the men who had left Johnston could still hear the stutter of his machine gun. And then there was a final burst, and silence.

That night the men of G Company waded through waist-deep water, through a mile of German entrenchments, until they finally rejoined their battalion. That night Johnston was listed officially as KIA.

But the next day, at another company outpost, a lone figure was spotted working his way toward our lines. He would crawl, rest, walk a few steps, fall, crawl again. When he got close enough to be identified as a GI, two men crawled out to bring him back. He could barely talk, and he had no shoes. He explained that a German medic had treated him, decided he was too far gone for a stretcher, and another German took his shoes and left him on the battlefield.

His name, of course, was Pfc. William Johnston of G Company.

During all this, we already had evacuated some 18,000 Italian civilians from the beachhead to Naples. We were not only thinking of their safety, but of ours. These Italians owed much to Mussolini. It was Mussolini who had set up the reclamation program that had given them the farms they owned. It was no surprise when our soldiers discovered an Italian shepherd maneuvering his flock of sheep to point out likely artillery targets for German observers in the hills. Once the shepherd would move his sheep out of the target area, the German artillery would pulverize the place.

When we discovered this, we almost pulverized the Italian shepherd. As for the sheep, even mutton tasted good after a steady diet of K-rations.

"If you want to hold a position, you can do it; the other fellow will quit first," said one of our generals at Anzio.

The other fellow did quit first, and our lines held.

The war moved into March, and settled down into a battle of big guns.

The beachhead only had two main roads connected by an ox-cart path which our engineers had graded and widened to accommodate the heavy flow of traffic. It was only a mile behind the front and the enemy watched it most carefully.

Our MP's set up a traffic pattern allowing only one vehicle at a time to cross the road, and at different intervals. The idea was not to race across the open stretch at top speed, but to suddenly vary the speed to confuse the enemy gunners. If you didn't confuse them, you were dead.

It was one of the small items of war—a decision on the future of two soldiers. Both of them belonged to a tank battalion on Anzio. One was a corporal and the other a private, both from Binghamton, N.Y. They had taken their basic training together and fought through the war together. Now the Army was sending the corporal home for permanent duty in the United States. It was a sad day when Cpl. Roderick R. Loop said goodbye to his son Pvt. William R. Loop.

Cassino was such a classic case of an impregnable natural defense barrier that they studied it for years as a special course at the Italian Military College. If the Americans didn't know this, the Germans did. While we were still sixty miles away from Cassino, their engineers were busy making this natural impregnable defense even more impregnable. They had three months to enlarge existing caves, dynamite new ones, camouflage gun positions so only their muzzles showed, dig mortar emplacements into deep gullies to fire at such a steep angle that there was small danger of being searched out and destroyed by counterbattery. The stiff gorse thickets on the mountainside were embedded with barbed wire, and trip wires set off flares and mines.

In Cassino itself, even the strong stone walls were reinforced, tanks concealed in some of the buildings, tunnels constructed between them, pillboxes built inside. They also had portable pillboxes, five inches thick, on wheels, drawn by tractors.

From Monte Cassino, observation was so sharp that they could see our every move in the valley, even pick out the hills four miles away in the moonlight.

Of course, we had our own observation.

They called them "grasshopper pilots," and they had a lyric to describe them:

> *We don't need spurs or boots*
> *And we fly too low for 'chutes.*

They were also called, "the eyes of the artillery." Their Piper Cubs, or "flying jeeps," or "Maytag Messerschmitts," flew fifty miles an hour at low altitude, their engines often sounding like the clatter of sewing machines.

"I don't worry so much about flak," Smitty told Sgt. Jack Foisie, "but when Jerries start firing 88-mm air bursts, then it is time to go." Smitty was S/Sgt. James Smith, Jr., Alexandria, Va.

The *Wilma Elaine* lifted slightly, and then dropped slightly.

"It is time to go," announced Smitty.

Smitty told Foisie how the artillery observer adjusted fire by radio from his frontline box seat, normally stayed up about an hour, giving the observer time to kill three or so targets. Then the plane went back, refueled, and started all over again.

"My job," explained Smitty, "is to keep the planes on the target and watch out for ME's. They always come out of the sun. I watch for our own ground flak. That tells me there's an enemy about. I watch for vapor trails."

"See that light streak in the sky over there?" he said, pointing westward toward the sea. "That's coming from something. There are fighters—two, three, four, five, six of them. Making for the sun."

"Ours?" asked Foisie.

"I don't know," said Smitty. "Keep your eye on them."

A Piper Cub pilot has no parachutes.

"Wouldn't have time to use them," Smitty said quietly.

The first battle for Cassino lasted for three weeks.

171

Our net Allied gain was a small snaking bridgehead over the upper Rapido north of Cassino along a ridge we called Snakeshead. It was a skinny appendix curling through the mountains, within a thousand yards of Monte Cassino. It was a slippery foothold, painful to supply. The final fifty GI's there were so numbed from exposure that many of them had to be carried out on stretchers. The stretchers were ripe targets, and many of them never made it.

When the wounded arrived, the ambulances were ready. One of the Fifth Army ambulance units was French, and female.

The old Italian victrola was scratching out some music, and a pretty French girl, with flowing black hair, was waltzing around the room, with a dreamy look in her eyes and an imaginary sweetheart in her arms.

"Tonight I am not here," she said, her voice musical. "Tonight, I am in Paris, wearing a long red evening gown and silk stockings and satin shoes and a beautiful white flower in my hair."

The scratched record finished its song, and she walked over to start it playing all over again. It was the only record in the room.

She was smiling wistfully. "We are still very feminine girls, yes?"

There were still traces of lipstick and powder on the faces of some of them. They still knew how to giggle girlishly. A few of them were still pretty enough to be pin-up girls—despite their GI fatigues, leggings and muddy boots.

These two dozen French women ambulance drivers were far away from Paris. They were in a cramped room in a damp, cold farmhouse, with garlic hanging from the ceiling.

"When we first came here, the soldiers they laugh at us," said Rénée, who used to be a Social Service secretary. "They say we are girls and we will wreck our machines, and lose our way, and we not able to stand all this dirty living of war.

"But we stand it," Rénée said. "It is hard at first, and we are frightened when we are first shelled and when we see soldiers die in our arms, but we stand it. And our ambulances they are clean, and we never have accidents, and now the soldiers they no longer laugh at us.

"We do not come here for adventure," Rénée added, her tired eyes shining. "We come here to work seriously, to work hard."

And they do. All day and all night there are three ambulances (two girls to an ambulance) making the twenty-mile round trip to the front line, within one kilometer of the actual fighting, to pick up the wounded and bring them back to the collection station. The other girls in other ambulances take the wounded back to the field hospital, and when there is a battle going on and the casualties are heavy, quite often all twelve ambulances are out on the road.

In the blackout, they often have to guess at the road, try to bypass the water-filled shell holes, hold tightly onto the wheel when the machine starts to slide in the slippery, slushy mud. If they get a flat tire in the pouring rain, they must hurry to fix it, because the wounded are waiting.

Finally, when the wounded are loaded inside, the girls alternate with the driving. One stays back with the patients, giving them cigarettes, water, peeling oranges for them, injecting morphine if they need it, trying to make them comfortable, talking to them.

"We love music," said a little brunette named Nanou, "but we have no radio, no nothing, and we feel a little lonely and empty, sometimes."

The pat phrase was: "Large German forces are being contained." But for the soldier sticking out on a skinny salient, a tremendous finger of force surrounded by superior forces looking down at him from all sides, the question was: who is containing whom?

We suffered a sharp defeat in that first battle for Cassino. One division of GI's had some 2,000 casualties in trying to cross the Rapido, another American division lost more than 2,200 men fighting for this mountain bridgehead. Both these divisions were temporarily finished as a fighting force. The British and French suffered similar losses in their areas.

And why? Our Cassino offensive had been launched prematurely, mainly to support the Anzio landing. Our troops were tired when they started, and some of them were green and untested. But the main reason was that our force was not powerful enough to face the situation—we sent in regiments where we needed divisions.

But if we suffered, so did the Germans. Their victory was sweet, but it was bittersweet. Some frontline companies suffered up to 75 percent casualties.

Excerpts from a German diary at the start of the Cassino battle:

JANUARY 22d. I am done. The artillery fire is driving me crazy. I am frightened as never before, and cold. During the day, one cannot leave one's hole. The last days have finished me off altogether. I am in need of someone to hold onto.

JANUARY 25th. I am becoming a pessimist. We are on half-rations. No mail. Teddy is a prisoner. I see myself one, very soon.

JANUARY 27th. The lice are getting the better of us. I do not care any longer. Rations are getting shorter —fifteen men, three loaves of bread, no hot meals. They say we are to be relieved by some mountain troops. My laundry bag has been looted. Now ten men, one loaf of bread.

The Germans best expressed their loneliness in a song they sang, a song which some of our GI's translated and also sang, a song called "Lili Marlene." It began:

> Outside the barracks, by the corner light,
> I'll always stand and wait for you at night,
> We will create a world for two.
> I'd wait for you the whole night through.
> For you, Lili Marlene, for you, Lili Marlene.
> When we are marching in the mud and cold,
> And when my pack seems more than I can hold,
> My love for you renews my might,
> I'm warm again, my pack is light.
> It's you, Lili Marlene, it's you, Lili Marlene.

The dramatic feature of the second battle for Cassino was the bombing of the Benedictine Abbey. It sat on top of the 1,703-foot-high Monte Cassino with the majesty of an impenetrable fortress of history. Inside the cathedral were the pipes of a celebrated organ, the high altar containing some work supposedly done by Michelangelo, choir stalls of incredibly fine carving, and the tomb of St. Benedict. It was St. Benedict himself who opened the original Abbey in A.D. 529. It had already been destroyed and rebuilt three times.

Our GI's had been pulled out of the front line, replaced by New Zealand troops, and their general complained that any enemy in the monastery could "watch and bring down fire on every movement on the roads or open country in the plain below." Whether or not the Germans were inside the monastery, he said, it was an obvious observation post. A single observer with a single pair of binoculars and a radio could direct the fire of an unlimited number of guns on any target.

"Wherever you went," said a soldier, "there was the monastery looking at you."

His commanding general, Alexander, agreed. The building had been spared, said Alexander, "to our great disadvantage, but it was an integral part of the German defensive system, mainly from the superb observation it afforded. It was impossible to ask troops to storm a hill surmounted by an intact building such as this, capable of sheltering several hundred infantry in perfect security from shellfire, and ready, at the critical moment, to emerge and counterattack."

The bombing would largely be an American Air Force show, and so one of our Air Force generals flew over the Abbey in a Piper Cub. Flying at less than two hundred feet above it, he flatly said that he saw a radio aerial on the Abbey, and enemy soldiers moving in and out of the building.

We then dropped pamphlets in the Abbey area, warning all civilians to leave. It was addressed to "Italian friends" and said, "We have until now been careful to avoid bombarding Monte Cassino. The Germans have taken advantage of this. The battle is now closing in more and more around the sacred precincts. Against our will, we are now obliged to direct our weapons against the monastery itself. We warn you so that you may save yourselves."

First came the waves of big bombers on the morning of February 15. Only ten percent of them hit the Abbey but it was enough to obliterate the beauty of its interior and make the lovely cloisters look like broken teeth. Then came the medium bombers, which were much more accurate.

"They dipped slightly," an observer wrote. "A moment later, a bright flame, such as a giant might have produced by striking titanic matches on the mountainside, spurted swiftly upwards at half a dozen points. Then the pillar of smoke, five hundred feet high, broke upwards into the blue."

We had converted a piece of history into a piece of rubble. Monte Cassino Abbey was now nothing more than Hill 516.

"I certify," said the Abbot of the monastery later, "to be the truth that inside the enclosure of the sacred monastery there never were any German soldiers."

The pity of it was the waste of it.

"They told the monks," said the soldier afterwards, "and they told the enemy, but they didn't tell us!"

We had not synchronized any proper attack plan to follow up the bombing. The Nazis still controlled the rocky road that zigzagged up to the monastery and we had not had any proper patrols of the forward area, any built-up reserve of troops, or even any sufficient mortar ammunition. (Two trucks with mortar ammo plunged off a mountain road and were never replaced.)

When our forward troops did take off toward the hill, they were immediately beaten down by withering fire from grenades and guns. Wriggling on the ground, they tried to outflank the enemy, without success. They went nowhere.

The bombing had achieved nothing and helped nobody.

Some of our positions were only seventy yards away from the German positions. The litter of loose rocks made any silent night movement almost impossible. Here was the most mechanized war in history with hundreds of available airplanes, tanks, artillery pieces and some 70,000 vehicles, and yet all of them were practically useless compared to the mule and the man.

And the time would even come in Cassino when our communication would be so cut that we would depend completely on a pigeon to carry frontline messages of desperate need.

Our war in Italy had come to this: a mule and a pigeon.

The combined concept of Anzio and Cassino was a failure of full proportion because the German resistance held firm on both fronts. We had underestimated the enemy and overestimated our strength.

Our bombers then began the third battle for Cassino, again an obliteration bombing, this time on Cassino itself.

Cassino—known as Casinum in ancient Roman times when Marc Antony held his orgies there—had long before been cleared of civilians. Our bombing there was regarded as "a choice of difficulties."

Cassino was a half-mile square, a highly fortified strongpoint. Our plan was to bomb it into extinction, then move our tanks in behind a creeping artillery barrage, follow with infantry moving through the town to Highway 6, then fanning out toward the Liri River valley.

The bombing date was March 15.

A German soldier nearby recorded in his dairy:

MARCH 15th. Today, hell has let loose at Cassino. Cassino is a few kilometers away to our left. We have a good view of everything. Almost a thousand aircraft bomb our positions at Cassino and in the hills. We can see nothing but dust and smoke. The boys who are lying up there must be going mad. In addition, the artillery puts down a concentration of fire throughout the whole day. The ground is shaking as if there was an earthquake.

MARCH 17th. In spite of all the bombs and shells, we still hold Cassino. Today we were relieved quite unexpectedly. It does not appear to be a good thing, for it comes too suddenly, but the main thing is that we get out of these hills.

MARCH 22d. We are back in the hills beyond Cassino. What we are going through here is beyond description. I never experienced anything like this in Russia, not even a second's peace, only the dreadful thunder of guns and mortars, and there are planes over and above. Everything is in the hands of Fate, and many of the boys have met theirs already. Our strongpoint is built round with stones. If one is dropped among them, then we'll have had it.

MARCH 25th. There has been a heavy fall of snow. It is whirling into our posts. You would think you were in Russia. Just when you think you are going to have a few hours' rest and get a sleep, the fleas and bugs torment you. Rats and mice are our companions, too.

It was the last entry he made.

Our 500 bombers dropped 1,400 tons of bombs—although they dropped some on our own troops in Venafro, fifteen miles away, causing 140 casualties; and some more on a Moroccan military hospital, causing another 40 casualties, and even more on one of our headquarters. But we still successfully completed a saturation bombing of Cassino.

As a British soldier said, quoting the Duke of Wellington, "I don't know how they will impress the enemy, but, by God, they frighten me!"

And our tanks did take off at noon, as planned, behind a creeping barrage of more than 600 guns.

Describing the bombing of Cassino, an observer wrote: "The enemy was strangely, horribly silent, and very eerie it seemed. A little half-hearted ack-ack had greeted the first wave or two. Then we heard it no more. I remember no spectacle in war so gigantically one-sided. Above, the beautiful, arrogant, silver-gray monsters performing their missions, with what looked from below like a spirit of utter detachment. Below, a silent town, suffering all this in complete passivity."

We found Cassino a ruin of rubble in vast heaps, blocking roads, and huge deep craters instead of streets. In that first hour of battle, we needed bulldozers instead of tanks, engineers instead of infantry. And then came the rains, torrents of them, making lakes out of craters, mud and mire out of dust and rubble. But, somehow, the Germans were still alive and so now it became a battle from one pile of rubble to another, a battle of flooded cellars, a battle of a sniper's paradise.

It's one thing to move forward into a generalized firing area; it's another to know there is a patient sniper, selectively concerned about killing you. To pull such a sniper out of position, so that you can kill him before he can kill you, is a thing of high art and cold courage. The courage is to expose yourself deliberately, while your buddy cocks his gun and tries to kill the sniper in the split second before he gets you.

Pfc. Jackson Wisecarver, back in the mountains, tried another tactic. Wisecarver, a machine gunner, was faced with the knowledge that a sniper was only a hundred yards away, when he took over the gun pit of another gunner. For several days, Wisecarver tried every trick imaginable to get the German to expose himself, but none worked until the thirteenth day. Wisecarver had started, each preceding day, with a burst of gunfire in the general direction of the sniper, and throughout each day, there would be an exchange of fire without results. On the last

178

day that Wisecarver would be occupying the position, he refrained from his usual morning exchange. The sniper, suspicious at first, finally concluded that he had eliminated the American machine gunner during the night; and after a great length of time, he emerged from his protective niche. It was only a short burst, but it enabled Wisecarver to turn over the gun pit to his relief GI, without having to warn the new gunner of a sniper out front.

We waited almost six weeks, until mid-May, before launching the fourth and final battle of Cassino. Our new axiom was: only numbers can annihilate. Alexander brought in the British Eighth Army from the Adriatic coast, packed them next to the Fifth Army on a twenty-mile front between Cassino and the sea. The two armies were to smash the Gustav Line and move straight for Rome. Then the reinforced Anzio army, now with six divisions, would break out of the beachhead, and cut off the retreating German Tenth Army in the Alban Hills, trap them in a powerful pincers.

Anzio had settled into its own strange way of war. Waiting for the breakout, "the greatest jailbreak in history," were some 70,000 men, 18,000 vehicles and 356 tanks. There was still "Anzio Annie," the huge railroad gun, carefully hidden in tunnels until time of firing. But its huge projectiles, fired from so far a distance, were highly inaccurate. They rubbled our dock area but they sank few ships.

All over the beachhead were signs saying, "42nd Street and Broadway," "The Good Eats Cafe," "Beachhead Hotel—Special Rates to New Arrivals."

Makeshift stills, using copper tubing from fallen planes, distilled a potent kind of brandy. Supplementing K-rations were a surprising amount of hamburgers made from strolling cattle who "just happened to trip over a mine." Sheep didn't trip over mines as often because GI's weren't overly fond of mutton.

Homemade entertainment came from an exchange of bands by GI's and Scottish bagpipers; a GI magician named Pvt. Roland Ormsby, better known as "The Baron," who even brought his own tuxedo; beetle races (painted different colors) and even an Anzio Derby.

The Derby was born in the brain of an old Baltimore handicapper, Sgt. Bill Harr, who laid out a race course with white engineer's tape, collected enough mules and horses to make a race, set up a public-address system and even recruited some pretty nurses to give prizes to the winners.

The odd part of it was that the Derby was in plain sight of enemy guns, and the collected crowd made a most inviting target, and yet not one enemy shot was fired. Maybe the German gunners were betting, too. But the odds were now stacking up against them.

The addition of the Eighth Army to the Fifth Army front was made in absolute secrecy, and successfully so. The Eighth Army even left behind dummy tanks when they moved an armored division. We had increased our artillery to 1,600 pieces, made all our troop movements at night, built no new roads which might arouse suspicion, maintained a sporadic artillery exchange on a daily basis.

We knew the Germans were building a new defense line, six miles behind the Gustav Line, and we had the added spur to break it before it was built.

Our troops now were international—American, British, French, New Zealand, Polish, South African, Italian, Goums and Gurkhas.

They were always smiling, always laughing, like a bunch of kids just young enough to think the whole world was a big joke.

But when night came, these smiling, laughing little guys would creep quietly with their kukris, their eighteen-inch knives, and when they came across a big guy, they would hack at his thighs; if somebody came at them with a bayonet, they would chop at his arms; otherwise, they just confined themselves to lopping off heads, which they do quickly, cleanly, with a professional touch.

The Gurkhas are a peaceful, pastoral people, and they're not really Indians. They come from Nepal, sixteen thousand feet up in the Himalayas, on the northern fringe of India, between China and Tibet. They're so far away from everything and everybody that they get five months off to take a three-months' furlough. That's simply because it takes them a full month to walk home from the nearest railroad station.

But there's the old story about the English-speaking German who spotted an English-speaking Gurkha in a foxhole and lunged at him with a bayonet. The Gurkha twisted his body a little, just in time. "You missed me," he said, and then whipped out his kukri and slashed. "You missed me, too," said the Jerry. "Hell I did," said the Gurkha. "Wait until you shake your head."

"Those Goums don't fight fair," one English-speaking German prisoner complained. "They are crazy."

That was true. But these French-Moroccan native troops had been taking hill after hill, bringing back hundreds of German prisoners, leaving behind many more Jerries, quite dead.

All of them had intimate knowledge of the French light machine gun, the American tommy gun, and the 81-mm mortar. But give them a bayonet and a bunch of grenades and they'll charge any position, anywhere.

After getting into positions at night, clambering as quietly as goats, the Goums would make a cold-steel attack, preceded by several dozen well-aimed grenades. When they got within fifty yards of the top, the Jerries would open up with machine guns. Instead of falling flat on their faces, hunting for cover, the Goums rushed straight in for some hand-to-hand fighting. For that, each Goumier had a ten-inch knife, a *"koumia,"* which he sometimes used to cut off heads.

Most of the men were lean, with closely cropped, crinkly hair and a plaited pigtail. The pigtail is to give the Lord something to grab onto when He yanks them up to Paradise, after they die. The Goums are all Mohammedans in religion, Berber in origin. (Berbers are natives of North Africa; Arabs are not.) Practically all of them wear beards. "They believe that a man who has not seen action and does not have a beard, is not a man."

There is the story that Goums were offered a bonus for every pair of ears they brought back. After they brought back a lot of ears, too many of them, their officer investigated and discovered that they were not German ears, but "British ears."

There is also the story of a favorite Goumier trick of sneaking in on two sleeping Germans and cutting the head off of one of them quietly, and then leaving the other one asleep, to wake up to a surprising sight.

The night of May 1 was misty after some rain, but then the sky cleared and the stars looked sharp. An hour before midnight came the voice of a thousand guns from Cassino to the sea, all aimed at preregistered targets located by air reconnaissance during the previous month—communication centers, command posts, enemy artillery. However disorganized by this massive artillery, the Germans still managed to flood the river area with smoke so thick that our soldiers had to edge their way to the boats by holding onto the bayonet scabbard of the man in front of them. The smoke turned to our advantage during the morning, mixing with the mist to enable us to complete much of our bridging operation.

The half-measure days were over. We had come in force. And then the Abbey was ours, Cassino was ours—now both of them just names and numbers on the map. We were streaming into the Liri River valley with 2,000 tanks and 20,000 vehicles, a victorious Army on the move. Before we could reach the Adolf Hitler Line, the Germans hurriedly changed its name to the Dora Line.

And now it was time for Anzio.

The Anzio breakout began just before dawn on the twenty-third of May, also with intense artillery followed by tanks and troops.

It was about a mile northwest of Borga Grappa, a tiny village beaten into rubble by air attacks. Some GI's from a tank destroyer outfit met some British Tommies. They were tired, but they grinned and they shook hands—Anzio shaking hands with Cassino. And now both forces would head for Rome.

We had twenty-eight divisions chasing twenty-one German divisions and General Clark decided to change the Fifth Army direction. Instead of cutting off the German Army in the planned pincer, he switched his troops to head for Rome. Those Germans we might have captured would live to fight us in the Apennines months later, north of Pisa in their Gothic Line.

We were not fighting this war only with soldiers and armies. Behind the German lines, cutting into the enemy in a hundred harassing ways, were bands of Italian partisans.

Yank correspondent Sgt. Harry Sions told the strange story of a partisan from Brooklyn:

"A rough-looking, oddly dressed character walked up to the entrance gate of a parachute battalion's encampment here and said he wanted to go inside. The stranger wore

British Army shoes, mustard-colored cotton pants, a torn GI paratrooper's jacket and an Italian straw hat with an orange band. Cpl. Milo Peck, of Barre, Mass., who was standing guard at the gate, was not impressed.

" 'And what do you want inside?' asked Peck.

" 'I want to report to my outfit,' the stranger said. 'I'm Manuel Serrano. Don't you remember me?'

" 'Serrano!' said Peck. 'I thought you were dead a long time ago, back in Tunisia. Where the hell have you been all this time?' "

And that was how Sgt. Manuel Serrano, first American soldier known to have fought with the Italian partisans, returned to his outfit after an absence of twenty months.

Serrano was a six-footer, deeply sun-burned and husky. He had a small black mustache and thick black hair streaked with gray. Born in Puerto Rico, twenty-four years before, he had lived in Brooklyn, N. Y., since he was five, and before the war played the maracas and drums in a rhumba band in a Greenwich Village hot-spot.

Captured in North Africa, and shipped to Palermo Prison Camp and then to Italy, Serrano escaped after the grapevine heard of the Italian surrender.

"They taught me a lot of tricks at Benning and in England, but Fascist-hunting wasn't one of them. I was pretty nervous," said Serrano. But he helped them hunt for a lot of Fascists, and killed many of them—but always after a fair trial.

One of the most important partisan jobs was to help escaped American and British prisoners. Serrano estimates that his band helped more than a hundred prisoners back to the Allied lines. Three girls worked with the partisans on these deals, getting the names, ranks and serial numbers of escaped prisoners who had taken refuge in farmhouses in the area. The partisans radioed this information to Allied headquarters at Bari.

One morning in March, while the partisans were camping in the hills near Comunanza, in the La Marche region, a farmer reported that the Fascists had captured and killed six escaped Allied prisoners. They had stripped the prisoners of their identification and clothes, he said, and had taken them to a field nearby. There they had forced the prisoners to dig a long, shallow ditch. When the ditch was dug, the Fascists machine-gunned the prisoners, threw their bodies into the ditch, then covered them with a few shovelfuls of dirt.

"That night," Serrano says, "three of us made for the field. We saw the ditch, but the bodies had disappeared. We checked around, and learned that nuns had taken the bodies to the convent in Comunanza after the Fascists left. We went to the convent, and there were the six bodies, wrapped in white sheets and lying on slabs of wood. The nuns had cleaned the bodies and wrapped them in the sheets. I lifted up the covers from the faces, and recognized them all. Four were GI's and the other two were British. The nuns said they would give them a decent burial. Then we left.

"I walked out of that convent and back up the hills to camp. When I got to the top of the first hill, I turned around toward the convent, and those six dead soldiers, and I swore that for each one of those soldiers I would kill a Fascist with my bare hands. I think for the first time, I really knew what it meant to be a partisan."

On the day Serrano left, he made a speech in the town piazza. "I told them I'd be back some day," he said, "and that I would tell the American soldiers what I had learned from the partisans. They begged me to stay. They even wanted to make me mayor of the town. In fact, they wanted to give me the town's prettiest girl for a wife. But I guess I'll wait till I get back to Brooklyn and find a nice Italian girl there. I like these Eyeties. Maybe it's because I'm a Latin, too, and understand them a little better than some other American soldiers."

There were two rows of apartment houses where the Appian Way ends and the city of Rome begins, and crowds surged out of them, laughing and singing and shouting and crying. They were soon handing us bottles of wine. A girl put a flower behind a GI's ear. An old lady with white hair kissed a tank.

Our line of tanks and troops were completely stopped. "These crazy people don't know it," said a tall, thin, anxious captain, "but they're holding up the war."

As our troops moved through Rome, one GI took a long look at the ancient ruins of the Colosseum, whistled softly and said, "Gee, I didn't know our bombers had done *that* much damage to Rome!"

Before prices soared out of sight, GI money could buy a bottle of wine for five cents, a prostitute for twelve cents. San Carlo Restaurant kept open for business, as usual, serving Americans instead of Germans, serving the same best cuts of horsemeat and the finest wines. Rome was almost unscathed by the war, and water, gas and electricity were all in working order. Nor had the Nazis planted any time bombs in public buildings, as they had in Naples.

Some lucky units were bivouacked outside the city, and one GI engineer, a sergeant who used to be a railroad foreman in Kansas, told Sgt. Paul Green about some of the fun he had.

"I gets to town," he said, "and just friendly-like, offers a gal a piece-a gum, I din' think nothin' would come of it. She busts out cryin'. So I gives her the whole pack. She's about middle-height, and has dang-near blonde hair. Then I sez, by golly, does she want a drink and somethin' to eat? She nods her head. So we gets on a streetcar and go downtown. She tells me it's-a goin' to cost plenty, but I sez, by golly, what's the good of money if you don't spend it.

"We had a swell meal . . . steak and all that, plus cognac. She likes cognac . . . It all came to about ten bucks, but was wu'th it, every cent.

"The next day, I gets back to camp and walks up to the captain. It was a little after eleven. 'You look sober,' he sez. 'By golly,' I sez, 'I ain't had a drink all mornin'. But I ain't sayin' what I had last night, and I ain't sayin' what I brought back with me.' He gets interested. 'So you brought somethin' back with you,' he sez. 'Sure did,' I sez. He scratched his head. It was that licorice-tastin' stuff . . .'"

"Anisette?" Green prompted him.

"That's right. Annie-zette. Pretty powerful strong, too. So I give the captain the rest of the bottle.

"Well, the next day, he sez all of us can go into town, if we come back when we're supposed to. I went to my pal and ast her how many friends she can get. 'How many do you need?' she sez. 'By golly,' I sez, 'all you can find.' So I goes outside and counts them. Fourteen there were, besides me. 'Fourteen,' I sez. She sez nothin', but sits down at a phone, and don't you think in a couple-a minutes, she's got a gal for every one of them fellas?" He shook his head in admiration.

"Soon we wuz all scattered. I starts drinkin'; I'm-a gettin' high. But she sez, 'By golly, a fella can't have any fun when he's drunk.' She's right, too. So she takes out two white capsules and gives me one. But I figure maybe it's dope. The Germans been here for a long time, and you

185

never can tell. So I sez, 'Give me them.' I puts 'em both in her bag and mixes them up. 'So you don't trust me,' she sez, and laughs. 'Gotta make sure, by golly,' I sez. I gives her one, and I takes the other. I swallow it. What do you know, in half an hour, my head's clear as a bell. Still don't know what was in them capsules.

"We get a pass every two days now," he said, "I'm a-goin' back tomorrow."

For the outside world, Rome was only a one-day headline. The day after, the Allied armies invaded France. Eisenhower notified Field Marshal Alexander that three veteran GI divisions of the Fifth Army would be diverted from the Italian front to make the invasion of southern France.

Alexander protested:

"I cannot overemphasize my conviction that if my tried and experienced commanders and troops are taken away for operations elsewhere, we shall certainly miss a golden opportunity of scoring a really decisive victory, and we shall never be able to reap the full benefits of the efforts and gains we have made during the last few weeks. I feel strongly that it is of the greatest importance not to let go the chance that has been so hardly won."

But Eisenhower's decision was firm.

And so the main strength was pulled out of the Allied drive in Italy, giving the retreating Germans an unexpected breather, a longer time to consolidate its new Gothic Line, a line of mountain defenses four miles deep.

The war in Italy would go on for many months more. At the year's end, the Allied Armies would have moved 315 miles in 365 days, past three major fortified defense lines, at the cost of more than 50,000 combat casualties.

For the GI's still there, Italy would be the same giant minefield, the same war of mud, mules and mountains, but, now, more than ever, it would be the forgotten war.

Mechanized War

STAY OUT O
OLD RUTS

"Fresh, spirited American troops, flushed with victory, are bringing in thousands of hungry, ragged, battle-weary prisoners . . ." (News item)

*"Th' hell with it, sir. Let's go back
to the front."*

The Prince and the Pauper

"Beautiful view. Is there one for the enlisted men?"

"Why th' hell couldn't you have been born a beautiful woman?"

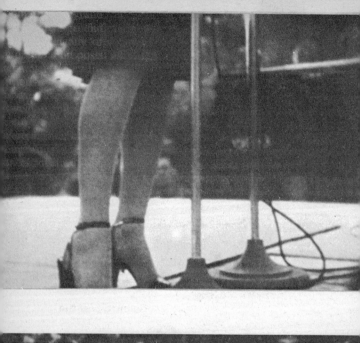

FRANCE AND GERMANY

Stretch me out on the barbed wire—
You with the long fingers.
If I scream,
And I may scream,
Twist my pulp into a question mark
And call it a pattern of man.
                    —S/Sgt. Ralph G. Martin

From D-Day to St.-Lô

Most of the plans were neatly filed in a fat folder labeled "Operation, Overlord." Everything had been figured out, on paper. There would be so many personnel and vehicles on so many boats, so much ammo, so many rations, so many stretchers. Each truck would have its gas tank full, carry enough extra for a 150-mile trip, and each soldier would carry a K- and a D-ration. All officers would send their trunks to storage.

There had been dry run after dry run, with soldiers seldom sure whether or not it was the real thing. There had been a final date set, and changed, postponed a day because of bad weather. It all depended on weather, tide and what the moon looked like.

This was the plan:

Simultaneous landings on two main beaches: near St.

Laurent-sur-Mer on the northern coast of Calvados, and near Varreville on the southern part of the east coast of the Cotentin Peninsula; with two airborne divisions dropping inland the night before around Ste.-Mère-Eglise. The British and Canadians would come in north of Caen near Le Havre.

There would also be a one-hour air bombardment and continuous naval bombardment of the sixteen German coastal guns and the myriad of six-foot-thick concrete pillboxes, things the Nazis called *Widerstandsnests*. And there would be three companies of Rangers going in to destroy a battery of big German guns at Pointe du Hoc, which commanded both beaches. And there would be engineer special brigades with the big job of blowing gaps in the thick concrete wall lining the beach, cutting through the rows of barbed wire, bulldozing roads out of nothing, and sweeping the mines.

According to COSSAC (Chiefs of Staff of the Supreme Allied Command), there would be a maximum of five German infantry divisions and one panzer division along our whole front on D-Day.

It was there in the folder, everything you could think of. Somebody had even sat down with a pencil and paper and figured out that by D plus ten our troops would have had 43,586 casualties.

An invasion ship is a lonely ship. Down below in an LST you sit and sweat and nobody says anything because there is nothing to say. You look around and wonder who will be dead soon. Will it be that tall, tough-looking sergeant busy double-checking his rifle; or the guy stretched out in his upper bunk who keeps praying aloud all the time; or the kid sitting next to you who wet his pants? Who will be dead soon?

Then the thought comes, swelling inside of you, a huge fist of fear socking at your gut, hammering and hammering . . . "Maybe it's me. Maybe I'll be dead soon . . ."

Communiqué No. 1, Tuesday, June 6, 1944:
    UNDER THE COMMAND OF GENERAL EISENHOWER, ALLIED NAVAL FORCES, SUPPORTED BY STRONG AIR FORCES, BEGAN LANDING ALLIED ARMIES THIS MORNING ON THE NORTHERN COAST OF FRANCE.

The sea was choppy, and Omaha Beach was a long

seven miles away when the first wave of soldiers lowered into their assault boats. Coming in, there was Allied naval gunfire bursting all along the beaches; large, medium and fighter-bombers swooping down by the dozens, dropping their loads on gun positions, troop concentrations, coastal batteries, bridges, highways, railroads. With so much air-navy pounding, everything looked easier. Some even thought that it might be a walk-in.

But nobody walked. They came in running fast, falling flat, getting up again, crouching, running fast, falling flat, hunting for a big rock, a shellhole, anything. Then digging in, because the Germans still had plenty of guns and ammo and deeply dug-in defense positions behind the bluffs.

From these hundred-foot-high bluffs, their guns not only commanded the beach strip of 7,900 yards but also the five small valleys opening out into the beach. If the Germans could keep these exits closed and pin down our troops and shoot up our ships and vehicles, the show would soon be over. But if we could force the exits, then our troops could fan out behind the hill defenses, neutralizing them and consolidating the beachhead. We would be able to do that because the German defense was not in depth. They were concentrating most of their strength along the beaches.

It looked bad at first. The Germans had been practicing anti-invasion maneuvers just two days before, and many of them sat safely inside concrete pillboxes pouring enfilading fire on billiard-table beaches. After a half hour, assault teams succeeded in establishing a ragged fire line in some sectors.

Everything was confusion. Units were mixed up, many of them leaderless. Shells were coming in without letup. Boats burning, vehicles with nowhere to go, bogging down, getting hit; supplies getting wet; boats trying to come in all the time, some hitting mines, exploding; some thirty tanks never reaching shore because of the high seas or because German guns picked them off on the way in; only six out of sixteen tankdozers reaching the beach; everything jammed together like a junkyard, so much so that the naval beach-battalion commander radioed ships to stop sending in any more vehicles for a while.

Soon, though, scattered units got assembled; one of the valley exits was forced open, and trucks started moving off the beach. Some gaps were blown through the wire and concrete, and troops began pushing southward across the high ground into a position near Colleville-sur-Mer.

"If you want to live, keep moving," everybody said.

When the British ship slowly pulled into port, all the newspapermen crowded inside because it was the first boat back from the beach. The boat was loaded with dead and wounded. One of the wounded talked quickly, excitedly.

He told how he got soaking wet wading ashore with a load of explosives on his back. He was part of a demolition team of twenty-eight who were supposed to blow gaps in the concrete wall.

"I was just coming out of the water when this guy exploded right in front of me. There just wasn't anything left of him except some of his skin which splattered all over my arm. I remember dipping my arm in the water to wash it off. I guess I was too excited to be scared."

Then he told how they blew this tank barricade, and then he got hit with this hunk of shrapnel in the elbow.

"It wasn't as tough as I thought it would be," he said.

The other soldiers in the hold of the ship didn't say anything. The war was still in their faces.

Twelve hours after H-Hour only one of the planned exits was in operation on Omaha Beach. Most of our artillery was underwater, but by 1600 hours the field artillery had five howitzers just off the beach, supporting the infantry. Two hours later there were ten more howitzers in action.

During all this, the Naval Shore Fire Control parties, who had come in with the assault troops, were talking to their big gray ships telling them what to shell and with how much.

By midnight, the tired, dirty assault forces of V Corps were spread out on a strip of Free France about 10,000 yards wide, straddling the coastal road, with their deepest inland penetration estimated at 3,000 yards and their forward positions sitting on the high ground which divided the sea from the Aure River.

The two small boats floundered around in the rough waves, and shells kept plopping close. The big ships seemed far away, and the fifteen guys in the two boats kept working on their radio sets. At H plus 15, they finally got through. "Testing . . . one two three four, can you hear me . . . over . . ."

Four of these radios had started for Utah Beach. Two had been put into waterproofed jeeps, but were knocked out long before they got to the beach. The other two were in these small boats—DUKW's—boats with wheels so that they could keep moving when they reached land. If they got knocked out, too, then the distance from shore to ships would be like a million miles and a million years.

At H plus 3, the two DUKW's wobbled on shore, tried to race up the beach to reach cover. One was smacked square, killing one guy, wounding several others, smashing the radio. The other got through. For fifteen hours this single radio did the job of four, filling one hot-priority order after another: change of fire direction, more boats for the wounded, more this, more that, more everything.

For fifteen hours, "Can you hear me . . . can you hear me . . . Over . . ."

They started dropping by the light of the full moon at 0130, five hours before the first waves of infantry hit Utah Beach. They started dropping from 800 invasion-decorated planes (black and white stripes) on six predetermined zones. Twenty planes never got back.

Of the two airborne divisions, one was widely dispersed because of thick flak and fog. Even as late as June 8, it still had only 2,100 combat effectives under unified control. But that didn't stop them from storming Pouppeville, a tiny town which was important because it blocked the causeway entrance from Utah Beach. Before glider reinforcements arrived the next night, they had also taken stubbornly defended Varreville, pushing down Purple Heart Lane toward Carentan, to link up Omaha and Utah Beaches. Purple Heart Lane went through canals, swamplands and across the Douve River. To get out of the swamp, they used bayonets for the first time in the invasion.

Meanwhile, paratroopers landed mostly west of the main Carentan-Cherbourg road, west of Ste.-Mère-Eglise, which the troopers promptly walked into, cleaned out, and took over. That was the first town taken in France, and the Germans shoved in several tank attacks trying to get it back. There were two paratrooper bazooka teams who took care of five tanks all by themselves. Finally the Germans pulled out.

The paratroopers had done their job—elbowing enemy reinforcements away from the beaches.

Now they were waiting for the infantry.

"Just before we pulled out, the CO read us this message from Eisenhower about how we were all crusaders and all that, and it made us feel pretty good," said Sgt. Robert Miller, who was in the sixteenth plane over France.

"It seemed like a long trip, but it was only two hours. It was a long two hours though, because it was so hot in the plane, and with all that hundred and twenty pounds of stuff on us, most of the guys got a little sick.

"You don't talk much. I didn't say a damn word. And don't ask me what I was thinking about because I don't remember. I guess I was thinking a little about everything.

"And don't ask me what I saw when the chute opened, because I don't remember that either. But I remember everything after I hit the ground. Seeing a guy burning in the air. Things like that.

"The most terrible thing is when you hit the ground and you don't see anybody and you don't hear anything and you're all alone. Being lonely like that is the worst feeling in the world."

The landing at Utah was smooth and quick compared to Omaha. That's because Utah was a mistake—some units landed 1,500 yards southeast of the beaches at which they were supposed to land. They still got plenty of fire, almost continuous, from some German battery in nearby Fontenay, but this was only a small sprinkling of the stuff they would have got if they had landed where they had intended to.

It was so smooth where they did land that 30 amphibious tanks were launched 5,000 yards offshore in two waves, and came in with the loss of only one tank.

Soon after five forts were cleared around the beaches, the infantry moved up to relieve the waiting paratroopers. By midnight, they had cleared an arc-shaped area which averaged from four to seven miles inland.

The expected Luftwaffe show of strength never materialized. Instead of an estimated 1,800 Nazi sorties over the beaches on D-Day, the antiaircraft crews spotted several single planes which didn't stay around long enough to be shot at. The first ack-ack crew moved in at H plus 17; the first barrage balloon was floating in the breeze at H plus 225 minutes. Even our artillery came in early, delivering supporting fire as early as H plus 90.

But despite the smoothness and quickness of everything, there were still plenty of red crosses scattered along the beach. (A total of 832 wounded were evacuated from France that first day; the others were stretched out behind cover somewhere.) As for the dead, they lay where they fell. There was no time to bury the dead that first day.

This was his fourth D-Day, he said. Arzew in Africa, Gela in Sicily, Salerno in Italy and now this one. He was a medic with the combat engineers, Pfc. Stanley Borok of Center Moriches, Long Island, N.Y.

"If you're shooting dice," he said, "how many lucky sevens can you roll before you crap out? I figured that this time maybe I was gonna crap out, and I didn't want to crap out. Not that I've got any wife or kids back home, but I just didn't want to crap out. Nobody wants to. But it was rough; it was sure rough."

The waves slapping and banging and the landing craft floating around in circles for two hours before H-Hour and everybody sits with a helmet between his knees puking his guts out, so sick that he doesn't care what happens to him. But suddenly the boat starts moving in and somehow you stand up and swallow what you've got in your mouth and forget you're sick.

"I took five steps and this 88 shell lands about thirty feet to my left. Then I run to the right and bang, another 88, and this time my buddy is staring at his hand because his thumb is shot off. Then two more, just like that, and I found some backbone and ribs and the back of a skull with the whole face cleaned out, all of it right near the pack next to me."

His first patient was a guy who had his front tooth knocked out by a piece of shrapnel. His second was in a foxhole buried up to his thighs.

"I didn't even notice it at first but he had blood spouting from his chest. Two big holes. You can't plug up a guy's lungs, brother. We did all we could, though. I spotted this bottle of blood plasma that we were giving some other guy and then I noticed this other one was dead so I just took out the needle and put it in this guy's arm. But it didn't do much good. He died in my arms."

The British were having it tough those first few days. They had landed near Bayeux, two British divisions and one Canadian. Their foothold near Caen was the hinge of the whole beachhead. Three German armored divisions were hammering away at them, throwing in attack after

203

attack. The Germans rightly figured that if they could crack through the British-Canadian position with tanks, they could race down the beaches, cut off our supplies, surround us, separate us and chop us up.

The Germans were also particularly sensitive about our threat to Carentan and the possible linkup of the two beaches into a firm front. To keep the two beachheads separated, they threw in a single extra paratroop division which was like adding meat to a grinder because our buildup was steady, with more and more troops pouring over the beaches.

At Isigny, divers of an Engineer Port Construction and Repair Group opened the canal locks to relieve the flooded countryside where our troops were fighting.

"I'll never forget that swamp," said Pfc. Vito Dziengielewski. "It was stinking, scummy, gray-looking water and it came up to our knees. I'll never forget that stink. It just made you kinda sick. As if a lot of things had died there. Then there were millions of bugs buzzing around, biting the hell out of you, and you were even too tired to shoo them away. You were so tired that you just wanted to fall down in the swamp and stretch out for a while. Some of the guys did slip and fall. If you didn't see a guy fall, it was hard to spot him because the weeds were so high and thick, just like Sea Breeze Bay in Rochester."

"But even when you crossed the swamp, there was no time to sit down and take off your shoes and wipe your feet and wiggle your toes in the sun and change your socks. You could feel the wet socks sucking down in your shoes with each step, wet socks heavy with mud and scum. Some of the Joes threw their leggings away and rolled up their pants so that their legs would dry a little quicker. But nobody had a chance to change his socks for three days. Some of them soon didn't have to."

At the Auville Bridge, somewhere between Carentan and Isigny, a paratrooper shook hands with an infantryman, and the newspapers back home headlined the fact that Utah and Omaha were now one solid front.

But they weren't. Temporarily the junction was thin because troops on both beaches were heading away from each other, trying to swell out and make some elbowroom for maneuvers. Besides, the Germans still held some high ground, which meant that they could throw artillery fire any time they wanted to on both the Isigny-Carentan highway and the vital Carentan bridge. It was the bridge we were particularly worried about, because if the Germans got the bright idea of breaking through in strength to retake it, it would have sliced an unhappy wedge into our supply line. For protective insurance, the engineers built another bridge, 2,000 yards downstream.

Troops and supplies were still flowing over the beaches in a steady stream and one of the forgotten units with a private headache was the Traffic Headquarters Subsection of G-4.

"There was one vehicle for every six men in the invasion force, so you figure it out," said Sgt. Francis Scanlon, an accountant from West Medford, Mass.

"Our phone used to ring all day and all night long and people wanted to know where their unit was and which was the best way to get there and which roads were open."

He remembered something and smiled.

"The last question was the easiest to answer because there were so few roads open to anywhere. The only lateral road we had was the N-13 highway which went from Caen to Carentan. Then we had these skinny little roads branching off to the beaches. At one of these side roads, GC-5, we had to knock down a wall and a flower garden to widen a turn, and at another place tear down a church and cut through an apple orchard to break up traffic jams by some homemade traffic circles."

Besides that they had to make records of every vehicle hitting the beach, which unit, and where it was going. They did this twenty-four hours a day.

At certain critical sections of the road there was an hourly flow of more than 1,700 vehicles.

"And there were only seventeen men in our section," said the sergeant. Then he remembered something else.

"I'm the only one who's alive now," he said.

There was something special about taking the town of Quineville but nobody thought much about it at the time, especially the soldiers who did it. Taking Quineville meant that the beaches were now finally free of any enemy artillery fire, and the reason that Division G-3 didn't get excited was that their big job was just coming up—to sweep across and cut off the peninsula.

Cutting off the Cotentin Peninsula would stop Germans

205

from getting in or out of the Cherbourg area. It would give the Allies an important port, a big bag of prisoners and a broad front for future action.

The Germans knew this, expected it and tried to get ready for it. They called in elements of six divisions, forming two battle groups. We needed tanks.

Back at Southampton, England, on D plus ten, the three mechanics were getting ready for their first night off in weeks when the emergency call came. There was a tank that had broken down just out of town and they were bringing it in to be fixed, and it had to be ready before breakfast because it had to catch a convoy with the rest of its division.

It was a big Sherman tank with a sick motor, and the three mechanics told the tank crew to sleep in their beds because they wouldn't be using them that night. It was almost midnight when they started operating.

S/Sgt. Edward Seaman, Jr., of Toledo, O., kept razzing his boys to keep them sharp. And they razzed him back. They were tired and busy, and they were running into complications. No time to smoke. Only a quick cup of black coffee to keep the sleep from their eyes. Twenty straight hours operating on machines and guns. Another day tomorrow. There goes the air-raid alert again. Nobody ever writes any stories about an Ordnance Medium Automotive Maintenance Company.

There was no waiting or debating about the jump-off for Cherbourg. Our troops started moving northward the morning after they reached the sea.

Cherbourg got its worst plastering of the war on June 22, the first concentrated air bombardment on a target since D-Day. That's when ten squadrons bombed and strafed targets for a full hour. They were followed by twelve groups of fighter-bombers and eight groups of medium bombers clobbering pinpoint targets.

But, like the D-Day bombing, all this air effort softened the orange and squashed some of it, but didn't peel it.

The peeling had to be done by the infantry who came in fighting yard-by-yard, farm-by-farm, against stiff resistance.

On June 26, three divisions finally moved into the city of Cherbourg itself.

Sniper fire was persistent, the streets had to be flushed

house by house, but people streamed into the squares to greet their liberators.

"We were living in this house in the outskirts of the city when this Frenchman and his wife came back," said T/3 Bernard Crystal, who was with the engineer liaison section.

"We saw them coming up the hill slowly, both looking a little scared. Then they both suddenly stopped to stare at the house, staring at all the shrapnel holes and the partially busted roof, just staring, not saying a damn thing. Then the wife pointed to the garden, shaking her head, and the two of them came into the yard and started pulling weeds.

"They told us later it was their house. The Germans had kicked them out, and they hadn't been back for three years.

"I'll never forget the way they were pulling out those weeds . . ."

The beachhead was a front now. There were Americans spread over a thousand square miles of France. The price for this mileage was 2,245 killed, 11,670 wounded, 3,137 missing. It was much lighter than anybody expected. But if you saw faces instead of numbers on the casualty list, it wasn't light at all.

Other statistics for the three weeks: 36,006 Germans sitting in prisoner-of-war cages somewhere; 301 out of 1,249 German planes shot down after 125 day raids and 579 night raids. This air-raid total for three weeks was less than we had expected on D-Day alone.

As for the Cherbourg port, it was a mass of wreckage —every single one of the thousand installations had been at least partly destroyed. But engineers were already working on it, trying to get the port in shape quickly enough to make up for the serious loss of a specially built dock which had been wrecked in a three-day storm. Artillery shells were getting so scarce that artillery outfits were rationed.

It was going to be a slow, grudging push, and everybody knew it. You can't sweep across country when it's sliced up into small, square fields, each field walled on all four sides by hedgerows, sometimes ten feet thick and four feet high, and with trees and shrubs growing out of the top of them. And each hedgerow a possible strongpoint of Nazis, waiting for you.

"We hardly ever saw any Jerries. This is the way it was: we'd get inside a hedgerow and dig into it and down. If there were any holes, no matter how deep they were, we dug them deeper. Then you sent a squad to draw fire, and if they drew fire and came back, then you knew where the Germans were. After that, maybe you'd fire some shots and they'd fire some shots, you'd fire mortars and they'd fire mortars.

"That's all there was to most of it. Nobody did much during the day. We just lay in our holes and soaked in some sun. It wasn't a good idea to get too far from your holes. They got a whole squad with a single mortar shell once because they got too far from their holes.

"We usually got pretty busy at night. There were these sunken paths in between hedgerows and that's what we traveled on. And we never made a frontal attack on a hedgerow; we always tried to outflank it. Sometimes we bypassed a hedgerow filled with Germans and didn't know they were there until they opened up at us from behind. It was a funny kind of war."

Coming up from Cherbourg, we sweated out the heaviest German artillery barrage of the campaign on July 15.

Fighting here was particularly tough because of the swampy terrain, making it necessary for each division to fight separate actions. Coordination of corps strength would have to wait until they got onto solid ground. Meanwhile the great danger in single division action was that then the Germans could concentrate their strength and reserves. By July 18, it was evident that the Germans had done just that, also that they had shifted their main strength from the coastal area to the hilly ground.

With the whole corps, including a newly arrived division, closing in on St.-Lô, it was a special task force which finally forced an entrance into the much-battered town, pressing down slowly from the east. That was 1900 hours, July 17.

"We were dug in at this cemetery right at the edge of St.-Lô. Two platoons of Company C. And we stayed there three nights, and everybody was kidding about this was sure a helluva place to dig in, a helluva thing for our morale. But nobody laughed very loud because it wasn't very funny. We had just taken Hill 122 outside of town, and out of 200 in the company there were only 40 left. That's not very many. And we had to stay there in this cemetery, because our artillery was still shelling the town. So we stayed there, but they knew where we were and the Krauts shelled the hell out of the place. All these dead being unburied again and all these caskets and then the terrible stink of fresh dead horses and cows. We lost some of our boys, too. There was one guy who was split right in half. I remember that specifically. No, we didn't bury any of our own dead. The quartermaster does that. I think they take them back to an American cemetery, don't they?"

The Battle for France

Operation Cobra was our second D-Day. It was the yes-or-no answer to the type of war we were going to wage in Europe—whether it would continue to be grudgingly, painfully slow, or what?

COBRA called for a blitz: infantry breakthrough piercing powerfully on a narrow front with armored exploitation. Heavy artillery preparation and heavier air bombardment.

After an intense aerial plastering of an area 2,500 yards deep and 6,000 yards wide near the St.-Lô.–Perriers road, we were to jump off.

Bad weather twice postponed the jump-off date. Finally, on July 25, the show started. Our frontline troops withdrew 1,200 yards from the target area, and the planes came.

"We were five miles behind the front when we saw all these planes come over and everybody was feeling pretty good about it," said Pfc. Thomas Shaw of a Military Police battalion. "And then we saw some of the bombs dropping short, and we just looked with our mouths open. They brought the wounded boys back and we saw some of them. The ones we saw were really hysterical. One of them was crying like a baby.

"But nobody's perfect. The infantry makes mistakes, too. Everybody makes mistakes."

Only a fraction of the bombs had fallen short—the smoke over the target had drifted and some leading planes mistook the St.-Lô.–Perriers road for a similar road parallel to it, 2,500 yards away. But most of the other bombs had done their job—twenty minutes of bombardment by 350 fighter-bombers, one hour of clobbering by 1,500 bombers, twenty more minutes of bombing by another 350 fighter-bombers—all this on a small, narrow strip of front. German frontline troops were hurt, stunned, disorganized.

The first day, we moved at least two miles all along the front. Two days later, the Germans seemed to realize the danger of a strong breach in their central position. That's when they withdrew all along the sector leaving behind blown bridges and thick minefields.

The Germans had an estimated 29 light-sized divisions opposing the breakthrough, with 33 more divisions scattered elsewhere over France.

All indications were that the Nazis were quickly pulling divisions out of Brittany and away from the British front to help form a new defensive line. But their critical mistake had been made more than a month before, when they had elected to keep divisions in position to protect the rocket bases in the Pas de Calais area.

Since then, the Nazis had not only lost about 160,000 men, including 20,000 prisoners of war taken during the breakthrough, but they had also lost heavily in vehicles (2,500), tanks (400) and generals (11).

During all this, enemy air was still weak. The Luftwaffe's greatest show of strength came on July 29 when it sent up 82 sorties. Our air was busy everywhere. In the five days before August 1, the Air Force flew 400 armored-column support missions. Tank-plane coordination never worked better.

The 50-caliber machine gunner from Charlie Company was telling how it was on Hill 318.

He told how the regiment had beaten back counterattack after counterattack, how they just sat on the reverse slope of a hill with some of their antitank guns looking over the top and how one day, the Germans sent in 50 tanks with SS troopers yelling their goddam heads off.

Lots of dirty underwear got dirtier, then and there.

Then came the lovely, lovely sight of eight of our B–47's swooping so low you could almost see them smile, dropping 500-pound bombs kerplunk on the tanks. They were so close that one lieutenant even had his eardrums shattered.

These German tank-riding infantry were already jumping off by the dozens, scramming as fast as they could, and the soldiers of Charlie Company were picking them off like shooting-gallery ducks.

When it was all over, there were 14 burned-out German tanks sitting in a neat semicircle at the bottom of the hill, almost as if somebody had posed them that way.

Everybody just loved the Air Corps that day.

By the beginning of August, the hedgerow hell was far behind, and the door at the bottom of the corridor was open, and our combat commands were racing fast, ready to fan out in several directions, one toward the Brittany peninsula, the other in the direction of Paris and the Seine.

It was at noon on August 1 when the fifteen American divisions in France were split up into two Armies, the First and Third. The first specific mission for General George Patton's Third Army was to drive west to capture the Brittany peninsula and open the Brittany ports.

Before the first seven days were over, we had cleared the greater part of the peninsula, mopping up scattered pockets. Still resisting were St.-Malo, Brest, Lorient and St.-Nazaire.

The tanks got all the headlines. No matter what newspaper you picked up, the tanks got all the headlines.

Okay. Good.

But the infantry was there, too. Infantry sprawled all over the tops of tanks, riding a hundred miles a day that way sometimes, acting as the eyes and ears for the blind tank. Flushing out housetop snipers, hopping off to clean out an antitank gun hiding around the curve, deploying to wipe out a roadblock. Sitting naked on top of tanks . . .

Still, they were lucky in a way; they were riding. There were all those infantry divisions who walked long forced marches into boobytrapped towns, through minefields and always snipers, snipers and more snipers. The dirty job of mop-up that never made any headlines, seldom crept into any stories.

Walking for miles and miles and days and days until your feet were dead and your body was lead and your mind kept mumbling, "I'm so goddam tired . . ."

For the Germans, the situation was getting desperate. The Nazi high command finally agreed on a plan called

"LIEGE" which involved an immediate counterattack to cut through our narrow bottleneck between Mortain and the sea, thereby isolating all our troops in Brittany. For the job they had both the German Seventh Army and the Panzergruppe West.

Plunging first with tanks, the Germans struck in strength in the center of the line at Mortain, reaching the dominating ground west of town.

By August 9, two days after it started, the German semi-blitz already had been blunted and our own tanks and troops had bounced back. Field Marshal von Kluge of the German Seventh Army blamed it mostly on our air superiority. In one of his messages, later captured, he said: "Our own air support which is requested becomes engaged in air battles at the very start and does not reach the place of commitment as ordered."

It's a little like Hollywood. You pick up the phone at the air control office and you talk to a pilot in a plane somewhere in the sky.

"This is Sugar Baby One. Here are the coordinates for that tank column. Over."

You talk quietly as if you were ordering groceries at the A & P.

Or else you don't talk; you listen. You listen to a pilot saying quietly, undramatically to another pilot, "Jerry coming in at two o'clock." You listen to that and try to picture a German plane zooming down out of the sun right at you, guns shooting at you. You try to imagine that and you can't. Yet all of it is upstairs somewhere, not too far away. Then you listen to silence. Loud, long silence, and finally you hear a boyish voice in a semiscreech saying, "Whoopee, I got the sonofabitch. I really got him."

It's a little like Hollywood.

While First Army troops were pressuring the German Seventh Army from the rear into an oval-shaped pocket, Third Army troops were applying pressure from one flank at the same time as the British Second Army squeezed down from the other. This was the Falaise Gap.

The gap closed finally when we contacted the Canadians at the little village of Chambois, which sat at the mouth of a three-mile valley, through which the Germans had managed to evacuate some of their panzer units.

But most of the rest of the German Seventh Army, scattered in this pocket, was shelled and bombarded day and night, hour after hour, without letup. The high ground northeast of Chambois was aptly named the "Balcony of Death," because from there, our artillery observation posts had a perfect view of the whole valley. It was a valley littered with hundreds of burned vehicles, thousands of dead and wounded, smashed artillery pieces, overturned loot-laden carts, and dead horses and cattle swelling and stinking in the heat.

Artillery fire stopped long enough at certain intervals to accept mass surrenders, which became increasingly larger, until there were more than 10,000 prisoners in our stockades by August 19. By then there was no more Falaise pocket.

"Everybody asks me what the Falaise Gap looked like and they look at me kinda funny when I tell them I don't know. All I know is that we were green as hell because this was our first big action. We were so green that we didn't even dig in. I remember they brought up these tanks and fired pointblank direct fire at us and they hit our battalion CO. We were there five days and we lost a helluva lot of men. We were just green, that's all. And I never did get to see this Falaise Gap. There was just this small hill and there was a little town right next to it. I don't even remember the name of the town."

We were still containing the 30,000 Germans entrenched in Brest and an armored division was sweating out Lorient and St.-Nazaire. Resistance had ended elsewhere on the peninsula.

Third Army troops meanwhile crossed the Seine north and south of Paris, taking the high ground west of the city commanding the Seine River valley.

Then General Patton asked his engineers to do something supposedly impossible. There were seven railroad bridges from St.-Lô to Le Mans in different stages of demolition. Patton wanted the whole thing to be ready to receive ammunition trains in forty-eight hours. In addition to rebuilding them, it also meant repairing and laying new main lines in three marshaling yards, laying miles of track approaching bridges and yards, providing service and water facilities along the lines.

"I was there at one bridge," said the major. "It was

pretty bad. One edge of it had been blown into the stream and some ranking brass looked it over and said it couldn't be done. But there was a master sergeant who used to be a bridge designer and he got together with some noncoms and figured out how it could be finished in time. It looked kinda impossible to me, mostly because they didn't have enough of the right equipment. But goddam if they didn't do it. It was finished in forty-seven hours.

"When they first got started, it looked like a circus, everything all jumbled up and confused with guys doing different things.

"No I didn't see anybody cheer or yell when the train passed over the bridge. I guess they were too tired."

The Germans tried to shove across the remnants of their Seventh Army at a narrow shoulder of the lower Seine near Elbeuf, and four American divisions closed in rapidly to stop them. For two full days and nights, massed artillery fire destroyed everything, almost, which tried to cross the Seine at Elbeuf. On August 25, Elbeuf itself was reached, the American troops making contact with the British to the north.

That was the end of the German Seventh Army. Conservative estimates on casualties included 100,000 prisoners, 15,000 Germans buried by our Graves Registration people, plus an estimated 35,000 other German dead and wounded. Six full divisions had been liquidated. Von Kluge himself had committed suicide after the Chambois shambles.

But elsewhere on the Third Army front, the Germans were very much alive, deeply entrenched in small towns and big cities where they had to be rooted out, cities like Chartres. . . .

"Me and this other guy had a bazooka and an M-1 and we were parked on the second floor of a building right in the town square of Chartres and we were just sitting there waiting for things to happen when this Frenchman crawls up and puts us wise to some tanks running around town, Jerry tanks. So we kept our eyes peeled," said Pfc. Billy Barnes, of Dallas, Tex., who was with A Company of an armored division.

"Nothing happened until almost suppertime, when a Mark V tank comes breezing through the town square, and just when it passed us, we let loose with a rocket and it went right through the turret and the five Krauts piled out.

"After we knocked out the tank we moved up with the rest of the boys. But then we started to get artillery on us, the real heavy stuff. So we started running, but the faster we run, the more stuff we run into. So we stop running.

"When we got up a little further we found one of our noncoms. Somebody got him with a potato masher but we found four dead Krauts right next to him so we gave him credit for all four. What the hell. You know it took us six days before we really mopped up that town. That was what you call a tough sonofabitch."

We weren't supposed to go into Paris. We were supposed to outflank it.

But we hadn't counted on the French Resistance known as the FFI. Highly organized, spread out all over the city, the FFI started their own sniping street fighting on a big scale on August 19.

For the Germans in Paris, the situation got so serious that General von Choltitz arranged a verbal agreement. If the sniping would stop, he would permit food convoys to come into Paris. The FFI agreed not only because their food situation was so critical but because they had an acute shortage of ammunition and they couldn't fire much longer.

As soon as they learned all this, the Twelfth Army Group Headquarters, under General Omar Bradley, decided to enter Paris as soon as the armistice ended on noon, August 23.

The Germans resisted only in a group of buildings east of Vincennes, shooting down both the German and American officers who walked toward them with a white flag. It wasn't until the next morning that we reduced this strongpoint, and it wasn't until the day after that all street fighting and sniping completely stopped and Paris was formally returned to the French people.

When the other troops started moving northeast, a newly arrived division was paraded through Paris en route to the front.

"After all, we didn't have a damn thing to do with the taking of Paris. We just came in a couple of days later when somebody got the bright idea of having a parade and we just happened to be there and that's all there was to it. It wasn't right that we should get the credit, but what can you do—that's just the way it goes," said Pfc. Verner Odegard of Gonvick, Minn.

"As long as I live I don't guess I'll ever see a parade like that. Most of us slept in puptents in the Bois de Boulogne the night before, and it rained like hell and we were pretty dirty, so they picked out the cleanest guys to stand up front and on the outside. I had a bright new shiny patch, so they put me on the outside. It was a good place to be, too, because every guy marching on the outside had at least one girl on his arm kissing him and hugging him and marching right alongside him.

"We were marching twenty-four abreast right down the Champs Elysées and we had a helluva time trying to march because the whole street was jammed with people laughing and yelling and crying and singing. They were throwing flowers at us and bringing up big bottles of wine.

"The first regiment never did get through. The crowd just gobbled them up. They just broke in and grabbed the guys and lifted some of them on their shoulders and carried them into cafés and bars and their homes and wouldn't let them go. I hear it was a helluva job trying to round them all up later."

To take immediate advantage of a disorganized enemy, the general tactic was now an axis of advance northeast of Paris toward Belgium, with the First Army in the center, the Third Army on the right, the British on the left encircling Le Havre and driving up north toward Dieppe, and the Canadians on the coast cleaning up the strongpoints.

It was this startling speed all over the front that made the supply situation so tough. The impossible problem was to try to move supply depots far enough forward to meet the needs of the front when few people ever knew where the front was—and, on top of this, build up reserve supplies in critical materials.

The biggest responsibility rested on the Red Ball Express, a setup of truckers with top priority on special highways.

The trucker's voice got wistful when he remembered. The short hauls weren't so bad, he said, but those long hauls at night were so goddam lonely it was like poison. Sure, you had an assistant driver but there are only so many things you can talk about and then the talk gets dried up.

He had carried everything on his truck—mail, ammo, gas. There was one long run, 764 miles round-trip, 52 hours of steady driving from Ste. Marie Dumont to St. Elroy. They started at 8:30 P.M., got into St.-Lô just before midnight for a cup of hot coffee and then they'd got into Alençon just before daybreak.

When the war moved so fast, there were *beaucoup* enemy pockets on the rear that the trucks had to pass through. Once Stone even had an armored escort. And when they'd finally reached the tankers, the tankers would say, "Here comes the goddam QM with the gas. What are you guys doing so far front anyway?" And Stone would just laugh and say, "Charge it to Stony Pony Jr., Truck 43 of the 4002 Quartermaster Trucking Company.

"I called my truck Stony Pony after a gal back home in Chicago who used to slap my face all the time."

By the beginning of September, the whole German western front was just a number of fugitive battle groups, disorganized and demoralized, all painfully short of equipment. Our push from the Seine was so swift that we had shattered any German hopes of reorganizing and holding at the Somme-Marne line. The Nazi field marshal was in the embarrassing position of issuing field orders for his troops to hold at a certain line only to find out later that we had passed the line long before his orders had arrived.

By this time our Army high command had a military headache almost as bad as the Germans'. We had moved so fast that our headache was the gas shortage. It got so bad that C–47's were used. But even that didn't work. Daily gas consumption during the first week in September was as high as 665,360 gallons. The most popular, most important, busiest place anywhere was the gas dump.

"We didn't like to call it a gas dump," explained Pfc. Mel Rapp, Wernersville, Pa. "We called it a POL, just like the British did. Stands for petrol, oil and lubricants. Very fancy.

"Our place was Q339 right at St.-Lô, the 3938 QM Gas Supply Company, 32 nozzles pouring out 285,000 gallons a day fresh from the pipe.

"You could never point to a truck at the end of a convoy and say that was the last truck, because they never stopped coming, day and night. And if we ran out of gas, nobody would go away. They'd just stay there and wait.

217

Most of the drivers would flop where they were and grab some sleep, and so would we, because when the pipes opened up again we had twice as much work waiting for us.

"Lots of guys passed out. The gas fumes get you after a while. Sometimes you just keel over and sometimes you really get sick. You get lead poisoning. Looks something like poison ivy. On a real hot day, you could actually see the gas fumes. It looks like heat coming off a railroad track. I remember we were in this apple orchard with the little apples just coming out and goddam if the whole orchard didn't die in a week from the gas fumes."

The liberation of Belgium began at 1107 hours on September 2 when reconnaissance units crossed the border in the heavily wooded area near Momignies.

During all this, the confusion of the German high command was incredible. For example, there was a huge mass of German troops, almost twenty disorganized divisions, moving eastward from the British front, who were completely surprised to find American troops between them and Germany.

Our artillery went to work and the planes went to work and our troops pressed in chopping the big pocket into smaller pockets, netting a total of 30,000 PW's, several thousand more German dead and buried and tremendous amounts of materiel captured or destroyed.

This pocket annihilation called for an immediate switch in tactics, because it meant that Germany itself would be less strongly defended if we could get there before reinforcements did.

By the middle of September, Third Army troops were deployed along the Moselle waiting for more orders.

You cross the river in small rubber boats late at night, feeling wonderfully thankful that you're in a reserve battalion coming up late and nobody is going to get killed crossing this part of the river now because other battalions have secured the high ground on the other side and the Jerries don't have any more direct observation on the river. But then you stop feeling thankful because it's raining like hell and every part of you is wet and you're going to have to sleep in the mud and you're going to have to dig your hole into it and you know that you are going to have to dig with your hands because the mud will stick to the shovel. And you know you're going to have a choice

218

soon: dig a hole two feet deep and sweat out the incoming shells more than usual, or dig it deeper so that the water seeps in and you're practically swimming but you get better protection from the shrapnel.

You have a choice.

The German Army's first defense line since the Seine was the line of the Meuse River. Remnants of four infantry and seven German panzer divisions were dug in to stop us.

Elsewhere, our troops had moved into Luxemburg, reached the Albert Canal, pushed onto Maastricht. But then the Germans started throwing heavy concentrations of artillery. By September 12, the First Army's sustained drive had stopped. The war had settled down to slow-moving, bitter fighting.

The Sweep from the South

Berlin radio had been blaring the usual baloney for weeks after Normandy, but for once they sounded smug and sure, as if they had been sitting in on a lot of Seventh Army G-3 planning conferences. They kept saying that they knew all about the upcoming invasion of southern France, that they knew where and when and how much. And they were ready for it, they said.

But when Operation Dragoon started landing its troops on the forty-five-mile stretch of coast east of Toulon in the gray, foggy morning of August 15, the Germans weren't even remotely ready. Seldom had an invasion been so smooth and simple and perfectly executed as this one. It was something generals dream about during Louisiana maneuvers.

It was so smooth for several reasons:

The three American D-Day divisions were all veteran outfits which had made either two or three previous amphibious landings at such places as Africa, Sicily, Salerno and Anzio.

The Germans who knew we were coming didn't know

where. They had concentrated their strength in the Marseilles-Toulon area and our main landings about forty miles east of Toulon had caught them flatfooted and off-center.

Seventh Army G-2 correctly doped out expected resistance. The staff knew how many pillboxes were manned and how many weren't, and which beaches would be toughest. It knew that the German Nineteenth Army had only seven divisions stretched out all along the coast from the Pyrenees to the Alps. It also knew that the Germans had little armor and less air support.

Then there was the FFI—the Free French Infantry—giving the Germans a terrific internal bellyache.

The word spread fast. This was the night. Tomorrow was freedom. There was so much to do. Bridges to blow up, roadblocks to destroy, minefields to mark.

This is how you fight a tank when you have almost nothing to fight it with . . . Here is the approved method of digging mines with your hands from the beaches during the blacked-out night . . . If you wish to kill a German quietly, you must cut his neck *comme ça.*

Freedom comes expensive.

Task forces Romeo, Rugby and Rosie would hit at different times and different places before H-hour. Then at 0800 hours, Kodak would come in at Alpha, Delta and Carmel beaches scattered from Cap Cavalaire to Agay.

The mission of Romeo—a small unit of French Commandos—was to neutralize coastal defenses on the left flank and push on to the high ground. Rosie was a force of French Marines with the job of blowing up coastal defenses on the right flank. Romeo worked beautifully, but Rosie ran into mines. Only six survivors of Rosie made contact with GI troops the next day.

Rugby was something much more special, a task force of 10,000 paratroopers, British and American, dropping eighteen miles inland on three zones near Le Muy.

Then, Kodak—three divisions of infantry.

"It just didn't seem right. It was like somebody giving us something for nothing. It was just too goddam good to be true," said 1st Sgt. Robert Elliott of Leadville, Colo.

"The trouble was we were too busy and too scared to be happy. We never knew when they would start opening up on us from somewhere. So even though it was easy, you still sweat it out. One thing about war, as long as you live you're always sweating it out."

Perfect as it almost was, with six out of eleven assault battalions landing exactly at 0800, with the others coming in within four minutes—there were still some slight inevitable screwups.

One screw-up turned out wonderfully. It was during the Rugby show when the ground fog was so soupy that 29 planes dropped their loads of paratroopers in the wrong place. They dropped them three miles south of St.-Tropez in an area being bombarded by our own naval guns. But the bombardment soon stopped and the troopers were able to wipe out some important coastal guns and move into St.-Tropez way ahead of schedule.

Our troops came in so fast that some of the boys walked into a camouflaged dugout near the beach to find hot coffee boiling on the stove.

A mortar squad is only a temporary family. The faces are always changing in a mortar squad. The same goes for an infantry squad or a machine-gun squad; the faces are always changing.

If any one face hangs around very long, it gets older fast. War makes a man out of a kid who never shaved, or it breaks him.

"I came in at Sicily brand-new," said Sgt. William Spencer of Baker Company. "I didn't know my tail from third base. I was only nineteen. I was only a private then, too. Then pretty soon one guy gets knocked off and another guy and another guy and pretty soon I'm the oldest guy in the squad and so they make me the squad leader.

"Then Salerno and some of my new guys get knocked off and I keep getting more and more new guys, and they keep getting knocked off. They pulled us out of Cassino and shipped us to Anzio, and it was the same old story. I guess I must have had about five different squads.

"I don't know how I happened to hang around all this time. Maybe I'm just lucky."

Once in, the troops moved fast. There was no battle of the beaches on this invasion.

The Germans didn't seem to have much more than guerrilla defense, an uncoordinated checkerboard setup of isolated strongpoints. During the first few days our air reconnaissance reported German reinforcements streaming southward to the beaches but then their traffic did a complete about-face. Then it was just a rat race.

Before D-Day ended, we had completely cleared the St.-Tropez peninsula. After a two-day fight for Brignoles, we were sweeping up Highway 7, the best military road from the target area to the Rhone valley.

Our own losses were small. Of the 66,000 soldiers who landed on D-Day, less than 500 were casualties.

A thin tongue of land slipping out into the sea. It was a nice slice of scenery, green and wooded and curving.

But it was hot and loaded. Things like 20-mm guns firing direct fire, and patient German snipers sitting everywhere and machine guns all loaded up for a busy day. The important thing about all this was that this tiny tongue of land stuck out at Cavalaire-sur-Mer, giving the Germans a perfect field of flanking fire on incoming landing craft.

A battle patrol got the simple order, "Clean it up."

A direct hit of a German 20-mm shell tore apart the first American platoon leader. A sniper got the second. The third got an exploding mine fragment in his neck. When it was all over: 36 casualties.

A simple order, a tiny tongue of land.

In a special order of the day, Lt. Gen. Alexander Patch asked his Seventh Army to keep advancing regardless of fatigue or shortages because "The enemy is perplexed and stunned and the opportunity for decisive results is ahead of us."

For this occasion, Task Force Butler was born.

It was shaped out of hodgepodge units detached from each of the three divisions. It was to be the spearhead of the spearhead, the long exploring finger sticking into the confused mass of German troops, poking hard and fast and moving somewhere else.

The whole front now was nothing more than a widely dispersed, disconnected series of pockets and strongpoints. The front was so fluid that nobody knew for sure where the Germans were and where we weren't. Task Force Butler swept right into Sisteron, eighty miles from the beaches.

"Ever see one of these boxers, one of these guys who's really fast on his feet, bobbing and weaving all the time? Well, that's the way the whole outfit was," said T/5 Sol Feingold of Jersey City, N.J.

He told of the time near Livron when they spotted a long bumber-to-bumper convoy moving as fast as it could. Task Force Butler broke up and moved in, one section smashing at the head of the column, another shooting up the rear, then some tanks busting through the middle. Short jabs hitting where they hurt, with Germans too shocked to do much, either coming out with their hands up or stupidly trying to make a run for it.

How can you miss with 37-mm guns firing at targets 50 yards away?

When American troops streamed up the Rhone valley, the French Army, landing on D plus one, was busy cutting around Toulon and Marseilles.

Because, actually, the German military logic was correct. Geography had dictated our strategy. We badly needed the deep-water ports of Toulon and Marseilles. Without them, our whole sweep through France was almost valueless. We needed gas, food, ammunition in huge quantities, and quickly.

But the Germans knew our need. That's why the German high command, while pulling everything else out, was willing to sacrifice two full-strength divisions, one in Toulon and another in Marseilles.

Their job was suicidal. They were to fight to the last man, the last shell. They were to destroy everything destroyable.

The French moved fast, fighting from house to house into the city's heart—Goumiers, Spahis, Senegalese, Foreign Legionnaires and native Frenchmen fighting for Free France.

It was the same story at Marseilles, at the same time. By August 28, the 7,000 Germans and their commanding general decided it was slightly stupid to fight to the last man, so they surrendered the city. Toulon fell the same day.

"We were sitting around listening to the radio when some sugar-voiced announcer mentions the fact that Marseilles has been completely cleared. Well everybody's feeling good, and before I know it there are four of us jeeping to Marseilles to find us a nice little bar someplace and a nice little barmaid as well as a good story," said Sgt. Charley Green of XII Tactical Air Command Public Relations.

"Everybody was still feeling pretty good, even when we

223

started weaving around the French tanks moving into the city. But then things happened. First we heard some shells going over us one way and then we heard some more shells coming over us the other way and then we realized we were right in the goddam middle. Then we weren't feeling so good anymore.

"Then a machine gun opened up about a hundred yards away and it started getting dark and some air bursts came in and the tanks started moving around a little in the streets and some snipers opened up and we had a helluva job just trying to get out of that place.

"The whole payoff was when we finally got back to the Press Camp and the radio was still on and sure enough this same lying bastard of a radio announcer sitting on his fat ass in a beautiful studio somewhere is telling us all about how all the shooting had stopped in Marseilles. How do you like that?"

The Rhone valley was flooded with American troops. General Truscott's order to the three divisions was, "If you run out of gas, park your vehicles and move on foot."

The Nazi plan of retreat was very comprehensive. Resistance during the daytime with strong rear-guard action, long forced marches at night.

And all German soldiers were warned not to wander around unarmed.

German pockets all over the Rhone valley were quietly folding up by the dozens, anxiously hunting for Americans to whom they could surrender. They wanted Americans specifically because they knew the hate that filled the Free French forces. There were too many Frenchmen who knew about too many German concentration camps.

Grenoble was an FFI hot-spot. Women collaborators there had all their hair shaved and were branded with a swastika. For Americans, there was everything, all the wine, all the women, all the song that any GI ever dreamed about.

On the front page of the Grenoble newspaper, there was this:

Welcome!
Yesterday, without warning, we saw them suddenly rising up at the far end of the Cours Jean Jaures . . .
At first no one dared to believe it. The Americans?

They are here? Already? They are here? At last, astride their funny little jeeps, perched high on their heels, reminding one of the far West, piloting their General Sherman tanks, henceforth so well known along the Route Napoleon.

The crowd massed all along this fine avenue, just as it used to in the good old days of the Tour de France. What a glorious Tour de France this is . . .

Welcome to you all! You who have come from the distant provinces of Illinois, Ohio, Alabama or Texas . . . Welcome to the citizens of New York and San Francisco, you all who have come to help France get rid of a nightmare which has lasted four interminable years, and to aid her to rediscover her true soul.

Welcome to Grenoble, our town. Welcome to Dauphine, our province.

Our G-2 was worried. The way our divisions were thinly stretched out, we had almost sixty miles of exposed flank near the Italian frontier. If the Germans accumulated any strength there, especially some armor, they could break out and hit us where it hurt, badly crippling our entire supply setup.

But if we could persuade the Germans to move back out of the mountains on the Franco-Italian border, we would have a strong line which we could adequately defend with a minimum of troops.

The airborne boys and the FFI persuaded the German mountain troops to do just that, and we moved through the Riviera wonderland.

What the paratroopers said was, "If this is war, we want more." They said it softly, though, because up in the cold snow of the foggy mountains, patrols had a way of going out and never coming back. It was an eerie war, too.

But what they were talking about was Nice itself, sitting within shell-fire range of the front, with its neon lights blazing, its modern little nightclubs filled with real Scotch whiskey and beautiful women dressed in soft silk, and hot pianos beating out boogie-woogie just like it was Café Society Downtown in Greenwich Village.

Occasionally the glass in the windows shivered from the nearby naval shelling but the beautiful babes weren't paying any attention and neither was the pianist, and neither was the bartender. But then one of the paratroopers looked

225

at his watch and said, "Well, this has to be the last drink because I have to go on patrol pretty soon."

N 925540 was the map coordinate for Montélimar. Montélimar was just another French town sitting at the edge of a T-shaped plain which extended seven miles south. Control of the town and the high ground northeast of it would give us command of the whole valley and highway, closing the main German escape route across the Drôme River.

The whole German Nineteenth Army was moving up here now, five divisions including the 11th Panzer, and if we could keep them trapped here in this valley, we could annihilate them with our artillery.

But it wasn't so simple. The Germans had most of the good cards stacked on their side. Their defensive positions were excellent; we didn't have enough troops to contain them just as we didn't have enough armor to stop the 11th Panzer; we didn't have enough air support, because of the terrific distance between the front and airfields. (Six airfields were opened up on D plus six. Before that, most fighters still came from Corsica.)

In addition to all this, the Germans had an ace up their sleeve. Somehow, somewhere they picked up a copy of Top Secret operations, including a map overlay showing our relative strength at different positions.

Our weak spot, according to the map, was at Bonlieu, and that's where the Germans broke out of the trap, punching Mark VI tanks and infantry in between two regiments.

German tanks kept the trapdoor open for two days until August 28, when the trap was reset again, but only after much of the Nineteenth Army had sneaked out.

Throughout the eight-day battle, our artillery was shooting up everything. Highway 7 was just a series of roadblocks created by the masses of wrecked vehicles littering the road. The Piper Cubs were overworking that week.

"From up there it's like a box seat at a Broadway show. The only thing is if you go too high you're liable to get hit by Jerry planes or flak and if you go too low, even small-arms fire will knock you down.

"Still it's an awful peculiar thing to sit way up there and spot something and call for fire on it and just sit there and wait sixty seconds and watch something blow up. Sometimes it's a whole convoy, and you keep adjusting fire until you pick the whole thing to pieces. Or sometimes maybe it's just a house that the Jerries use as an observation post. Whatever happens we always pass on the report to the boys of the 158th Field Artillery Battalion because they never get to see what they hit. We're their eyes."

The terrific speed of our push had bitched up a lot of things, mainly supplies. Gas shortage was an old story, but then the lack of ammunition became almost equally serious. You can walk to war but you can't fight without bullets and shells. The shell shortage became so acute that artillery sometimes had to pass up juicy targets, even observed targets, because they were down to their last 25 rounds. The rule was to save the last 25 rounds for a possible counterattack.

Another section with another headache was the Signal Corps.

The truck moves slowly, reeling off both the cable and the galvanized wire. As the truck moves up, the soldiers walk more quickly to keep up with it, their hands stringing the two wires together to make sure they don't get entangled, and hanging it up on trees to make sure the tanks don't tear it up.

They walk like this all day long, until dark, catching up to the unit in front of them, the company sometimes laying fifty miles of wire a day, trying to keep up with the spearheads.

"It's like sleepwalking," said Sgt. Edward Flannery of Company C of the 1st Signal Battalion. "We've been doing this all through Africa and Sicily and Italy, and we can do it blindfolded. I got so used to it that I walked all through France stringing wires together and knocking nails in trees, and all the time I was back in Philadelphia."

Using the Swiss border as a hinge to protect their flank against encirclement, the Germans were able to swing their columns northeast, heading for the Belfort Gap, aiming for the Rhine. The whole Seventh Army was chasing them.

Southern France was now entirely liberated and Lyon was waiting impatiently. South of Lyon, there were still 10,000 German combat effectives trying to pull out as fast

227

as possible because all Germans south of the Loire and west of the Rhone and Saone Rivers faced soon-coming isolation. The Third and Seventh Armies were getting closer together.

The Germans moved so fast, backwards, that they simply didn't bother to put up even a show of resistance for Lyon.

Our casualties were small. In a rat race you don't have too many.

"Seems like every time we just finished putting up our tents, we had to pull them down again and move somewhere else. We must have moved at least a dozen times in less than thirty days. But a surgical team is just no good to anybody unless it's right behind the front," said Sgt. Henry Mahnken of West New York, N.J., of the Second Auxiliary Signal Group. Sometimes he passed the instruments, sometimes he helped the anesthetist, sometimes he subbed as assistant surgeon, holding the belly open while the surgeon cut.

They'd only operate on those patients classified as nontransportable, patients who would die if you moved them. Each such operation was a long sweaty job, three to four hours.

"The war moved so fast that we never knew where it was exactly. But we never had to go anywhere to find it; it always came to us."

The French attempt to close the Belfort Gap escape hatch didn't work out because the Germans counterattacked with tanks in strength, thereby partially maintaining a defense line generally east-west along the Doubs River. The French had their two armored divisions divided among the American Third Army and the Seventh Army. On September 10, elements of both French armored divisions made the first junction of the two American armies near Sombernon. That same day, other French troops went into Dijon.

Both armies were now facing east. East was the Moselle.

But the champagne campaign was *finis*. Now it was a slow war. Plodding through hills and woods on ground too mushy for tank maneuvers against an enemy dug into excellent defensive positions. And the autumn rains had started.

228

Siege of the Siegfried

German real estate suddenly got expensive in September. The Germans were selling space for a time, but they were selling it at so many casualties for a town or a river or a hill or a forest or a pillbox.

They sold it stingily because they didn't have too much to sell, and they were trying to stall in front of the Siegfried Line until winter set in.

Seventh Army was crossing the Moselle into the Vosges, threatening the whole Alsace plain; Third Army was pressing closer to the Saar valley and into the Siegfried Line area; First Army had already crossed the German border in the Aachen area and British Second Army on the extreme north was hitting hard at Siegfried's weakest point.

Extending from the Dutch frontier almost to the Swiss border, the Siegfried Line looked formidable enough, deep belts of elaborately connected pillboxes, some of them eight feet thick and steel-plated. Along natural defenses like the Rhine, Siegfried defenses were sketchy, but in the vulnerable Moselle River valley and the Aachen plain, there were pill-boxes zigzagging in depth for twelve miles.

Aachen was Germany's most sensitive spot in mid-September. Goebbels' propaganda drums were thumping defiantly that Aachen would be Germany's Stalingrad, that we could never take it.

The Aachen area was important because if we could punch through there we could fan out north and south, racing up and down the rear of the whole Siegfried Line.

Our operations tactic here was simple: pinch it off. Completely encircle the area, cut the supply roads, take the high ground to the east and Aachen itself would be an isolated rear-echelon pocket.

But the Germans had five divisions there and were rushing in reinforcements fast. Of the seventy German fortress battalions in the Siegfried, twenty now faced the First Army. Most of them were parked in these pillboxes, as many as forty to a jumbo-size pillbox, and a large part of these pillbox defenders were Germany's 4–F's, the Volkssturm.

It made an awfully good story, a wonderful story.

"GERMANY'S VOLKSSTURM MADE UP OF OLD MEN, STOM-

ACH CASES, CRIPPLES WITH GLASS EYES AND WOODEN LEGS . . ."

Most people back home thought that was very funny.

"Those Germans are really scraping the bottom of the barrel, aren't they? Well, it won't be long now . . ."

But the GI's up front didn't think it was so funny.

"I don't care if the guy behind that gun is a syphilitic prick who's a hundred years old—he's still sitting behind eight feet of concrete and he's still got enough fingers to press triggers and shoot bullets . . ."

When the ring around Aachen tightened, the Germans stepped up their evacuation of most of the 165,000 civilians and pulled out their prize SS troops.

General von Schwerin, commander of the city's defenses, then recommended that Aachen surrender rather than suffer any more hell. That was the last anybody ever saw of von Schwerin.

The German high command continued to strip troops from other quiet sectors and speed them to the Aachen area, committing them wholesale. They kept throwing in counterattack after counterattack, as many as six in one day, all tank-supported. They also used the familiar "mousetrap" tactic of sucking in our troops, allowing them to penetrate just so far and then opening up with enfilading cross fire.

Fighting for Crucifix Hill, northeast of Aachen, the 1st Division had to give separate flamethrowing-flushing treatment to every pillbox on the hill. All of them had to be destroyed because the Germans had a habit of infiltrating, climbing back into them and firing at our troops from the rear. One infantry company took care of 19 pillboxes in one day.

Pillbox fighting was something new to us.

"We didn't know exactly how much demolitions to use at first," said Cpl. Frederick Griffin of Geneva, N.Y., and Company A of the 120th Engineers.

"The first time we put twenty packs of tetratyl inside and let her go. She just went up into the air, turned a half flip and came down. After that we used less and less. It all depends how big and thick it is.

"When we were in a big hurry, we sometimes blew up only certain ones so that we'd break the chain and they couldn't cover each other even if the Krauts did get back. Lots of these pillboxes weren't manned and we never knew

230

which was which, especially if the infantry bypassed them. That bothered the hell out of us because when we're loaded with tetratyl like that and a shell lands anywhere near us, there isn't enough left of us even to make a good memory."

At the end of the first week in October, the pincers circling the Aachen area were only three miles apart with our troops running into repeated counterattacks. By controlling the high ground, we were able to direct observed artillery fire not only for counterbattery but to break up attempted German armored thrusts. By October 16, the ring around Aachen was closed.

Aachen was a rubble dump. Twelve battalions of our heavy artillery had pumped in 5,000 rounds and our Tactical Air Command fighter-bombers continually pounded it after the Germans refused our surrender note.

With the city sealed off, the Germans supplied their Aachen garrison by parachute. Remaining resistance centered in the Technical High School on the western edge of town where fanatic Nazis were fighting from sewer to sewer. In the street fighting, it took our big 155-mm self-propelled guns to clean them out. But on October 21, Col. Gerhard Wilck came out of his four-story air-raid shelter and surrendered his 600 men. When this news swept around town, 1,000 more surrendered. But before they came out yelling *"Kamerad,"* those snipers killed a lot of American soldiers.

The sniper's finger presses the trigger and the bullet passes through the helmet, scalp, skull, small blood vessels membrane into the soft sponginess of the brain substance in the occipital lobe of the cerebral hemisphere.

Then you're either paralyzed or you're blind or you can't smell anything or your memory is gone or you can't talk or you're only bleeding or you're dead.

If a medic picks you up quickly enough, there's a surgeon who can pick out the bullet, tie up the blood vessels, cover up the hole in your head with a tantalum metal plate. Then, slowly, you learn things all over again, whether it's talking, walking or smelling.

But if the bullet rips through your medulla region in the back of your head (about twice the size of your thumb) or if it tears through a big blood vessel in the brain—then you're dead, buddy.

It all depends how your head is curved when the bullet hits.

First Army's Aachen push wasn't an isolated drive. In the big SHAEF picture, First Army was protecting the right flank of the British-Canadian 21st Army Group which was making the main Allied drive from the Arnhem bridgehead, trying to envelop the Ruhr valley from the north.

Three paratroop divisions of the First Allied Airborne Army had landed in the Arnhem-Eindhoven sector on September 17, at points both north and south of the Rhine. After the British Second Army moved up to make a junction, the force marched another thirty miles to Nijmegen, capturing the bridge intact, but they couldn't punch a corridor to reach Arnhem where British paratroopers were bitterly fighting. When a Polish paratroop regiment and elements of the British Second Army finally broke through, the British paratroopers were pulled out in the dark of night wearing blanket strips on their shoes to deaden the sound. About eight hundred were evacuated before the Germans sent up flares, saw what was happening and heavily shelled the whole length of the skinny corridor.

In the nine days' fighting there had been an estimated 4,800 casualties, of which 1,200 wounded had to be left behind.

While the big push was going on in the north, Third Army had orders to outpost its lines and patrol constantly to keep contact with the enemy and keep them from reinforcing other critical areas. In addition, it had been stripped of most of its transport because the military logistic was that it's better to supply one army fully so that it can punch rather than supply all armies only partially.

But the big job then was the mop-up of Metz, 39 natural fortresses, all fanatically defended by Nazi noncoms and officer candidates. Like most of war, this was an infantry job.

Toughest fort in the ring was Driant. Inside its maze of corridors were 900 Nazis so well placed and equipped that they could have held off a force three times their own. Driant would have cost too many casualties and it wasn't worth it then, so our troops pulled out under the cover of darkness.

What's a fort worth? A big, bell-shaped historic fort with fancy secret chambers and underground passages and even a ventilation system. What's it worth? Fifty casualties? A hundred? A thousand? How much is it worth? Do we have to take it now or can we take it later? How long shall we keep our troops there? Shall we do this or do that? Who wants to be a general?

Some of the Nazis' strongest natural defenses were in the thick forests of the Vosges Mountains on the Seventh Army front. Before our troops could even reach that, they first had to cross the Moselle.

Long-range plans called for us to take Epinal, secure a Moselle crossing and then advance northeast and force open the Saverne Gap which separates the High and Low Vosges, and open up the Alsace plain. The only other approach into the plain was through the Belfort Gap in the French sector.

The big division brass were all having headaches. They knew just how tough the Moselle crossing was going to be. The Germans were all dug in ready and waiting. It would be a bloody business.

Somebody announced that the mayor of Raon-aux-Bois wanted to see them on urgent business. They must have cursed to themselves and said what the hell does he want, and somebody went to find out.

He was Monsieur Gribelin, retired French naval officer, sixty years old if you please, and when they found out what he had to say, they almost kissed him. His was a gift of American lives.

There was a jeep-sized pass that led to a shallow part of the Moselle where the water was only waist-deep and the current was slow and there was plenty of cover for vehicles. It was a short cut to Eloyes where he went to see his daughter on Sundays. It would take them right behind the German positions.

It made a peculiar parade in the dark, cloudy night, with the rain coming down in drizzles and the old man walking proudly with his face shining and his chest out, and the tired GI's and their jeeps trailing close behind. . . .

Incapable of a large-scale attack but still strengthened by their junction with the German Army in the north, the Germans were selling space by the yard now, their bitter resistance at Grandvillers being typical. Trying to stabilize a slightly fluid front, they were digging deep in the Vosges foothills, sweating out the first October snow with the hope that mud would mire us down to slow-motion war. For the next two weeks, the rains made mud of everything. But where jeeps couldn't go, mules could.

Our supply situation had now improved considerably. Instead of gas, the emphasis was now on winter clothing and ammunition. Other critical items included soap, shelter halves, shoes of EE width and toilet paper.

Except for occasional bombings, strafing and sporadic artillery, all was generally quiet on the front throughout October.

What do you do up front when it's quiet?

If there's sun, you take off your shoes and socks and wiggle your toes in the warmth of it. If it rains or snows, you try to get under cover somewhere. The chow gets better and you eat hot meals a little more often maybe. You put in for a three-day pass to anywhere. You sleep as much as you can.

You sweat out your turn for a hot shower and you stand in it as long as you can. You want to stay in it for hours and hours and you rub yourself with soap again and again trying to get the stink out of your body and the mud out of your mind and the war out of your soul, for a few minutes anyway.

Then you climb back into your dirty smelly clothes and go back to your muddy foxhole up where the war is.

Before the beginning of November, 12th Army Group ordered a general attack all along the line.

First Army objective was the Rhine River in the Cologne vicinity, with the Ninth Army making a coordinated attack and Third Army enveloping the Metz defenses.

Basically, the idea was that if we hit hard everywhere, the Germans would crack somewhere. Wherever that "somewhere" was, we would then break through and exploit.

Besides an eighty-one-minute artillery preparation, our troops would also have a comprehensive air cover and a bombardment program known as Operation Q. It called for 1,204 heavy bombers and 485 fighter-bombers from the Eighth Air Force; 1,188 heavy bombers from the British RAF; 107 American mediums from the IX Bombardment Division and additional fighter planes from IX and XXIX Tactical Air Command.

Bad weather kept postponing the jump-off until November 16 when our bombers thoroughly rubbled their targets, especially Duren and Julich. Besides that, our planes caught two whole divisions in the process of changing positions and enemy casualties were terrific.

But the toughest fighting of all was taking place in the fifty square miles of the Huertgen Forest which the GI's called a "death factory." It was a "must" objective because it blocked approaches to Cologne and the Ruhr and was too big to outflank.

German guns long ago had been zeroed in on all conceivable targets, steep hills, deep belts of mines and barbed wire, booby traps almost everywhere, thick woods with dug-in machine gun positions, visibility zero, temperatures near freezing, weather always wet.

It took almost two months to clear the Huertgen Forest.

"One morning we looked up and there was a perfect blue sky and we knew that this was the morning of the attack," said Pfc. George Barrette of Hillsgrove, R.I., a radio operator.

"Our artillery gave us good support but we didn't get very far because the Jerries started throwing mortars all over the place and we all got orders to dig in. Then their 88's came over and we traded them one for one. It rained like hell that night.

"Next morning we moved into a patch of small pines and they must have pinpointed our command post because they threw in a six-hour barrage right on top of us. Me and this buddy of mine were in the same hole with only a little brush on top, and I remember I was actually bawling. We were both praying to the Lord over and over again to please stop the barrage. We were both shaking and shivering and crying and praying all at the same time. It was our first barrage . . .

"When it stopped, both of us waited for a while and then we crept out of the hole and I never saw anything like it. All the trees were torn down and the hill was just full of holes. They hit everything, even the battalion aid station. Every officer got hit except one.

"They sent me back to an aid station for a while and I guess they treated me for shock or something. Then they sent me back to my outfit. Everything was just as cold and

235

slimy as it was before and the fog was so thick you couldn't see fifteen yards away.

"And it was the same shells, the same goddam shells. Soon as I got there, the Jerries started laying them on again. They started laying them all over the road and I tried to dig in and then I started shaking and crying again. I guess I must have banged my head against a tree or something because I lost my senses. I couldn't hear anything. I don't remember exactly what happened but I was walking down the road and I remember seeing this soldier crawling out of a tank with both arms shot off. I remember helping him and then I don't remember anymore. I guess I must have gone off my nut."

We had breached their Siegfried Line defenses east of Aachen but they had built a strong new line of field fortification on the Roer River's east bank by large-scale community digging. Likewise, they converted whole villages into formidable strongpoints, with house cellars broken through to give a continuous underground defense works.

But we were not only fighting Germans, we were fighting wet and cold; we were fighting trench foot.

"They pulled us out of the line and when I got out of my hole and started walking, I couldn't feel my feet. They were dead," said Pfc. Noble Gardner of Ridge Farm, Ill., and Able Company.

"So I just sat down first chance I got and took off my shoes. It was the first time I took off my shoes in two weeks and my feet looked blue and frozen. I started to rub them but I was too tired and I fell asleep.

"When I got up the next morning, my feet were like balloons, so red and swollen that I couldn't put my shoes on. And when I tried to walk, it was like somebody giving me a lot of hotfoots and sticking needles in my feet.

"They kept me in the hospital for about ninety days before they let me go. But some guys had it lots worse. Some guys had big black blisters and a couple guys had to get their feet cut off. The doc says you get that from not changing your socks when your feet are wet. Christ, what the hell you gonna do when you're living in a hole for two weeks and the water's up to here and Jerries are shooting at you so you can't go no place. Christ, I'm lucky I'm here at all . . ."

Sensitive against any Ninth Army progress toward their Roer River, the Germans were throwing in fifteen tanks at

236

a time in support of their infantry. When Schleiden fell on November 19, the Germans rushed four infantry and six panzer divisions to the Ninth Army front.

But the Ninth Army kept pushing closer to the Roer, finally reaching the river south of Julich on November 28, after street fighting in Altdorf.

Meanwhile on the First Army's right flank, Third Army was poised in a north-south line along the Siegfried, a thirty-mile stretch of Franco-German border from Merzig to Sarreguemines. On its left flank, we were punching through the Maginot Line, pushing into St.-Avold.

Nobody slept very well. Everybody in Division Headquarters was clock-conscious these few days. When any officer or enlisted man got an assignment to go up front, everybody quietly sneered at him as if he was running away from the war instead of going to it. Because for those few days, the war was in St.-Avold.

No shelling, no air raids, nothing like that.

But at least a dozen time bombs scattered somewhere around the city. Huge demolition charges that could make rubble out of a big, brand-new building.

All of them set for certain times of certain days and nobody knew when or where. Several already had gone off outside St.-Avold. For several days, the engineers went through roofs and cellars and closets and everybody imagined that he heard a clock ticking somewhere.

For several days, there was no such thing as a rear echelon.

After bridging the Moselle River north and south of Thionville, our troops pushed for the Metz forts, and entered Metz from five directions on November 20.

Meanwhile our tanks raced for the German border, penetrating Saarlautern and reached the Saar River inside Germany, crossed it at four places north of Saarlautern.

By the end of the first week in December, Saarunion had fallen.

Far to the rear, some forts still stuck it out and we had to reduce them one at a time.

"I was tired like a bastard. Everybody was," said Pfc. Harry Bauman of Pitman, N.J., and Company L.

"They brought us to this Fort Driant the day it fell, so we could spend a night inside a building for a change. It wasn't much of a place because everything was all banged up. But it had four walls to cut off the wind, and we'd be dry, too.

"Then just as we start settling down, we get the order to pull out again. We were gonna march a couple miles to somewhere else. Everybody was bitching like hell. But you know the way it is in the Army. Nobody asks 'Why?' If you do, they just say 'Because.' So the best thing is not to ask any questions, just do it and keep bitching until you feel better.

"Now get this. The very next day we find that another company moved in when we pulled out, onto that same room, and a mine or something went off and killed about seventeen guys. Now how about that?"

The Germans' *Vosegen Stellung* defense line stretched from the Saverne Gap southward to the Swiss border, manned by four infantry and two armored divisions.

To outflank these Vosges Mountain defenses, Seventh Army's plan was to aim for the Schlucht Pass, most southerly of the east-west depressions, cutting through the High Vosges. Taking Schlucht would also force the fifteen-mile-wide Belfort Gap, opening up the whole Alsace plain.

Another objective was Strasbourg.

Sitting on the bank of the Rhine on flat ground, Strasbourg had no natural defenses and when the cryptic message "Cloth in iodine" arrived at headquarters, everybody knew that our troops had penetrated the city.

With the capture of Strasbourg, the Seventh Army front assumed the outline of a large reverse "S." Starting with the Third Army junction northwest of Strasbourg, it cut through the Vosges at right angles to the mountains to reach the Rhine at Strasbourg, then reversed direction across the Alsace plain back into the Vosges then reversed again southeast to join the First French Army pushing northward down the plain.

South of Strasbourg, the Germans continued to hold onto their Rhine bridges to supply their bulging Colmar pocket. Clean-up job of this Colmar area was the First French Army's mission while Seventh Army attacked northward to help crack the Siegfried, and sweep the Germans completely out of Alsace.

When the soldiers hit a big town, some of them buy picture postcards to send home to the family. Picture postcards of big-bosomed babes holding bunches of grapes between their toothpaste smiles and wearing picturesque Alsatian clothes, or else pictures of beautiful mountain scenery with healthy, happy people and an overripe yellow moon in the background.

They look at them without recognizing either the people or the places.

The beautiful babes weren't so beautiful anymore. The healthy, happy people were hungry and thin. Those picturesque clothes have been lying in the bottom of trunks for years. And this wasn't the season for grapes.

As for scenery, that forest full of snow-covered Christmas trees was lousy with snipers; those thin winding streams running through the valley in soft curves only made their feet wetter; and that time the full moon shone on the row of dimpling hills in front of the fast-running Rhine, the GI's just looked at it, cursed quietly, thinking of the long fucking climb and the fucking mud and the fucking mortars on the other side.

To frontline soldiers, Europe isn't picture postcards; it's scared bitter people and dirty slush and wild little kids yelling for bonbons.

That's why the fat majority of GI's want to go home, stay home. They've seen all they want to see of Europe even though most of them have never really seen it at all.

Seventh Army G-3 filed away the Rhine-crossing plans for future use and concentrated on cleaning up the area this side of the Siegfried.

First there was the Hagenau Forest, eighteen miles long and six miles wide, and then there was the Maginot Line running northward along the Rhine from Strasbourg to Fort Louis and from there parallel to the German border through Bitche.

Bitche was the toughest nut. Guarding the junction of the pass through the Vosges, the Ensemble de Bitche consisted of a cluster of the strongest Maginot forts. Modern forts like Schiesseck and Simserhoff, twenty-three floors deep, equipped with heavy artillery and interconnecting blocks.

"There we were on this hill about a thousand yards from this fort and we see these eight-inch shells bounce right off the walls. Honest to God, eight-inch shells, the heaviest stuff we've got and they didn't even make a dent.

They just chipped off a little concrete. Me and the boys had never seen anything like that before and if we didn't see it with our own eyes, we wouldn't have believed it.

"I guess we were all thinking the same thing when we saw those shells bounce off. We were thinking, 'How in the hell are we going to take that place?'" said the sergeant boss of the machine-gun section, Harry Garman of D Company.

Hagenau Forest was a huge headache because the Germans had formidable strongpoints in the quarry and château and were defending the area with heavy artillery positioned along the railroad tracks. After clearing the woods, we still had to clean out the town, building by building, until the Germans finally retreated across the Moder River, blowing the bridge after them.

Until Seventh Army pushed back the Germans into their Siegfried Line, the war here was a continuous series of desperate small-scale battles for tiny towns converted into strongpoints.

Obermodern, Kindwillder, Pfaffenhoffen, Gundershoofen, Bischwiller, Schirrheim, Soufflenheim, Reichshoffen, Mertzwiller, Schweighausen, Niederbronn, Ingwiller, Mielesheim, Bienwald.

Just a lot of places where soldiers died.

In early December, Goebbels had stopped referring to Allied gains as empty victories in "mere outpost zones." Ninth and First Armies were pushing slowly forward on a heavily fortified forty-mile front on the rim of Germany itself.

By opening the dikes and flooding the Arnhem-Nijmegen area, the Germans did stall the British Second Army push. But they couldn't stop the Canadian cleanup of the Scheldt Estuary, which opened up Antwerp to Allied shipping.

Meanwhile the Ninth Army smashed to the Roer on a twelve-mile stretch from Julich to Linnich.

Action was heaviest on the First Army front where the Germans had concentrated sixty-eight battalions of artillery, mostly in the sensitive Lammersdorf-Inden sector.

At the top of the Roer River were two vital dams, the Schwammenuauel and Urfttalsperre. These dams could flood the river and not only increase the width of the river up to a quarter mile and the depth five extra feet, but they could increase the velocity from five to sixteen feet per second, making continued crossings almost impossible.

Two attempts to bomb these dams, once by 573 planes, were both unsuccessful. This, again, was work for infantry.

By December 15, our troops were in possession of all defended areas on the west bank of the Roer in this area.

The next day was December 16, the beginning of the German counter-offensive in the Ardennes.

Battle of the Bulge

Germany's war of the Siegfried had been a war of attrition, constant commitment of reinforcements in driblets, quick shifting of troops from one weak spot to another, giving ground grudgingly, always giving ground but seldom taking any.

For the German high command, there was no future in such a war. Supplies and replacements got chewed up without anything to show for it. Ebbing morale became an important factor. Plus all this, the undermanned, undernourished Siegfried Line had started to crack.

Seventh Army troops were ripping through the northwest corner of it in Alsace, striking for the Rhine, and the nearby industrial center of Karlsruhe. Third Army was smashing hard at the gateway to the vital Saar region. First Army was getting closer to the important Roer dams and the Cologne plain. Ninth Army was poised along the Roer River, waiting to punch an offensive which would probably be coordinated with the Russian offensive in the east.

Germany's time was getting critically short, but Field Marshal von Rundstedt had a comprehensive plan and a timetable and two full-strength panzer armies.

His broad plan was to strike toward the Meuse River and on to Brussels and Antwerp, with the Sixth SS Panzer Army on the right driving to Liége, and the Fifth Panzer Army thrusting toward Namur, breaking through between Monschau and Trier on the First Army's lightly held southern sector. Eighteen divisions busting loose on a sixty-mile front after an intense artillery preparation of almost three hours. Also scheduled were strong diversionary attacks to temporarily screen the main push, including dropping paratroopers to set up roadblocks at important points.

Of most of this, we knew little. However, First Army's G-2 Estimate No. 37, dated December 10, said:

> "It is plain that the enemy's strategy in defense of the Reich is based on the exhaustion of our offensive to be followed by an all-out counterattack with armor between the Roer and the Erft supported by every weapon he can bring up."

Our G-2 even knew that the Nazis were planning something called Operation Grief, special details of saboteurs dressed completely like American soldiers, even down to their dog tags and accents.

We knew all this, but we still didn't know the scope of what was coming, and we didn't know where or when. Few could conceive of an offensive through the thickly wooded Ardennes.

The day was December 16.

"It had been awful quiet for weeks," said Cpl. David Gordon, a rifleman with A Company.

"We were living in the town of Befort, sleeping between sheets and lazying around in the sun with nothing much to do, and then this day came and it all happened at once. They piled us all in half-tracks and shoved us up front. We didn't even have time to pick up our stuff. And when we got to a roadblock about a mile out of town, we could hear all kinds of Jerry fire blowing off around us. First time I ever heard Screaming Meemies. We had our CP in a little caboose, and guys were running in and out all the time and nobody seemed to know what the hell was happening.

"First guy killed in our platoon was a twenty-one-year-old kid, about six feet two, a helluva nice kid from the midwest. I remember once he got hold of a Danny Kaye record of 'Dinah' and he must have played it twenty-five times. Awful nice kid, a college boy, too.

"Just before we pulled out, I remember spotting his Christmas package on the table in the CP. He never even got a chance to open it.

"We left a lot of guys behind when we pulled out. Nobody seemed to know where the hell we were going or what we were going to do or what the deal was. All we knew was that we were getting out of there in a hurry . . ."

Penetrating the Belgian-Luxemburg frontiers at three places, von Rundstedt's SS troops hit hardest at a boundary between two Army corps, bending the flank back into the Bucholz Forest and smashing straight through the thinly held sector, sweeping as fast as they could with almost nothing in front of them. At first the front looked like a shallow arc beaming northwest toward St.-Vith but it soon started swelling into a bulge with the two hinges at Butgenbach, on the north, and Echternach, on the south.

For the Germans, it was beautiful weather: soupy fog, thick clouds and zero visibility, keeping our planes grounded.

The Germans were desperately anxious to bust through this Butgenbach hinge so that they could rush toward Liége, their first big objective, and fan out toward Antwerp and Brussels. Liége was the heart of our supply setup and von Rundstedt had banked heavily on capturing huge food and fuel dumps along the way. In two gas dumps near Spa, there were three million gallons of gas. But we held at Butgenbach, so the Germans kept pushing westward, probing everywhere on the north shoulder for weak spots. Their next big stops were Malmédy, Stavelot and Stoumont, all three of which sat in a row about twenty-four miles southeast of Liége. Each was an entrance.

But at Malmédy, elements of an engineer combat battalion set up roadblocks and stayed put, for the first time fighting with bazookas and M-1's.

The German SS troopers had captured 150 prisoners near Malmédy. They herded them in a field, then shot them down with machine guns and pistols. Forty-three somehow escaped. One of them was Pfc. Homer Ford of the 518th Military Police Battalion. Homer said:

"Men were lying around moaning and crying. When the Germans came over, they would say, 'Is he breathing?' and would either shoot or hit them with the butt of their guns. The closest they came to me was about ten feet. After they fired at us, I lay stretched out with my hands out and I could feel the blood oozing out. I was lying in the snow, and I got wet and started to shiver, and I was afraid they would see me shivering, but they didn't. I had my head down and they couldn't see, but they were walking around the whole bunch, and then they went over toward the road junction. I heard them shoot their pistols right next to me. I could hear them pull the trigger back and then the click. The men were moaning and taking on something terrible. I also heard the butt hit their heads and a squishing noise. . . ."

At Malmédy, the German column sideslipped to the south, bypassing the town. At Stavelot they met similar resistance from an engineer platoon, a company of armored infantry, and a platoon of tank destroyers who held out behind a blown bridge and then formed a roadblock north of the town until more infantry moved in to reinforce them. And at Stoumont it was still more of the same, with a tank battalion and elements of an antiaircraft battalion helping block the road net to the north with a conglomeration of all kinds of weapons and vehicles, even a 155-mm self-propelled gun, all of which they had drafted from a nearby ordnance depot.

Each of these tiny towns had become the meeting point of all kinds of small units—clerks, cooks, military police, antiaircraft, Belgians, bakers, mechanics—all drafted to dig in as soldiers and hold at all costs against a highly mechanized German Army of picked troops.

"Tom here was a clerk and I'm a mechanic," said Cpl. Vincent Consiglio of Buffalo, N.Y., "and neither of us ever held a rifle since way back in basic training.

"So you could have knocked me over with a feather when they give us rifles and ammo and tell us where to stay. There were just a few of us in this house near Stavelot and pretty soon sure enough somebody tells us that we're surrounded and I almost fill up my pants. I say to myself, Consiglio, what the hell you doing here anyway? You're a mechanic, not a fighting soldier.

"But that's not the end of it. There's about thirty-five of us in this house and the Jerries open up with a helluva lot of stuff and some of the guys get knocked off and finally we decide to send somebody out to make contact with some outfit to let them know what the hell's happening up here and for chrissakes send reinforcements.

"Yeah, you guessed it, I'm the jerk who volunteered. I'll never forget that as long as I live. Running through the

244

open gates, across the street down the hill through the creek. I was going so goddam fast I didn't even feel the water. Then another eighty yards across a field with burp guns opening up all over the place. Then through the woods and over the railroad track. I remember every inch of that trip, to the minute some GI was getting ready to plug me because they thought I was a Jerry.

"When I convinced them, though, they did send a tank and got the rest of the guys out of that house. There were only twelve left then."

"We gamble everything now—we cannot fail," Field Marshal von Rundstedt told his troops in a dramatic order of the day. But his prize troops and tanks kept running into more and more trouble, especially in the Malmédy-Stavelot-Stoumont sector. There they kept attacking and counterattacking again and again, but by this time our reinforcements had poured in and the Germans never did smash a hole big enough to pour through and fan out. We had built a stone wall backed by a continuous flood of reinforcements, and the Germans were just knocking their heads against it.

But while these panzer units were probing for a breakthrough on this northern shoulder, other tanks and troops had swept straight westward, overrunning northern Luxemburg by December 19, crossing into Belgium with a penetration of at least twenty miles, putting them seven miles south of Bastogne.

That was the broadest, deepest penetration. The other was on a narrow front north of St.-Vith. The original penetration had been divided in two because of the stubborn resistance around St.-Vith in an area ten miles long and eight miles wide.

Frustrated in its drive north at these points, the desperate Nazis hit two other sections: the Elsenborn Ridge, at our northern hinge and the Amblève River area.

Unable to punch through anywhere to sweep into Liége, the Germans were still raining V-bombs into the city by the hundreds. Everything was still confusion.

The two correspondents walked into a big bare building where First Army headquarters clerks were unloading the records and hanging the maps. They had just come from Spa.

Stretched out on a bedroll on the floor was the G-2

officer who had given some of the briefings. He wasn't sleeping so the two correspondents wandered over and said hello and then asked him what was the military situation.

The colonel just looked at them and said in a slow, tired voice, "I don't know. I don't know what's happening. You know as much as I do."

The first phase of the German winter offensive ended December 22. After six days, the Nazis had penetrated fifty miles into our lines at some points. But both von Rundstedt's strategy and timetable were now fouled up. Nowhere had the Nazis been able to break through to the north and take over the vitally necessary fuel and food supply depots. Without our supplies, the Nazi panzer divisions couldn't go anywhere.

An airborne division in Bastogne was cut off from everybody, getting supplies by air from C–47's which flew 850 supply drops during the Bastogne isolation. Bastogne had become a serious thorn in von Rundstedt's side because it cost a lot of casualties without yielding any dividends. It was a constant threat to von Rundstedt's rear, even if he should smash through to Liége. With its road net, Bastogne would also have aided von Rundstédt in supplying his forward troops.

But inside Bastogne we had more than 15,000 troops. In addition to the paratroopers, we had parts of two divisions, plus assorted small units of all sizes and descriptions.

When the Germans completely surrounded Bastogne and sent a surrender ultimatum, Brig. Gen. McAuliffe said, "Nuts."

SHAEF's strategy first called for blocking the northern shoulder of the bulge, which had been done, and then taking care of blunting the extended tip of the Nazi salient which had pushed almost sixty miles to nowhere. Nowhere, because they failed to reach any of our vital supply dumps, and we still had a natural defense line in front of them—the Meuse River, which the British were defending.

To bolster the First Army, other armies, particularly the Ninth, were stripped of much of their strength. Third Army was ordered to make a fast switch from the Saar front to the southern shoulder of the breakthrough—three divisions to cut a corridor to relieve the troops in Bastogne. Seventh Army had to stop its Siegfried push—which had put it within eight miles of Karlsruhe—and take over most of the Third Army front. This meant prepared defenses on an eighty-four-mile front westward from the Rhine. This also meant pulling out of some towns we had taken to get on better defensive ground.

Just a few days before, they had been laughing and singing in the streets, waving flags, bringing out the best wine, racing alongside our jeeps so that they could touch our hands or get a smile. Only a few stayed inside behind closed shutters. But everybody knew then who was on whose side.

Now the happy, laughing ones were crowded in close clusters on the street corners, staring intently at all the military traffic, considering carefully how many trucks were empty, how many were full, which way they were going.

The news had spread fast: "The Americans are leaving . . . The Germans are coming back . . ."

Those to whom this meant death were already on the road, whole families piled onto sagging horse carts, sometimes riding, sometimes walking, women, children, old people.

And jeering at them, spitting at them, walking down the streets laughing and happy and singing were the handful who had stayed indoors behind shutters when the Americans had come.

Estimated German strength against the First Army at this time was fourteen divisions and one armored brigade, about 100,000 combat troops and 500 tanks.

Most of our planes were grounded because weather had been bad. Thick fog, zero visibility, icing conditions. But some planes got up anyway. On December 18, when an L-5 spotted a stretched-out convoy of tanks and armored cars speeding for Stoumont, Tactical Air Command came out in force. It destroyed at least 126 tanks and armored cars, damaging the rest badly enough to make the remnants turn tail.

In the five days beginning December 23, TAC flew 2,856 sorties, destroying 206 tanks and armored vehicles and 1,921 motor transport.

German air support was heavier than it had ever been since the invasion. But most of their planes came out at night to bomb all along the front, especially trying to knock out our airfields in the Maastricht-Brussels-Eindhoven triangle. Of an estimated 300 German planes up one day, 125 were shot down.

Von Rundstedt was having other headaches with his spearheads. Our troops were holding firm on the northern shoulder. On the southern shoulder, the airborne division was still holding isolated Bastogne waiting for Third Army troops to come up. It was to be their Christmas present.

The wet cold had crept inside their clothes several days before when they first came up to the observation post. It was the misery of this numbing, dirty dampness that first made them start talking about soaking in warm baths and climbing in between soft white sheets. Then the talk shifted to Christmas and good food and how they'd give their right arms if they could only be home for Christmas.

One guy said he had a kid he never saw before because his picture hadn't come yet and he felt pretty bad because he wasn't able to send him a present; another guy said he always went home for Christmas and this was the first Christmas he couldn't make it and his folks must be terribly lonely; and the third guy said that if he had one wish now he would wish that he could be back home in bed with his wife.

They said all this as they stood around a small fire, wet and dirty and cold and hungry and miserable and full of hurting emptiness. And another three guys came up later to relieve them and one guy said, "Merry Christmas," and the three guys looked surprised and one of them said slowly, "We thought tomorrow was Christmas."

Stalled, but not stopped, von Rundstedt had fresh plans for a continued offensive.

As of December 26, the southern German spearhead had pushed through all of northern Luxemburg above the Sûre River. The northern attacking force was moving northwest toward Namur with its armored spearheads only fifteen miles south of the city, near Dinant, within sight of the Meuse River where the British had dug in their tanks.

Von Rundstedt's new plans, however, had been based on a serious misinterpretation. German G-2 had thought that XVIII Airborne Corps was in a process of a major withdrawal when they pulled back a few miles to better defensive positions. Consequently the Germans expected only slight resistance at the Manhay and Marche Road junctions, which they badly needed for any new jump-off.

248

In a fierce night attack, they did take Manhay but an armored division recaptured most of the lost ground the next afternoon.

The Germans also made still another attempt to take Elsenhorn on December 27, following a heavy artillery preparation. But our artillery was even heavier, more concentrated. All along the northern shoulder, our artillery had broken up counterattack after counterattack just before it was launched. Mostly we used 105-mm guns.

Shell, Fixed, H. E., M-384A1, W/Fuse, Time, Mechanical, M-43 (All modifications), 105-mm Gun, M-3, Intended for fragmentation and blast effect against aircraft targets.

Components consist of: M-6 cartridge case; M-28 type primer; a loosely loaded propelling charge held in position by a distance wad and igniter assembly; and a fused M-38A1 projectile. Standing bursting charge is TNT but 50-50 amatol may be used as an alternative.

Weight of complete round, 63.73 pounds; length 45.31 inches; type of base, boat-tailed; radius of ogive, 8.37 caliber; muzzle velocity, 2,800 ft. per second; maximum range horizontal 20,000 yards.

Within a twenty-foot radius, there are 1,160 effective fragments which can cause casualties, either death or long-term wounded; or else 975 fragments capable of penetrating one-eighth of an inch mild steel.

Pull the lanyard which releases the hammer, hits the primer, shoots the flame through the vent into the powder and high pressures the shell to somewhere miles away.

Heavy snow channelized the Germans to the roads, and they didn't have as many roads as they needed. Supply columns were having a tough job reaching the armored spearheads at the tip of the salient. Capture of thirteen German self-propelled guns intact near Celles because the vehicles had run out of gas was as significant as the reports that the 6th Panzer SS Army had started digging in between Bullange and Stavelot.

Unable to break out of the bulge, either north or south, the two panzer armies had little space to maneuver. This flank-chipping of his spearheads caused von Rundstedt to pull back west of the Marche–St. Hubert Line, the first real bulge-shrinkage of the offensive.

Seventeen days after its all-out offensive—after breaking through on a thirty-five-mile front to a depth of sixty miles within sight of the Meuse—the Germans were finally stopped, and the front around them began to shape into a hard wall.

Von Rundstedt's "On to Antwerp" of December 16 was now changed to: "We have succeeded in disrupting the enemy's planned winter offensive."

Act Two of the Battle of the Bulge began on January 3 when First Army launched attacks on a twenty-five-mile front against the center of the salient. Thick winter weather prevented close air support, and icy roads slowed down our vehicles, but our troops still registered advances up to 4,000 yards daily.

While British troops pushed back the nose of the salient, First and Third Armies were trying to smash through the shoulders and split the bulge in half, with Houffalize as the objective.

However, the Germans had put their greatest strength in their shoulders to keep their bulge corridor open for possible evacuation of their prize panzers, and so advances were grudgingly slow.

Both American armies were fourteen miles apart when the Germans pulled in their armor from the Bostogne sector to protect these key lateral roads from St.-Vith to Houffalize. Von Rundstedt also withdrew as much armor as he could from the bulge nose to protect his shoulders.

Houffalize itself was bitterly defended. When the armored broke into the city on January 15, it found the Germans there well organized, fighting without confusion. But the airborne made contact with an armored division, and we now controlled the whole highway of Liége (except for a small sector between Houffalize and Bastogne). This was the most important highway in the Ardennes.

It took more time to clear the whole western end of the corridor because of the heavy minefields.

The minesweeper is in front of the whole war. For the GI's walking not too close behind him, slowly, the minesweeper is one of the world's wonderful people. The minesweeper walking with a heavy, dragged step, his shoulders hunched, his eyes staring at the ground, his arms slowly moving the vacuum cleaner contraption from side to side.

And when he hears a loud buzzing, he stops. And when

he stops, the whole war waits a minute. First he double-checks the buzzing. Then he sits down and stares at the ground as if he were watching an ant fight. Finally he pokes a little with something sharp and then he digs with his hands, gently, very gently.

But usually in war a soldier is his own mine detector. A guy on a patrol can't take a minesweeper with him. He takes his chances, strains his eyes looking at snow, grass, horse dung, looking for three prongs in disturbed earth. Because underneath the ground somewhere may be powdered picric acid waiting to get excited. Foot pressure in the wrong place and a complicated human being becomes hamburger meat.

When Third Army troops pushed northward into the bulge, the German line bent but didn't break. Our daily gains were small. Farther north the British front had bogged down largely because of floods. In counterattacking the bulge we were never able to smash through and chop it up. It was a matter of slow squeezing so that it kept shrinking from a fat bulge to a narrow arc.

The weather cleared suddenly and for the next several days our troops had plenty of air support. During two days—January 22 and 23—the Ninth Air Force flew 2,500 sorties, dropped 1,375 tons of bombs, destroyed 2,557 motor transport, 993 railroad cars, 40 tanks, 53 armored vehicles, 25 locomotives, 62 gun positions and probably destroyed or damaged at least as many more.

The major sweated out each plane, because it was tricky trying to land on icy runways.

But they came in all right, and like always the pilots half ran into the briefing room.

And this time everybody had something to tell. They had been moping around the dayrooms for so long now, waiting for weather, waiting with all the buildup of nervous tension that goes with waiting. Now they had gone out and really done a job, and now they were back.

After the major had calmed them down and pumped them dry, the room was empty again except for a pilot who was slumped in a chair and said half-aloud, "I was just thinking. All us guys flying planes are such lucky pricks. We go through some hell but then we come back to a bed and a hot meal and a good night's sleep. But those poor goddam bastards in the fucking infantry . . ."

251

As soon as the bulge started visibly shrinking the scene of big action shifted south to the Seventh Army front.

The German buildup here had become obvious. As soon as von Rundstedt saw that the Ardennes offensive had flopped, he shifted what remaining reserves he had to the south. Bigger patrols crossed the Rhine more frequently north of Strasbourg to see what we had, and we didn't have very much.

At the end of December, Seventh Army G-2 came out with the flat statement that the Germans might be expected to launch a series of attacks from the Bitche-Sarreguemines sector to try to seize the Saverne Gap and possibly fan out to the Rhine with as many as eight divisions to recapture the Alsace plain and cut off a large part of the Seventh Army. Such a drive might also be coordinated with a breakout of the Colmar pocket, which the Germans were also reinforcing. Another possibility was a Rhine crossing to establish a bridgehead in the Gambsheim area for the recapture of Strasbourg.

All these things happened to a limited extent.

Because Seventh Army had taken over the Third Army front, too, it was so overextended on a thinly held front that General Devers' order to his troops was, "Be prepared to yield ground rather than endanger the integrity of your forces."

As was expected, the Germans shoved enough troops across the Rhine at Gambsheim to hold a bridgehead two miles deep and five miles long, about six miles north of Strasbourg. The Germans now held 82 miles of the Rhine to our 32. And there wasn't too much we could do about it because our lines were so stretched out.

The Germans then broke out of the Colmar pocket and raced up along the Rhine to Erstein, only ten miles south of Strasbourg. Strasbourg sat surrounded by German forces on three sides. It was a piercing probe into strong German territory and our troops were ordered to evacuate the city. Then that order was changed because of the psychological importance of that city to the French.

The Colmar pocket now resembled a panhandle-shaped area extending fifty miles along the Rhine and thirty miles at its widest, including the High Vosges. We went in to clean up Colmar after a junction with the French. From then on it was a matter of chopping up the pocket, corralling some 20,000 prisoners.

252

It was Sunday in Colmar and all the people were dressed in their best clothes, walking down the Beethovenstrasse, going to church.

High in the dirty, misty sky, several Messerschmitts were slipping inside the flak, peeling off, diving to bomb the city's outskirts. Shells were zooming so low over the city that you kept wanting to fall flat on your face. Tanks, trucks and troops were rushing through the streets of the city in several directions. And on Beethovenstrasse, lying in a sticky pool of blood, there was a dead German sniper.

But except for a small circle of kids staring at the dead Nazi, the civilians didn't seem to notice him, just as they didn't seem to notice the trucks or the tanks or the shells or the planes.

It wasn't that they were trying to separate themselves from the war by ignoring it. It was just that they had been seeing and hearing war for weeks now and it had become a part of them.

Now it was Sunday and Colmar was free and they were going to church.

Before February was a week old, the French had come up to punch through the bottom of the bridgehead. They took Gambsheim and the rest of the pocket folded quickly after that.

Up at the northern end of the Allied front, the British had cleared the whole area of the Roer-Maas triangle west of the Roer River. The Canadian First Army had mopped up pockets twelve miles north of Venlo in the flooded Nijmegen area, clearing the northern end of the Siegfried on February 12.

Along the Ninth Army front there was comparative quiet, with our troops practicing smoke-screen demonstrations along the Roer.

While final plans were being readied for the Roer crossings, SHAEF announced final casualty figures for the Battle of the Bulge:

Of the 25 German divisions thrown into action, 17 had been "critically impaired," having lost an estimated 90,000 men, of whom 40,000 were prisoners and the rest either killed or badly wounded. The Germans also had lost 600 tanks and assault guns plus a terrific amount of all kinds of equipment.

Our casualties up to January 11 were 55,421, of whom 18,418 were missing.

The Payoff

The hayloft was filled with the stink of dirty, sweating feet, but nobody seemed to notice. The men of the squad were stretched out in the straw, packed close together. Most of them were talking in low whispers; some were sleeping, a few were just lying still, smoking cigarettes, staring into the darkness.

In a couple of hours, this first squad of the first platoon of Able Company would be piling into an assault boat to cross the Roer River in the first wave.

Everybody in the squad had written letters that day. This was partly because there was nothing else to do, nowhere to go. The CO had ordered everybody to stay inside that day for security reasons. One of the boys had an ancient issue of some magazine and it had made the rounds, everybody reading every word of it before it was put into the toilet-paper supply.

"We were playing casino in the afternoon because I'm the only one who has enough dough to play poker," said Pvt. Cletus Crawford of Tama, Ia., who had joined the squad a month before. He was the assistant bazookaman.

"I've got forty bucks in my shirt pocket," continued Crawford, "and I told the guys that if I kick off on this show, they're supposed to split the dough between them and play at least one hot game of poker in my memory."

The whole squad was wide awake now, everybody laughing.

One private said he was getting hungry and somebody told him to chew on his bedroom slippers and everybody got hysterical again. The private had asked for bedroom slippers when he was in England. They had just arrived that day.

"I don't know what to do with them," he said.

Several soldiers suggested he should stick them up his ass and that set off more laughs.

Sgt. Herbert Harding, acting squad leader, explained why everybody laughed so much.

"If we didn't laugh, we'd go nuts," he said.

When the whole Ninth Army and part of First Army jumped off across the Roer on February 23, everybody crossed fingers, watched and waited. Most people had stopped playing guessing games about the war's end because the memory of Ardennes was still fresh. When anybody said it would be all over by spring, the bitter reply was, "Which spring?"

The black fascism of Germany still made a big blot on the map and there were still hundreds of thousands of Germans with guns. There were lots of mountains, too, and thick forests and hundreds of villages which could be easily converted into strongpoints.

Besides all that there were big fat rivers like the Rhine and the swollen Roer.

The Roer was swollen because the Germans had blown up the floodgates of the river dams just before we got there. It had swelled from thirty yards to three hundred with a six-mile current. But by February 23, the swelling got skinnier and the speed slowed down, and our troops crossed at ten different points on a twenty-two-mile front from south of Düren to north of Linnich, following a forty-five-minute artillery preparation.

By February 25, all our division bridgeheads were linked in a continuous twenty-five-mile strip of front, each division bulging fast. The Germans couldn't seem to form any cohesive defensive line west of the Rhine, and our motorized infantry divisions, sometimes spearheaded by tanks, were busting through everywhere all along the front.

From the observation post on the river bank, you could see everything: the mortar shells lobbing in at close range, a hand grenade exploding, some soldiers running fast to somewhere, falling flat. That was the war of the river bank.

Several blocks the other way was the center of the city where the soldiers still sat behind machine guns at different street corners because there were still a few snipers in business. You could hear the war very clearly from here, but most of the artillery was outgoing. That morning, though, the stuff had been coming in, heavy and everywhere.

A soldier behind a machine gun in the city's center, Pvt. John Martiz of Cumberland, Md., said:

"I haven't been down to the Rhine yet, and I'm not curious at all. I'll see it soon enough."

Down at Third Army, our troops had cleaned out a sizable bump of land called the "Vianden Bulge" and also worked on a triangle of bitterly held land between the Moselle and Saar Rivers. That done, they branched out in different directions, smashed into Trier, attacked toward the Moselle, capturing two bridges intact over that river.

Farther south, on the Seventh Army front, some of the roughest fighting was in the Saarbrücken area, one of the Siegfried's key points. Our troops pushed to within two miles of that city.

Up at the First Army front, the drive to Cologne quickened, clearing the city of the enemy by March 6.

"The main thing I remember about Cologne was the zoo," said T/Sgt. Chester Stasack, a platoon sergeant with F Company.

"Only things still alive were a couple monkeys and a hippo. The hippo was my favorite. We stayed there a week and I used to come around all the time and feed that hippo D-bars. As soon as I came over, he'd open his mouth big and I'd throw it in. He was an awful nice hippo. I even got brave enough to touch him once.

"But it was a shame the way the dead lions and zebras and elephants were lying around. I used to go to zoos a lot when I was a kid . . ."

Except for two pockets—a small one in a Rhine bend south of Neuss and a larger one in the Wesel area, sixteen miles long and eleven miles deep—Allied armies had cleared the west bank of the Rhine as far south as Cologne. The Normandy landings were now nine months old.

But von Rundstedt had managed to keep a defeat from being a disaster by pulling out the bulk of his troops from the Rhine's west bank. March estimates placed his strength at 20 divisions between Cleves and Cologne, another 40 divisions elsewhere on the western front.

Below Cologne, First Army was attacking on a broad front, sweeping to the Rhine at Remagen where they found the Ludendorff railroad bridge still intact. First patrols crossed the Rhine at 1630 hours March 7, after demolition charges had been removed from the bridge. From then on it was a race, with everybody pushing as quickly as possible. The established bridgehead was a firm one, and by March 13 had a depth of almost five miles and a length of more than ten.

Spotlighted into the world's headlines overnight, the Remagen bridgehead was the single greatest threat to the German defenses. It was the hole in the dike, and the flood poured through.

Von Rundstedt knew what it meant, and German divisions, especially panzer divisions, were soon racing from all over the western front to try to beat back the Remagen bridgehead, to plug the hole.

In addition, considerable German air was up to try to destroy the bridge. Of 43 planes which came over, 23 were shot down.

She told how scared she was when the ambulance crossed the bridge, but nothing happened then. It happened later. It happened quickly. A German plane, roaring down, strafing like mad, ambulances or no ambulances.

"I just got out and ran," said nurse Mildred Judkins of the 51st Field Hospital. "There was a hole on the side of the road, but there was a dead Jerry there and I didn't want to stay with him, so I kept running and running through the field, not thinking about mines or anything, just running. Then there was some brush and I flopped right into it."

While the spotlight focus was on Remagen, other First Army troops reached the Rhine between Remagen and Cologne. By the eleventh, the whole west bank had been cleared as far as Remagen, and the Germans had blown all the bridges at Bonn.

Third Army was also driving swiftly to the east. Covering fifty miles in two days, the tanks reached the Rhine north of Coblenz and other tanks made a parallel dash to the Rhine at Andernach. These two narrow armored thrusts were soon joined to form a single six-mile wide salient which turned south toward the Moselle. By March 12, the whole west bank of the Rhine had been cleared from the Moselle way up to Nijmegen, a distance of one hundred and thirty-five miles. The Germans still held one hundred and fifteen more miles, from Coblenz to slightly north of Strasbourg.

Worms fell. Then Kaiserslautern, focal point of a wide roadnet including an autobahn west to the Rhine. Prisoners taken were from twenty German units, indicating wide disorder.

Germany's Saar defense rested in the hands of approximately 125,000 soldiers: twelve divisions from the Nazi First Army and another seven divisions which had been salvaged from the Moselle trap and were badly in need of reinforcements.

But for Germany, reinforcements were nowhere. Since the beginning of the Canadian offensive on February 8, the Germans had had close to 275,000 casualties—killed, seriously wounded, and prisoners.

While Third Army pressed in against the Saar sector on one side, Seventh Army troops gave the old squeeze play from the other side. Almost all of the Saar Basin was sealed off on March 20. Immediately afterwards, we were rushing more troops to the walls of the pocket to start pressing in and slicing up.

East of here, Seventh Army troops were still moving slowly through the Siegfried.

Back at Remagen, the famous Ludendorff Bridge collapsed on March 17, after the bridgehead was twenty-three miles long and eight miles deep. But by this time we already had built several pontoon bridges to supplement it, so the loss wasn't too serious. Before it collapsed, the Ludendorff had been attacked by a total of more than 350 enemy planes of which 111 were shot down.

Aside from persistence at Remagen, the German air strength was relatively scattered, and isolated antiaircraft crews didn't get too much to shoot at.

For the fourteen soldiers of Section One of D Battery of the 548th AAA, parked somewhere in the middle of nowhere—for them, their daily bull session is their whole life.

It always starts out by razzing somebody. They'll razz "Shortstop" because a barmaid in Chicago wouldn't give him a double Scotch because she thought he was too young—she gave him a small root beer instead; they'll razz "Brooklyn" for the night he thought he saw a German paratrooper and it turned out to be a helmet liner on a fence post; they'll razz Hank because he never says anything but always has a smile on his face; and they'll razz Kirkovich because he's the only "cherry" in the section.

Then whenever there's a lull in the conversation, somebody will pop out of the quiet with:

"And what's so hot about Texas?"

For hours after that, the two Texas boys in the outfit will tell all over again about the size, production, independence, beautiful women and cattle of Texas.

And that's the way it goes night after night.

When the talk is done, somebody will stick his head out of the hole and say that maybe tomorrow will be a nice day, maybe we'll get some new magazines, maybe we'll get some visitors, maybe we'll see some planes to shoot at.

Comes dawn, they'll all pile out of their holes, rain or shine, strip and clean the guns and somebody will say:

"And what's so hot about Arkansas?"

Then the day will have begun.

Field Marshal Montgomery's long awaited offensive in the north began on the night of March 23, after a heavy air and artillery preparation. Rhine crossings were made on both sides of Rees with Commandos seizing Wesel in a surprise raid.

However, at the Remagen bridgehead, our growth was slow because the Germans had brought in elements of eleven divisions to poke at the perimeter, trying to punch holes in it, which they couldn't do. On March 25, our tanks finally broke out, driving twenty-two miles east toward Giessen.

Third Army meanwhile had broken through to the Rhine as far south as Worms to cut behind the German First Army front. By holding firm on the Siefried flank along the Rhine, the Germans managed to prevent collapse of the small remaining bridgehead. But it wasn't to last long because an armored column entered the big city of Ludwigshafen while other troops closed in. By March 24, Third and Seventh Armies had taken almost 200,000 prisoners from this Saar Palatinate pocket.

But the Third Army already was deep across the Rhine. They crossed on March 22, without air or artillery and the only surprised Germans on the other side were police or home guards. Seventh Army troops made their Rhine crossings on March 26, also without air or artillery preparation. By the next day we held a strip ten miles deep and seventeen miles long and were already fighting in the northern part of Mannheim.

Again our air was all-out with TAC forces flying 33,163 sorties in a week of close support of their armies. Our medium and heavy bombers also were busy bombing enemy airfields, the same airfields which our aviation engineers would soon have the dirty job of cleaning up and rebuilding.

With the whole western front now bulging out everywhere, the newspapers were filled with all kinds of queer stories of strange reunions.

Pfc. William Bohlenberger of Battery B piled on top of a truck going through little towns one after another and finally stopping for five minutes for piss call. And Bohlenberger, looking around as if in a dream and then running like somebody gone crazy, running to a little house off the road and yelling, "Mom . . . Mom . . ."

To make everything even more Hollywood, his mother was washing dishes in the kitchen and his brother was in the living room, still wearing his German uniform. It had been fifteen years since they had all seen each other, and the American soldier and the German mother were incoherently crying the way you'd expect them to cry. But the American soldier and his German soldier-brother didn't say a word to each other.

Some of the guys had to come in and practically drag Bohlenberger away from his mother because everybody had taken his piss and the driver was in a hurry and the war couldn't wait.

That's the end of the story. Corny, isn't it?

At the beginning of April, the whole German defense setup had begun to crumble like a piece of dry bread. We had crossed the Rhine in more than six places, meeting less and less resistance. To the north, the British Second and American Ninth Armies had crossed the Rhine in strength, driving sixteen miles deep, holding a solid strip thirty miles long, already entering Germany's all-vital Ruhr industrial area.

Farther south, Germany's front had been cut in two. Armored columns broke out of the Remagen bridgehead, punching fifty miles east to the Rhine while the Third Army bridgehead on the east bank had grown to forty miles. A junction of the two would close another pocket between the Lahn and the Rhine. Finally, still farther south, the Seventh Army had completed this Rhine crossing cycle, swelling swiftly near Mannheim.

Allied troops now held one hundred and thirty miles of the Rhine's east bank. The Germans were desperately cannibalizing their divisions trying to stop us somewhere. They could no longer shift troops quickly enough. Von Rundstedt was out and Kesselring, the master tactician of the Italian campaign, was in. But the war's end was now only a matter of time, a short time.

It was a strange front with these armored fingers poking so deep into Germany, as much as forty miles a day, sometimes leaving wide gaps between the spearhead point and the rest of the Army—gaps where the Germans still were, with *Panzerfausts* (antitank grenade launchers).

Some spearheads weren't having it so good. They were running into fanatical resistance at different points. Ninth Army troops, for example, were having it tough on both sides of the Lippe River until an armored division managed to break out angling southeast where they made junction with another armored division. This sealed off a large area between the Ruhr and Sieg Rivers containing major elements of twenty Nazi divisions, including four of Germany's eight armored divisions in the west, an estimated 30,000 troops.

Counterattacks came quick and heavy and the Germans did push out in some places but they were all checked and more of our troops came up to contain the trap.

The roads were clogged with slave workers who had been liberated.

To those soldiers who had never thought about it much, the war's meaning was beginning to sink in deep . . .

"You mean they took all these people and worked them like slaves? Back home I used to think that was just a lot of propaganda . . ."

Soon to come were more of the same, piled up thick. Soon to come were the concentration camps, the huge piles of naked, stinking, beaten bodies of prisoners piled up like cordwood, the living dead with skin so tight over their gaping bodies that you expected it to crack when they bent over. Soon to come were the walls of torture chambers covered with the imprints of feet which had kicked and kicked before death finally came. And the stories, the incredible stories which you didn't believe until they took off their clothes and showed you. People's asses beaten into rawness by big clubs and then the wounds cut open and salt rubbed in. People whipped like dogs never would be whipped. People burned alive, women's breasts cut off, men hung by their balls. How many millions of people, how many millions of stories?

Soldiers who never knew what fascism really was knew it now.

With the loss of the Ruhr, the German high command lost its last great industrial area. But there were other things almost as serious. More than 100,000 German troops looked like they were going to be bottled up in Holland because of the British and Canadian drives to the Zuider Zee and the North Sea.

And farther south, American spearheads were advancing eastward toward Hannover and Leipzig and southeastward toward Nuremberg and Munich, threatening to cut the Reich in two. Prisoners were streaming into our PW cages now at the rate of 20,000 a day.

Typical of the toughest infantry fighting was at Aschaffenburg—six days of fighting against fanatic resistance from house to house, room to room, where sixteen-year-old German girls fought side by side with the German Wehrmacht.

Housecleaning a town always means sudden death for somebody. It means kicking in a door and lobbing in a grenade fast, and then running in to see who's still alive and who wants to surrender and who wants to die. Then it means yelling upstairs for the bastards to come down and give up. If nobody answers it means creeping upstairs to double-check, throwing up another grenade, praying like hell that there isn't any Jerry with a waiting grenade in his hand, hiding in the bedroom or the closet or the toilet.

And when one house is cleaned out, there's another house and another house and another house.

Our front in Europe on April 11, was a great arc extending three hundred and twenty-five miles from Arnhem to Karlsruhe with long columns socking deep into the Reich. On the left flank, the First Canadian, Second British and U.S. Ninth Armies were attacking northwest to the Zuider Zee and due north to the North Sea to cut off Holland, and then northeast toward the great ports of Hamburg and Bremen.

In the center of the arc, another series of columns of the First and Third Armies were attacking generally east toward Leipzig, Dresden and the Czech frontier. On the right flank, the U.S. Seventh Army and the First French Army were attacking southeast toward Nuremberg, Munich and the upper Danube plain. Behind these columns, elements of the First and Ninth Armies were pressing the Ruhr pocket into a shrinking ball.

On every section of the front now, we were liberating Allied prisoner of war camps.

Back at the Red Cross Club in Brussels, the four of them were sitting at a table loaded with sixteen bottles of

Coca-Cola and eight plates of doughnuts. One of the guys quickly got up and made a beeline for the toilet. Pfc. Joseph Kennedy of Brooklyn, a former forward-artillery observer, smiled a weak smile and said, "We all have the GI's. He's got it worse than we have. He's got it bad. We can't eat too much, but we couldn't resist this."

They had lived on watered soup and bird-specks of bread. One of the few times they had meat was when a bomb killed a couple horses.

"We used to dream up menus in the camp," said Kennedy. "Our favorite menu was a Super-Dagwood with a pancake, six link sausages, another pancake, a layer of bacon strips, another pancake, then two fried eggs, another pancake, then a melted pound of butter and finally sprinkle the whole top of it with chocolate chips. We used to have chocolate on every menu. All of us love chocolate. . . ."

Biggest talk of mid-April concerned the possible German retreat to the National Redoubt because the narrow waist of Germany was being pinched tighter and tighter, threatening to cut Germany in half at any time.

Complete collapse of the Ruhr pocket was quickened when we made contact, cutting it in half. After that, the Germans started surrendering en masse. When the PW's here were counted, the figure was 317,000, three times the original estimate.

South of the Ninth Army, the First Army tank columns reached the Elbe, cutting off an estimated 10,000 Germans in the Harz Mountains. The armored pushed to within seven miles of Leipzig, meeting more fanatics, including a large number of Hitler Youth, many of them only twelve years old. They were using flak guns for direct fire. Leipzig (population prewar, 720,000) was mostly a large aircraft-assembly center although it had everything else including V-bomb material.

He was a mealy-mouthed runty guy, and he hit the floor every few minutes, every time the GI hit him. The soldier would pick him up, sock him a few times and let him fall, then pick him up and do it all over again. The runty guy was a scientist who had helped invent the V-bombs.

They found him in a huge underground factory set up at Nordhausen with a half dozen corridors a kilometer long sliced by several dozen other corridors, all air-conditioned and lit by fluorescent light. Some of the V-bombs were still in the assembling stage.

. . . Those hundreds of kids back in London lined up around the building with their mothers, waiting to get into the store, because they were selling ice cream again after so many years, and so many kids had never had any ice cream before . . .

And then the V-2 bomb coming out of the soundlessness of nowhere blasting kids into pieces for blocks around.

The photographer said to the GI, "Would you please lift that runt up again once more and sock him again so I can get a picture of it?"

"The pleasure's all mine," said the soldier.

Third Army rolled all the way to cut the Berlin-Munich highway, the main escape route from the capital to the Bavarian hills. All the Germans had left now was a complicated, curving route through Czechoslovakia.

On the Seventh Army front, the ball-bearing center of Schweinfurt had fallen and the next big stop was Nuremberg, Bavaria's second largest city, shrine of the Nazi Party.

Southwest of Heilbronn, resistance temporarily stalled the French thrust toward Stuttgart. Reason for this resistance in this southern sector was presumed to be a defense of the Bavarian and Austrian Alps, where the Germans had planned their last stand in the National Redoubt, their *Alpenstellung*.

It had been such a long day. All day and all night riding in trucks with the same old K-rations to eat, sleeping in your clothes as usual, a single blanket maybe to cut off the night wind. Just some sniper fire, and a few isolated machine guns to wipe out. Nothing much.

Two buddies stretched out together off the road:

"You know, Willie, I'm scared, I'm so goddam scared . . ."

"Are you nuts? The way we're going now, the whole thing will blow over in a couple weeks. Then you can go back to your wife and make babies and tell all your kids what a wonderful hero you were."

"That's what I'm scared about, Willie. It's almost over and I'm almost home, and I'm scared that maybe just a lucky fucking shot will get me. And I don't want to die now, Willie, not when it's almost over. I don't want to die now. Do you know what I mean?"

"I know what you mean . . ."

Germany was quickly being broken into bits and pieces. To the north, the Germans still held a funnel-shaped area limited by the Oder and the Elbe with a narrow westward extension along the North Sea. To the south they had a larger oval-shaped area, most of Bavaria and Austria and parts of Czechoslovakia.

Armed civilians were trying to put up a small-time imitation of Stalingrad in Halle. Slightly south of that city, a motorized division rode into Czechoslovakia cutting off most of Germany's remaining roads into the Redoubt.

The Redoubt had been built up as the probable last center of prolonged fanatic resistance where the Germans would hold out to the death, exacting an expensive price in casualties before their final defeat. But that wasn't to be. The Redoubt defense busted like a big empty balloon.

During all this, the British pushed into Bremen and the Russians smashed into Berlin. The big news everywhere was the Russian-American linkup at Torgau on the Elbe River, twenty-eight miles northeast of Leipzig, on April 26. Unofficially the junction was made the day before when a GI patrol met the 58th Russian Guards Division.

The rest came quickly. Munich fell on May 1 to the Seventh Army. Berlin fell. Nine hundred thousand Nazis surrendered in Italy and west Austria. Von Rundstedt was captured. Seventh Army pushed through the Brenner Pass to link up with the Fifth Army in Italy. Berchtesgaden fell. Salzburg fell. Hamburg fell. All forces in Holland, Denmark and northern Germany surrendered, 500,000 of them.

All this was one-two-three, one after another, every day a headline streamer, everybody waiting for the big one.

It was a week of confusion like no other week of the war. Everybody said it so many times that nobody would believe it any more. Nobody believed it because the radio and newspapers had kicked it around unofficially since the night of April 28.

It wasn't until midnight of May 8 that it was official.

The war was over.

"Sure, there were lots of bodies we never identified. You know what a direct hit by a shell does to a guy. Or a mine. Or a solid hit with a grenade even. Sometimes all we have is a leg or a hunk of arm," said T/Sgt. Donald Haguall of the 48th Quartermaster Graves Registration.

"The ones that stink the worst are the guys who got internal wounds and are dead about three weeks with the blood staying inside and rotting and when you move the body, the blood comes out of the nose and mouth. Then some of them bloat up in the sun, they bloat up so big that they bust the buttons and then they get blue and the skin peels. They don't all get blue, some of them get black.

"But they all stink. There's only one stink and that's it. You never get used to it either. As long as you live, you never get used to it. And after a while, the stink gets in your clothes and you can taste it in your mouth. If you think about it too much, you go Section Eight.

"You know what I think? I think maybe if every civilian in the world could smell the stink of death for an hour, or even ten minutes, then I think we wouldn't have any more wars. What do you think?"

The War Was Over

It started out phony. It started when a photographer staged a shot with some French babes kissing some slightly overhappy soldiers in front of Rainbow Corner. Watching the whole thing curiously, quietly, were several dozen soldiers sitting at the tables outside the Red Cross Club, sipping Cokes.

That was Monday, the afternoon of the unofficial announcement.

"I keep telling everybody that the war is really over," said the MP at the door who was no longer checking passes, "but nobody believes me. I told one guy and he just said, 'What . . . again . . . ?'"

That was only part of the mood that afternoon. There was something else. There was this:

Two paratroopers were just standing in front of the club when an excitable Frenchman ran up to them, waving a French newspaper, yelling, *"La guerre est finie . . . La guerre est finie . . ."* After he raced by, spreading the news, one of the paratroopers simply said, "For him, not for us."

Then there was another soldier who listened to somebody tell him that the war was over and then said bitterly, "Which war, the war they're fighting in Paris?"

That was Monday afternoon, and then the mood changed.

It changed slowly. You could feel it change; you could hear it. First the singing by small crowds, loud singing by people who had drunk lots of cognac and were walking down the Champs-Elysées arm-in-arm until they had a small parade. Then the parades getting longer and the crowds getting bigger and the planes swooping down low dropping flares and dozens of people piling onto any jeep that slowed down.

The Champs-Elysées was the center of it and every soldier had a girl or two girls or a dozen girls. And everybody was singing and everybody was everybody's buddy.

"Hiya Army . . . Hiya Navy . . ."

"Hello beautiful . . ."

"Goddammit, don't call me sir . . . today I'm a civilian."

"Hiya civilian . . ."

It spread fast. Some of it was forced. Some guys were getting drunk not because they really wanted to, but just because they felt they had to. But most of the soldiers on the Champs were just letting themselves go, catching the spirit of it.

"Show me the way to go home . . ."

"Roll out the barrel, we'll have a barrel of fun . . ."

"We're forgetting about the CBI tonight. We're forgetting about every goddam thing," said Pfc. Nat Mangano of Company H. "We're just gonna have a helluva time, that's all. Why not?"

There were very few lonely people.

"I can't find anybody to celebrate with. I don't know anybody here. I'm just on a three-day pass. Every time I find me a girl she disappears. And I can't get a drink. All the bars are closed. But don't worry, I'll make contact before the night's over. I've gotta make contact. I'm going back to the outfit tomorrow."

It looked like that about midnight at the Arc de Triomphe. It looked like it was going to last all night long and not stop for days and days.

At one of the big cafés at the Rond Pont, Pvt. Robert Sullivan put his arm around the lieutenant colonel. Both of them had all kinds of ribbons and all kinds of clusters. Both were smiling and looking at the empty champagne bottles.

When they had drained their glasses, Sullivan pointed to the lieutenant colonel and beamed. "This wonderful sonofabitch," he said. "If he wanted my right arm, I'd cut off my right arm right now and give it to him." The lieutenant colonel kept beaming and refilled the glasses.

"He was a second lieutenant and I was a private in his squad, and he was the best second lieutenant in the business and now he's a lieutenant colonel and I'm still a private and if he wants my right arm, I'll cut it off right now and give it to him. Honest to God." They were both still beaming when they finished off another glass of champagne.

In another café, some Wacs were singing, *"Mister Monsoor from Armentieres, parley-vous . . ."*

On the Rue de Berri, in front of the WAC hotel, a soldier and a Wac were in a clinch and the soldier said something and the Wac's voice came out of the darkness, "Nope, not even on V-E Day . . ."

In the dayroom of the 108th General Hospital, a few boys were playing checkers, not listening to the radio. The radio was announcing the official end of the war in Europe.

There were two soldiers sitting right next to the radio, listening very intently, as if they wanted to make sure they got every word.

After Winston Churchill had finished speaking, I asked one of the soldiers how he felt about it. He turned around to stare with wide-open eyes and then his words came out so slowly as if it was painful for him to talk, as if he had to drag out every word separately. He said:

"I have no feeling at all."

Then he pointed to his head. "I got hit on the head with a dud," he said. "I don't remember too much. I don't remember what battalion I was with. I don't even remember what my rank is. I think I'm a T/5 but I'm not sure. Isn't that funny?"

The other soldier was Pvt. Ernest Kuhn of Chicago. He had just been liberated after five months in a Nazi PW camp. He still had some shrapnel in his throat.

"I listened to Churchill talk and I kept saying to myself that I was still alive. The war was over and I was still alive. And I thought of all the boys in my division band who were with me in the Ardennes who are dead now. We used to be a pretty good band."

The nurse told how all the patients crowded to the balconies the night before to watch the planes drop the flares and how some of the planes spotted the hospital's red cross and all the crowded balconies and how they came back and buzzed the hospital again and again, wiggling their wings, dropping so many flares that it looked like daylight. Then somebody started singing "God Bless America," and everybody joined in and some of the soldiers looked like they were crying.

In one of the wards, Pvt. Junior H. Powell told how he felt:

"It's a great thing all right," he said, "but I kinda wish it'd all happened a month ago."

Then he pointed to his missing leg.

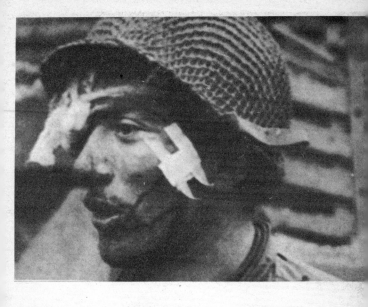

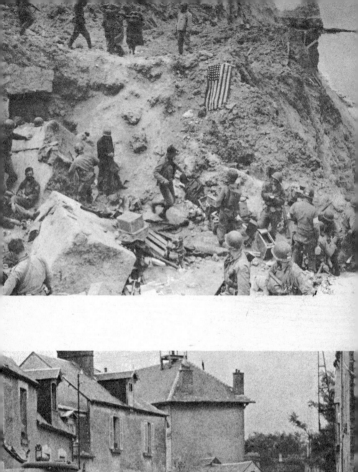

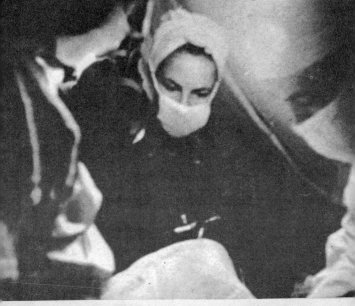

Dream

"Don't look now, but there's old 'Coo-shay Awvec' back in town!"

THE PACIFIC

Lullaby

. . . you have come a long way to lie on the sand.
Forgetful of the motion of
the slow, incessant waves
curving and falling, the white foam lifting
the white sand drifting
over your face, your outflung hand,
drifting and creeping,
slow and incessant and cool . . .
you have come a long way, a world away, to
sleep. . . .

—Sgt. Charles E. Butler

Midway

The Battle of Midway turned the tide of the war and yet it was a battle in which nine-tenths of the men involved never even saw the battle. It was one of the great battles in naval history, and yet it was not a battle of ships —it was a battle of planes.

The importance of Midway rested in its name—it was midway across the Pacific. Two tiny islets inside an encircling reef: Sand Island two miles long, and Eastern Island only half that size. Yet Midway was not expendable. We had spent twenty million dollars to convert it into an unsinkable aircraft carrier, a naval airbase second in importance only to Pearl Harbor. The 121 planes there were old, many obsolete, but every dawn they patrolled more than a million and a half square miles of ocean.

One of the many reasons the Japanese wanted Midway was that they saw it as the source of the sixteen B-25 bombers that had bombed Japan on April 18, 1942.

The English-speaking Japanese propagandist from Tokyo was explaining over the radio that Japan was the only country at war free from any threat of attack. Then he went on to say what a fine day it was in Tokyo with the Festival of the Cherry Blossoms and the two baseball games. And, then, you could hear the air-raid siren.

Sighted by a Japanese fishing boat, our carriers let loose their B-25's. During the takeoff, one of the planes skidded on the slippery deck and it cost a sailor his arm. Otherwise they were all away without incident. But everybody knew this earlier departure forced them to fly four hundred miles more and most of the crews would either have to jump or dump before they reached the friendly airfield in China.

Their mission included selected targets in several Japanese cities, particularly Tokyo. They flew low enough for Sgt. Jake Eierman to see a cleaning woman rush out and shake her mop at them. Sgt. Ed Bain remarked how drab the city looked. Sgt. Jim Macia remembered how hungry he was and how he ate a peanut-butter-and-jelly sandwich. A Sgt. Wayne Bissell spotted a baseball stadium and wondered how the game was going.

The planes rose to 1,500 feet for the bomb run. Bomb-bay doors have a clanking sound when they open and you could see the red light blink on the instrument panel, watch it pulsate each time it dropped a 500-pound incendiary.

They called it the Doolittle Raid after the colonel who commanded it. It was his force and his planning that helped shape the raid, and he survived. But he would be among the first to share the credit with all those men who were crashed and caught, starved and beaten, and the ones who were beheaded. Only one of the sixteen planes reached the intended Chinese airfield. But no sixteen planes had ever made a more memorable mission at a more important time. It was a kind of bravado psychological slap.

The mop-up of Midway was only part of Admiral Yamamoto's grand-scale plan, called "AF." Yamamoto knew the time would come when American forces would try to breach the 3,000-mile perimeter of his Pacific. To wipe out any such possibility, he knew he must kill the core of our remaining Pacific fleet—our aircraft carriers. Only those carriers stood between the Japanese fleet and the American coastline.

To do this, Yamamoto assembled a massive task force of some two hundred ships including eleven battleships, eight aircraft carriers, twenty-two cruisers, plus several dozen destroyers and submarines. From this group, he would split off a feinting force to occupy some Aleutian Islands near Alaska, to attract a strong part of the U.S. Fleet. Then his main Japanese force would move in on Midway, occupy it, and then search for and destroy our remaining big ships.

Their carriers had some seven hundred planes to devastate the tiny islets, and then 5,000 veteran Japanese combat troops planned to leave their twelve transports and walk ashore "where only the maggots moved."

It didn't quite work that way.

It didn't work because we had broken their secret code. MAGIC told us all their plans, and this time we not only knew when but where.

We had a month to prepare. We had to quickly collect our scattered fleet into a task force. Our aircraft carrier *Yorktown* had been badly hit in the stalemated naval air battle of the Coral Sea, and the repair crews at Pearl had to compress the work of months into days. We needed the *Yorktown*. Even with it, we only had three available aircraft carriers. We didn't even have the reserves to reinforce our small cadre of 3,600 combat men on Midway.

But MAGIC still gave us the edge, and the edge was sharp. Knowing their plans, we refused to be decoyed to defend the Aleutians. We went where the war was.

It was at 0600 hours on June 4, 1942, that a Midway-based PBY recon plane first spotted the oncoming Japanese fleet.

Japanese planes were then already on their way with plan "Organization Number Five," to blast the Midway islands. The island's radar spotted their 108 attacking planes 93 miles away and our planes scrambled to intercept them. But our old and obsolete planes hardly dented their attacking pattern. It took the Japanese planes only twenty minutes to convert these tiny islets into a litter of broken buildings, destroying planes and hangars and burning fuel-storage tanks. The sands were covered with thousands of dead birds. Still, we were lucky. Our runways were still usable and our casualties light—twenty killed.

One of the bombs landed squarely on the Post Exchange, scattering everything from cigarettes to beer cans. A GI machine gunner, after being hit in the solar plexus by a beer can, was quoted as saying, "I never could take beer on an empty stomach."

We were lucky, too, because the Japanese were so slow in spotting our ships. Had their 25 submarines been given the more flexible order of sweeping their areas instead of staying static, some of them would have seen us long before. So would one of their carrier search planes, if it had not developed engine trouble at a critical time, and had to turn back.

So the surprise element was still ours, and our carrier planes were already on their way.

Meanwhile, our big bombers from Midway made their initial attacks.

One Flying Fortress soon reported that its bombs had attacked a Japanese cruiser and saw it sink in fifteen seconds. The cruiser, however, turned out to be an American submarine which had managed to crash-dive safely out of harm's way.

The fact is, throughout the Pacific war, these high-altitude bombers failed to sink a single ship. The reason was clear: from 30,000 feet, a ship is a thin matchstick. At 20,000 feet, a clear deck can be distinguished from one covered with aircraft. At 10,000 feet, an individual plane on a flight deck can be made out.

But, even at 10,000 feet, trying to bomb a ship is like trying to "drop a marble from eye-level on a scared mouse."

The first three waves of our carrier planes didn't seem to have any better luck. The Japanese Zekes could zip in and out of our plane formations at twice our speed. They could outmaneuver us, outclimb us, outfly us, outshoot us. They also outnumbered us.

In the flurry of an air fight over many miles at great speed, the first job was always identification.

"Anybody who says he can identify an airplane more than a couple of miles away is nuts," said Radio Technician Second Class Richard Walker. "At that distance, a plane is just a black speck and you don't know what it is. The way we would know for sure was our IFF [Identification, Friend or Foe]. Our plane would see that speck in the sky, send off a code on his IFF box, and if the code didn't come back right, then he'd get ready to start shooting.

"The IFF box was my department. I'd be waiting for them on the catwalk of the flight deck when they landed, to check the IFF and ask the pilot if everything was O.K. If it wasn't, then I'd rip it out and put in a new one while I fixed the old one. Each IFF box was really a complicated mess and everything had to be just perfect, and didn't I know it! And you want to hear something funny? When I first got into the Navy, I didn't even know what a fuse was!"

Our first raid of carrier planes took nineteen minutes. The sky was all colors: floating black tennis balls of ack-ack, red streams of fire from automatic weapons, bursting shells of blue and yellow and pink and red and white and even lavender. All this beautiful color killed ten of our first fourteen torpedo bombers.

We had scored no hits.

Our second wave was worse. Due to a signal mix-up, fifteen more of our Devastators found themselves without fighter cover as they dived onto their targets. To have any hope of a hit, a torpedo-bomber pilot must maintain steady course in altitude for at least two minutes.

"Johnny One to Johnny Two . . . How am I doing? . . . My two wingmen are going into the water . . . I'd give a million to know who did that . . . Watch those fighters . . ." SPLASH . . .

We lost every one of those fifteen planes, and only a single pilot survived.

And we still had scored no hits.

The pilots were the glory boys. Nobody deserved it more. They had grace and courage and style. But at the rear end of each torpedo bomber was a radio gunner, an enlisted man, fighting and dying with the same grace, the same courage, the same style.

When the twin .30-caliber machine guns broke loose from their mount, Sgt. Floyd Adkins somehow held these 175-pound guns in his lap until his plane pulled out of a dive. Then, when a Japanese fighter moved in for the kill, Adkins managed to manhandle his clumsy-shaped guns well enough to shoot down the attacking plane. Back aboard ship, Adkins later tried to carry the gun again. "Look," he said. "Now I can't even lift it."

By the end of the third wave of our air attack, at 1024 hours, we had lost 35 out of 41 attacking planes.

And we still had not scored a single hit on any enemy ship.

Six minutes later, the Battle of Midway was won, and the victory was ours.

Six minutes.

On the flight deck of the Japanese aircraft carrier *Akagi,* the admiral had given the signal to "Launch When Ready." Planes were in position, engines warming up, and the carrier started turning into the wind—a carrier's war is a war of wind. The first plane picked up speed, started to whiz off the deck, when the ship lookout yelled, "Helldivers!"

"The terrifying scream of the dive-bombers reached me first, followed by the crashing explosion of a direct hit," later wrote Mitsuo Fushida. "There was a blinding flash, and then a second explosion, much louder than the first. I was shaken by a weird blast of warm air. There was still another shock, but less severe, apparently a near-miss. Then followed a startling quiet, as the barking of guns suddenly ceased. I got up and I looked at the sky. The enemy planes were already gone from sight.

"Looking about, I was horrified at the destruction which had been wrought in a matter of seconds. There was a huge hole in the flight deck, just behind the amidships elevator. The elevator itself, twisted like molten glass, was dropping into the hangar. Deck-plates reeled upwards in grotesque configurations. Planes stood tail-up, belching livid flame and jet-black smoke. Reluctant tears streamed down my cheeks as I watched the fires spread."

Within six minutes, the tide had turned. Within six minutes, our planes had destroyed three Japanese aircraft carriers.

There was more to come.

Japanese carrier planes had found the U.S.S. *Yorktown* and hit her with three bombs. A bomb hit whips a carrier like a musical saw. It pops rivets, starts fires, springs doors, shorts power. Into action went the waiting Damage Control parties, sailors with gas masks, explosimeters, axes, rescue-breather apparatus, fire extinguishers, wedges and sledges, coils of all kinds—fire hose, emergency power, foam wire. Sailors wearing oversize helmets with telephone headsets got their orders from a battery of talkers who had completely diagrammed all the danger places on the ship—the fuel oil, the gas, the ventilation systems, the steam and electrical and water systems. Damage-control teams soon moved in among the shattered machinery, slipping in the blood and oil, fighting the flames, searching for the wounded men and the broken mains, and the dead. Sometimes all they found of a dead sailor was a small piece of skull left in a scorched helmet.

It took two hours to put out the fires, reline the boilers, clear and repair the flight deck, refuel her planes and get underway again. By then the Japanese bombers were back. Some of our fighters got up to meet them, and Machinist Reid and Radio Electrician Bayers shot down three enemy planes and Ralph Rich got a fourth. But the Japanese dropped four torpedoes and two of them hit.

When a torpedo hits a ship in its vital areas, she shudders like a startled horse, almost seems to leap out of the water. Sailors are often hurled overboard and sucked into flooding compartments, decks heave, oil spouts, ankles and legs snap. And the sailors deep down below decks are sometimes buried alive.

As the captain prepared to abandon ship, an officer spoke on the intercom to some men caught down below on the fourth deck of the *Yorktown*.

"Do you know what kind of fix you're in?" he asked them.

"Sure," answered a sailor, "but we've got a helluva good acey-deucey game down here."

The sailor, however, had a single request:

"When you scuttle her," he said, "aim the torpedoes right where we are. We want it to be quick."

There was no need for scuttling. The *Yorktown* listed fast, slipped over on her port side and sank with all her flags flying while the surrounding ships saluted her.

The acey-deucey game was over.

But the score still wasn't settled. Planes from the U.S.S. *Enterprise* found the fourth Japanese aircraft carrier, landed four heavy bombs on her deck, sank her. And, only then, did all the planes come home.

An aircraft carrier comes alive only when its planes are readied for war and catapulted into the sky.

An aircraft carrier comes alive when its huge hangar decks smell of sweat and gas and oil, noisy with the intensity of many men at work checking engines, guns, radios, control cables, landing gear.

An aircraft carrier comes alive when the planes return and you can count the dead.

When Torpedo Eight returned to the U.S.S. *Hornet,* and the quiet crewmen checked into the Ready Room for Intelligence reports, there were twenty-five planes missing. Fifty men. The returning crews no longer had any illusions of immortality. "Give them each a bottle and see to it personally that they go to bed," said the admiral. He had kept the lights on long after dark in the hope others would return. When warned of all the subs in the area, he said, "To hell with the subs."

For those returning planes, the main man is the man with waving paddles. On the U.S.S. *Enterprise* it was Bert Harden.

As each plane turned toward his ship, Bert used his paddles to tell the pilots whether they were coming in too high or too low, too fast or too slow, whether or not their wings were level. Then with a final flurry or a slash, Bert was the one who decided whether to wave them off to try again or else let them cut and come in.

Each signal had to be sharp and slashing. Slash down the right paddle, slash it across his body to the left, slash it. No hesitations or question marks, everything certain, absolute, immediate.

If a plane came in too fast, it might snap the arresting cable which had such tremendous springs that it could whip around and cut a man in half, as it sometimes did.

After the long day of returning planes, Bert suddenly yelled to his helper.

"For God's sake, how many more?"

"Dunno . . . We already have a couple more than we launched."

The thought hit Harden and it shook him. "Call the bridge," he yelled. "Have them check all the planes for meatballs." (This referred to the round red ball of the Japanese insignia.)

It took time but the word came back—No, there were no Japanese planes aboard, just five extra planes from the *Yorktown.*

A Japanese sailor later reported that when Admiral Yamamoto was told of the loss of four Japanese carriers, he groaned aloud. Midway became an unmentionable word at Japanese naval headquarters. Wounded Midway survivors were taken ashore to Japan at night and kept in isolation, away from visitors, like prisoners.

When the forty-eight-hour battle was all over, the United States had lost a carrier, a destroyer, 150 planes and 307 men. Japan had lost four aircraft carriers, a heavy cruiser, 253 planes and 3,500 men. It was Japan's first naval defeat since 1592, when the Koreans used history's first ironclad ships to drive the Japanese fleet from Chinhae Bay.

Pearl Harbor had been partially avenged, exactly six months after December 7. The Battle of Midway had restored the naval balance in the Pacific. The initiative was now ours. Our own grand plan, Operation Watchtower, called next for the seizure of Guadalcanal.

We had ended the beginning, and now we were beginning the end.

Guadalcanal

> *And when he gets to Heaven*
> *To St. Peter he will tell:*
> *"One more Marine reporting, sir—*
> *I've served my time in Hell."*

Hell was Guadalcanal, and that verse was the epitaph found there on a Marine's grave.

Some military historians call the Guadalcanal campaign the most bitter in our history since the campaign of northern Virginia in the Civil War. It stretched out six months and saw seven major naval engagements and at least ten land battles.

"What do we want with a place nobody ever heard of before?" a Marine asked just before the invasion.

310

We wanted it to protect our supply lines and provide a stepping-stone for future offensives. And we wanted it fast because the Japanese were busy building a big airfield there. From that airfield they would have a sweeping air control of the South Pacific.

Almost all we knew about Guadalcanal was that it was on the southern end of the Solomons, the second largest island in a 600-mile double string of seventeen islands—about a thousand miles northeast of Australia. We had a Navy hydrographic chart made thirty-two years before and the description of it in a short story by Jack London which even misspelled the name of the place. We did order aerial reconnaissance photos, but they arrived too late to do much good.

Our timetable called for 37 days to plot, plan and prepare a full-scale invasion, our first major amphibious operation of the war. This meant the assembling of sixty warships, sixty days' combat supply, and the 19,000 Marines on 31 transports. Final training was intensive.

Question: "If an enemy soldier jumped from a tree, what would you do?"

Correct answer: "Kick him in the balls!"

The Japanese put it more delicately:

"As the dying leopard leaves its coat to a man, so a warrior's reputation serves his sons after his death. . . . If you unite with me, our courage and power shall illuminate the whole earth."

Part of the preliminary plan was to mop up some small offshore islands close to Guadalcanal.

Guadalcanal is for the history books, but who ever heard of Tulagi, Gavutu and Tanambogu?

> *We asked all the doggies to come to Tulagi,*
> *But General MacArthur said, "No."*
> *When asked for his reason—*
> *"It isn't the season.*
> *Besides, you have no USO!"*

Tulagi had been British, a small boot-shaped island that even had a cricket field. Now banzai attacks had replaced cricket: mass charges by fanatic soldiers yelling: "Japanese boy drink American boy's blood!!!!"

When an American tank stalled, they stormed it with Molotov cocktails until the crew climbed out and ran for it. Last man out of the tank was Pfc. Eugene Moore, who came out feet first and found himself surrounded by 42 frenzied Japanese. They grabbed him, punched him, tore his hair, kicked him in the face and stomach, ripped his pockets for his money, knifed him, even stuck a pitchfork into him, and finally they grabbed him by his feet and arms and swung him back and forth against the tank, again and again and again, literally trying to beat the life out of him. So intense was all this that they didn't even notice Pvt. Kenneth Koons and a few other riflemen carefully picking them off one by one. When it was all over, Pfc. Moore was still alive and rushed to a battalion aid station, and all 42 attacking Japanese were dead.

Gavutu and Tanambogu were twin islets, small but steep, ringed by coral and joined by a narrow causeway. Both places were pocked with armored caves. Since we couldn't force them out, we sealed them in. Sgt. Orle Bergner became known as "the one-man stick of dynamite." He strapped explosives to the ends of long poles, fitted them with five-second fuses and threw them into the mouths of caves. During one of the blasts, another cave-sealer, Harry Torgerson, lost the seat of his pants. Told about it, he said, "Screw the pants . . . get me more dynamite."

It was just a small scene, a short conversation: Communications Sgt. Robert Bradley, a forward observer for a mortar section on Tanambogu, was hit in the throat, his voice box smashed. As a doctor tried to stop the blood, Bradley indicated he wanted to write something and so the doctor gave him a pencil.

"Will I live?" he wrote.

The doctor nodded yes.

"Will I speak again?" he wrote.

The doctor hesitated, then nodded again.

Bradley grinned and wrote with a flourish, "What the hell's the use in worrying?"

The unknown islands with the forgotten names were captured at the cost of 144 Americans killed, 194 wounded.

But these were still sideshows. The main event was

312

Guadalcanal, about eighty miles long and twenty-five miles wide.

It looked lovely: a slender green island with a graceful spine of mountains, beautiful white beaches washed by gentle waves and fringed with the exotic lazy look of coconut groves.

We landed 10,000 Marines on August 6, 1942, almost without opposition. Instead of sticking bayonets into bodies, we used them to cleave the tops off of coconuts.

For the next few days, the enemy was almost invisible. We captured the almost-completed airfield without much combat, found half-eaten breakfasts, large stores of rice, a complex of power and oxygen plants, wharves, radio stations, bridges, blast pens and even ice plants all ready and waiting for us.

There was a grassy knoll overlooking the field from the south that the general insisted our troops capture quickly. A soldier wondered why.

"Maybe it's because it's the only place with a view," said a private.

"So?"

"So where else they gonna put the officers' club?"

But the Marines didn't do badly either. They liberated a warehouse full of Japanese beer and sake, used rickshaws to empty the place and bury the evidence from prying officer eyes. Some of the nighttime trigger-happy shooting came from men who had soaked up a little too much sake. One such soldier, challenged by a Marine sentry, found he couldn't persuade his lips to pronounce the difficult password and finally said, "Aw shit—shoot." And the sentry collapsed in laughter.

Two days after the Guadalcanal landings came the naval battle of Savo Island, also known as the Five Sitting Ducks. We were the sitting ducks.

It was a night battle that ended at dawn, and we seemed to have the odds on our side—we had radar and they didn't. But their sailors had been trained to see things at night miles away. "The Americans build things well," a Japanese officer said, "but their blue eyes are no match for our dark eyes in night action."

By the time our ship blinkers had signaled to each other "Warning, warning, strange ships entering harbor," the Japanese had spotted us, and started firing. Before it was over, they sank four of our cruisers and one destroyer. They escaped almost without a mark. Our defeat might have been a disaster if their ships had stayed to destroy our defenseless transports on the beach. But they overestimated our reserve strength and sped away from the scene. So did we.

Our naval exit from the combat area was so complete and so sudden that our ships didn't wait to unload the rest of the food and ammunition our Marines badly needed.

The code name for Guadalcanal was Cactus but Admiral William Halsey later suggested that it should have been Shoestring. "They might have won a reasonably quick victory if we had been able to protect them, supply them and reinforce them, but we weren't. We didn't have the ships, either cargo or combat, and the enemy did."

Some of our Marines later had a medal made in Australia showing a rear admiral dropping a hot potato into the hands of a kneeling Marine and the Latin motto read, *"Faciat Georgius."* Translated, it said, "Let George do it." Or, as one less gentlemanly Marine put it, "They left us bare-ass."

The Guadalcanal potato soon became hotter. Undisturbed by enemy ships or planes, the Japanese began heavy reinforcement of troops and constant bombardment by ships and planes.

Japanese soldiers, however, wrapped up their war with all the etiquette of their mystique. Before entering battle, they made out their wills, cut off locks of hair or pieces of fingernails and sealed them in envelopes, wound round them the belts of a thousand stitches made by loved ones to protect them from bullets. "Remember that death is lighter than a feather but that duty is heavier than a mountain."

Then they were told:

"When you encounter the enemy after landing, regard yourself as an avenger coming at last face to face with his father's murderer . . . if you fail to destroy him utterly, you can never rest at peace. And the first blow is the vital blow."

Henderson Field's most memorable night was The Night of the Battleships. The familiar droning Japanese recon plane, Louie the Louse, lit up the place shortly after midnight with his usual green flare, and then it began.

Sixteen 14-inch guns from Japanese battleships opened up ten miles away and the shells raced through the blackness like flaming boxcars, "PAH-BOOM . . . PAH-BOOM . . . PAH-BOOM."

It was a sledgehammer of sounds coming again and again and again and it brought a terror to the soul. You could see the flesh around men's mouths starting to shake, their eyes coating with a hot shine as if the tears were close, the blood draining from their faces leaving them white like watery milk. It made the young look old, the firm seem flabby and the only human sounds heard were the cries of pain and prayer, the rattling of teeth, and an almost animal whimpering. One sergeant crawled among his men on his hands and knees begging them to shoot him because he couldn't stand it anymore.

It lasted an eternity of ninety minutes.

It didn't happen again, because we finally drove them off with a whole series of naval actions in Ironbottom Bay —so called because it became a graveyard of ships, theirs and ours.

During one such action, our aircraft carrier U.S.S. *Enterprise* was hit hard.

Deep in the stern of a carrier is the steel box called the Steering Engine Room. Two large electric motors and a control panel get their signals from the Bridge. At the given signal, one of the motors pumps hydraulic oil against the plungers which control the rudder. The other motor rests in reserve. And if the control from the Bridge breaks down, there's a wheel and compass in that steel box of a room ready to take over the steering.

Seven men have the worry of this room. Without their work, the ship is dead.

On the U.S.S. *Enterprise*, bomb hits had torn 24 craters throughout the three steel decks of the ship. Six-foot holes in the waterline let in the sea. Everything else seemed a shambles of choking smoke. Steering control was lost and the ship feebly floundered.

The Steering Engine Room was such an oven that it seared any exposed flesh and baked any sweat like the quick sizzle of water on a hot skillet.

Thirty years in the Navy, Machinist William Arnold Smith knew every stir and twist in that steering engine.

Wearing an RBA mask (Rescue-Breather Apparatus), Smith got halfway down through the wreckage before he collapsed and was dragged out by his lifeline. Filling his lungs with fresh air, Smith again went down, along with another helper, Machinist's Mate First Class Cecil Robinson.

This time they reached the charred hatch before they both collapsed. Again dragged out, again revived, they again went down, somehow opened the watertight door and stumbled into the superheated steering room. Smith quickly saw the drowned starboard motor in its half-completed shift to the port. Carefully his fingers moved to complete the operation. Hydraulic oil hit the rams, moved the three-story rudder and the helmsman could report to the captain, "Steering control regained, sir."

It all took 38 minutes.

Sailors were similarly busy elsewhere:

Seaman Henry Dunn, in an asbestos suit, plug in an emergency power cable.

Seaman Reuben Fisher, aim the high velocity fog of your fire hose at some five-inch powder cases before the flashing fire gets there.

Machinist W. E. Fluitt, drain and vent the gasoline system, flood the pipes with carbon dioxide before the hot bomb fragments tear into it.

Shipfitter Jim Brewer, move into the heart of the hottest fires, find the source, and direct fire-fighting action.

Shipfitter First Class Larry Wyfels, reestablish water pressure, then search for wounded.

Storekeeper Jesse Crowder, head into the Paint and Pyrotechnic Storeroom and operate the CO_2 smothering system.

Boatswain Edward Hatchell, trim the splintered timbers around holes on flight deck and cover them with square steel sheets of boiler plate.

Carpenters W. L. Reames, Leon Brown and Helmuth Bentz, work armpit-deep in seawater under emergency lighting, build a planked cofferdam to cover the huge holes in the skin of the ship.

Ray Owens, trip releasing mechanism to dump overboard large tank of high-octane gas.

The ship must be ready to receive the returning planes.

Admiral Halsey visited Guadalcanal on an inspection trip and Major General Vandegrift's cook worked hard to make a special dinner, including apple pie. The admiral was pleased enough to send for the cook and personally praise him in great detail and with many adjectives for the fine meal. The cook was Butch Morgan, a tough sergeant with a red walrus mustache, who had seen action in

316

France in World War I. Butch's face grew as red as his mustache during the praise and finally he blurted, "Aw, bullshit, Admiral . . . you don't need to say that."

The Japanese said that the Marines were not genuine jungle fighters because "they always cut the jungle down."

It was true that Marines liked to clear a field of fire up to a hundred yards so they could see the enemy coming and cut him down before he came. They dug deep connecting pits called spider holes where they could stand and shoot, cushioned them with sandbags, banked them with cut-up sections of coconut logs, covered them with clumps of grass for camouflage, then interlaced the field of fire with barbed wire. They mined and booby-trapped the approaches, set up hand grenades—their pins partly withdrawn—to trip the unwary, zeroed in their artillery on likely trails and assembly points, registered interlocking machine guns for massed night firing, arranged cans of gasoline in the trees with a pre-fixed, preset rifle that would fire a bullet a night to set the can afire. And then they waited.

Jungle war is a war of silence. An extra sound and you're dead.

We caught a whole Japanese battalion that way at the bottom of a ravine, and our pinpointed 105-mm howitzer shells blasted them. Every time the Japanese broke for cover, our Marines drove them back again with machine-gun fire and 81-mm mortars.

> We have a weapon that nobody loves
> They say that our gun's a disgrace,
> You crank up 200, and 200 more—
> And it lands in the very same place.
> Oh, there's many a gunner who's blowing his top,
> Observers are all going mad.
> But our affection has lasted,
> This pig-iron bastard
> Is the best gun this world ever had.

Before it was over, we had killed some 700 of them.

Then our souvenir-hunting Marines swept in to collect samurai swords, flags, watches, anything. One Marine private even had a pair of pliers to pull gold teeth which went into a bag that once held Bull Durham tobacco.

If war takes some of the human out of the human being, it soon returns.

Almost all the Japanese there were killed, but a few survived. One of the survivors was a sad, starving, sorry little man who said he hadn't eaten in seven days. He was given a can of beans and even some pogey-bait. Pogey-bait was the hard-to-get candy, often rationed only a bar to a squad. You drew lots to win it and then you ate in the bushes, away from the hungry eyes of your buddies.

Somebody also gave him some cigarettes and he smoked them one after another, said he hadn't smoked in 103 days. His feet were too swollen to walk and so Cpl. Tom Walker, of Quincy, Mass., carried him on his back to the battalion aid station. It made quite a picture, the small man with his pants and shirt split widely at the rear, riding on the back of the highly embarrassed Walker.

Tokyo Rose described our Marine invasion as "summer insects which have dropped into the fire by themselves." Soon she would be referring to the Marines as the "butchers of Guadalcanal." And Guadalcanal would have a new name, Death Island.

With more death came more hell.

Hell was sharp-edged cogon grass higher than your head.

Hell was red furry spiders as big as your fist, giant lizards as long as your leg, leeches falling from trees to suck blood, armies of white ants with a bite of fire, scurrying scorpions inflaming any flesh they touched, enormous rats and bats everywhere, and rivers with waiting crocodiles.

Hell was the sour, foul smell of the squishy jungle, humidity that rotted a body within hours, a sticky, stinking wet heat of dripping rain forests that sapped the strength of any man.

Hell was an enemy hidden in the dark deep of shadows, an enemy so fanatic that it used its own dead as booby traps, an enemy that whispered at night, "Come here, please . . . come here, please . . ." or else charged in a banzai attack, climbing over its own dead, yelling, "Fuck Babe Ruth!!"

We sent out daily patrols, sometimes a dozen men, sometimes a full company of a couple of hundred. They smeared mud on their faces, covered their bodies with

318

branches, walked slowly and silently at spaced intervals of a dozen feet to the left or right of trails, often covering only a mile a day. They learned to carry an inch of beef suet to grease their feet daily to avoid blisters. They learned to look for the rustle of a leaf, listen for the cry of a strange bird. Ambushes were everywhere.

Sometimes they stayed alive by playing dead.

Digging in for the night near a tree, a Marine's shovel hit the covered body of a Japanese soldier. The Marine brushed off the body, but the Japanese didn't move. The Marine lifted the soldier's arm and let it drop. It dropped limply, the face motionless. To double-check, the Marine again lifted the man's arm and let it drop. This time, the Japanese eyelid twitched. A bullet stopped the twitching.

Pfc. Harry Dunn was a better actor. He played dead when some Japanese soldiers overran his outpost, jabbing the wounded with their bayonets. Nearby, Dunn later found his buddy, Pvt. Jack Morrison, badly wounded in the chest but alive. For two days Dunn dragged him gently through the thicket into the water where they drank for the first time. Morrison sometimes cried out from the pain and Dunn sometimes passed out from exhaustion, but Dunn swam down the river, his buddy on his back, fearfully watching out for the V-wakes of crocodiles. By daybreak, Dunn managed to reach the perimeter of our lines. His buddy was still alive. The act was over.

The so-called Bastard Air Force was in business on our captured airfield within two weeks.

All of them wore long-billed blue baseball caps and identical faded khaki shirts. The crews learned all kinds of trade tricks. Gunners soon knew the need of wiping guns free of oil because oil froze at altitudes above 25,000 feet. Mechanics used a hand pump and a chamois strainer to get the gas out of the big drums. And, since there were no hoists, they learned how to lug and load the 500-pound bombs by hand.

It was a hodgepodge group of planes. The newly arrived batch of fourteen P–40's was soon cut to three. It was too slow for a fighter but we soon found it fine for strafing and close-support bombing because of its light nose cannon and heavy weapons. To fight off the faster Zekes, we developed a system of flying fighters in pairs, wing to wing, each watching the other's tail. It worked well. Six days after their arrival, a group of Dauntlesses shot down sixteen Japanese planes.

Diving in and out of the sun, naval enlisted-man pilot, Machinist Donald Runyon, shot down three planes. The thin skins of the Japanese fighters flamed easily because their gas tanks were not self-sealing. He remembered the first exploding into a flaming rag doll of a plane, the second flaring like a struck match falling in a steeping glide, and the third igniting and falling in a driving left turn. Our daytime air superiority soon forced Japanese transports to confine their reinforcements to the night only. We called them Rat Runs of the Tokyo Express.

The Seabees had it all figured out. A 50-pound Japanese bomb landing on the runway tore up 1,600 square feet of steel matting. So, as soon as the Japanese bombers started heading home, these Seabees raced toward the blasted area, tore the twisted matting from the crater, filled it with fresh earth, packed it with compressors, covered it all over again with the new steel matting—which was already cut up and waiting alongside the strip.

Seabees (named after the first initials of Construction Battalion) were mostly older men, past the draft age, all volunteers, all craftsmen in some construction specialty.

The younger Marines constantly kidded them. "What the hell, Pop! They running out of men back home?" But the Seabees smiled, worked, and answered softly. These young Marines might have been their sons.

Bloody Ridge was a humpbacked mound of earth sticking out of the jungle like the spine of a whale. It was the perfect approach to Henderson Field, running gently down to it out of the jungle. For the Japanese, breaking the back of this ridge meant the mop-up victory of Guadalcanal.

We knew that. We dug in. We waited.

Through a spread of smoke, before the dawn of September 15, several thousand crack Japanese troops attacked in waves, yelling, "U.S. Marines be dead tomorrow, U.S. Marines be dead tomorrow."

And the loud, unforgettable answer of one BAR man was, "You'll eat shit first, you bastards!"

The CO put it simply to his men: "If we don't hold, we will lose Guadalcanal."

We held.

Occasionally, when a dazed Marine drifted back, he was

320

told, "The only thing that they have that you don't is guts." Then, back in the line again, somebody gave the World War I Belleau Wood cry, "You! Do you want to live forever?"

Pfc. Jimmy Corzine saw four Japanese setting up a machine gun on a small rise of ground, rushed them, bayoneted the gunner, then swung the gun around to spray the enemy from their own weapon before he too was finally killed.

Do you want to live forever?

Three Japanese broke through a gap in the barbed wire, jumped into the foxhole of Cpl. Gene Wilson. Wilson squeezed the trigger of his BAR. It jammed. "Marine, you die," said a Japanese soldier with a thrusting bayonet. Wilson slashed with his machete, and the enemy sank to the ground, his entrails slipping through his clutching fingers.

Wilson then jumped from his hole hacking the others to similar death with his thick-bladed knife.

Do you want to live forever?

A Japanese soldier had his bayonet into the leg of Cpl. John Shea, his bayonet slashing in and out again. Shea kicked the soldier with his other foot, slamming him against the side of the hole and finally finished him off with his tommy gun.

Do you want to live forever?

By nightfall we had counted more than 700 Japanese bodies. Amazingly, our own dead only totaled 34 with 75 others wounded.

"The attack of the Ichiki Detachment was not entirely successful," Japanese headquarters reported.

One of the few Japanese prisoners said, "Make no matter about us dead. More will come. We never stop coming. Soon you all be Japanese."

More did come. During their fierce offensive in October, the Japanese were told, "Do not expect to return, not even one man, if the occupation is not successful."

"Use grenades," Sgt. Mitchell Paige told his men. "Don't let them spot the guns. Fire only when you have to."

Most of the battle took place on both sides of the nose of a ridge.

"I was so wound-up that I couldn't stop," said Paige later. "I rounded up the skirmish line, told them I was going to charge off the nose and I wanted them to be right behind me. I picked up the machine gun and without noticing the burning hot-water jacket cradled it in my arms. Two belts of ammo I threw around my shoulders. The total weight was about one hundred and fifty pounds but the way I felt I could have carried three more without noticing it . . . The skirmish line came over the nose whooping like a bunch of wild Indians. We reached the edge of the clearing where the jungle began and there was nothing left either to holler at or shoot at. The battle was over with that strange sort of quietness that always follows.

"The first thing I did was to sit down. I was soaked in perspiration and steam was rising in a cloud from my gun. My hand felt funny. I looked down and saw through my tattered shirt a blister which ran from my fingertips to my forearm."

They estimated that there were a hundred and ten Japanese dead in front of Sgt. Paige's sector.

"They started to smell so horribly," added Paige, "that we had to bury them by blasting part of the ridge over on top of them. On the third day we marched twelve miles back to the airport. I never knew what day it was, and what's more I didn't care . . ."

The Army took over from the Marines on December 9, and by the end of that month most of the Marines were gone. Some of them had been in the line for 122 consecutive days without relief and they came out bearded and bony and ragged. Some of them didn't have the strength to climb up the cargo nets of the ships. But almost all of them stopped off at the cemetery to search for the names of their buddies. It was a neat square cleared area cut out of the coconut grove and each grave was covered with palm fronds.

Compared to the estimated 30,000 Japanese casualties, the American graves were few. All Marine ground losses totaled 1,592 dead and 4,183 wounded. The Army would add another 550 dead and more than twice as many wounded.

Describing the capture of Kokumbona toward the end of the campaign, *Yank* combat correspondent Mack Morriss told of the courage of two GI's: a conscientious objector and an Army Signal Corps lineman.

The conscientious objector was Pvt. Orville Cox, of

New Richmond, O., a draftee with only nine months' service. Cox went 350 yards up the face of a hill under heavy fire to bring out two wounded men. It took him two hours, but he brought them both out.

"When I went in, I said I was willin' to do first aid," he said, "but I wasn't aimin' to help kill."

And there was Pvt. Sam Russell, an Apache Indian from Camp Verde, Ariz., whose job was to lay down wire to keep communication intact with frontline units and headquarters. One particular unit was cut-off and nobody knew where. Sam worked his way through a Japanese encirclement, dragged the line into the middle of the outfit, set up the power phone and tested. With that phone, the platoon leader was able to direct artillery fire onto the surrounding enemy so they could break through them.

"I just ran a piece and crawled a piece," said Sam.

Before the campaign was all over, the Japanese evacuated some 12,000 troops in daring destroyer runs.

We would kill them later.

New Guinea

General Douglas MacArthur described the New Guinea campaign as "the determination to clear the enemy off our lawn so that we could go across the street and play in his yard."

It was not quite the language the GI's would have used.

There was no lawn, there was no play, there was no yard.

The world's second largest island—1,300 miles long— New Guinea was a country of high peaks and deep gorges, swollen rivers and sodden mountains, dense jungle and stinking swamps. It was a fever country, a nightmare country, a country of torrential rains, tropical ulcers, and a steaming, sucking heat.

In the cool planning rooms of the Pentagon, New Guinea was only a prong, part of a twin with Guadalcanal, aimed at the key Japanese base of Rabaul. Instead of storming Rabaul, our plan was to isolate it, blast it and let it starve.

The situation was this: we sat on one coast and the Japanese sat on the other coast. Dividing us was the backbone of the Owen Stanley Range of mountains, more than two miles high: connecting us was a single, slimy jungle trail. The Japanese had pushed down this trail to within thirty-two miles of Port Moresby before the Australian troops finally stopped them. By this time, our GI reinforcements were pouring in.

Flanked by Bootless Inlet and Caution Bay, Port Moresby was a microscopic metropolis set in the back curve of a beautiful blue-green harbor, surrounded by a cluster of native huts on stilts on the water's edge and white and yellow houses farther back in the green hills. We had the natives on our side, the friendly Fuzzy-wuzzies.

Fuzzy-wuzzies called everybody "Joe." Betel-nut juice made red gashes of their mouths, stained their teeth scarlet. They loved color, wore red blankets like a sarong. A Fuzzy-wuzzy bought a mature twelve-year-old wife for two pigs, and if she didn't work hard enough, he got his pigs back. But he would probably trade his wife or his favorite snakeskin drum for a bottle of peroxide to dye his bushy, frizzly hair orange.

The men hunted fish and snakes with spears, acted as carriers and guides for our GI's, and it was not true that they were really cannibals. Fuzzy-wuzzies only ate their enemy when they were very, very emotionally stirred up.

In the Valley of Silence, every sound had an eerie ring to it. The night noise that sounded like a man brushing against your tent turned out to be a leaf fallen from the tree on the canvas, a leaf with a stem as thick as your thumb, a leaf that measured almost three feet long and more than a foot wide.

Then there were the pythons. Sgt. Sam Feldman later told of a GI of average height who had been found stretched out almost eight feet long, every bone in his body broken. "The way these pythons worked it," said Feldman, "was to keep one end of themselves firm onto something solid and then just wrap around their victim and squeeze. A good-size python was about forty feet long and liked to swallow its victim whole."

Intelligence officers reported that some of our men threw away their weapons and ran to the rear, that we had trouble getting soldiers to go out on patrol, that our GI's wore long, dirty beards, lived on inadequate rations, wore torn clothes and worn-out shoes and had little observance of military courtesy. One Intelligence officer also reported that he found a regimental headquarters almost five miles behind the line and that its officers had never been forward to the front.

MacArthur soon gave orders that he wanted all officers removed who wouldn't fight. "If necessary put sergeants and corporals in charge of companies . . . I want you to take Buna or not come back alive."

First they had to push the Japanese back across the Bloody Track.

The GI's called it the Golden Staircase.

Two thousand steps cut into the mud, each step two feet high made of young trees packed into the black glue, each step so slimy that you slipped at least once every few minutes. No place to rest, no time to stop because there was always another soldier right behind you.

There was one break in the mold: a skeleton of a Japanese soldier still on a stretcher, only remnants of his uniform still sticking to his bones. Each GI solemnly shook the skeleton hand as he passed it by.

There was less humor in the news that the Japanese had used some Australian soldiers for bayonet target-practice and left a crude sign beside their bodies saying. "It took them a long time to die."

And then there was this note in the captured diary of a Japanese soldier: "Because of the food shortage, some soldiers have been eating the flesh of Australian soldiers. The taste is said to be good."

The Australians had called the New Guinea war a "Q" war. "Q" meant quartermaster and the supply problem *was* critical. Reefs were so rough that you couldn't bring boats in too close. Unloading heavy ammo from a bobbing boat to a pitching canoe on a moonless night had its disadvantage, but not as much as being bombed and strafed during the day by the zooming Zero fighters.

Twenty Zeroes one day set four American supply ships afire. "Those damn planes threw cannons, machine guns, belly tanks, sukiyaki and everything else at us," a GI told Sgt. E. J. Kahn. "I would shoot one of those Zeroes if it was nursing a baby."

Swimming ashore after a strafing, Pvt. George Crisp of

Caro, Mich., found himself faced with the choice of releasing his rifle or his helmet. He kept his helmet. Later asked why, he pointed to a sizable dent in his helmet where a bullet had hit. How could he let it go, he said, "after it did this for me!"

Unloading was only the beginning. GI's from quartermaster then had to carry it up front. During one such trip Sgt. Owen Gascall found his supply squad facing a Japanese machine-gun nest. A bullet grazed Gascall's head and he motioned his squad to make a wide detour while he drew enemy fire to himself by tossing grenades. He turned to leave only when his squad was safely away. But Gascall never made it. The next bullet killed him.

The supplies were delivered.

But to deliver supplies, you also needed roads, bridges, airports; you needed engineers.

Everybody complained about the engineers. If there were no roads, it was their fault. If there were roads, then why were they so bumpy? If they weren't bumpy, why weren't they wider?

But the engineers were at Moresby before the foot soldiers, the engineers were there to get the airstrip ready for the first planes landing the first troops. And when there was a pillbox controlling some high ground, it was the engineers who squirmed up alongside it to blow it up. And when there was a rough stream that needed fording, it was the engineers who went in under fire to build the bridge. And when there was a scummy swamp that needed a rope or wire tied down on both sides for GI's to hang onto, it was the engineers who swam through that scum first.

GI's learned to love the engineers.

He was thirty-seven years old, a staff sergeant named Herman Bottcher, and he took advantage of his age and friendship to tell his younger officers, "If you guys would get off your goddam tails and start fighting maybe we'd get something done."

Finally, one night, Bottcher made his own move. He took a squad of thirteen men, slipped through to the sea between the Japanese positions. When morning came, here was Bottcher's Salient, deeply dug in on a tiny spit of land, flanked on both sides by Japanese, but facing both sides with a clear field of fire along the beach.

Before the first day was done, the beach was littered with the bodies of forty attacking Japanese. That night, there were many more. Bottcher even managed to creep out at night to destroy a persistent enemy machine-gun nest all by himself.

We somehow managed to resupply Bottcher with ammunition and food, while the enemy dead around them mounted to more than a hundred. One night, an admiring American general made it into their position and asked Bottcher's men if they wanted anything, anything at all.

One of the GI's turned a half-somersault in the sand, exposed his bare ass where the dampness had rotted away his trousers, and then said, excitedly, "Pants . . . for God's sake, General, pants!"

He got them.

Buna fell and the organized resistance in the Papuan Peninsula ended by January 23, 1943, but the Japanese decided to reinforce their bases in northeast New Guinea. In early March, they sent a convoy of destroyers to protect some 20,000 troops in sixteen transports. We sighted them and carefully planned a coordinated attack. It became known as the Battle of the Bismarck Sea but it was more of a slaughter than a battle. Not only did we blast them without bombers, but we sucked them into the range of our fighter-bombers and the results were devastating.

We had perfected a system of skip-bombing attack which used 500-pound bombs with a five-second delayed fuse. This permitted bombers to make low-level attacks with increased accuracy, and still get away before the bombs exploded. Within a half hour every Japanese troop transport had been hit at least once, and at least eight transports and four destroyers were sinking. There was no mercy for the 3,805 swimming enemy soldiers in the sea. The strafing was a massacre. In the same way, the Japanese fighter pilots had no compunction about shooting down any of our air crews forced to parachute out of a doomed plane. But we only lost four planes—they lost almost fifty.

Compared to the jungle below, air war was a clean war. But a plane can have its own concentrated share of hell: twenty Zeroes coming in on a Flying Fortress five at a time, their guns blazing; an explosive bullet hitting with the shearing force of an ax blade; and the sudden explosion of fire inside a plane.

It was only afterwards that radio operator Cpl. Dick

Hemphill of South Carolina could reminisce to Sgt. Don Harrison and say, "Hot lead whistled through our compartment like buckshot and reminded me of the time I got caught in a melon patch back home."

Hemphill was the first to sight the fighters and announced, "Zeroes ample, ack-ack limited."

And when gunner Pvt. Jimmie Wilson found two holes in his chest, it was Hemphill cradling his friend's head, giving him first aid and wiping away the red foam coming through Wilson's clenched teeth. Another gunner came to help and was told, "Get back to your station. We have only four guns working now."

Bullets were coming everywhere. Four control cables shot away, the left aileron damaged, the hydraulic system completely gone. Another bullet severed the cord on Bill Ritenour's neck microphone and another hit his canteen but he was still alive, still able to yell, "Head for the ceiling . . . we're on fire." A bullet had exploded into a box of ammunition. The pilot climbed into the clouds while the crew shoved the burning box out of the open bomb bay.

But they still didn't head home. They had their job to do. They returned to the target area, dropped bombs where they were supposed to drop them, and only then turned toward their base.

Somehow the plane landed intact, with or without brakes.

Four men injured, nobody killed, just another mission.

This New Guinea war would drag on for another year, our troops edging up the coast, capturing Lae in September 1943. After that, we leapfrogged some strong amphibious landings to seize the more strategic areas on the western end of this huge island, isolating large strongholds of Japanese troops.

At first the Japanese maintained their fierceness. A captured Japanese soldier might bite off his own tongue to prevent himself from revealing any military secrets. And there was the story of the wounded Japanese, being operated on in an American hospital, suddenly grabbing the scalpel from the surgeon's hand and stabbing him.

But, gradually, with their increased desperation came increased despair:

"Our troops do not come," a Japanese soldier wrote in his journal. "Even though they do come, they are driven away by enemy planes. Every day my comrades die one

328

by one and our provisions disappear. . . . All I can do is shed tears of resentment. Now we are waiting only for death . . . Comrades are you going to stand by and watch us die? Even the invincible Imperial Army is at a loss. Can't anything be done? Please, God."

Somebody called the war of New Guinea a war of mud, mountains, malaria, mosquitoes and monotony. All this was true. But while the war dragged here in the wet, weary months, it flared elsewhere.

The Aleutians

The Aleutian war was a waste. Strategists on both sides afterwards agreed on this. It served little purpose except to consume troops, planes and ships that were badly needed elsewhere in the Pacific.

Attu and Kiska were just two tiny, bleak, treeless, frozen islands far off the coast of Alaska and the Japanese occupied them in June 1942 strictly as a sideshow to the Battle of Midway. When they swarmed over Attu, they found a total population of 39 Aleuts plus an American missionary and his wife. When they invaded Kiska, the only Americans there were running a small weather station.

Patrolling the area was impossible. The fog was a white wall, thick and always. So clinging and everlasting was it that you seldom saw the end of your own ship. When two of our destroyers collided in the area, a third one came to help and rammed into both of them. The only time our destroyers got close enough to battle enemy destroyers, we fired five torpedoes and they fired forty-three—and all of them missed.

Pilots had trouble seeing their landing strips, much less their targets. We dropped four million pounds of bombs on those islands with minimal effect and our ships bombarded them repeatedly, with even less effect.

Pentagon strategists, however, felt that we needed to take these islands to clear the area for safer shipping to Russia—in case Russia ever came into the Pacific war. And, that's why, on May 11, 1943, we invaded Attu.

The Japanese had their guns and mortars set into steep

crags just above the fog line, forcing our GI's to fight a ghostly war, shooting at sounds instead of sights.

GI Rule Number One was that if you saw any soldiers on a cliff, they were Americans; but if you saw nothing, and only heard them, then they were Japanese.

Pvt. Raymond Witherstine, of Youngstown, O., was part of an attack up a ridge to give the Japanese "a red hot goose." But the fog lifted suddenly and there were the enemy, their guns aimed directly at them.

"They heard our noncoms yelling out orders," said Witherstine, "and plugged them first. It's lucky any of us got out alive. All of us didn't. Only way we could get the wounded back to the bottom was to cram them into their sleeping bags and slide them down through the snow."

The tundra made it tough to move anywhere. The tundra was a drippy layer of muck, often four feet deep. Tractors towed supplies on mud slides, pulleys and bucket brigades were used to pass up the ammo, hundred-foot ropes hoisted the 37-mm guns, signalmen climbed cliffs with 80-pound reels on their backs.

"First we are instructed how to behave as camels," said Pvt. Joe Resandes, "and now we are mastering the ways of the mountain goat."

For every plane shot down by the enemy we lost six to the weather. For every casualty from a bullet, we lost even more from the cold.

But the dead didn't stink.

"A body was as good as ever after thirty days," said Cpl. Edward Stratton of Nashville, "only it couldn't talk."

Trapped on a ridge near the harbor, the Japanese launched a screaming, suicide banzai charge, hundreds later killing themselves with their own hand grenades. We buried almost two thousand of them. We took only eleven prisoners.

The twenty-day campaign cost some 700 GI lives with twice as many wounded.

In one of the captured Japanese letters, it said, "Is war such a thing as this? Soon after firing ceases, birds are singing and flying around above the quiet and frozen ground."

We expected the same kind of fanatic resistance when we invaded nearby Kiska several months later. Before we moved our troops into Quisling Bay in the predawn hours, we subjected the island to a prolonged preliminary bombardment.

GI's had their midnight breakfast of grilled steak and

potatoes, camouflaged their faces a gray-green and listened to the ship chaplain say, "And now we commit ourselves, our bodies and our souls to Thy keeping."

But the landing was eerie quiet except for a short, sharp sound in the distance. Sgt. Clyde Patterson, an Alaskan fisherman, identified the sound as a fox bark. This is the season when the fox are whelping, he explained, and if there were any human beings around, "the fox would have killed their young."

The omen was good and Patterson was right. The Japanese had evacuated more than five thousand troops onto a sixteen-ship convoy within a single hour of a single night.

Souvenir hunters found three yellow dogs, coats with sea-otter collars, a Japanese edition of *Gone with the Wind*, several cases of whiskey, and the wreckage of an American P–40 fighter plane with this plaque in English alongside it:

SLEEPING HERE, A BRAVE HERO WHO HAS LOST YOUTH
AND HAPPINESS FOR HIS MOTHERLAND, JULY 25.

At Kiska Harbor, there was a bigger sign, boldly lettered: "WE SHALL COME AGAIN AND KILL OUT SEPARATELY YANKI-JOKER."

For the men in the Waiting War, there were few bullets fired in anger, and yet all of them were parts of the massive mosaic.

Pvt. Donald Parks, Cleveland, O., ran a banana boat bringing supplies to an antiaircraft unit on a remote island off Panama.

Cpl. Ed Plaut, Greenwich, Conn., helped run an Army radio station in Alaska.

Pvt. Alfred Eccles, Atlantic City, N.J., drove a truck on a regular run from Iran to Russia.

Sgt. Bill Rowe, a former milkman from Durham, N.C., taught Chinese soldiers the GI way of war.

And what about the GI engineer units cutting a road through the Himalaya Mountains from India to China?

The Waiting War had its own motion, its own need.

Australia

It was a "Dear John" letter in reverse, a girl from Nebraska complaining because her GI was deserting her for an Australian girl. "What has she got that I haven't got?" the American girl wanted to know.

"Nothing," wrote her former boy friend, "but she's got it here."

Almost all the arriving GI's had it made. They came here to a staging area, en route to where the war was, and the Aussies treated them like heroes. The beer was warm and the whiskey sweet, but the GI's drank the pubs dry. When invited to Australian homes for dinner, they brought butter and cigarettes, and they couldn't have been more welcome. The Red Cross had taken over the best hotels with the softest beds and you could get triple-decker sandwiches on toast and hamburgers and steaks.

But, best of all, the women were everywhere, and the women were willing. Fresh-looking, friendly, with marvelous legs, the Aussie girls found it perfectly normal for strange GI's to approach them on the street and ask for a date. When 600 Australian girls were invited to entertain 800 GI's at a local dance, more than 900 girls showed up.

In learning the lingo, however, a GI was slow to understand that when an Australian girl said she was "knocked up," it meant she was exhausted, not pregnant.

Not everybody had it so good, even in Australia. Some GI units were stationed near the desert towns, places like Oodnadatta and Alice Springs and Darwin. For GI's, Darwin was considered a disaster area, hot, dry and buggy. They sang this verse to the tune of "Red Sails in the Sunset":

> Red dust in your navel
> Red dust in your shirt
> See beautiful Darwin
> See beautiful dirt.

Or, as one GI put it:

"Listen, Buddy, here's how it is in Darwin. After a while, you find yourself talking to yourself. Then you find yourself talking to the lizards. Then you find the lizards talking to you. And pretty soon you find yourself listening."

But not for long. There was still lots of war left.

New Georgia

Halfway up the ladder of the Solomon Islands was the New Georgia group. We had two naval battles there that ended without any clear-cut victory. But Japanese air losses were heavy. During our invasion of Rendova, they attacked continuously on the landing area, and we shot down some 121 enemy planes. Within the next six weeks, the Japanese were to lose another 350 planes. Our own losses numbered about a hundred.

Some days it doesn't pay to get up in the morning.

Bill Coffeen was a staff sergeant, one of the few enlisted-men pilots in the Marines at the Guadalcanal air base.

His Corsair engine started smoking so badly that he had to jump somewhere over the Kolombangara area.

Landing in the water, he pulled the cord on his Mae West jacket. It had a hole on it.

He inflated his rubber raft. His paddle was missing.

He saw some friendly planes coming in close and waved at them. They didn't see him.

He finally reached a small island. It was uninhabited.

A mosquito bite infected his hand to twice its size. After he cut it open, he noticed that his right foot was also infected.

He hand-paddled to a bigger island, saw a house on it, crawled to it. It was deserted.

When he was finally found by a Melanesian native, he had paddled for thirty-two days, lost forty pounds, had malaria, a body covered with ulcers.

Finally returned to his base a month later, he found that his squadron had finished their first tour of duty, had a wild liberty in Australia.

One of his buddies smiled when he said, "We told the Aussie girls all about you."

Our main goal was Munda Airfield. It took five weeks of war to move five miles. So strict was the rule for utter silence, that when a mortar shell hit one of our foxholes at night, it wasn't until dawn that two GI's in that hole saw that the third soldier had his arm torn off at the elbow, and had bled to death—in silence.

A Japanese soldier could stand up in front of his hole, his shadow clear and obvious on a moonless night, and twenty GI's could see him plainly and not one of them would fire. Firing at him would reveal our positions, would result only in a quick hail of grenades.

Sgt. Lester Goldstein of Collinsville, Conn., had the same strict orders not to fire back at night. "We were curled up in our foxholes with a machete in one hand and a bayonet in the other. The first night . . . they killed three of our men. The second night we lost three or four men and on the third night we lost nine."

On the third night, though, some of the grenade-throwing Japanese crept too close to some of our foxholes and our GI's dragged them in and killed them quietly with the bayonets and the machetes.

And there was this kind of pleading at night from English-speaking Japanese:

"Aid, aid, doc . . . give aid to me . . . I am wounded . . ."

"Christ, he's got me in the guts! I'm stabbed! Water, water!"

"Buddy, are you there . . . please . . . please answer me . . ."

Or even more simply, a Japanese would say quietly, "Got a match?"

Answer them, and you were dead.

It was the kind of war where Platoon Sgt. Clarence Terry of Arco, Ida., borrowed empty plasma bottles from the medics and gasoline from the jeep drivers to make homemade Molotov cocktails to clear the enemy from a ridge called Hastings.

No wonder it took five weeks to go five miles.

First Sgt. Orville (Pappy) Cummins of Spokane, Wash., described to *Yank* correspondent Mack Morriss the results of some mortar fire on a Japanese gun position during a day's action. He told how the Japanese soldier "went forty feet in the air, over the tops of the trees, just floated up lazylike, turned over one time and came back down. Then there was another that went up like a pinwheel, all arms and legs twisting in the air. He was an officer, I think, because I saw a saber go one way and a pistol the other." There was still another soldier, he said, "blown plumb out of his pants. We found the breeches hanging way up the limb of a tree."

We had our own casualties.

"I'm hit," said a GI to his buddy. Then, as he fell forward, he said, "I'm dead."

He was.

New Georgia was cleared, but at a high cost. Next stop was Bougainville.

"What time is it?" asked one GI, during a firing interval.

"Who cares," answered another. "It's my birthday."

"Happy birthday."

Bougainville

Mud and muck, that was Bougainville. No lovely beaches, no coconut groves. But it was the last Japanese-held stronghold in the northern Solomon Islands. We had no plan to clear the 130-mile-long island of its 60,000 enemy troops; we wanted only to operate three airfields in the Empress Augusta Bay area, and protect its perimeter. If we did, we would push closer toward closing the pincers on the giant air-sea-troop base of Rabaul, only 210 miles away.

The Japanese knew this, too.

When some 14,000 Marines landed in November 1943 in this Empress Bay area, the communiqué described the beaches as "lightly defended." But a Marine combat correspondent, who was there, called the fighting "savage, close, primitive."

The weather was the worst, one of the wettest places in the world. A GI described it in a letter home: "Bougainville, November 1, 2, 3, 4, 5, 6, 7, 8, 9—it rained today."

Once off the beaches into the jungle, visibility was often only five yards. Our heavy artillery felt forced to fire as close as twenty-five yards in front of our own lines. "They dig in while you're shooting at them," said one GI. "If they get three shovelfuls out, you can't hit them."

The Japanese had to cross through that dense rain forest and mountains and jungle to get their main force against us, and it took them more than two months. By that time, we had not only built our airfields, but we had strengthened a defense perimeter around them about ten miles long and five miles deep. We now had a hundred planes to beat back their bombers, defend our front, and start hitting Rabaul more regularly. We had PT boats to dart at their barges of reinforcements that crept around the coast at night. Our Navy beat back their Navy in two bitter battles, so they couldn't come in and shell our invasion area. And our Army reinforced our Marines.

"Our battalion was very very lucky," said Cpl. Joseph Bennett. "We had this flat land in front of us. It was a little jungly, but not too bad. Some of the other outfits faced hills or swamps or real jungle, but we could see anything that came at us.

"Well, we had all been on patrols, including me, and we found Japanese or traces of them all over the place. We knew they were coming and we were ready for them. We had reinforced our foxholes with logs and zeroed in the machine guns and set up the mortars.

"I was an instrument corporal in an 81-mm mortar platoon. It was my job to keep track of all the mortar fire for six mortars. Somebody would say 'Target Six' and I would pick up the phone and say 'Section Two' and tell them where we wanted them to lay down the fire, and they would do it. You had to be fast and you had to be right."

The Japanese planned a massed attack on March 9. Because of the distance and the weight, the heaviest artillery they brought with them were the 75-mms. Not only did we have heavy concentrations of big guns surrounding the edge of the airfield, but we also had the directed fire of a half dozen destroyers parked in the Bay.

To pinpoint all this vital fire, we needed a tiny thumb of earth sticking high above the jungle overlooking everything. But it was some five hundred yards in front of our lines, and there were no trails, and the climb was tortuous. The Japanese used it during the day to direct their fire on us, then retired at night over the edge of the ridge to escape our counterfire and get some sleep.

We sent 51 men to try to make it up there, and they did. They moved in while the Japanese were out. Because of the rough climb, they had minimum supplies, three grenades apiece, no food, and only eleven belts of machine-gun ammo. In the valley in front of them were several thousand Japanese.

The Japanese didn't know we were there and they would soon return and Sgt. Richard Murphy and Sgt. Slim Tierney each set up a machine gun facing one of the two trails. With such little ammunition, each bullet had to hit. The morning heat was a hundred degrees, but it seemed even hotter. And then they came, in small, surprised groups, and we cut them down in brief bursts. Our artillery fire came in close support, almost too close. A single shell falling short could have wiped out our whole position. But we held, radioed back for more men, ammo, food, and more came, along with three mortars.

We had men at the rim flanking the hill and they were the first casualties. Pfc. Jacob Solomon went down into the heavy fire to bring back Pfc. Charles Skinner of Franklin, O., a BAR man. "I found this guy firing even after they got him," said Solomon. Skinner was bloody, glassy-eyed, but alive. One of the bullets had gone up the back of his helmet, made a circle around the scalp before it fell out. There was still another soldier who had been hit, and Solomon went back through the open fire to bring him back, too. He was weak from loss of blood, but he kept saying, "I'm O.K., I'm O.K."

Thanks to them, so were we.

That thumb of earth was a prize without price.

They came down in wave after wave from the southeast slope of "Bloody Hill," thousands of them attacking frontally, climbing over their own dead as we shot them down. Our naval guns swept the front up and back and sideways and made big gaps in their lines, but they kept coming. So desperate was the fanaticism of their banzai, that a Japanese soldier even charged an American tank with a bayonet. And, all the time, they kept yelling.

"For God's sake, shut up!" complained a BAR man, yelling back at them. "Us bastards are mad enough already!"

And there was a Japanese soldier who jumped into a foxhole, yelling in perfect English, "I'm too young to die!"

"So am I," said the GI, as he killed him with his knife.

They made two other banzai attacks that same week, and then it was over. We counted almost 6,000 dead in front of a single hill. Their broken remnants returned through the spine of mountains and jungle from where they came, and we let them sit and starve while the war moved on.

Here's how quickly a front became rear echelon:

By the fifth week after the invasion, 3,500 soldiers were seeing movies as often as three times a week.

Within five weeks, the Engineers had cut ten miles of "improved" highway into the jungle, plus one hundred and thirty miles more of jeep trails. They had also built five bridges, making their own two-foot-long bridge nails out of artillery cases. For wood, they built their own sawmill which they called "Thick and Thin Lumber Company." Next priority after bridges were latrines and mess halls.

Within six weeks, the Signal Corps had laid 5,000 miles of wire. S/Sgt. Jim Smith of Cleveland Heights, O., even had a French phone to call his men.

Dentists were filling and pulling teeth within two weeks after the Army landed. Within that same period, the Postal Service was delivering mail regularly from home.

Private GI improvements included a coconut tree felled across a stream and notched at the middle to make a washboard; the huge roots of the banyan tree converted into an air-raid shelter and dining rooms for private beer parties; and everybody seemed to have a pet wombat— wombats are the size of dogs, furry like a bear, with a kangaroo pouch.

Because of heat, men wore almost no clothes. The only woman anybody saw in the area was nude—tattooed, on the chest of Pvt. Albert Herron, once a Toledo, O., cab-driver.

There was nothing anybody could do about the air raids, often as many as six a night during the early weeks. But as one GI said, "War is bad enough without being any more uncomfortable than necessary."

Tarawa

Take a square mile of coral reef. Crisscross it completely with some 500 pillboxes so set up that when you push past one pillbox, you move directly into the cross fire of two inner ones. On each pillbox, pile layers of armor plate, palm-tree trunks eighteen inches deep, five feet of concrete, plus added layers of coral, railroad steel, sand. Strew area liberally with barbed wire, mines, booby traps. Garrison all gun emplacements with 4,800 picked Japanese troops, half of them Imperial Marines. Zero in all guns at all possible landing beaches.

That was Tarawa.

That was why a Japanese admiral boasted that Americans could not conquer Tarawa "with a million men in a hundred years."

We had a simple way to tell the exact Japanese troop strength on Tarawa. An aerial photograph revealed the number of latrines throughout the lagoon which the Japanese built out over the water. Knowing the Japanese Army regulation of building a latrine for a specific number of soldiers, it all became a matter of easy arithmetic. The Japanese are a very precise people.

To a degree, the strength of Tarawa was our own fault. We had sent in a battalion of Marines early in August 1942 to make a hit-and-run raid on nearby Makin atoll. All they did was to destroy a radio station. Before that raid, all the Gilbert Islands, including Makin and Tarawa, had very few Japanese troops. But, after that raid, the Japanese reinforced the whole area with considerable strength.

An invasion is a measured thing.

An attack cargo ship carried:

Twenty-four days' B rations for the entire force; approximately 3,000 five-gallon cans of water; sufficient gasoline for 8 days' operation for all motor vehicles; approximately 18,750 gallons of white gasoline; over 70,000 gallons of diesel oil; 28,200 gallons of high-octane gasoline for the amphibian tractors; 7,684 gallons of motor oil; 3,655 pounds of grease; 5 units of fire for all weapons on board; 5 units of fire for one battery of 105-mm howitzers; 4 units of fire for the weapons of the medium tanks; 4 units of fire for the two 30-caliber and one 50-caliber machine guns on each of the amphibian tractors carried aboard the 3 LST's; slightly more than 30 days of medical supplies; 30 days of maintenance for all items in ordnance; about one and a half tons of chemical-warfare supplies; approximately 30 days' quartermaster's supplies for the entire force; 30 days' signal supplies; and 30 days' engineer maintenance for an engineer combat battalion; and 20 days' maintenance requirements for an infantry division, less the combat battalion.

Average weight of supplies per soldier on board the three attack troopships—1,322 pounds. This included 1,600 half-pints of ice cream that were supposed to be sent ashore after the battle was over—on the first day.

The fifteen islands of the Gilberts had the strategic importance of serving as a protective screen at the entrance of the central Pacific, the main islands of this group were Makin, Apamama and Tarawa. Through the central Pacific we could cut off Japan from her overseas empire. Winning the Gilberts would not drastically change the way of the war except that it would put our planes within closer striking distance of the vital Marshall Islands, so much nearer Japan. We already had moved 2,100 miles southwest of Pearl Harbor.

First we hit Makin, about a hundred miles from Tarawa.

We expected no trouble from Makin. Since there were so few troops and fewer defenses, our preliminary naval bombardment had done its greatest damage to coconut trees and native huts and a few dummy-gun positions. But the Japanese had cached guns and water gourds and even sake in the top fronds of certain trees, which they had carefully marked with notches cut for easier climbing. The sniping caused too many trigger-happy soldiers to fire at too many tops of too many trees, and it slowed our movement.

First Sgt. Thomas Valentine remembered that the snipers were more of a nuisance than an obstacle, and that the casualties were relatively few. "We learned that by taking careful cover, and moving rapidly from one concealment to another, we could minimize the sniper threat." Besides, Valentine added, "we knew our reserves would get them, if we didn't."

But before the general could tell the admiral, "Makin taken," we still had a couple of hundred casualties. We had outnumbered the enemy 25 to 1, but for every three of the enemy killed, two Americans were either killed or wounded.

Navy critics later said the cost of Makin was too high and the speed "infuriatingly slow." In the Makin harbor, the Navy lost an escort carrier with more than 600 men aboard. Had Makin been taken earlier, they said, that ship would not have been there.

But the detractors of the Makin campaign were reminded, "When the Marines land and meet the enemy at bayonet point, the only armor a Marine will have is his khaki shirt."

Everybody knew Tarawa would be tougher.

Shaped like an upside-down bird, Betio was the most strongly defended islet in the Tarawa atoll because it had an airfield.

To neutralize the Betio beaches, an admiral planned two-and-a-half hours of preliminary bombardment, and said, "We do not intend to neutralize it, we do not intend to destroy it. Gentlemen, we will obliterate it."

But we had much to learn. Tarawa, in November 1943, was our first major amphibious invasion of a heavily defended atoll. With the possible exception of Iwo Jima, Tarawa's beaches were the best protected.

Our planes blasted it with 800 tons of bombs.

Our Navy threw in more than 3,000 tons of shells.

Our Navy fighter planes came in with full fire support, flying only sixty feet above the water.

Our destroyers acted as artillery, coming within seven hundred yards of the beaches.

"It seemed almost impossible for any human being to be alive on Betio," an admiral said.

But they were very much alive, only waiting for us to come close enough.

They waited until the clumsy-looking but maneuverable amtracks (amphibious tractors) started arriving at the reefs with the first wave of Marines. Suddenly everywhere amtracks were burning, blowing up, sinking. Pfc. Donald Libby was hit in both thighs, then hurled out of his amtrack by a mortar shell which killed almost everybody else. He had seven shrapnel wounds, bleeding heavily, when he spotted a life preserver and hung onto it. The battle shore was full of clanging and screaming and he could hear it vaguely as he barely kept himself afloat. Hours later he felt the tide going out and he saw somebody wading out toward him wearing a Marine helmet and carrying a bayonet.

"What state are you from?" the voice asked Libby.

"Maine," he said, and he stood up in the water, "and where are you from?"

The man from Japan answered by lunging at Libby with his bayonet. Libby put up his left hand and the bayonet went through it. Libby then grabbed the bayonet blade with his right hand, wrenched it away, swung at the Japanese soldier with the hilt and hit him behind the ear, then hit him again on the forehead as he fell in the water. Libby then held the soldier's head under the water until he drowned.

More hours later, another amtrack found Libby floating in his preserver, still bleeding, looking shriveled but still alive.

Before that D-Day was done, we had sent in some 5,000 Marines and more than a thousand were dead, twice as many more wounded and the rest pinned down on the beaches.

On Red Beach One, our heavy tanks were ready to come in and the platoon leader had a quick decision to make. No matter where he brought in his tanks, he would have to ride over the dead and wounded bodies of our Marines who littered the beach. He wouldn't do it. He ordered his waterproofed tanks to go back in the water, back around the right flank of the beach from which he then hoped to move inland. In doing this, four tanks were drowned in the potholes in the reef, and the two which made it ashore were quickly knocked out by waiting guns.

Our reinforcements kept coming continuously all afternoon. The Higgins boats couldn't climb the reefs like the amtracks and the men had to wade the last half mile to shore, dead-duck targets for all the enemy guns.

A bullet hit Pfc. Richard Lund in the right chest, came out his right arm. It spun him, dropped him. He picked himself out of the water, kept walking in, still carrying his radio.

On the beach, a young Marine, his chest ripped open, cried out for a cigarette.

"I'll light one for you," said another Marine.

"No time," said the gasping, dying soldier. "Gimme yours."

The lit cigarette put in his mouth, the young Marine inhaled once, the smoke coming out of his open chest—and then he died.

Report of the first day: "The issue is in doubt."

Second day report: "Casualties many; percentage dead unknown; combat efficiency: we are winning."

Some of that efficiency came from men like Pfc. Adrian Strange, a blond, almost beardless Marine from Knox City, Tex., who walked into a Command Post saying, "Somebody gimme a pack of cigarettes. There's a machine-gun crew out there in a shell hole and there ain't one of 'em's got a butt." Then, as he lit one for himself, he said, "I just got me another sniper. That's six today and me a cripple. Busted my ankle stepping into a shell hole yesterday."

The bullets started coming in more thickly all around him. Strange simply turned and yelled at the enemy gunners, "Shoot me down, you sonofabitch." And then he limped away to deliver the cigarettes.

We started winning only by clearing out pillbox after pillbox after pillbox, using tanks as attacking screens, using bulldozers to heap sand against exits and gun openings, pouring gasoline and grenades down air vents.

On the third day, our situation rapidly improved and the Japanese radio sent out its last message: "Our weapons have been destroyed and from now on everyone is attempting a final charge. May Japan exist for ten thousand years."

We cut their attack to pieces that night.

Of the Japanese garrison of 4,800, only seventeen surrendered. The rest were killed, or killed themselves.

Some had committed suicide by cutting their throats. Those who had no knives would bump their heads against some wreckage. Those who couldn't hit their heads hard

343

enough, tried to dive and drown. "They would come to the surface, gasp a little bit, try to save themselves instinctively, then realize that they didn't want to be saved and dive down again. Sometimes it took a man four or five dives before he could commit suicide in that way."

Our own casualties: more than a thousand dead, more than twice as many wounded.

We used bulldozers to bury the dead, theirs and ours. The 'dozers scooped out trenches only three feet deep because the sand was so soggy that you hit water when you went four feet deep. They were laid out in rows without blankets.

"What a hell of a way to die," said a correspondent staring at the mangled bodies.

A Marine rifleman just looked at him and said quietly "You can't pick a better way."

They later found one body on an isolated part of the beach, broiled from the sun, gaping wounds all over him a muzzle pointed at his throat. He had tried to kill himself but he hadn't the strength to pull the trigger. When they told him he was safe he could only say, "Water—pour water on me!"

The whole horror lasted seventy-six hours. Some six years later, the Marine general who was there was asked if it was worth it.

He said no.

"Tarawa had no particular strategic importance," he said. "Tarawa should have been bypassed. Its capture was a terrible waste of life and effort."

Other strategists disagreed. Capture of the key Gilberts made it possible to use land-based planes against the Marshall Islands which enabled us to hit them with shorter flights and heavier loads and photograph them thoroughly for the future invasion.

Even more than that, Tarawa was our testing ground that made all succeeding invasions so much less expensive.

We learned lessons: the need for longer, slower naval bombardment against observable targets; the need for continued help from the big guns of the destroyers even after the landing; the need for putting heavy artillery on adjoining islands to help in early fire support; and the vital need for more and more amphibian tractors.

The war was different on the third atoll in the Gilberts, Apamama. Our Marines walked in without worry and the bare-breasted native girls greeted them, singing in English, "Brighten the corner where you are . . ."

New Britain

Our continual air bombardment of Rabaul had flattened most of the huge harbor, driven its installations underground, destroyed much of its air power. Thanks to our new airfields in Bougainville and New Guinea, we shot down at least 230 planes over Rabaul during that month of December. Our own losses were remarkably small.

> *If the engine conks out now*
> *We'll come down from forty thou'*
> *And wind up in a rowboat at Rabaul.*

Despite this pounding, Rabaul maintained its impregnability as a fortress area in northeastern New Britain; and we still needed to neutralize it. To do this, we invaded New Britain in the Cape Gloucester area, in the northwestern part of the island, just before Christmas of 1943. Again, all we wanted of this 250-mile-long island was an area large enough for some protected airfields to complete the air ring around Rabaul. Then, and only then would Rabaul empty its airfields, and then and only then would Rabaul die.

Our landings at the Cape looked like the best possible Christmas present—they were virtually unopposed. That's because the Japanese never expected anybody to invade such a swampy jungle area.

One regimental sector map was marked "Damp Flat."
"It's damp, all right," a Marine complained. "It's damp clear up to your ass!"

The swamps had rotted the forest and the giant trees were called "widow-makers." The first Marine invasion casualty was caused by a falling tree, and there would be nineteen others smashed to death that way in the next six weeks.

We cleared the Cape within a week, captured the Japa-

nese airfield, then moved deeper into the jungle to protec
the perimeter against counterattack.

And, suddenly, it stopped being so easy.

How did we know it wasn't just a creek?

It was only a few feet deep with a rocky bottom, maybe
twenty feet wide at its widest and it had a twisting way
through the steep banks of the jungle. Our scouts crossed
it, and the area looked clear and our foot soldiers followed. Then everything exploded and the jungle was littered with our dead and wounded.

Cpl. Lawrence Oliveria, Fall River, Mass., saw a
blinded Marine trying to crawl away. "The boy didn't
moan or pray or nothing," said Oliveria. "He just kept
saying, 'I can't see, I can't see. . . .' " But he would wait
uncomplainingly near Oliveria who would pull him back a
few feet at a time, back toward the creek.

Pfc. Charles Conger, hit badly in both legs, had to drag
himself by inches, head first, then belly, down the bank,
tumbling into the water through the thick of bullets. Two
Marines, who already swam across to safety, came back to
get him.

Platoon Sgt. John White saw a friend of his get it. "You
could hear the bullet hit him in the stomach," said White.
"He just stook there a minute. He said, 'Them dirty bastards!' Then he fell down. He was dead." White also saw
another guy he knew. "He didn't have his head. He just
had a neck with dog tags on it."

We spent several days probing different sides of that
creek for weak spots, but there were none. The Japanese
were deeply dug into fortified positions all along the other
side, completely camouflaged, so that we seldom even saw
a Japanese soldier. Every time we crossed, we were always
forced back with heavy losses.

"It don't do any good," said a young rifleman to Platoon Sgt. Casimir Polakowski.

"What the hell are you beefing about?" said the sergeant. "You get paid for it, don't you?"

The young rifleman grinned, went back to his gun.

Before we finally cleared the creek, we gave it a new
name—"Suicide Creek."

It soon became suicide for the enemy too. We brought
346

up some tanks on some dry ground to outflank them. Later, on the dead body of a Japanese soldier, we found a letter that read, "Now we are waiting only for death."

Aogiri Ridge, Sweet Cookie Hill, Hill 660—it all took six weeks to clear. The wetness made clothes moldy, swelled pencils, decomposed cartridge belts, turned food into slop. Every day you had to check the grenade pins for rust, and the only way you could keep matches dry was to seal them inside a contraceptive—which had no other purpose there anyway.

The Sixth Army moved in on the southern shore of New Britain.

Diverted by a small group of commando-trained troops in rubber boats coming in at nearby Umlingolu, the Japanese let the main American force come in unopposed elsewhere on Arawe. The Umlingolu reception was so hot that S/Sgt. Bill Hughes of Grand Prairie, Tex., said, "Anyone who got out of that—God was on his side."

But the unopposed main force fanned out quickly, took over the air base, cleared the area in five days, dug their defenses in depth. Our P-38 fighter planes came in constantly to provide air cover against frequent enemy bombers.

"When I get out of here," said Sgt. Oakley Askers of Dallas, Tex., "I'm going to kiss the first P-38 I find."

Other landings at Green Island, the Admiralties, New Ireland and the drive farther up the New Guinea coast left Rabaul at long last isolated, its 50,000 troops left there for the rest of the war with nowhere to go and no way to get there. Then the last hundred planes left the Rabaul airports for Truk. Then, Rabaul was dead.

PT boats

They lived in jungle creeks and the Japanese called them "cat-eyed devils" while our own admirals more affectionately referred to them as our "spitkit navy" or our "splinter fleet."

From the air, they looked like water wasps, the same

347

darting speed, the same sudden energy. If they had a slogan, it should have been: "Give me a fast ship, for I intend to go in harm's way."

PT technically meant, "Patrol, torpedo." These PT boats, or "Petes," were only seventy-seven feet long, plywood eggshells without any armor but many said they carried the hardest punch per ton of any ship in any navy. Four torpedoes, five machine guns, rockets, mines, depth charges, two officers and nine men.

> *Oh, some PT's do forty-five*
> *And some do thirty-nine;*
> *When we get ours to run at all,*
> *We think we're doing fine.*

In the early days, sailors on bigger ships called PT boats "tinker toys." The Japanese had the Tokyo Express, they said, "and we got the Toonerville Trolley."

Compared to the formal names and numbers of the bigger ships, PT boats had such sprightly ones as *Cock of the Walk, Malaria* and *Ball of Fire.* Compared to the rigid discipline and red tape of the bigger ships, a PT-boat base had no typewriters, and both officers and enlisted men worked without shirts and with the feeling of a small family.

Their main mission early in the war was to cut off the Japanese stream of supplies and reinforcements to their advanced forces. This meant night war close to uncharted reefs against bigger armed power barges. They operated with radar and one Japanese diary said of them, "They seem to have excellent night binoculars." On a single night, two PT boats sank ten of these barges and silenced a shore battery. Tactic of the barges was to hug the reefs, suck in the PT boats closer to shore within range of their bigger shore guns.

PT boats moved with a power and a grace, their lifted prows cutting huge waves, the thick wake of white behind them. "One hit in the right place might blow our thin mahogany hull to smithereens," said Machinist Mate First Class John Burg. So they raced in, hit hard, raked the enemy from stern, beam and stem, from every angle, raced away, in and out, again and again, until they sank their barges.

348

On a typical night mission, passenger-soldier Sgt. Dave Richardson remembered the yell at 4:30 A.M. from Louis Schaff, Quartermaster Third Class, of Pekin, Ill.: "Barge two points off the port bow!"

Before the dawn came, they shot up and sank three barges, two of them 70-footers and armor-plated. They had boarded one of the big ones, but there was little time to look. Came the first light, and the shore batteries would spot them and enemy planes would chase them. So back they sped to the peace of their hidden creek to wait for the next night, and the next night.

Before the war's end, PT boats acted as a cordon thrown across the Surigao Strait to locate the approaching Japanese naval force; landed recon units behind enemy lines; attacked everything from submarines to a battleship, and sometimes sank them; rescued General Douglas MacArthur from the Philippines; delivered mail and evacuated wounded; and two of them even held their own against 30 enemy planes who dropped 40 bombs on their area in a forty-minute fight before friendly air-help arrived.

In a three-month period, PT's sank 147 barges near northern New Guinea, forcing the Japanese to send more of their supplies by submarine.

But they were small and they were expendable.

The Japanese destroyer saw the PT boat and swerved on it, slicing it in half, and the water soon flamed from the exploding high-octane gas. One of the survivors, Machinist Mate Patrick McMahon, was burned badly on his face, hands and arms. Another survivor later said of him, "You could see that he was suffering such pain that his lips twitched . . . You'd watch him and think, if you were in his place, you'd probably be yelling, 'Why doesn't somebody do something?' But every time you asked Mac how he was doing, he'd wrinkle his face and give you a grin."

McMahon's skipper—everybody called him "Shafty"—had been on the college swimming team, and managed to tow him for three hours to a small island. The other survivors had come in on an improvised raft. But only McMahon would be able to say that his life had been saved by the President of the United States.

The Marshalls

SHORE: "Come in please."

SHIP: "Go ahead."

SHORE: "At present time I cannot give you the front lines but will do so as soon as possible. I have no targets for you but you may fire at targets of opportunity that you can see in Zone T."

SHIP: "Roger. We have a possible blockhouse in Zone T and will fire a few salvos at it."

SHORE: "Are you firing now?"

SHIP: "Affirmative. We are firing at possible blockhouse in Zone T."

SHORE: "I would now like to fire on a real blockhouse in Square 105. I will give you coordinates on this point. Fire at emplacement 486474 in Square 105. I will adjust fire."

SHIP: "Firing ship ready."

SHORE: "Commence firing."

SHIP: "Wilco."

   (SALVO, SALVO)

SHORE: "No change in elevation. Left 200."

   (SALVO, SALVO)

SHIP: "No change. No change. Rapid fire. Three salvos."

  (SALVO, SALVO, SALVO)

SHORE: "Down 25. No change. Three salvos."

  (SALVO, SALVO, SALVO)

SHORE: "Cease firing. Target neutralized. Good shooting."

SHIP: "Wilco."

One of the recon pilots who helped direct fire whistled loudly over the intercom and said, "Hot damn, I'm glad I'm on your side."

"If you took twenty necklaces of different lengths," wrote Samuel Eliot Morison, "composed of beads of different shapes and sizes, threw them into the bottom of a tank and let in just enough water to cover the smaller beads, you would have a fair chart of the Marshalls."

They stretched out some 650 miles with 36 true atolls containing some 2,000 islands and islets, all of them blocking the way to Japan. The ones we wanted most here were Kwajalein and Eniwetok.

Kwajalein was the world's biggest atoll, a hundred islands and islets scattered over an area sixty-six miles long and eighteen miles wide. Deep inside that atoll, the crescent-shaped island of Kwajalein was less than three miles long and only eight hundred yards wide. It served as a communications and replacement headquarters, and the Japanese considered it so rear-echelon that they never dreamed we would invade it.

Our paper plan called for landings on thirty islets, mostly for reconnaissance purpose, with three full-scale landings.

It was the kind of naval embarrassment that only a few isolated historians might remember.

We landed a small recon outfit to occupy a tiny islet called Gea, sitting at the mouth of the Kwajalein lagoon. In the darkness before dawn, the loaded rubber boats moved against the reefs without opposition. Ashore, the GI's fought a small single skirmish. The result: four dead enemy and two prisoners. Somebody found the tallest palm tree and climbed up to fly the American flag.

But then, suddenly, their ship sent an urgent message telling all troops to return immediately. It seems somebody had made a mistake. They had captured the wrong island. The islet they wanted was Gehh and not Gea.

Back on their converted destroyer, before going into the right island, the GI's had a shave, shower and a hot meal. "It was a gentlemanly way to fight a war," said the squad leader, Sgt. Chester Chagnon, Burlington, Vt. But it *was* embarrassing.

We then made larger landings against Roi and Namur, twin islands connected by a causeway. Our bombardment left the Roi airfield littered with the skeletons of some seventy planes. A thousand-pound bomb had blasted a shelter killing every senior officer on the island, leaving the Japanese soldiers literally leaderless. Some hid in the huge drainage system under the airfield, and had to be forced out by flamethrowers. The rest raced over the causeway to Namur. Our troops landed at noon, in the middle of a squall, and by evening the island was ours.

Namur took another day. Meanwhile the bombardment of nearby Kwajalein continued and we had landed heavy artillery on an adjoining island called Ennebuj.

351

When their big guns were cool, they were cooks and clerks and truck drivers; but when their guns were working, all of them were ammunition handlers, sweating all through the day and night, with only short rest periods. The big guns almost never stopped firing and their CO said, "The men can stand it more than the guns." We even had the wind on our side for this one, a strong wind sweeping away the smoke and cooling the crews. But the CO was right about the guns. The tube of a 155-mm got so hot that it burst, a large piece of it hurling four hundred yards in the air, killing four GI's and wounding thirteen others.

But nobody knew better than the artillery that their cost was small, their price was right.

Before the bombardment, Kinichi Ijiya had written in his diary, "Since landing on this island . . . most of my time has been spent digging ditches." But the ditches were not deep enough. Besides the artillery, and the 15,000 tons of shells from fifty warships, our big bombers had also joined in on the three-day preliminary bombardment.

"The entire island looked as if it had been picked up at twenty thousand feet and dropped," said a naval observer.

So complete was our preliminary destruction that our combat engineers found little to do, only a few beach obstacles left to destroy.

The whole invasion seemed story-book perfect. Our eighty-four amtracks loaded with troops arrived on the beaches in almost synchronized formation. In the twelve minutes after H-hour on that February morning, we landed some 1,200 GI's without a single casualty.

Our shells had so defoliated the trees that there was no hiding place for snipers. Not a single enemy plane appeared. By the end of the first day, both invasion beaches had been cleared of explosives, the shell holes filled and smoothed, a graded beach road linked to the main road that ringed the island, and even the supply setup fully organized.

We advanced over one-fourth of the island on that first day.

The official communiqué described our progress as "methodical and unspectacular."

But how unspectacular is it when you fire all night from your hole and the next morning find bullets through your helmet, field glasses and canteen?

How unspectacular is it when you see a blockhouse explode, killing and wounding a hundred men and throwing a GI a hundred and fifty feet out into the lagoon—where somebody fishes him out, still alive?

How unspectacular is it when you see a Japanese soldier race up to one of our tanks, hold a grenade against the tank wall until it explodes—not hurting the tank, but blowing off his arm?

How unspectacular is it for two platoons to find themselves attacking different entrances of the same blockhouse, each not knowing about the other, with the Japanese suddenly rushing out of both doors throwing everybody in complete confusion?

And how unspectacular is it for Pfc. Paul Roper and Pvt. Parvée Rasberry in a routine attack of a routine pillbox? Lob in grenades without effect, fire flamethrowers and watch the flames bounce off, finally crawl right up to the pillbox and drop in a white phosphorus smoke grenade through the gun slit. That drives out some of the soldiers, and you kill some. But the rest run back in again, and you have to repeat the whole scene all over again and again, until you run out of phosphorus grenades, until you kill all of them. Just to make sure, somebody creeps up to the top of the pillbox, empties an M-1 rifle into the opening. And just to make doubly sure, you call up a tank to fire its flamethrower directly into the pillbox slits. Unspectacular? It depends who writes the communiqué.

Radio Tokyo announcer with the Oxford accent said how sad he felt for his American friends because the Japanese troops in the Marshalls had shot down all the attacking planes and sunk most of the invading ships. For the Japanese troops on Kwajalein, this seemed like sick humor. The only planes they saw were ours, and our undisturbed ships in the harbor had maintained a support fire that never seemed to stop. And the sickening stink on the island, was the stink of their dead, not ours.

One of the few Japanese prisoners said that his superiors had told him that Americans would cut off his ears if they caught him. It explained some of the fanaticism of the Japanese soldier who yelled, "Come and get me, you sonofabitch souvenir hunters."

And so we did.

We caught seventy Japanese in a tank trap, killed all of them.

"When you get past ten, you lose count and lose interest," said BAR man PFC. James Carrigan of San Saba, Tex., who had killed a dozen that day. Before it was over we would kill 7,870 of their 8,675 soldiers on the island.

There was little of the island left to take by the third day. Smoothest coordination came from tanks and troops. In earlier invasions, a GI had to bang his rifle on a tank to try to persuade the tank commander to open up and listen. In the heat of a war action, tank commanders were highly reluctant to open up because they never knew what they would find. But we had now put in phones in metal boxes in the rear of each tank.

Sgt. Melvin Huggins saw this deserted enemy machine gun, almost moved up to it until he saw a ditch just behind it. It was camouflaged just enough to make him suspicious. So he moved back to the nearest tank, picked up the tank telephone, told them to rumble over and check the ditch. The hunch was good. The ditch was alive with the enemy who were using the machine gun as bait to tempt, and kill, the curious GI's. The tank quickly flushed them out, cut them down.

The telephone is a wonderful invention.

By the fourth day it was all over on Kwajalein. But the bitter GI subject of the day was that a 37-mm antitank gun had been ordered to fire and destroy a building, which it did. Only afterwards did everybody find out that this building housed most of the Japanese beer, sake and candy.

But the GI's soon found other pleasures. Some went swimming in the surf—wearing shoes because of the sharp coral. A few found salvageable Japanese bicycles they could ride. T/5 Robert Fuller of Kansas City repaired a shot-up truck, gave his friends free rides. The first barrack bags started arriving, and the GI search was on. And somebody even noticed that hundreds of white tropical birds had started to return to the defoliated trees.

The joys however were few and there was this crudely printed sign:

HOTEL ATOLL
No beer Atoll
No women Atoll
Nuthin' Atoll

354

The island was still full of bodies to bury and a GI expressed the general feeling when he said, "Everybody hopes the next island will smell better."

Next stop was Eniwetok, 330 miles and two weeks away.

Its invasion wasn't timetabled for another three months, but the quick Kwajalein success was unexpected, and we had all the uncommitted reserves ready to go.

To confuse the enemy, we made a diversionary attack on Truk, a thousand miles from Kwajalein. The Pentagon regarded Truk as "The Japanese Pearl Harbor," "The Gibraltar of the Pacific," the best fleet anchorage in all the Japanese-held islands, an impregnable position garrisoned by some 50,000 soldiers and hundreds of planes.

"I heard many radio broadcasts from the United States describing Truk as an impregnable bastion," said the Truk commander afterwards. "We could not help but laugh at this, knowing how weak we really were. I had the South Sea blues for fear that you would find out the truth."

We soon found out. We sent in Task Force 58 on a two-day raid, with a core of three aircraft carriers. Our carrier planes destroyed 340 enemy planes in the air and on the ground, sunk 32 ships including two cruisers, four destroyers and 200,000 tons of shipping. Our own loss was less than two dozen planes. The fearful Truk bomb turned out to be a bubble.

"This is the easiest yet," said Pfc. Albert Lee of Los Angeles, who had made three previous invasions. And Sgt. Matt Toper of New York City felt so safe and comfortable after the Eniwetok landing that he lit up one of the twenty cigars he had hoarded. Our first two waves walked in without any sight of any enemy.

Then the weather changed, and so did the war. A cooling rain cut down visibility, and Japanese guns seemed to open up from everywhere.

"Underground," said Sgt. Chris Hagen of Fairmont, Minn. "The sonsofbitches are underground."

And so they were. They had dug hundreds and hundreds of spider holes, all carefully camouflaged, covered with corrugated iron topped by palm fronds and dried leaves. Some were for single soldiers, others large enough for a half dozen, and still others interconnected by tunnels

355

made of opened oil drums. In one area, not forty yards square, we flushed out twenty holes, killed more than fifty Japanese.

Working with a tank, Pfc. William Hollowiak made these spider holes a specialty, using all the guns and grenades of the dead, theirs and ours. It was like playing peek-a-boo, but for keeps.

Our quick movement cut off the Japanese from their supply areas. "What will the soldiers have to look forward to?" wrote one Japanese soldier in his diary. "There is nothing more important than eating."

Japanese officers soon notified them of their future:

"Sick and wounded who cannot endure the battle will commit suicide. Others will reorganize, return to the battle as a unit, and die fighting."

"We cut them down like overripe wheat," said a soldier, after a few futile banzai attacks. "They lay like tired children with their faces in the sand."

We had killed and buried 2,677 enemy at Eniwetok. Our own dead: 339. But our gain was strategic in its importance. The key to Eniwetok was in its name, which meant, "land between east and west."

We had now pierced the outer perimeter of the Japanese empire.

The Marianas

Resting between battles in a scatter of areas from Upmadung to Ennugenliggelap, the GI's made "jungle juice," listened to the native "sing-sings," discussed the news that a captain had his arm chewed off by an alligator, and continued their never-ending campaign against Atabrine.

Atabrine was a bitter, yellow pill all GI's were forced to take three times a day to prevent malaria. What made the pill even more bitter was the unquenchable rumor that Atabrine made men sterile.

Refusal to take the pills became widespread. "You think I want a broken arrow?" said a GI.

To counter this revolt, the medics started a desperate campaign, even intimating that Atabrine actually heightened sexual powers. One of their posters showed a curvy nude, with the message, "COME BACK TO THIS—TAKE ATABRINE." Another showed a bare-breasted blonde with the caption, "TWO REASONS WHY YOU SHOULD TAKE ATABRINE."

GI's answered with their own kidding campaign of posters:

"HEMORRHOIDS? GIVE ATABRINE A 30-DAY TRIAL."

"WHY WEAR A TRUSS? TAKE ATABRINE."

But even Atabrine didn't break their boredom. One big sign read, "RIFLE AND GUN CLUB—WHERE LIFE IS A THIRTY CALIBER BORE."

At rare intervals isolated Japanese soldiers strayed into camp, some covered with fungus, crawling on their hands and knees because their legs were too rotten to support them. And, occasionally, there was still the enemy soldier coming in to kill as many as he could before he himself was killed.

Sgt. Phil Mottola shot one such enemy soldier on New Britain long after the campaign was over.

"I'm shot," screamed the Japanese soldier in English.

"Shot, hell!" yelled Mottola, "you're dead!" Then he fired a few more bursts to finish him off.

Such shooting would soon no longer be a novelty. The Saipan invasion was next, and soon.

We had swept a thousand miles closer to Japan in a single summer. So carefully had we picked our strategic points of attack that we had isolated 135,000 Japanese troops. But now we had a new need: now we wanted some islands to serve as unsinkable aircraft carriers for our new B–29's to bomb Japan itself. We needed the Marianas, specifically Saipan, Tinian and Guam.

Tokyo headquarters passed on the word: "If Saipan is lost, air raids on Tokyo will take place often; therefore you must absolutely hold Saipan."

Saipan was one of fifteen Mariana islands in a 425-mile string. No coral atoll like Kwajalein, no jungle like Guadalcanal, Saipan was something different for us. Twelve miles long with a curving mountainous spine, narrow beaches, scrubby trees, vermillion flowers, and honeycombed with caves, Saipan was also a heavily populated, intensely cultivated island with three good-sized communities. What made it ideal for defense was its 1,554-foot Mount Tapotchau, smack in its center with masses of hills

357

and ridges radiating from it. From their defense setup within all that craggy high ground, the Japanese could pinpoint its artillery anywhere.

The surgeon on the ship warned all the invading soldiers:

"In the surf, beware of sharks, barracuda, sea snakes, anemones, razor-sharp coral, polluted waters, poison fish and giant clams that shut on a man like a bear trap. Ashore, there is leprosy, filariasis, yaws, typhoid, dengue fever, dysentery, saber grass, hordes of flies, snakes and giant lizards."

He had some final advice.

"Eat nothing growing on the island, don't drink its waters and don't approach its inhabitants.

"Any questions?"

A GI raised his hand.

"Yes?" said the surgeon.

"Sir," said the private. "Why in the hell don't we let them keep the island?"

In the six months before our June invasion, the Japanese had been regularly reinforcing their Saipan garrison, up to a strength of 40,000 men. Three of our submarines had sunk troop transports in one of those convoys, and half of some 3,000 surviving troops straggled ashore without equipment. Planes from seven aircraft carriers swept in on Saipan, shot down some 200 enemy planes.

"For about two hours, the enemy planes ran amuck, and finally left leisurely amidst the unparalleled inaccurate antiaircraft fire. All we could do was watch helplessly," wrote a Japanese soldier in his diary.

Japanese reaction to the three days of naval bombardment was similar:

"Naval gunfire was too terrible for words . . . There was no way of coping with the explosions. We could do nothing but wait for them to stop." And a Japanese naval officer wrote, "I quietly opened the quart I brought along and took my first shot from it. There is something undescribable about a shot of liquor during bombardment."

From a more simple soldier, came this comment, "I have at last come to the place where I will die."

At first, everything seemed to go according to plan. Our three underwater-demolition teams—each with sixteen officers and eighty men—made their preliminary check and found nothing. Our 34 LST's moved into position at 0700 hours, dropped anchor about a half mile from the beaches, opened their big bow doors, lowered their ramps and out came the seven hundred amphibious tractors and tanks, loaded with troops. A dozen other LST's nearby started disgorging their light artillery. Within twenty minutes, we had landed some 8,000 GI's—not a single collision among the landing craft. By nightfall we had more than 20,000 ashore. But the Japanese had registered their guns on the beaches, even using flags on the reefs to zero in more accurately. And they had massed sixteen 105-mm howitzers and thirty 75-mm artillery on the high ground and the reverse slopes and their fire was both intense and accurate. By the darkness of the first day, although we had taken two-thirds of the area of our expected objective, we had suffered heavy casualties.

Two stretcher cases on the beaches, one a private, the other an old-time sergeant. The private said he had to take a shit and the medical corpsmen quickly grabbed the sergeant's helmet and handed it to the private. The sergeant boiled, "That I should live to see the day when a private should do that in my helmet."

The Japanese had the great advantage of terrain, and an intimate knowledge of it. During the earliest beachhead fighting, they maintained a strong wedge of troops right in the center of our extended beachheads. It was the marshy area of the Lake Susupe region, and the Marines who went in there to search and destroy found themselves moving in muck up to their waists. It was a bad day for the laundry units of both armies.

The Saipan invasion had ended the research by Commander Hayashi of the Japanese Imperial Navy Medical Corps:

CONCERNING THE SOILING OF NAVY MEN'S CLOTHING
1. Throughout the four seasons, the shirts of cooks, firemen and general duty personnel show a remarkably high degree of soiling. This is also true of their socks, which in the case of barbers, radiomen and nurses show a low degree of soiling.
2. The progress of soiling is generally proportionate to the passage of time and is cumulative in effect. However,

in the case of cooks, firemen and general duty personnel the degree of soiling exhibited on the first day is equivalent to that noted on the fifth to seventh day for barbers and nurses. Taking an average for all branches, the soiling of shirts and drawers tends to show a cumulative increase, and this process accelerates sharply in the summer.

In the case of drawers . . . the seat gets dirtiest . . .

. . . The soiling of drawers increased sharply during the invasion . . .

On our first night on the beaches, the Japanese charged in a screaming banzai, blowing bugles, waving sabers, carrying land mines in their hands in a desperate attempt to drive us into the sea. They had started with an old-fashioned political rally with stump speeches and flag waving, and were whipped up to such an emotional pitch that they began marching toward us down the shore road behind their tanks in columns of platoons. We spotted a couple of thousand of them just behind our lines having a final pep rally, and pinpointed a naval bombardment right on top of them. But they kept coming. We finally stopped them with tank guns and concentrated rocket shelling from our ships only 1,250 yards offshore—the rockets sounding like the sudden snap of an enormous whiplash.

It took almost six bloody days of fighting to clear the beachhead area. We had two Marine divisions and an Army division ashore, plus seven battalions of artillery and two tank battalions and we needed them all in the early days.

It was a phrase some of our soldiers learned, but it seldom worked.

The phrase, in Japanese, was: *"Tay-oh-ah-geh-tay-deh-tay-koi."* It meant, "Put up your hands."

We cut across the island, captured the airfield, found only one Japanese in the whole installation, hiding between double doors of a control tower.

The enemy had retreated to the high ground.

"Those who cannot participate in combat must commit suicide," the Japanese troops were told. "Casualties will remain in their present positions and defend Nafutan Point." The password for enemy troops was, *"Shichi Sei Hokoku"*

(Seven lives for one's country).

It was a nice shady hill, and the two sergeants, Ben Livesey and Onel Dickens, stopped their tanks for some chow, started heating their C-rations.

Just before they could eat, they heard firing. Below their hill they saw three Marine amtracks stuck in the swamp, and three Japanese tanks approaching them and firing. Livesey and Dickens rushed back to their tanks, buttoned down their turrets and raced onto the Japanese tanks' tails, each firing their 75's as soon as they got into range. Each shot up one enemy tank and then both concentrated on the third one, shot away its treads. Marines meanwhile jumped out of the stalled tanks and killed the Japanese tank crews as they were flushed out.

The Marine amtrack crews then joined the two tanks on their tree-shaded hill as they all had their heated C-rations.

While the land war moved grudgingly, the air-sea war took on a crucial emphasis.

Submarines reported the movement of a Japanese force of aircraft carriers heading toward our invasion area. We outnumbered them in carriers, our seven to their five and we had the greater strength of planes, but the Japanese had the advantage of operating within range of their land-based planes from Guam. Their carrier planes also had a greater range than ours because they were lighter, had less armor.

The first raid of Japanese carrier planes never reached our ships. Our planes intercepted them, shot down 45 of their 69 planes. Their second raid was even more disastrous—we shot down 98 of their 130 planes, and one of our submarines sank an aircraft carrier with a single torpedo.

Lasting three days, it was the greatest naval carrier battle of the war. When it was over, the Japanese had lost 400 planes and two aircraft carriers. We had lost only thirty planes, and one battleship had received a minor hit.

The unknown story was that, back in the Aleutian campaign, we had captured a Zeke fighter plane intact—the Japanese pilot had broken his neck on landing. Brought back to the States, that Zeke was tested exhaustively and we designed our new Hellcat fighter plane to have all of its advantages and none of its weaknesses. Our Hellcat was twice as powerful and could outspeed, outclimb, outdive and outgun the Zeke. That captured plane was almost worth a fleet of carriers.

We called our victory "The Great Marianas Turkey Shoot."

It gave us complete command of the air and sea around the Marianas, and that advantage was enormous.

There was none of this sharp high drama in our land war. The limestone cliffs surrounding Mount Tapotchau all seemed to rise like knife blades, each ravine a bitter battlefield. The names we gave that area told the story: Death Valley, Purple Heart Ridge, Hot Potato Hill, Hell's Pocket, Bloody Acres.

The Battle of Bloody Acres took place on a narrow shrub-covered strip, only 2,000 yards long, an area broken by gullies, with the Japanese artillery up above in the caves of the cliffs on the right. It lasted thirty-six hours.

"I lost fifteen pounds in the Bloody Acres fighting," said First Sgt. Arthur Bradt of Schenectady. "In close combat, there's so much ducking, dodging, jumping and sprinting that only a tough body can take it."

And Sgt. Norman Olsen of Hempstead, N.Y., had a more technical observation. "All through Bloody Acres, I saw only two guys firing from the shoulder, and they were down in holes. When you fire from the shoulder, you're too good a target. Hip firing is a must." Olsen was happy that he had been taught in his jungle training course to fire at dummies thrown at him from the other side. "You had to plaster those dummies in nothing flat."

Other lessons learned: slit trenches are best against small arms fire but Y-holes are what you want against artillery and mortars. In a Y-hole, three men lie feet to feet with the forward man in the stem pointing toward the front. A shell would have to hit square on the junction to wound all three—but in a slit trench a single shell can get everybody. On the other hand, the disadvantage of a Y-hole against infiltrators is that an enemy moved into one Y-hole and knifed two of the men before the third knew what was happening.

And there was another basic lesson: Get your digging done before dark.

"The fight on Saipan as things stand now is progressing one-sidedly," the Japanese commander reported to Tokyo. "Step by step he comes toward us and concentrates his fire on us as we withdraw, so that wherever we go we're quickly surrounded by fire."

After we captured Mount Tapotchau, a Marine told Sgt. Larry McManus, "Everytime I look back at the beach from here, I wonder how any of us got ashore."

The first town we captured, Chalan-Kanoa, gave our GI's a chance to take some baths—each house having a cistern well. Houses also often provided warm beer, bananas, and Japanese phonograph records for background. But our soldiers quickly learned to wear their helmets inside the houses—they were built for small people, and the low ceilings caused bumped heads.

Up in the hills, near some called "The Pimples," the Japanese moved their artillery pieces out of the caves to fire at our troops, then pulled them back again to avoid observation and counterfire.

They also stepped up their infiltration.

"Everything was quiet," said T/Sgt. Mike Mele, Albany, N.Y. "It wasn't even dark yet. I noticed this guy sitting in the sand minding his own business like he was one of the boys. So, when I took a short break, I offered him a butt. He refused it, shaking his head. When he did that, I plugged him in a hurry. No one in my outfit ever turns down a smoke."

A GI found a sleeping Japanese soldier, brought him to headquarters where he revealed details of an upcoming banzai attack near Hara Kiri Gulch. The scorched crisp fields of sugar cane were still thick enough to conceal the enemy. We called the area Paradise Valley, but the Japanese referred to it as the Valley of Hell. "We felt this was an unpleasant hint and suggestion concerning our future," wrote of the Japanese officers.

Despite our readiness, the Japanese banzai was big enough to overwhelm our perimeter position.

"The first thing I saw was a long thin glistening object waving back and forth in the half-darkness down the road," said 1st Sgt. Norman Olsen, Hempstead, N.Y. "Then another one glistened over by the beach. Then I saw one in the bushes toward the cliffs. In a second it seemed as if there were hundreds of them all over the area waving wildly back and forth."

"The .30's mowed them down like tall grass but they kept coming," said T/Sgt. Frank Mandaro of Jackson Heights, N.Y.

Water gave out, medics stripped branches for splints, made tourniquets from gun slings, took clothes from the wounded for bandages. The wounded helped to load guns, picking up ammo from the dead and giving it to men on the firing line. S/Sgt. Richard Hiffay of West Sand Lake, N.Y., said, "There's no word to describe the guts of some of our wounded."

Pfc. Thomas Daley, Brooklyn, N.Y., walking calmly toward the enemy, kept repeating, "I'm staying right here. I'm staying here and fighting."

Pvt. William Hokoana of Hawaii killed 200 with his BAR from the fork of a small tree.

A Japanese bayoneted Pfc. Robert Postal but Postal killed him with a rifle bullet as he struggled to withdraw the blade. Another charged Pfc. Ken Rayburn with a lowered bayonet. Rayburn's carbine jammed but he knocked down the Japanese by hurling a mattock at his stomach.

Sgt. Claude Moore was bending over to count bodies when he was shot in his ass. A medical corpsman nearby examined him quickly and said, "Damned if it didn't go in and out of both cheeks."

A smile wiped away Moore's pain.

"Four purple hearts," he said, "and all with one bullet."

"It was like a movie stampede staged in the old wild west movies," said a GI. "We were the cameramen. It didn't make any difference if you shot one, five more would take his place. They ran right over us."

Our artillery firing forty rounds a minute in our support, we finally formed a line, beat them back, wiped them out. A Japanese soldier wrote near the end of the twenty-four-day campaign, "I felt we were entirely surrounded and lost all hope. I felt that the final hour was drawing near."

One of the most sickening sights of the war came at the very end. The Japanese civilians had been told that we would torture them horribly if we captured them. Driven into them was the idea, "I will never suffer the disgrace of being taken alive."

Most of it happened at Marpi Point just beyond the physical reach of our GI's. But we could see it happening.

Whole families hand in hand, jumping off the cliffs onto the sharp rocks below. Men waiting patiently for the officer to hack off their heads. Mothers cutting the throats of their babies, then killing themselves. Fathers stabbing or strangling their children, hurling the tiny bodies off the cliff, then jumping after them. Three women on a rock combing their black hair, then standing erect, joining hands, and slowly walking into the sea until it covered them. A naked woman in the last stages of childbirth wading into the water right after them to drown herself, too.

At times the water below Marpi Point was so thick with floating bodies that our small naval craft were unable to steer any course without running over them.

We had secured the island by July 9, wiped out a Japanese force of 30,000 troops at a cost of some 14,000 killed and wounded. In those final few days, some of our own Marines were killed by our own men because they had thought it fun to dress up in Japanese generals' uniforms and strut down the roads waving their samurai swords.

Two weeks later we landed at Tinian, about three miles away. Army artillery had massed 156 guns on the southern tip of Saipan, blasting Tinian continuously to soften it for our troops. Our P–47 fighter-bomber planes were already using Saipan airfields.

Ten miles long and five miles wide, Tinian looked like a broad elevated limestone plateau, surrounded by a barrier of abrupt cliffs. But there was still landing space on two hundred yards of beaches. Commenting on the preliminary bombardment by the ships, a Japanese soldier wrote wishfully, "It became quiet after the enemy warships left . . . Maybe the enemy is retreating."

But the Marines swarmed in, swept easily across the island. "After Saipan," a Marine told Sgt. H. N. Oliphant, "Tinian was almost like maneuvers."

Our troops were soon picking cucumbers to eat with their C-rations, and eight days later, the island was ours.

A hundred miles away, and twice the size of Saipan, Guam had the tougher terrain of jungle as well as mountains.

First we blasted it by air.

"There were nine B–24's, but not one of our planes went up to meet them," wrote Lt. Imanishi, after one of our raids. "We felt disheartened. Just how desirous our air force is of fighting is open to doubt." And then, a later postscript, "It is especially pitiful that we cannot control the air. We can only clench our fists with anger and wait."

Our frogmen found 640 underwater obstacles of palm-log cribs filled with coral and connected by wire cable—and blew them up. Our naval fire support was so close that we killed some of our own men. The Japanese ashore made effective use of tree bursts, causing increased casualties.

Medic Robert Law saw eight Marines hit by a shell burst, hurried to the one with a shattered leg, gave him morphine, saw that he had to amputate. The Marine asked only for something to hold on to and Law put dirt clumps in his hand which the Marine squeezed while Law cut with his combat knife. The Marine did not utter a sound throughout the operation but squeezed the dirt to dust. As the medic was binding up the stump, the Marine smiled at him, then fell unconscious.

Another Marine volunteered to wear a microphone to record his stream of consciousness as he hit the beach:

"I am thinking of my wife and my little daughter. Hope they are all right and I can see them again. Hey, Dave! Keep your eyes on this stuff in case I get hit. I am walking behind the amtrack. The water is about two and a half feet deep. I am stumbling. Getting tired. Just losing my breath. Say, you fellows, don't leave me all alone.

"Bullets are kicking up the water all around. One landed right next to me. Hey, everybody spread out! Spread out, you guys. . . . How the hell are we going to get to that beach? . . . One of our men has been hit. He is lying on his side. I can't tell who it is. Another one has just been hit. Bullets, bullets.

"We are about a hundred feet from the beach. Everybody's mouth seems drawn. Another one just got hit. Another one just next to me on my right. Hey, Dave! Are you all right? One has been hit and is on his back. Blood is pouring out of his mouth . . . Can't tell where the fire is coming from . . . I am still running, out of breath. . . . It is a strange thing . . ."

Then the sound stopped.

There were the usual banzai charges on Guam and some Marines even kidded about it, passing out this mimeographed announcement:

TONIGHT
BANZAI CHARGE
Thrills   Chills   Suspense
See Sake-crazed Japanese charge at high port
See Everybody Shoot Everybody
See the Cream of the Marine Corps Play with Live Ammo
Sponsored by the Athletic and Morale Office
Come along and Bring a Friend
Don't miss the thrilling spectacle of the Banzai Charge
Starting at 10 P.M. and lasting all night
ADMISSION FREE

Guam was the liquor locker for the Japanese in the central Pacific and the enemy had all the beer and sake it could swallow. They would come into some of their banzai attacks singing drunkenly, even laughing, attacking tanks with bare hands, even beating tanks with their fists and kicking them. They were buoyant with booze. We poured in 26,000 shells in two hours after midnight, and it was a massacre. A single platoon killed 258 enemy without the loss of a single man. We would watch as they committed suicide by taking off their helmets, placing primed grenades on top of their heads, replacing the helmet, then awaiting the end with folded arms.

We did take more prisoners than usual, though. One of them was asked why he surrendered and he said that his unit had been ordered by his commanding officer to fight to the last man.

"Well?" asked the GI interrogator.

The Japanese soldier blinked and said, "I am the last man."

Secured by mid-August, Guam soon became part of the rear echelon along with Guadalcanal.

Some real liquor was filtering through although most GI's still made their own, often by straining a bottle of after-shave lotion through a loaf of bread, mixing it up with raisins, sugar, vanilla extract or coconut milk. Medical alcohol gave it all an extra flavor.

As for the coffee, there was this lyric, often sung:

The coffee that they give us, they say is mighty fine,
It's good for cuts and bruises, in place of iodine.

There was also this GI comment on officers:

The officers they give us, can stand up to the worst,
You find 'em every weekend, shacked up with a nurse.

One of the better-circulated stories concerned an MP ordering the driver of a Marine jeep.

"Put those goddam lights out."

The driver did. However, his passenger, a general, told the driver,

"Put those goddam lights back on."

The driver did. Now the MP yelled even louder. "Put those goddam lights *out!*"

"I *can't,*" the driver yelled, "I got the goddam general with me!"

Last barrier before the Philippines were the Palaus, directly east of it. Before any invasion, we had to clear them to protect our right flank. On the island of Peleliu, in mid-September, Bloody Nose Ridge became another bitter battle star for the Marines, a month of fighting to wipe out 12,000 fanatic Japanese defenders from caves and pillboxes.

"Any souvenirs?" a U.S. naval officer asked a wet, weary, wounded Marine as he scrambled aboard ship, after the battle.

The Marine patted his rear end.

"I brought my ass outa there," he said. "That's the only souvenir I wanted."

Leyte Gulf

When a ship crossed the Equator, even the war waited a minute. That's pollywog time, the time when the formal dignity of the United States Navy gets dumped overboard.

A pollywog is anybody—no matter what his naval rank —who crosses the equator for the first time. At this point he must suffer all the initiation indignities before becoming a "shellback."

Heads get shaved, except for decorative tufts and

fringes. A variety of viscous liquids including shellac, banana oil, egg yolk, lemon extract, iodine and assorted almost-permanent dyes are used to anoint the initiates. Pollywogs, particularly junior officers, may be decorated in sun bonnets or hand-painted brassieres, forced to act as servile waiters at enlisted-men's mess, and perhaps lined behind the boilers for a half hour and baked at 140 degrees. Specially selected pollywog officers were given two Coke bottles to use as binoculars to search for the Equator.

When pollywog officers came into the court of King Neptune—usually the fattest sailor aboard—they had to bow, often recite a complicated poem and sing, "I Love You." They also had to grovel and kiss his well-greased belly. And, finally, all pollywogs had to run the long gauntlet of "shellbackers"—each of whom was equipped with a canvas tube stuffed with wet paper ready to whack the ass of every parading pollywog that passed by.

It was a small smile in a grim war.

Navy war is a waiting war.

A ship is an oil speck in a vast sea and even an armada only makes a small blot. To find a fleet to fight takes time and luck and steady search.

Except during an invasion. If the prize is rich, then the enemy must fight for it with everything.

The prize of the Philippines was rich indeed. It was crucial. To protect this prize, the Japanese Imperial Navy had a sweeping plan called Sho Operation Number One. *"Sho"* meant "victory."

It was simply this: to converge on the landings at Leyte in three prongs. The northern prong was to bait Admiral William Halsey's Third Fleet, suck it away from the scene of main action. A center Japanese fleet was to slip through the San Bernardino Strait, move on to Leyte Gulf from the north. A southern force would simultaneously come through Surigao Strait, between Mindinao and Leyte, and the two groups would form a pincer on the invasion ships and destroy them.

It turned out to be one of the great sea fights in history, a naval action sprawled over an area of more than 500,000 square miles, twice the size of Texas. Few other battles in the war came so tiptoe close to complete disaster.

For the Japanese, it was their great gamble:

369

"If we lose the Philippines, even though our Fleet remains intact, it will be of little use to us," said Admiral Toyoda, explaining the purpose of SHO–1. "For with the Philippines in enemy hands, our shipping lane to the south will be completely severed. If we draw the Fleet back into Japanese waters, it will be without fuel. If we leave it in the south, it will be without arms and munitions. There is no sense in saving the Fleet at the loss of the Philippines."

Their gamble was great because we outnumbered them —166 warships against their 70, 1,280 planes against their 716.

Besides, our ships were ready.

To ready a ship for war, the stern cranes on deck are lowered and secured, any items that might burn or splinter are heaved overboard or stowed below; torpedomen check each torpedo to make sure it is alive and deadly; stanchions and lifelines are taken down and stowed; radio and radar technicians check the rig on their secondary stations, in case their main stations are knocked out; firemen triple-check all their hoses and fire equipment; the gunners inspect their guns and ammunition; sailors put on long-sleeved shirts to save their skin from heat blast; the paint is scraped down to the steel and then, and then only, are the decks ready for action.

First contact on October 23, 1944, came from the *Darter* and the *Dace,* two submarines which not only sighted the Japanese central force, but sank two cruisers and damaged a third.

Retaliation came quickly.

A lookout on the U.S.S. *Princeton* spotted a single Japanese divebomber coming in low out of the clouds, right off the port bow. It came so fast there was no time to dodge or maneuver, and the 500-pound bomb fell squarely on the flight deck from less than 1,200 feet. We shot the plane down but the damage was done.

The damage, at first, seemed slight—only a small hole. But it had gone deep, exploded on the hangar deck, ignited high-octane gasoline, reached six torpedo-loaded planes. Huge chunks of the flight elevator "as big as a house" hurtled through the air in successive blasts, and in a fraction of a second the ship became a charnel house. So violent were the explosions that they almost sank two ships nearby trying to save her.

370

Leaving a dying ship is like leaving home. Each bunk, however carbon-copy, is something special, something private. Pinups and pictures of family, the sounds and smells and warmth of nearby buddies.

Each seabag packed and crammed with memories: the small stacks of letters, two Alka-Seltzer bottles filled with quarters, a collection of Bing Crosby records, a well-worn deck of cards, a comic book, a Bible, a copy of *Main Currents of American Thought,* the last remnants of a box of cookies, good-luck charms—some of the great range of souvenirs.

Each corner of the ship was a memory of elbow grease, a job station, a quiet place in the wind.

Home is where the heart is.

At first, the Japanese luck seemed to hold. Admiral Halsey had been hooked hard by their decoy bait. His planes had spotted their northern force of aircraft carriers, decided that here was the main enemy strength, and raced after it. In the race, he took with him a whole fleet of 119 ships leaving naked our invasion transports at nearby Leyte Gulf. The Japanese decoy fleet consisted of only 17 ships, including the four aircraft carriers, almost empty of planes.

Meanwhile, the southern prong of the enemy pincer headed for the invasion area. Coming towards Surigao Strait, they found themselves facing a line of six old battleships—five of them reclaimed from the Pearl Harbor attack. We also had some 39 PT boats to skim in ahead of us at night and draw fire to find out exactly how many Japanese ships were where, and what was their speed and their course.

And then we moved in our screen of destroyers. Our radar was good that night, and theirs was bad. Our destroyers knocked out three of theirs, plus a battleship, and retired unhurt.

But the Japanese kept on coming, and so Rear Admiral Oldendorf had his chance to execute the classic tactic of "capping the T." This maneuver permits the ships on the horizontal bar of the "T" to let loose their guns broadside against the vertical column of the enemy, which can only fire its forward batteries.

The sea was smooth, almost glassy; the night black; the range 17,000 yards . . .

FIRE!

A terrific rolling roar, a moment of silence, the hiss of the air blast clearing the gun barrels, the whirring of reloading and the sound of the rammer, the grinding of the elevator gears, the noise of "Stand By" buzzer, then the flash and the fire.

"Most beautiful sight I ever witnessed," said a sailor. "The arched line of tracers looked like a continual stream of lighted railroad cars going over a hill."

The Japanese never knew what hit them, and their return fire only revealed their confusion.

Here was modern sea war at night—a war between ships where neither saw the other. And there was only one rule: Never give a sucker an even break.

Before daybreak, we had wiped out two battleships, a heavy cruiser, a light cruiser, five destroyers and many thousands of lives. Of that southern enemy fleet, only a single Japanese destroyer escaped intact.

Our own casualties were almost minor: 39 killed and 114 wounded, most of them on one of our ships that had been caught in a moment's cross fire, by our own "friendlies."

The ship's log of the U.S. destroyer *Albert W. Grant,* reported:

"The first shell landed at 0407 and exploded among a stack of empty powder cases. Several shells then hit amidships thirty seconds later, steam now pouring out of the forward stack. Forward firerooms and engine rooms were then out of commission.

"0408½. Additional shell hits begin to riddle ship. Hit forward at waterline flooded forward storeroom and forward crews' berthing compartment. Hit in 40-mm #1 exploded 50-mm ammunition and started fire. Hit through starboard davit exploded killing ship's doctor, 5 radiomen and almost entire amidships repair party. Other hits in forward stack, one hit on port motor whale boat, one hit and low order explosion in galley. One hit in scullery room, one hit in after crews' berthing compartment, and one additional hit in forward engine room. All lights, telephone communications, radars and radios out of commission. Steering control shifted aft."

The doctors and medics on the *Grant* were all dead except for Pharmacist Mate First Class W. H. Swaim, Jr. He drafted J. C. O'Neill, Jr., whose father was a doctor and who remembered something about makeshift tourniquets and how to rig up an emergency oxygen tent and how to bind up a huge open wound. They set up an aid station in the toilet, using emergency lighting.

But even then, there were so many casualties that the wounded had to take care of the wounded. W. G. Hertel, hit badly in both legs, asked to be propped up against the base of a boat davit and helped administer morphine syrettes to all within reach. Radio Technician J. M. Flaherty, still bleeding heavily from shrapnel wounds, tied a make-shift dressing on his badly torn thigh, and then maneuvered himself to give help to other wounded.

And W. N. Selleck, both legs torn off, looked up at one of the aid men and said, "There's nothing you can do for me, fellows. Go ahead and do something for those others."

And then he died.

Just as we had won the battle of Surigao Strait, obliterating the whole southern prong of the Japanese pincer, the main enemy force moved quickly through the deserted straight of San Bernardino—a fleet of four battleships, two heavy cruisers, two light cruisers and seven destroyers. The only thing that stood between them and a million tons of our shipping along the invasion beach was a peanut force called Taffy Three.

Taffy Three consisted of seven "small boys" (destroyers and destroyer escorts) and six puny escort carriers called CVE's.

CVE's were thin-skinned, brittle-bottomed ships better known as "Combustible, Vulnerable, Expendable." They were also called "baby tomato cans," "kaiser coffins," "jeep carriers," "buckets of bolts," "wind wagons" and "a runway slapped on a hull designed for a tanker." They were really baby flattops, carrying 18 to 36 planes, intended to supply air support for ground operations ashore. Their biggest gun was a five-incher, hardly designed for a stand-up, slugging fight with the 14-inch guns on a battleship.

The battle of Samar was a war of jeeps against giants. Or, as Rear Admiral C. A. F. Sprague put it, "It was like a puppy being smacked by a truck."

But it was a plucky puppy.

Sprague formed his six CVE's into a rough circle about 2,500 yards in diameter, put his "small boys" as an outer screen, then ordered, "Small boys launch torpedo attack."

The hawk had gone into the chickens and the chickens had attacked.

Sunrise, October 25, a small handful of American destroyers moved in to take on the major portion of the Japanese fleet.

Our attack confused the Japanese admiral. He now thought he faced a major American naval force, thought our baby flattops were big ones. Rain squalls heightened the confusion and the thick black oily smoke of our ships and the white chemical smoke screens from our fantails gave the sea war an unreal quality. Coming out of the smoke and squalls our own ships would barely avoid collision. "People could have touched as our bows missed each other," said a sailor afterward. The rough sea was soon full of aerial bombs, shell splashes, torpedo wakes.

Japanese shells contained a dye—different colors for different ships to help their gunners identify which shells were hitting which ships. Small boy U.S.S. *Johnston* got the whole rainbow.

"The red, green, purple and yellow colors might have been pretty under different circumstances," said a *Johnston* gunner, "but at this moment, I didn't like the color scheme."

She had used up all her torpedoes, firing futile 5-inch shells against a battleship which hit her with three 14-inch shells, and three more 6-inch shell hits, knocking out her fireroom, engine room, killing the power to her 5-inch guns. Steering orders had to be yelled through open hatches at sailors below. Three cruisers and several destroyers came in for the kill, circling her "like Indians attacking a prairie schooner" and not all the guts and gumption in the world could have saved her. As she went down, a surviving sailor saw the Japanese skipper on the nearest ship salute her bravery.

The "small boys" had moved within 440 yards of the enemy ships, raking the battleship superstructures with their five-inch popguns. Before being sunk herself, one of the destroyers reported to Sprague, "Exercise completed."

The Japanese admiral made a serious tactical blunder. Instead of sending in his destroyers with torpedoes and then forming a battleline with his big ships—which would have devastated our force within minutes—he ordered General Attack, every ship for itself.

But their power was still enormous.

"The enemy was closing with disconcerting rapidity and the volume and the accuracy of its fire was increasing," our Action Report noted later. "At this point it did not appear that any of our ships could survive another five minutes of the heavy caliber fire being received."

At this critical point, Admiral Sprague gave his orders, "Prepare to attack major portion of Japanese fleet."

Or, as Chief Gunner's Mate Jenkins aboard the U.S.S. *White Plains* told his crew, "Hold on a little longer, boys; we're sucking 'em into the 40-mm range."

Somebody said that the armor-piercing shells of the big enemy battlewagons ripped through the thin skins of the CVE's as if they were wet shoe boxes.

Every ship in the shoe-box fleet was hit at least once. Destroyer escort *Samuel B. Roberts* had her side torn open, her power knocked out, her fuel tanks destroyed, every gun knocked out of action except one.

Number Two gun on the *Samuel Roberts* had fired more than three hundred rounds of five-inch ammunition, scoring observed hits on a heavy cruiser, knocking out an eight-inch gun turret, demolishing a ship's bridge, and starting fires in the cruiser control tower.

First an enemy shell knocked out the gun's ammunition hoist, another disrupted its power, but the crew kept loading, ramming, aiming and firing six charges entirely by hand. They did this with the certain knowledge that without compressed air to clear the bore of burning bits of fragments from the previous charge, the silken powder bags could "cook off" and explode before the breech could be closed.

This happened on the seventh round, killing all but three crew members who were critically injured.

Gun captain was Gunner's Mate Third Class Paul Henry Carr. The Action Report later noted:

"The first man to enter the gun mount after the explosion found the gun captain Carr on the deck of the mount holding in his hands the last projectile (weight 54 pounds) available to his gun, even though he was severely wounded from his neck down to the middle of his thighs. He was completely torn open and his intestines were splattered throughout the inside of the mount. Nevertheless he held in his hand the projectile, held it above his head and begged the petty officer who had entered the mount to help him get that last round out. The breech of the gun had been blown into an unrecognizable mass of steel. The mount itself was torn to pieces. He was the only man capable of physical movement within the mount and yet his only idea was to get out that last round. He died within five minutes."

The *Roberts* took an hour to sink.

Somebody should have saluted *her*, too.

But we weren't only being hit—we were hitting back. Our ships and planes had sunk a light cruiser and a destroyer, and damaged many others. They had sunk two of our escort carriers, two destroyers and a destroyer escort, shot down 105 planes—a thousand of our sailors killed or missing. We were at the tiptoe edge of complete destruction.

Then, suddenly, almost miraculously, the Japanese naval force withdrew.

"I could not believe my eyes," said Admiral Sprague, giving most of the credit to the "definite partiality of the Almighty God."

Less pleased was a signalman on the U.S.S. *Fanshaw Bay* who yelled from the ship's bridge, "Goddammit, boys, they're getting away!"

The two-hour historic battle had ended at 0911 hours.

Why? Had the Japanese admiral persisted in his attack for another half hour, he could have wiped out the shoebox fleet, destroyed our defenseless transports, wreaked havoc on our invasion beach.

Then, why?

Nobody really knew. Did the Japanese imagine a huge trap waiting for them in the gulf, a fresh armada, a large force of land-based and carrier-based planes? Were they worried about the return of the Halsey fleet? Were they too dismayed by the destruction of their southern prong? Was his communication so bad that he thought his own caualties were heavier than they really were? In combat the line between a bad decision and a good decision is sometimes very thin indeed. But this was a disastrous decision.

For our side, naval historian Samuel Eliot Morison wrote, "In no engagement in its entire history has the United States Navy shown more gallantry, guts and gumption."

An officer of the *Roberts* said something of his men on his ship, which could have applied to all men on all ships of that day's action:

"To witness the conduct of the average enlisted men on board this vessel, with an average of less than one year's service, would make any man proud to be an average American. The crew were informed over the loudspeaker system at the beginning of the action of CO's estimate of the situation: i.e., a fight against overwhelming odds from which survival could not be expected, during which time we would do what damage we could. In the face of this knowledge the men zealously manned their stations . . . and fought and worked with such calmness, courage and efficiency that no higher honor could be conceived than to command such a group."

It was a coincidence of courage, but October 25 was also the anniversary of another battle, five centuries earlier, when a small force of English bowmen defeated the cream of French knighthood at Agincourt. That was on St. Crispin's Day, and part of the historic memory put it well:

> He that shall live this day and see old age,
> Will yearly on the vigil feast his neighbors . . .
>   and show his scars,
> And say, "These wounds I had on Crispin's Day."

There was still a third phase of the Battle of Leyte Gulf, Halsey's destruction of the four decoy carriers in the battle off Cape Engaño. We had sunk these carriers with three air strikes of 517 sorties. Halsey was all set to destroy the rest of that northern fleet of seventeen ships, when he got Sprague's harried request for help, and this message from naval headquarters:

FROM CINCPAC ACTION COM THIRD FLEET INFO COMINCH CTF 77 X WHERE IS RPT WHERE IS TASK FORCE THIRTY-FOUR RB THE WORLD WONDERS.

"The world wonders" was code padding, but Halsey read it as part of the message, brooded for an hour about the supposed insult, then headed south to help the Seventh Fleet. By the time he arrived, no help was needed and the main Japanese fleet was out of reach.

But our victory was a great one. We had sunk 26 Japanese ships including four aircraft carriers, three battleships, ten cruisers and nine destroyers, and damaged 25 others. We had lost six ships, with eleven more damaged.

Never again would the Japanese Imperial Navy return as a fighting force.

"After the battle," said Vice Admiral Ozawa, "the surface force became strictly auxiliary, so that we relied on land forces, special attack [kamikaze] and air power."

The Philippines

"People of the Philippines, I have returned," broadcast General Douglas MacArthur on the invasion beach of Leyte, October 21, 1944. "By the Grace of Almighty God our forces stand again on Philippine soil, soil consecrated by the blood of our peoples . . . Rally to me . . ."

He had not returned alone. With him, were 738 war ships, 133,000 men of our Sixth Army and 200,000 tons of supplies, all of which were landed on four beaches within three days. "Overwhelming force," General Ulysses S Grant had said, "is the answer to successful attack."

Back home in Chattanooga, Tenn., Pfc. Austin Harder was a telephone lineman and he was still wearing his climbing spikes when he landed on Red Beach. His job that morning was a special job of pride. There was a topless palm trunk he had to climb near the beach, the enemy mortar fire plopping not too far away. Twenty feet from the tree were three litters of wounded. Halfway up the tree Harder hesitated and his buddies below yelled, "Higher . . . higher . . . take it higher!"

Up near the top, the palm trunk started to bend slightly but Harder stayed with it, did what he had to do.

What he had to do was to take an American flag he had wrapped around his waist, tie it firmly on the tree, and smooth it straight because there was no breeze. It was a time for lumps in throats, some cheers, and a sergeant nearby yelling, "Get the hell off the beach."

Leyte was one of the largest of the 7,000 islands in the Philippines, and smack in the center. During the critical four-day naval battle in Leyte Gulf, our troops landed almost without opposition. The Japanese had their prepared positions, their pillboxes, their well-designed earthworks in the nearby high ground, but the men were missing. Our thousands of 4.5-inch naval rockets had landed on nothing and killed nobody.

Near one of the invasion beaches were some huts, filled with Filipinos. One had been hit by some shell fragments and our medics were soon fixing him up. A five-year-old girl found her hands quickly filled with C-ration candy and D-ration chocolate bars while her father was busy smoking American cigarettes.

Another hut was deserted, but it did have a sign on the door, crudely printed in chalk, "DO NOT BURN MY HOUSE."

By nightfall of D-Day, we controlled almost fifteen miles of coastline, and were moving through the knee-deep water of rice paddies toward the high ground. The Japanese had switched strategy from a beach defense to a defense in depth behind a range of jagged hills.

But there was no question about the character of the continued Japanese determination. "The Army has received the following order from His Majesty, the Emperor: Enemy ground forces will be destroyed."

"Though life and death are separated by a thin sheet of paper," a Japanese soldier wrote, after hearing the Emperor's order, "I will not die until I see the face of a Yankee."

Somebody said that the Japanese fought to die and the Americans fought to live.

Take the case of Pvt. Harold Moon, Jr., parked at the key point of his company's perimeter. Everybody else in his platoon had been killed. Nobody expected Moon to stay and fight alone, even for a short time. Nobody ever expected him to try to maintain that isolated perimeter position by himself against repeated attacks.

But he did, for four hours of constant fighting. He threw his grenades until they were gone, directed mortar fire on a nearby Japanese machine gun, carefully rationed the guns and ammunition of all his dead buddies, yelled curses at any enemy who could hear him—and they heard him well. There was a weird interval of an hour when he was wounded in his leg, unable to move much, and a single Japanese officer kept circling his position, throwing grenades until Moon finally shot him in the head.

With the arrival of early light, Moon deliberately exposed himself so that some nearby GI's could spot a camouflaged enemy machine gun, and knock it out. A whole squad of Japanese finally overran Moon's hole, but he had his machine gun supported between his legs and he killed eighteen of them. The Army later awarded Moon the Congressional Medal of Honor for that action. They sent it to his family, of course, because Pvt. Moon had been killed.

We took the town of Tacloban, and its airstrip, the first day. The monsoon season started soon after our landings, the downpour steady and drenching—thirty-five inches of rain within forty days—turning puddles into lakes and converting the airstrip into a sea of black mud. Truckloads of crushed coral disappeared into the runways like raisins in soft ice cream. It took all the steel matting we could get to make the boggy strip even remotely usable. Some of our carrier planes, fighting in the Gulf, ran out of fuel and had to make forced landings in that muck. Sgt. Sam Halpern had the headache of wig-wagging them in with his signal flags. The lucky ones somehow slid to a landing, were quickly refueled and sent off again before the field got worse, as it did. The unlucky ones were hauled out of their cracked-up planes, their wrecks bulldozed off the bog to make room for the next emergency landing.

The people of Tacloban had been waiting a long time. They greeted 'us with ripe papayas, bunches of bananas, liberated Japanese beer—and there was a neatly dressed middle-aged man handing out hard-boiled eggs, saying, "Thank you, sir, thank you, sir."

The story they told was a story of rape, murder and torture. For more than two years, their native guerrillas had fought the Japanese occupation troops with homemade shotguns, cannon built out of sewer pipe, and jungle traps set with spears of sharpened bamboo. They had helped us set up weather stations, radio stations, air warning systems long before our troops ever landed.

To retaliate, the Japanese would order the whole family of a suspected guerrilla to come and identify him. In front of the family, they would beat up the suspect into a mangle of blood and whimper, drag him in front of a member of his family, lift up his mashed head for recognition. If the relative denied recognition, the Japanese would smile and say, "So sorry," and then repeat the whole beating process before dragging him to the next relative. Once

380

identified, the suspect would be killed, of course, but never slowly.

None of that ever stopped the guerrilla war. And when we went through Tacloban, Sgt. Bill Alcine remembered a small elderly Filipino pointing to his home and telling a GI, "My house, my house," indicating that there was a Japanese sniper in there.

"O.K. Mac," said the GI, "but it'll look like Swiss cheese if he doesn't come outa there."

The GI went in. There were eight shots. The GI came out again, motioned to the elderly man that it was O.K. now to go back in.

"Thank you, sir, thank you, sir."

It was perfect sniper country. The cogon grass was shoulder-high, and thick enough to hide anybody. The Japanese tied some of the grass to their helmets to complete their camouflage, waited quietly for some of our troops to pass through before they started firing from the rear. They usually shot from ground level and most of our sniper casualties were hit from the hips down. Some of them also used pointed bullets made of wood and paper. Fired over a GI's head, the paper bullet would explode with a loud pop, causing the GI to turn in that direction. This gave the sniper more time to aim a more deadly shot with the real bullet.

We expected the snipers in the grass and the swamps and the trees, but we did not expect them to come out of the graves.

It was an old Spanish-style cemetery, about a hundred yards square, the weeds heavy and high. The stone crypts, above the ground, had been converted into pillboxes and holes had been drilled through headstones for gun slits. A whole company had passed through there before a tomb suddenly opened up with four Japanese firing at once, and a Japanese officer jumped out of a grave waving his sword.

During the fight, the company command post queried K Company radio operator Pfc. Roy Alvis, of Kane, Ill., whether the Japanese had broken through our lines. "Hell, no," said Alvis. "We've gone through theirs and are fighting for our own bivouac."

As Alvis later put it, "There was no peace for the dead that night."

The Battle of Leyte became a race of reinforcements. With more than 350,000 troops on assorted Philippine Islands, the Japanese decided to make a stand on Leyte. They had a force of some 30,000—started shipping in a steady stream of men and supplies—even though our bombers did catch some of their convoys. On one November day, our bombers sank six troop transports, drowning an estimated 10,000 Japanese. "The waters of the sea around us were tinted with blood," a soldier in the convoy afterwards wrote.

We were moving so fast that even the enemy didn't quite know where we were. At different times, we surprised Japanese platoons carrying tuna fish and rice, a group of truck mechanics, and several horse-drawn carts carrying Japannese ammunition.

By the first of December, our troops outnumbered the Japanese seven to one, but this was not the kind of war where mass means too much. Equally important was the enemy's lack of food and supply. The hills became homes for the flotsam and jetsam of the enemy, disorganized small bands, the forgotten wounded.

"I am exhausted," a Japanese soldier wrote in a letter he never mailed. "We have no food. The enemy are now within 500 meters of us. Mother, my dear wife and son, I am writing this letter to you by dim candlelight. Our end is near. What will be the future of Japan if this island shall fall into enemy hands?"

Japanese soldier Shohei Ooka wrote of a starving demented officer, from whose head the leeches dangled like tatters.

"Just before he died, he fixed me with the clear eyes of a policeman and in an excess of lucidity, such as visits patients at the moment of their death, said, 'What, are you still here? You poor fellow! When I'm dead, you may eat this.'

"Slowly he raised his emaciated left arm and slapped it with his other hand."

The Leyte campaign lasted longer than we expected. It had become a battle for individual hilltops, hills with cold numbers and bloody names. As a desperate but futile attempt to turn the battle, the Japanese dropped 450 paratroopers—fortified by sake. We later found some of the empty sake bottles still labeled with the warning that the contents should not be drunk until the paratroop planes were in the air.

It was a weird war.

Pfc. Clifton Riggins reported into an aid station—he had been attacked by a swarm of wild bees.

M/Sgt. Fred R. Thompson of Terre Haute, Ind., had a constant complaint about the two hundred miles of telephone wire the Signal Corps had unreeled in the first fifteen days: "The carabao get all tangled up in the wire and rip it all to hell."

Pfc. John F. Marias confided that he felt strangely at home sweeping up the debris in the Leyte branch of the Bank of the Philippines—his father had been president of that branch bank before the war.

Leyte was sloppy country for tanks and trucks, but they still filled a need.

"The roads may be muddy," said T/Sgt. Robert Mc-Grath of Grand Rapids, Mich., "but the trucks do finally make it with supplies. We get our barracks bags here and a change of clothing. On Attu, you had to carry everything on your back."

Tanks served as artillery against caves and pillboxes. But the GI's had to hover over them, watch them constantly so that an infiltrating Japanese soldier wouldn't rush up to throw a grenade at the tank treads. Or slap on one of those magnetic mines. Or incinerate it.

One of our tanks ran over one of our own shells, and blew up. A storm started at the same time, and the thunder and lightning mixed with the screams of the wounded men as the GI's tried to pull them out. Sgt. Ralph Boyce saw one of the GI's looking at one of the wounded men wiping the blood on his filthy sleeve. Boyce saw the GI pull out a handsomely stitched silk scarf that he had probably been saving to send to his girl. "He stared at it for a moment," wrote Boyce, "then walked over to the injured man and said, 'Here, Mac, let me do that for you.' And he wiped the blood and dirt from the man's face with the silk scarf."

The prolonged campaign had made it impossible to build up the island as a major air and supply base for the coming invasion of Luzon. But the Japanese decision to make a stand at Leyte meant that it no longer had an organized navy or an organized air force or even an organized army.

"Our defeat at Leyte," said Admiral Mitsumasa Yonai later, "was tantamount to the loss of the Philippines. When you took the Philippines, that was the end of our resources."

The enemy casualty count swelled to more than 80,000 after the mop-up.

Mop-up is a favorite communiqué word. It sounds like a postscript that doesn't count. The battle has been won, the campaign is over, the strategy decisions have been made. All that remains is a mop-up of men who are not afraid to die by men who don't want to die.

Mop-up is a tragic word. And who wants to die for it?

Expect to fight for every inch of beach and don't drink water, Sixth Army Intelligence officers advised our GI's just before our Lingayen Gulf invasion on January 9, 1945. But our Intelligence was as wrong about the water (you can't poison artesian wells) as they were about the invasion reception. The reception was warm and wonderful, the friendly Filipinos waiting for us with kisses and coconuts and short, stubby bottles of cider—and the Japanese nowhere to be seen.

The continued Japanese tactic was an abandoned beachhead but a defense in depth. By nightfall of the first day we had landed 68,000 troops, and controlled a fifteen-mile-long beachhead more than three miles deep. In fact, the heaviest casualties after three full days was a regimental loss of five men killed and ten wounded.

Such was the carnival quality of our invasion that our GI's even operated a midget-sized railroad we had found. Each railroad car was the size of a sofa, but it worked, and it was fun.

More fun came from the appropriation of a Chevrolet sedan which had been driving serenely down the coast road until it ran into one of our roadblocks. The two Japanese passengers were most surprised.

But the fun was short and the road was long.

The road to Manila was a winding, two-lane concrete road, and most of our GI's walked, as usual.

"We got the center road," said Sgt. Joseph Bennett, "the main road to Manila, that was our baby, go south on that

384

main road. And we got very little opposition for about four or five days, until we got to Clark Field. That was our first real fight because the Japanese had a big air base there. They used their antiaircraft guns as antipersonnel and that's how I got wounded. I was on top of a hill just outside the field and they were using 40-mm stuff, striking the trees near us, splintering the trees and the splinters dug right into us. They brought me back to a field hospital, patched me up in a few days and threw me out again and I hitched a ride up to my old outfit. Our recon sergeant had been knocked out so they made me recon sergeant.

"There was a river, the Pasig, running east and west across Manila. We had to cross it, and crossing the Pasig was like setting up a beachhead. We had to move men and material across the river, and then attack the Japanese who were in the main part of Manila.

"Three of us were sent to find the tallest house on the north side of the river, overlooking the Japanese on the south side. The main thing was to watch what was happening and not let them see us. We were there for three days, directing mortars, artillery, everything. We would call back and say there was a big house with five Japanese on the top of it that you could hit, or else that there was a window on the second floor that you guys oughta be able to lay a shot through. Things like that.

"Then they spotted us and they started throwing in shells at us, and knocked our house down. But when the first shell hit, we beat it.

"And that's the way it went, that's the way the war was."

General Tomoyuki Yamashita had decided he could not defend either the beaches or the central Manila plain against the superior American force. Nor would he crowd his 150,000 troops into the dead end of Bataan and Corregidor. Nor would he make a stand in Manila itself—its population of a million would be impossible to feed, its highly inflammable buildings and flat ground hard to defend. He preferred to base his strength in the mountainous areas of the northeast.

Yamashita had left behind in Manila a vice admiral to blow up bridges, maintain order, and protect his supply movements. However, the vice admiral had more heroic dreams.

He transformed Manila into a mass of barbed-wire entanglements, overturned trolley cars and wired together truck bodies as roadblocks, converted houses into machine-gun nests, sandbagged entrances, barricaded stairways, chopped gun slits through outside walls, planted mine fields on all the main street approaches, torn the big guns out of the ships in the harbor and dug them in at strategic street corners. Manila was all set up for siege.

When we heard this, we canceled our plans for a big victory parade in Manila.

Some of our advancing troops were stalled at the city outskirts not by mines or bullets, but by beer.

These GI's had had four days of forced march when they reached this blown bridge. Waiting at the bridge were smiling Filipinos with cold beer. The beer, they said, came from the nearby Balintowak Brewery, better known as BBB. There was no problem getting volunteers for a reconnaissance of the area. The recon unit found everything intact, including the refrigeration. Every GI was then permitted to fill up his helmet with the cold beer, and it was a long, long line.

Pfc. Daniel Catale of New York City even had a glass beer stein with him, something he had carried along for months, using it mostly for GI coffee or chlorinated water. Now he drank his cold beer in complete luxury, telling Sgt. Dick Hanley, "This is like a shot in the arm. Now I'll be able to walk into Manila like I was fresh."

But it was not a walk-in, and nobody was fresh at the finish.

Core of the Japanese defense was a semicircle of heavily fortified government buildings and schools in the Intromuros area. It became a battle of big guns against stone walls. The big guns of war usually stay in the protected rear, use Piper Cubs and forward observers to tell them the long-distance target and range. But at Manila, a big 155-mm gun often found itself on the front line firing pointblank at a couple hundred yards' range to blast a breach in a concrete wall for our GI's to rush through.

The battle of Manila was a battle for a shoe factory, the Far Eastern University, the Manila Club, the Medical School, and an assortment of other buildings, each a strongpoint presenting special problems of attack.

Typical was the fight for the police station. We blasted the building all night and the Japanese would leave their positions to take cover in the rear. Then before the Japanese returned at first light, we rushed in. Our mistake was in starting at the basement and working up. By the time we reached the first floor, we had a fire fight on our hands in the corridors. In one room alone, we had to wipe out three machine-gun positions. By the time we had cleared that first floor, the Japanese were on the second floor, destroying the stairway so we couldn't climb up, and then cutting holes in the floor to drop grenades on us.

It took eight days of heavy fighting to clean out that police station, and we did it only by virtually demolishing it with artillery.

That one police station cost us 25 dead, 80 wounded, and three medium tanks.

After that, we learned to attack a building from the top going down. T/Sgt. Robert Steele climbed on one roof, knocked a hole in it, poured in gasoline, then started a flash fire by dropping in a white phosphorus hand grenade.

And during this war of streets and buildings, it was not unusual to see a Filipino running past the guns, dodging among the tanks, ducking under the bullets, carrying a cup of steaming coffee for a new GI friend.

And so Manila was ours, and we moved on to Bataan and Corregidor, dropping paratroopers to hasten the end there. As part of their final gesture of mass suicide, a fanatic force of Japanese blew up themselves and their storehouse of tons of ammunition in the Corregidor caves. Debris from that blast hit a GI almost a mile away, and some of it even landed on a destroyer more than 2,000 yards offshore. Scattered everywhere were parts and pieces of people.

"As soon as I got all the casualties off, I sat down on a rock and burst out crying," said a medic. "I couldn't stop myself, and didn't even want to. I'd seen more than a man could stand and still stay normal."

There was a flag-raising ceremony after the cleanup, and a colonel announced loudly to General MacArthur, "Sir, I present to you, Fortress Corregidor."

It was a moving moment. It had cost much blood.

There was still a drag-out war in the mountains that would last six more months. ZigZag Pass was one of the bloodier areas—the road twisted violently through jungle so thick that you could step five feet off it and no longer see the road. And on every hill and every knoll of every zig and every zag of that pass, the Japanese had their honeycomb of camouflaged well-stocked pillboxes.

This was the lonely war of assault teams: two squads, one with eight men armed with BAR's, flamethrowers, demolitions, thermite grenades, everything; the other squad of six men armed mainly with rifles and light automatic weapons for covering fire. They had to climb knifelike ridges in rain so heavy that you couldn't see five feet in front of you.

In the small towns in the valleys, you drank the potent tuba juice made out of bamboo roots and the price of a whore was a can of C-rations.

Some GI's felt uncomfortable lining up in front of a house on stilts, brought there by a small brother, serving as pimp, and with the parents sitting amiably alongside the entrance, counting customers. The other girls, the nice ones, had a classic phrase, "No touch, Joe." You could smell coconut oil in their hair and see them on their balconies picking the bugs out of the oily strands.

Once in a while, a starving Japanese straggler came out of the hills. The Filipinos worked in the sugar-cane fields with their sharp bolo knives and if one of them found him first, they had a way of cutting off the soldier's hands before turning him into our headquarters.

By April we had raised some 200 sunken ships from Manila Bay and were processing 10,000 tons of shipping through that port every day. By mid-August, it was all over. We had two armies there then, the Sixth and the Eighth, and we had killed some 70,000 Japanese, destroyed the Japanese Fourteenth Army, cut off more than 300,000 of the enemy on other isolated islands throughout the Philippines.

But their defense was a grudging success. They had tied up a considerable part of our troops for an overextended time.

The war had moved on.

Submarines

"An exploding depth charge has three noises," wrote submariner George Grider. "First, there is a click. Then comes a clang, or crashing sound, like someone hitting your hull with a million sledgehammers. Finally there is a swishing noise, as though water is falling over a waterfall or pouring into a cavity the charge has created. The closer the charge is, the more closely together these noises come. When it is very close, you hear one horrible clang!"

There's also a ping sound, the sound of an enemy destroyer bouncing sonar signals off your hull. And, more than anything else, there is the almost unbearable sound of utter silence when all equipment has been cut off, and the heat of the engine seeps through the pigboat mixing with the smell of sweat and strain, and you await the arrival of the first depth charge. On land, a GI can race for a rock, find a hole to hide; in a plane, you can bail out in a chute; on a ship, there are lifeboats and lifebelts. All of them have a piece of hope. But in a sub, at the bottom of the sea, you can only sweat and pray.

With a crew of seven officers and seventy enlisted men, our subs carried enough supplies for sixty days. Surface speed: 20 knots; underwater speed, 9 knots; underwater endurance, 48 hours.

The old World War I subs had bad air, wet insides, a patrolling ability of only eight days. The new ones had air-conditioned movies, ice-cream freezers and could stay at sea for more than two months without refueling. One sub considered it a food crisis when, a month out at sea, it ran out of whipping cream and men had to eat the strawberry shortcake without it.

However, not all submarine life was simple comfort.

These were submarine instructions on the *Wahoo* for flushing a toilet:

"Before using, see that bowl flapper valve 'A' is closed, gate valve 'C' in discharge pipeline is open, valve 'D' in water-supply pipeline is open. Then open valve 'E' next to bowl to admit necessary water. Close valves 'D' and 'E' after pull-lever 'A'. Release lever 'A'. Open valve 'C' in air-supply line. Rock air-valve lever 'F' outboard to charge measuring tank to ten pounds above sea pressure. Open valve 'B', and rock air-valve lever inboard to blow overboard. Close valves 'B', 'C' and 'G'."

All these specific instructions assumed special importance when a captured Japanese told how one of their subs hit bottom near Hawaii and took such a terrible down-angle at one point that their latrines overflowed and filled every compartment.

Our so-called pigboats occasionally hunted in wolf packs. One such wolf pack of nine subs invaded the Sea of Japan, sank 27 merchant ships for a total of 57,000 shipping tons, within 11 days. They also picked up eleven survivors of a B–29. During the last year of the war, subs rescued 380 pilots and crews downed in the sea. Another wolf pack sank an entire convoy plus its destroyer escort and an aircraft carrier, and rescued 163 British and Australian prisoners.

But, usually, a submarine went out alone. Each sub had its own area to patrol. Such areas had designated code names, some of them set up with a touch of whimsey. One of them was called, "Hit Parade," and each of the ten subdivisions within it was named after a musical instrument. When a sub was ordered to "play the trombone in Hit Parade," it knew just where to go. It would not duplicate the effort of the sub which was "tooting the flute," or "strumming the banjo."

Within its area, though, each sub was a private pirate, with all the freedom and excitement of it.

"Motor Machinist's Mate D. C. Keeter was a good man to have on lookout, for he was one of the most alert lookouts I ever saw," said his sub commander. "He had a habit of freezing every now and then, like a good pointer that has come on a covey of quail, while he studied some speck on the horizon. At first it was distracting; you would forget to watch anything but Keeter, waiting to see him go on point. But it was a fine example of concentration on the job, and it paid off that night. Keeter froze, pointed, and sang out, 'Smoke on the horizon. Bearing one hundred and twenty starboard.'"

It was their first enemy ship, a freighter.

"Stand by to fire."

"Stand by for final bearing."

"Mark bearing . . . set . . . fire ONE!"

"Fire TWO! . . . Fire THREE! . . . Fire FOUR!"

BOOM! A torpedo takes one minute and twenty seconds to arrive. A hit ship breaking apart sounds like the sudden crumpling of cellophane close to your ears.

There was the new sub that scored 14 hits out of the first 14 "tin fish" fired; the sub that popped up in the Japanese-controlled waters near Truk, picked up 22 American aviators who were shot down; the sub that calmly photographed all the potential invasion areas of Japan; the sub that landed a whole party of Marine raiders on Makin; the sub that supplied the Filipino guerrillas with medicine and munitions; the sub that "up periscoped" so that an American airman in the water could hold onto it and be towed out of sight until it was safe for the sub to surface; the sub that surfaced right in the midst of a Japanese convoy, fired all its 24 torpedoes from the surface, scored 19 hits, sank 7 ships; the sub that sweated out some 400 depth charges and still survived; the sub that destroyed a whole convoy of two freighters, one transport, one tanker; and the sub that sank 24 ships and 90,000 tons of shipping within nine months of action; and still another that sank five destroyers in four days.

There was the sub that picked up a couple of our Javanese spies, pious Mohammedans who had to be told by the navigator four times a day where Mecca was, so they could bow to it.

And there was a sub ordered to evacuate 58 men, women and children on a twelve-day run to Australia. The whole crew packed itself in the after-battery compartment, putting the male passengers in the forward torpedo rooms and the women and children in the after-torpedo room. It was during that run that one of the crew saw a native woman puffing on a large cigar while nursing her infant, then letting her baby take a few puffs after it finished feeding.

Nobody knew any of this during the war, because we called the subs our silent service, and kept their successes secret. Among themselves, though, the lid was off. Submarine skipper of the *Sturgeon* felt obliged to report the sinking of his first ship, with "STURGEON NO LONGER VIRGIN."

The new subs were all named after fishes, and their crews learned to live like them. These were sailors of a special breed, each a specialist in several areas, all of them expert on such fundamentals as blowing water from the forward torpedo tanks to the after tubes and knowing how to pump from the forward trim tank to the negative tank.

Theirs was a tighter interdependence than most men on most ships. Maybe they spent more time in the sack, drank more coffee, played more cards, shared more bull sessions, knew each other more intimately than most sailors. But they also had a deeper respect for each other's privacy.

And, strangely enough, most of these men felt only a minimal feeling of cooped-up pressure. A sub spends as much time on the surface as under it and any sailor any time can request permission to get the fresh air of the bridge. The remarkable thing is that there were submariners who never went out to see the sky from the time they left port to the time they returned.

Once in port, though, everybody aboard was happy to receive a blinker signal from a neighboring sub saying, "I challenge you to a baseball game on the beach. You bring the beer."

Subs sank 201 out of the 686 Japanese warships destroyed during the war, and some 5,000,000 tons of enemy shipping.

The stagger of these statistics is that we only had 200 subs at the end of the war. We had lost 52.

So few had done so much so silently.

Iwo Jima

Code name for Iwo Jima was "Hot Rock."

It was. It was an ugly island shaped like a lopsided pear or a bloated pork chop with black beaches of volcanic ash that turned into thick gray goo during a drenching rain. It was full of hot fissures and steaming sulphur beds that caused a thick yellow smog to seep in everywhere.

It was a small island, not much more than five miles long and two miles wide, some scrub bush, a few trees, and no native animals. Population: a thousand natives and 22,000 Japanese troops.

And why did we want it, this small sizzling plop in the sea?

It was a halfway house to Tokyo. Crippled B–29 Superforts returning to Saipan from a raid on Japan could never hope to make the 1,300 miles and usually dumped and drowned. Before Iwo, we lost as many planes to the Pacific as we did to the enemy. An air base in Iwo could cut the pressure of a sixteen-hour round trip, give the crippled planes a haven. It could permit B–29's to take more bombs instead of more gas. And it could wipe out a persistent Japanese fighter base that served to intercept our bombers. But, in the words of the official report, the main reason we wanted Iwo was as a base "from which to attack the Japanese Empire."

The bitter defense of Leyte and Luzon had delayed our invasion schedule by at least a month. That extra month helped the Japanese add to Iwo's impregnability.

Facing a beach area 2,500 yards long and 1,000 yards inland were the following: 10 reinforced concrete blockhouses, 7 covered artillery positions, 80 pillboxes, seventy 120-mm defense guns, two 120-mm short coastal defense guns, four 120-mm dual-purpose guns, one 80-mm dual purpose gun; one 70-mm battalion howitzer, six 47-mm antitank, antiboat guns, three 37-mm antitank, antiboat guns, nineteen 25-mm twin-mount machine guns, one 13-mm machine gun.

Added to all that was a multitude of other gun positions, unseen or unidentified, such as hundreds of pillboxes hidden in the space of a good-sized baseball field. Some of them had walls of reinforced concrete nine feet thick, strengthened by several layers of steel. Ceilings were up to ten feet thick, sometimes topped with more than thirty feet of sand. Not only were most of them completely camouflaged, but they were mutually supporting, and could fire on each other in case one was captured. Every open area was under registered fire, every road, every ravine, every gully. Mines were planted everywhere, some of them as big as a bathtub.

Compared to the five hundred caves we found on Peleliu, Iwo Jima had some fifteen hundred, many of them in five levels tied into an underground network of almost thirty miles, tunnels thirty feet below ground that went everywhere. There was no defense line to breach; it was like a giant sponge—squeeze it and every hole showed its separate hell.

Facing it all from the island's top was the mustard-yellow Mount Suribachi, 556 feet high, where the Japanese general staff directed the changing strategy and the changing direction of fire from everywhere to anywhere.

Pvt. Shigeru Yoshida was a twenty-two-year-old former stonemason working on the Suribachi fortifications for many months. Specifications called for a seven-story gallery to be built inside the mountain with thirty-five feet of

393

overhead cover, plastered walls, steam and piped-in water, all entrances angled at 90 degrees to protect against flamethrowers and demolition charges.

Men could work no more than ten minutes at a time near the volcano because the temperature often rose to 160 degrees. They wore masks against the fumes.

There were few shirkers. Japanese soldiers were told by their officers that American soldiers would cut off the left forearm of each Japanese prisoner and carve it into a letter opener to be sent to President Roosevelt. And their heads would be cut off so that their skulls could be made into American ashtrays.

Yoshida, along with the rest, took the battle vow:

"Above all else, we shall dedicate ourselves and our entire strength to the defense of this island. We shall grasp bombs, charge the enemy tanks and destroy them. We shall infiltrate into the midst of the enemy, annihilate them. With every salvo, we will, without fail, kill the enemy. Each man will make it his duty to kill ten of the enemy before dying. Until we are destroyed to the last man, we shall harass the enemy by guerrilla tactics."

Came the morning of February 19, and you could see the invaders coming. Yoshida spread out his gas mask and his protective ointment nearby in the cave at the hill of the mountain, made a tiny fire to brew some tea, and waited. His stonework was over.

Our bombers thought they had pulverized Iwo; our ships thought they had left only carnage—more than 8,000 shells hit the beachhead area within thirty minutes. But the Japanese here were too deeply dug in to be hurt hard. It did do some damage. One destroyed enemy gun position dropped over the cliff "like a half-extracted tooth hanging on a man's jaw." And the rolling barrage did devastate some company areas.

Most of the invading Marines were handed a printed card from the chaplain with the words of the famous prayer written by Sir Jacob Astley before the Battle of Edgehill in 1642:

> *O Lord!*
> *Thou knowest how busy I must be this day:*
> *If I forget Thee, do not Thou forget me.*

And Cpl. Robert Blankenship, III, never forgot the words of a platoon sergeant named Goldblatt, just before they hit the beach. Said Boldblatt: "I'll kill the first sonofabitch who says, 'This is it!'"

Nobody did.

We landed some 30,000 troops that February D-Day. The Japanese strategy was to suck in our soldiers onto the plain, then annihilate them with concentrated fire.

You couldn't run on the black ashy beach, especially when you were a mortarman carrying 122 pounds, or even a medical corpsman with 55. You couldn't dig deep into it either because the sand kept crumbling. The good thing about the sand was that it swallowed up bullets that might otherwise ricochet and shells that might otherwise splatter.

One of the early boats coming out with casualties was intercepted by another craft, with a Navy captain. The captain requested permission to take one of the casualties aboard his boat. Permission was granted. The casualty was his son, his only son, Sgt. Charles C. Anderson, Jr. The sergeant had lost both legs and an arm from a land mine.

"I'm feeling pretty good," he told his father. And then, he said, "I wonder how Mother will take all this." And then he died.

When a Navy chaplain later called on Mrs. Anderson in Washington, she asked him, "Is it my husband or my son?"

Told it was her son, she said, "A force stronger than ours has taken charge." And then she dressed and reported for duty at her job as a volunteer at Bethesda Naval Hospital.

The military maps divided the assault beach into seven strips, each 500 yards wide. The northern part of the island was the plateau, its shores rocky and inaccessible, and the strip of beach stretched for two miles, north and east of the base of Mount Suribachi. On the other side of black beach was the pockmarked crumbling cliff. It was as if the invasion beach was flanked on one side by a 55-story building and on the other side by a 35-story building, both of them overseeing everything that happened, both of them bristling with every kind of gun.

And there was no pity, no safety for the wounded.

Men who carried stretchers remembered not to stay in step, because then it didn't bounce the body too much. But where do you put the wounded when there's no place to hide? The wounded waited on the beach, waited for the boats to come and get them, waited with the shells bursting among them, tearing up the torn. Most of them were too drained to cry, too scared for sound, but one of them gripped his stretcher poles, sat up straight, stared at the sky and screamed and screamed and screamed, the shells coming in closer all around him, the black cinders flying in his face. His screaming was an almost inhuman animal sound, sometimes gurgling and sickening, but so loud-pitched that it reached into the guts of everyone in the area, the sound scraping at their souls until some of them openly wished, "Why doesn't he die?"

And, finally, he fell slowly onto his shoulder, rolling over on his back, and lay still.

Assault was frontal, and throughout the whole of the war for Iwo, there was no room to maneuver, there were no rear areas. Invasion troops had to climb ten-foot terraces and it often seemed as if they were climbing a waterfall. The slippery gravel sucked at anything that touched it, and the formless sand seemed to fill every hole as soon as it was formed. Vehicles need wire mats before they could move. Wire-layers, unable to run in the ash, were the easiest targets. When you wanted to drink or urinate, you lay on your side to do it; when you wanted to defecate, you pushed yourself to the bottom of the hole—if you had time.

Conversation between Marine Privates Martin Culpepper and Lewis Wall, reported by Marine combat correspondent Sgt. Robert Leckie:

"There was an artillery burst not far off, and kind of back of me," said Culpepper. "It caught me off-guard, you know, kind of surprised me some, and I just jumped without thinking. . . . Well, I hit the side of the thing, and slid down on my right side. I was moving fast . . . Well, I started to climb back out . . . There it was . . . the crap was fresh as hell, too. And I had put my hand in it before I knew what happened . . ."

"Probably one of them Navy guys," said Wall.

"Hell, every hole's got crap in it . . . but it's on the bottom. Everybody knows that. I could have killed him . . . I mean it, I could have killed him right there, if I'd known who it was."

396

"It ought to be a death penalty on that sort of thing," said Wall. "It takes a worthless, selfish, one-way sonofabitch with ingrown hairs to do something like that."

"You know," said Culpepper, "they oughta make a movie showing war like it is. It would be sensational. People falling in crap, parts of people lying around, bodies flung about, people getting shot while they was trying to take a crap."

"And they could throw a little crap in the air conditioning, so that when you come out, you'd know how it felt."

"Serves 'em right, by God," said Culpepper. "They don't know and they don't care."

"And I don't blame them," said Wall softly.

The Marine joke was, "Don't hit a Seabee, he might be your grandfather." Seabees soon learned to spot the holes before they moved out into the open, learned to stay on that side of the hole where the fire was coming from.

This was the first time that Seabees landed with the second wave of an invasion—and it was the last. More than a thousand Seabees were ashore by D-Day afternoon, and their casualties were heavy.

Chief Carpenter's Mate A. W. Baker, a former Arkansas deputy sheriff, led a forty-man section ashore in the second wave. Before it was dark, half of them were dead or wounded.

Carpenter's Mate Third Class Delmer Rodabaugh had five large notebooks filled with mimeographed forms. He was supposed to be "a checker" on all the supplies, but he soon found himself carrying ammo to the combat men.

And Machinist's Mate First Class Elphenix Benard of Escanaba, Mich., was driving a bulldozer off the LST ramp, more bulldozers and tanks lined up behind him ready to come in on the beach. Directly in front of him were the crowded dead bodies of Marines and Seabees. He hesitated, closed his eyes, and kept going, his bulldozer over the bodies. His bulldozer was needed to open roads out of the beach, and the tanks behind him had to come in.

"I had no choice," he said. "I had no choice."

At the end of the first day, there were some 600 dead, either ashore or afloat, and almost 2,000 wounded. For the next twenty-six days, we would have a thousand more casualties every day.

Describing a dead American body on the invasion beach, Sgt. Thomas Grady Gallant wrote: "His face was drained of blood, and waxen, but strangely composed, reflecting only a mild impatience. And the face was unmarked and clean. The head was uncovered, the helmet nowhere to be seen, and the blond, close-cropped hair, neatly parted and combed, shone under the morning sun.

"From the shoulder down, the body was severed lengthwise, with the precise accuracy of a saw cutting down the backbone, leaving the corpse a strange half-man, with the left entirely gone, but the right half still dressed in a half-dungaree, which was neat and pressed. The right half of the body was complete. The head and neck, the right arm and shoulder, the right leg and foot, all were there. But there was no left leg or left arm, or left side; all these were gone. There was no sign of blood; neither were any of the missing parts in view, nor tattered shreds of uniforms; there was no pack or rifle.

"But, coming from the massive wound, crossing the right chest and strung over the right shoulder, just beneath the chin, there stretched a length of intestine that seemed to never end. Its very length, gently curving but untangled, was an unknotted rope of grayish-white, shell-like flesh that contrasted sharply with the smut-colored cinder-sand, to become a thing of horror. The ghastly thing, bathed in the sunshing of the beach, pale and revolting, a snakelike ribbon that rippled along the ground, lay directly in the path of the men charging from the tank."

A Japanese sailor on Iwo wrote: "Let me fall like the flower petals scatter."

But where are the flower petals when a tank rolls over a body?—the body is gone and there is only some wet dark soil and some scattered globs of mud near the tank treads.

And where is the scatter of flower petals inside a tank when a shell enters and explodes the ammunition inside, all of it whirling around and around inside the tank, acting like a beater in a mixing bowl full of eggs, turning human beings into a viscous mess of sticky fluid splattered all over the tank walls.

There are no flower petals in war.

Our troops seldom saw many Japanese dead. The Japanese buried them swiftly in the soft sand. Or, when there was no time, the bodies were burned where they lay. Our burial rules were much more formal. It's all properly printed in the rules of war: "Early problems of sanitation . . . in the order of importance: Disposal of the dead, disposal of human excreta, and the disposal of ration tins and food remnants."

Sgt. Frank Cedarwood carried only a carbine, helmet, canteen and ammo, and he seemed to be moving around more than most Marines. Wherever he went, he asked, "You seen any friendly dead around here, any Marine bodies? We're getting them gathered up."

"Hell," said a sergeant named Lupman. "We must be doin' all right. We got enough land for a cemetery."

We knew where our cemeteries would be. We already had marked the places on our recon photographs before the invasion. Graves Registration teams had bulldozers to push the black beach cinders into a huge mound so that the graves would be deep enough in the shifting sands. Six feet deep was the rule, but here it was eight feet because of the expected drift of the sand in the wind.

Bodies were first brought to the processing area for identification. Dog tags, identification bracelets, letters. Take fingerprints, make a dental chart of the teeth, spray the remains with sodium arsenate for sanitary reasons, then tag the personal belongings for shipment home. Full physical description of all bodies mutilated beyond identification, then marked "Unknown."

Wrap all bodies in blanket or shelter half or whatever available. Space between bodies, three feet from center line of body. Fifty bodies in a row. Locate each name on map of cemetery, for future reference.

The war was still too wide-open to collect too many of the dead, and this caused a problem of flies. They were huge blue flies, as big as pussy willows, and they didn't buzz or hover, they just clung to the bodies, thick and fat and full.

The corps surgeon solved the problem by having planes spray oily DDT on the whole battlefield—the living as well as the dead, the enemy as well as the Americans.

You have to stay healthy to fight a war.

Nights were the scariest. A shadow was death. A flash was destruction. A sound was fear. And the password was as important as your serial number.

399

That night the password was any President's name.

Seaman First Class Abe Levine of Brooklyn, standing guard near the beach, challenged a shadow, and the soldier answered, "Fillmore."

"All right, you sonofabitch," said Levine, "one more like that and you're dead."

Levine challenged another guy who sounded unsure and panicky when he answered, "Wallace."

"Goddammit," said Levine, "it's Presidents, not Vice-Presidents."

It took four days to take Mount Suribachi. Its capture pulled us out of the sand into the sky. It gave us the eyes of the island. It served as a symbol, but nobody knew then that the symbol would be caught in a picture that would ring the world.

A six-man patrol got to the top of it, and one of them tied a small flag onto a piece of pipe while Marine photographer Sgt. Louis Lowery snapped the picture. One of the six refused to pose with the others, jeered at them, called them "Hollywood Marines."

To make it more Hollywood, two Japanese raced out of a nearby cave, one running toward the flag with a drawn saber. A Marine named Robeson shot him and he fell inside the crater. The other Japanese threw a grenade at the photographer and Lowery hurried over the rim, slid down the side some fifty feet before he stopped, his camera smashed. But his pictures were undamaged, and the flag was still flying.

An hour later, Suribachi was safe and secured, and another patrol arrived with a civilian photographer to replace the smaller flag with a larger one. It was the second picture that became world-famous.

People like a larger flag.

The greatest concentration of Japanese defense stretched across the middle of the island. There was no line here either, but the cluster of pillboxes and gun positions was thicker, the interconnected chains tighter, the minefields heavier, the booby traps more ingenious. They not only booby-trapped their dead, but even their bottles of sake.

There was the amphitheater, a natural arena near one of the enemy airfields, the heights overlooking the exposed, bleak terrain; Turkey Knob an enemy-held mound of earth sticking out of the smooth flatness; Hill 362, a wild incline of jutting rocks and crevices and blind alleys where tanks were buried in narrow ravines as gun emplacements and every corner was a death trap.

Average division gain per day was 300 yards, and often it was nothing at all. In two days of fighting, casualties in one battalion alone rose to 68 percent.

"Among the Americans who served on Iwo Island, uncommon valor was a common virtue," said Admiral Nimitz.

Take Pfc. Douglas Jacobson. He was a rifleman, not a bazookaman. But when the bazookaman was hit, Jacobson grabbed his bazooka, raced forward to knock out a Japanese 20-mm gun, kept running, knocking out pillboxes, gun positions, at least sixteen of them, killing some 75 of the enemy.

Take Sgt. William Harrell. A grenade tore off his left hand, broke his thigh and a Japanese stood at the edge of his hole with a drawn saber. With his right hand, he shot the Japanese, fell exhausted while another enemy soldier put a grenade under his head. Harrell killed him, too, pushed the grenade as far as he could. It blew off his right hand, killed some nearby enemy soldiers. At dawn, Harrell was carried away, still alive, his post still secure.

Take Pharmacist's Mate Third Class Jack Williams. He ran to a shell hole to treat a wounded Marine when a sniper shot him three times in the belly and groin. Williams finished treating the wounded Marine, bound up his own wounds, gave first aid to another casualty, then headed back to the aid station when he was again shot by a sniper, this time killed.

Take Cpl. Tony Stein, a twenty-four-year-old former toolmaker from North Dayton, O. Toolmaker Tony made his own gun, a special machine gun converted out of the wing gun of a wrecked Navy fighter plane. He called it his "stinger." With that stinger, he killed a couple dozen of the enemy within the first hour, attacking one pillbox after another. And when he ran out of ammo, he took off his helmet and shoes and ran to the beach for more. He made eight trips like that, twice his stinger was shot from his hands. Once he was hit in the shoulder with shrapnel, sent back to the beach for evacuation, but went back front a few days later, until he was finally killed.

Death is the common price of courage.

The final days of fighting on Iwo mostly concerned caves and involved flamethrowers and white phosphorus grenades. If it was an ugly way to die, what was the good way?

"A flamethrower hit the Japanese, and his body was burning along the shoulders, and his back covered with fire. He rose wild-eyed, mad with the burning of his own body . . . fell, face downward, a few feet from his dead and flaming companion, fire leaping from his back and sides, his head burning particularly bright in a puddle of liquid from the flamethrower. George stood transfixed by the unreality of the scene. He felt completely detached from it. As he watched the bodies burn, the skin turning black and splitting as liquified fat burst the hide, a large bubble formed at the rectum of the last Japanese to die. As the flames shrank, to become jagged lines of fluttering, yellowish flickers of light, the bubbles slowly ceased to expand and did not burst."

As for the white phosphorus grenades, Toshihiko Ohno described one that casually landed in his cave at Iwo:

"Hurriedly we took off our clothes and rubbed them in the dirt, but when we managed to scrape the phosphorus off our clothes we found it starting to burn under our nails. If we got it off the right hand, the left hand would start to burn. For four or five hours we battled the phosphorus, and we completely forgot about the Americans. Later, we found that our clothes, in which we thought the flames had been completely put out, were burning again, sending up so much smoke we were greatly alarmed."

Ohno saw Americans bivouacked about three hundred yards away, and could hear them talking. "I scolded Kitagata for even breaking wind for fear we might be heard. Furthermore it was dangerous to have any smoke, but since the phosphorus was still burning, I took the opportunity to cook our rice properly with a fire, and we enjoyed a beautifully cooked dinner that day. We decided to make this our celebration of Navy Day, which fell about that time, and we talked about home and even managed to have some laughs."

The battle lasted 26 days. Of our five thousand dead, half had been killed in the first two days. There were almost no prisoners.

It was the costliest battle in 168 years of Marine history. More than twice as many Marines died in that battle as in the whole of World War I.

It was the most expensive piece of real estate the United States had ever bought—550 lives and 2,500 wounded for every square mile of it.

By early April, 7,000 Seabees, working ten-hour shifts, seven days a week, had moved three million yards of earth, leveling the central plateau. The island was mashed, rolled, paved into a giant B–29 airfield.

Grateful B–29 pilots named their planes for each of the Marine divisions at Iwo. Some 2,400 B–29's made emergency landings there before war ended. The 25,000 airmen lives saved "exceeded the lives lost in the capture of the island itself."

"Whenever I land on this island," said a B–29 pilot, "I thank God and the men who fought for it."

Long after the Iwo battle was over, Japanese infiltrators still came out of caves to kill.

"We covered ourselves with the soap and toothpaste we had managed to steal so that we would smell like Americans," said Toshihiko Ohno. "I started toward the line of tents. I thought if I managed to get into one with the hand grenades, I would kill as many Americans as I could. Choosing the largest tent because I thought it would have the largest number of the enemy, I found that it was the mess hall. Rolling up the flap of another tent, I spotted an American soldier fast asleep. Feeling a little sorry, I nevertheless made up my mind—I hit the grip on the grenade and threw it. It didn't go off. The second one, too, only hissed after the grip was struck. A second failure. I put all my frustrated feelings into the third. This also was a dud. The grenades had all been ruined by the dampness in the cave.

"Feeling I had to find some kind of weapon, I left the peacefully sleeping soldier and sneaked into another tent. There were several beds in this one and two soldiers were asleep. But there were no weapons to be found. After a while, a number of soldiers came in and I quickly dived under one of the vacant beds.

"When the soldier whose cot I was hiding under came back and got into his bed and drew up the blanket, I was sure that he had spotted me, because my rear end was protruding from under the bed. So I jumped up and tried to tackle him. He yelled and jumped out of bed. All the others woke at this and they grabbed me."

Ohno was lucky. He was alive. Four hundred other Japanese who tried a banzai attack on the airstrip—long after the island was supposedly secure—were practically annihilated. S/Sgt. Harry Hamilton, a P–51 mechanic, described how several of his buddies had fired fifteen bullets into one of the Japanese "and saw the soldier flinch with the impact of each one," but he was still alive. "I fired two more shots into him," said Hamilton, "and the guy still kept up his talking and hysterical laughter. I figured my carbine was shooting high, so I aimed at the bridge of his nose. The bullet drilled him right through the eyes, and he folded up like a rag."

You bury what you find, and they found a foot, with a Marine boot on it, a serial number on its tongue. It had belonged to a member of a tank crew and they buried it in a proper grave with proper honors.

Then came orders to exhume the foot. Its owner was in a Saipan hospital, still alive.

The conduct of war has a firm set of rules: you can't bury the same soldier twice.

But there is no rule about how many times you can die in war before you are buried. Ask the dead under the black beach of Iwo.

Okinawa

Midnight late in March 1945, somewhere outside Okinawa, at Picket Station Number Ten.

The sea was quiet, the battle over. Where were the 25 planes shot down, the two ships sunk, the eighty men dead or missing?

Aboard U.S.S. destroyer *Aaron Ward:*

A shapeless thing in a scorched life jacket near the No. 2 Fire Room:

"Who is it?"

"Damn, Chief, I can't tell. . . . He ain't got no head."

A hand, all by itself.

"That's all there was, Doc. Look, there's a high school ring, class of 1943. Do you know who it was?"

"Yes, Mac, I know."

A burned body without clothes, two bluebirds tattooed

on the chest:

"Oh I know him. That's Tony Olmeda."

"Doc, why does a guy want bluebirds tattooed on him?"

"Didn't you know? Bluebirds are supposed to bring happiness."

The living folded up the personal effects of the dead to send home to their next-of-kin, the folding gentle, the room quiet:

"Watch what you're doing . . . Don't send a pair of dirty socks back to his mother!"

Hunch your shoulders toward the wet breeze, keep your gun barrels elevated, search the sky for the slightest speck. Spot a speck five miles away and you only have a single minute to put up a curtain of ack-ack fire to kill that plane before it tries to kill your ship. Only a minute for your ship to move into violent evasive action. Only a minute for the proximity fuse on your shells to have any accuracy.

A picket destroyer sits on the outside of the outside screen of an armada, serves as its radar eyes. Above deck, it's all guns; below deck, it's all engine.

High-speed steam turbines in two engine rooms fed by four boilers and two fire rooms—the fire boiling water into superheated steam at 850 degrees, 600 pounds pressure, creating 60,000 horsepower at full speed.

Pipes, valves, blowers, generators, pumps, condensers, panels, alarms, dials, gauges, meters, fans—and the war above, a muffled thing, distant and unknown.

Read a magazine, wait for the coffee to perk, watch the gauges, make some small talk, try not to visualize the war that is above and outside. Then the weird noise, the explosion and an intricate engine room becomes a shambles of broken pipes, fierce flame, blackness.

"DELEGATE, DELEGATE, THIS IS MONGOOSE. OVER."

"GO AHEAD, MONGOOSE."

"DELEGATE, THIS IS MONGOOSE. WE ARE IN TERRIBLE SHAPE AND ARE SINKING. WE HAVE BEEN HIT TWICE AND ARE STILL UNDER ATTACK."

"WE KNOW IT, MONGOOSE, WE KNOW IT. . . . BLUENOSE IS ON HER WAY TO HELP YOU . . ."

The Japanese war had become a suicide war.

Out of this concept came the Kamikaze Tokuetsu Kogekitai (Kamikaze Special Attack Squad).

Kamikaze means "divine wind." It referred to a typhoon back in 1281 that dispersed the invasion fleet of Mongol Emperor Kublai Khan when he tried to take Japan. Now the Americans had sent another invasion armada to the Japanese perimeter of Okinawa—1,381 ships loaded with 183,000 troops and almost 800,000 tons of cargo. No longer having a fleet strong enough to turn them back, the Japanese counted on the crushing force of kamikaze planes—planes packed with explosives and aimed like a living missile to crash on our ships and destroy them.

Kamikazes had been strikingly successful at the Philippines and Iwo Jima. Now came the crucial test.

They were mostly young pilots with minimum training and maximum courage, and their orders were simple:

"It is absolutely out of the question for you to return alive. Your mission involves certain death. Choose a death that brings maximum results. Your bodies will be dead, but not your spirits."

There were only five planes left, all in poor condition, so the request was for volunteers. Everybody volunteered.

"As I turned to enter the shelter," said Captain Rikihei Inoguchi, "several of the pilots reached out to grab at my arms and sleeves, saying, 'Send me! Please send me! Send me!'

"I wheeled about and shouted, 'Everybody wants to go. Don't be so selfish!' "

Before they left, the kamikaze pilots attended their own funerals, wore white bands on their foreheads signifying death, handed their commanding officer little white boxes to be sent to their families, boxes that contained some of their hair or nails, since their ashes would never be found. And they wrote their final letters:

"Please do not weep because I am about to die . . ."

". . . I do not want a grave. I would feel oppressed if they were to put me in a narrow vault. A vagabond, such as I, has no need for it . . ."

"May our death be as sudden and clean as the shattering of crystal . . ."

Within thirty-six hours, 355 kamikaze pilots sank six of our ships, damaged 22 others. Before the campaign was over, the kamikazes sank 36 ships, damaged 368 others, killed or wounded 9,700 sailors, caused higher casualties in our Navy than in any other period in its history. One out of every seven naval casualties in World War II occurred near Okinawa.

"The lead kamikaze dives, dropping vertically into a barbed-wire entanglement of flak. He'll never make the carriers; that seems obvious. Instead, he's heading for a cruiser near the fringe. For a moment it looks as if he'll make it. But no—he's hit, and it's all over. His plane is a red flare, fading, dropping from sight.

"Everything is a blur now—a mixture of sound and color. Two more of them go the same way, exploding in midair. A fourth is luckier. He screams unscathed through the barrage, leveling inside the flak umbrella near the water. A hit! He's struck a destroyer right at the waterline. A bellowing explosion, then another and another. It's good! It's good! The ship is in its death throes . . .

"Tatsuno is alone now, still unhit, making a perfect run, better than they ever taught us in school. Tatsuno! Tatsuno! Fire spouts from his tail section, but he keeps going. The orange fingers reach out. His plane is a moving sheet of flame, but they can't stop him. Tatsuno! A tanker looms, ploughing the leaden liquid. They're closing! A hit! An enormous explosion rocks the atmosphere. For a curious instant embers seem to roll and dance. Now a staccato series of smaller bursts and one mighty blast, shaking the sea like a blanket. The tanker is going down. Gone. No trace but the widening shroud of oil.

"That was my friend."

There were 1,900 individual kamikaze attacks throughout the Okinawa campaign, and ten kikusui. A kikusui was a mass attack of kamikaze, a banzai with wings. Kikusui meant "floating chrysanthemums."

A more sophisticated kamikaze, the baka bomb, was not as successful. It was a glide bomb, launched from the belly of a conventional bomber, a Japanese version of the German V-1 missile. Guided at 600 mph by a single suicide pilot, the baka had a 2,640-pound warhead of trinitroanisol. Twenty feet long with a sixteen-foot wingspan, it carried three rockets as boosters. The pilot had to pull out of a dive into a glide toward its victim. Eight hundred were built, fifty were used and only three hit their target. Had they been perfected and used earlier, their effect could have been devastating.

There was also the "kaiten." "Kaiten" meant "turning the tide." That was the hope that didn't happen. It was a one-man ship that could move twenty knots at top speed, carry almost eight tons, so detonated that it was almost a moving mine ready to explode on contact. The Japanese had some four hundred kaitens parked on a small island outside Okinawa, which we fortunately found before they could use them.

Our invading troops expected the same pattern of suicide war on land.

"This is Zero Hour, boys," said Tokyo Rose, just before our invasion. "It is broadcast for all you American fighting men in the Pacific, particularly those standing off the shores of Okinawa . . . because many of you will never hear another program . . . Here's a good number, 'Going Home' . . . You boys off Okinawa enjoy it while you can, because when you're dead, you're a long time dead . . . Let's have a little jukebox music for the boys and make it hot . . . The boys are going to catch hell soon and they might as well get used to the heat."

If Iwo Jima was a pivotal pinpoint of an island, Okinawa's seizure was an urgent necessity. A key Japanese communications center, only 360 miles from Japan, Okinawa was the largest and most heavily populated island in the Ryukyu archipelago—more than 60 miles long and often more than ten miles wide—a settled island of small farms of fertile fields, cultivating sugar, rice and sweet potatoes. Most vital of all, it could handle 5,000 bombers.

"From Okinawa," our invading troops were told, "we can bomb the enemy anywhere—China, Japan, Formosa."

"And vice versa," a sergeant said.

The Japanese had over 100,000 troops on Okinawa, considered the island to be almost part of their homeland. The Japanese premier had said: "The enemy now stands at our front gate. It is the gravest moment in our country's history."

L-Day or Landing Day was April 1, 1945, Easter Sunday, and our troops expected the worst. But the Japanese let our troops ashore almost undisturbed. The Tenth Army landed 50,000 troops between 0830 and 1600 hours on L-Day, with only a few dozen casualties. It just didn't seem to make any sense. That's when we started referring to L-Day as Love Day.

Love Day continued into Honeymoon Week.

408

It was so easy that GI's changed slogans from "The Golden Gate in '48" to "Home Alive in '45."

Big joke was, "The Marines are going so fast that they have already contacted the Russians coming up from the other side of Okinawa."

And somebody put some lyrics to a song that started out, "Oh, don't you worry, Mother, your son is safe out here."

There were two landing fields just behind the six-mile strip of beaches, and we never expected to get them without a struggle, but we walked into them, too. The nearby dominating cliffs were honeycombed with caves and tunnels and fortifications—but the guns were dummy guns and the enemy was still invisible.

A Japanese plane landed smoothly on our newly captured field, the pilot getting out casually, walking toward our troops, suddenly saw his error, reached for his gun, and was quickly killed.

There's always one poor bastard who doesn't get the word.

Enemy resistance was much heavier on the nearby small island of Ie Shima, which we wanted for a radar station. One of the casualties, killed by a machine-gun bullet, was a shy, gnomelike civilian correspondent.

The simple monument on his grave read:

> At This Spot
> The
> 77th Infantry Division
> Lost a Buddy
> Ernie Pyle
> 18 April 1945

A skinny little runt of a guy with that wool knit cap of his and the thin gray hair on his thin face and those tired eyes of his. His eyes were always so tired. He saw so many things in war that lots of other people never saw. He saw the hurting loneliness of soldiers, how dirty and scared they could get, the look in their eyes when they passed around their pictures and letters, their sweating tenseness while waiting for the jump-off.

He saw all this because he lived with them, drank with them, shared their dreams and their war hell, squatted over the same slit trench.

More than anything else, Ernie wanted the people back home to know what war was, the monotony and misery of it. More than anything else, he wanted to puncture the phony overdramatic ideas that most people had picked up from too many movies. Somebody said he wrote a column as if he was giving away a part of himself. And so he was.

Not only did Ernie write what the GI couldn't quite put into words, but he was always on their side, always yelling for them. Ernie was the first to suggest that the combat soldier deserved extra pay, not as a reward—because there was no reward big enough—but as a sign of appreciation and recognition.

He was a part of the GI heart.

For them there was no other correspondent.

We cut Okinawa in two the first week, soon controlled three-fourths of the island, almost without contest. GI's were picking up farmyard pets—ponies, goats, rabbits. Some of them even moved into Japanese mess halls. The rice paddies seemed so picturesque, the climate so cool, the living so easy.

But not for long. The Japanese had concentrated their troops in the 85 square miles of the island's southern part —a maze of ridges fortified by large masses of carefully positioned artillery. Their plan was to pull us into the island, far away from the supporting gunfire of our ships— and then wipe us out.

We had five full divisions—three of them infantry, and two Marine—and we started a concerted push south by the middle of April. We counted our gains in yards—when we could count them at all. The *Nubai* had come—the incessant torrential rain that immobilized tanks and trucks, turned roads into rivers, foxholes into private pools, mud into lead.

Working day and night on the roads, engineers took their shoes off, tied sacking over their bare feet and fastened it around their knees. Mud clung to everything— food, clothes, guns. Mud in your C-rations, mud in your nails, mud in your ears. Blow your nose, and you blew mud. You kept your rifle under your body but how long could you keep it dry? If there was a common prayer then, it was, "Don't let me get wounded in the mud. Don't let me get killed in the mud."

Sugar Loaf wasn't just a hill—it was part of a small complex of high ground. Half Moon Hill on one side of it, and Horseshoe on the other. All of it had a flat ground

410

approach completely covered by their combined mortar and artillery. That ground became a meat grinder of casualties.

Our attack pattern was: barrage a hill with bombs and shells, move up the foot soldiers, hold it against counterattacks, fight down the reverse slope, then start on the next one.

We would attack during the day, dig in for the night—not for sleep, but for safety. A hole was never deep enough when the Japanese started their barrage. And then, at night, they would come, a screaming banzai or a single shadow.

Pvt. Evan Wylie described how Cpl. Alex Worden, of Roslyn, N.Y., was chewing some peanuts near his tank trying to keep awake when he saw some casual figure walking nearby.

"Hey, you," he called. "You want to get your butt shot off?" No answer, but the single shadow, suddenly multiplied. "Shoot those sonsofbitches," yelled Pfc. Junior Howell of Muncie, Ind.

"Don't let them get close," yelled somebody else. "They may have satchel charges."

Then, over the tank intercom, Cpl. Daniel Sullivan, of Los Angeles, Calif., pleaded, "Shoot 'em high, they may have nice sabers."

The next morning, when they looked at the dead Japanese, they noted that the bodies were clean, healthy, wearing new uniforms.

"If they're all like this," said one GI glumly, "then the bastards aren't even close to being licked."

But, finally, one day the word came, "SEND UP PX SUPPLIES. SUGAR LOAF IS OURS."

But there was also Conical Hill, Chocolate Drop Hill, Dick Hill, a dozen others. And the Japanese still controlled eight square miles surrounding the commanding heights of Mt. Yae Take. Nobody went up front without carrying something—food, water, ammo. Those coming back brought the wounded and the dead and the broken.

Every man has his breaking point. You can hear just so many shells, see just so many torn bodies, fear just so much fear, soak just so much rain, spend just so many sleepless nights—and then your irritability turns into silence, your silence into stupor, your legs twitch without

411

control, your eyes dilate, you urinate unknowingly, and your mouth opens and you scream.

There was the Marine on some island, hitting a tree screaming, "I hate you, goddammit, I hate you . . ." And another Marine nearby merely said, "Hit it once for me."

On Okinawa, he might have been hitting the mud.

We cleared out the complex of hills by the end of May, reduced the Japanese force to some 15,000 fanatical defenders holed up in caves. Then, again, came the spectacle of mass horror. Japanese soldiers running naked out of their caves, throwing dirt into the faces of bewildered GI's, then racing back into their caves to kill themselves. In one crowd of 350 Japanese soldiers and civilians, suicides mounted at the rate of one a minute: men killing their women, then blowing off their own heads with grenades; soldiers striking off the heads of their fellow soldiers, before killing themselves; and, everywhere, people simply cutting their throats.

Eighty-two days after our invasion, it was all over. The Japanese dead added up to 110,000 and our own casualties of dead and wounded were almost half of that.

A sergeant recognized a dead body, somebody from his platoon.

"He was a good guy," he said.

Another sergeant added quietly, "They were all good guys."

Airpower

Air war seemed as impersonal as long-range artillery. You bombed pinpoints, not people. You shot down other planes, not other pilots. No faces, no faces at all.

There were exceptions. Japanese pilot, Saburo Sakai, wrote:

"I could not believe what I saw—the Wildcat continued flying, almost as if nothing had happened. A Zero which had taken that many bullets into its vital cockpit, would have been a ball of fire by now. I could not understand it. I slammed the throttle forward and closed in to the American plane just as the enemy fighter lost speed. In a moment, I was ten yards ahead of the Wildcat, trying to slow down. I hunched my shoulders, prepared for the onslaught of his guns. I was trapped. I had popped 200 rounds into his cockpit, watching the bullets chewing up the thin metal skin and shattering the glass. But no bullets came; the Wildcat's guns remained silent. The entire situation was unbelievable. I dropped my speed until our planes were flying wing-to-wing formation. I opened my cockpit window and stared out. The Wildcat's cockpit canopy was already back, and I could see the pilot clearly. He was a big man, with a round face. He wore a light khaki uniform. He appeared to be middle-aged, not as young as I'd expected.

"For several seconds, we flew along in our bizarre formation, our eyes meeting across the narrow space between the two planes. The Wildcat was a shambles. Bullet holes had cut the fuselage and the wings up, from one end to the other. The skin of the rudder was gone, and the metal ribs stuck out like a skeleton. Now I could understand his horizontal flight, and also why the pilot had not fired. Blood stained his right shoulder, and I saw the dark patch moving downward over his chest. It was incredible that his plane was still in the air.

"But this was no way to kill a man! Not with him flying helplessly wounded, his plane a wreck. I raised my left hand, and shook my fist at him, shouting, uselessly, I knew, for him to fight instead of just flying along like a clay pigeon. The American looked startled; he raised his right hand weakly and waved.

"I had never felt so strange before. I had killed many Americans in the air, but this was the first time a man had weakened in such a fashion, directly before my eyes, and from wounds I had inflicted upon him. I honestly didn't know whether or not I should try to finish him off. Such thoughts are stupid, of course. Wounded or not, he was an enemy, and he had almost taken three of my own men, a few minutes before. However, there was no reason to aim for the pilot again. I wanted the airplane, not the man. I aimed carefully at the engine, barely touched the cannon trigger. A burst of flame and smoke exploded outward from his engine. The Wildcat rolled, and the pilot bailed out. Far below me, almost directly over the Guadalcanal coast, his parachute snapped open. The pilot did not grasp the shroud lines, but hung limply in the chute. The last I saw of him, he was drifting in toward the beach."

They did so much. Shark-mouthed P–40's flying out of China to protect the building of the Burma Road. The old PBY Catalina flying boats with two 2,000-pound torpedoes slung on their fat underbellies were converted into emergency torpedo bombers seeking out enemy transports. The workhorse plane of them all, the C–47 "Gooney Birds," flying unarmed everywhere, including the Hump over the Himalaya Mountains, carrying 15,000 tons of supplies per month from India to China; night-fighter planes that sought out kamikazes while they rested and refueled at nearby airfields; B–24 Liberators flying 2,600 miles from Australia to places like Balikpapan in Borneo, the Dutch East Indies, to knock out oil refineries.

Balikpapan supplied Japan with 35 percent of its oil. Oil is the blood of war, and 72 B–24's were sent to let the blood boil.

No bomber had ever flown so far before and no bombers had ever carried so much—20,000 pounds more per plane than the maximum specifications allowed.

The 72 took off on September 30, 1944, a sixteen-hour flight. Or, as somebody said, "Hours and hours of boredom . . . punctuated by a few moments of sheer terror."

One of its engines had been hit, oil started to burn on the cylinders, its tail was partly on fire, and the enemy fighters kept closing in.

All air gunners have rules:

Never shoot at an enemy plane unless it's close enough to do some good.

Always aim at a plane where it burns most easily—between the wing and the fuselage.

Go after bombers first.

Right waist gunner Sgt. Charles Held saw his gun shot out of his hands, the ring sight knocked off, the gun's back end broken apart. Held used his parachute for a cushion, pressing the loose gun against his chute pack. Holding the hot barrel in one hand, jolted by each recoil, he kept firing bursts at the attacking planes.

"I couldn't aim but my tracers were coming close enough so that the Japanese fighters at least knew this gun was still working."

At first the copilot tried to cheer up the crew, but then they heard him whimper over the intercom, "Oh my God, let me out of here . . . Please God let me out of here . . ."

Top turret gunner S/Sgt. Wilber L. Bowen later said, "Half the time I was praying hard enough to save half of the people in the United States. And half the time, I was cursing hard enough to put a good bishop in hell. When I saw three planes coming in at once with their wing edges sparkling, I just prayed they wouldn't hit us. And then when one of my guns jammed, I would pound on the magazine and cuss in the worst way I knew how."

Somehow the plane's fire was put out, its turrets chopped out with axes and thrown overboard to lighten weight, leaks in oil tanks stuffed with a pencil, a screwdriver, some rags and bits of candle.

And, somehow, they landed with broken brakes, plowing through palm trees, cutting through a parked truck, stopping in a sandbank. It took twelve seconds for every crew member to get clear of the plane.

Sergeant Held had a chest black and blue from the pounding of the gun he held, his hand burned through the glove he wore, his leg hurt by a stump of a tree that flew into the bomb bay during the landing.

But they were alive and they had done their job.

It took five such raids to destroy almost half of the Balikpapan Refinery, and put the rest of it out of action for six months.

> *God in your guts, good men at your back,*
> *Wings that stay on, and Tally-Ho.*

That was part of a poem by Gil Robb Wilson, and while it had some of the special spirit of the air, it told none of the daily detail of the drab and the dull and the lonely.

Let a bomb slip and it can crush your skull. Keep lifting them and they can break your back. Be careless about a fuse and you won't be around long.

Fix the fuel lines, change the cylinders, switch the engines, replace the wheels, instruments, radio, radar, hydraulic lines, the 55,000 separate parts all subject to steady strain.

And what about all the pencil-pushers with the daily headache of primary targets, secondary targets, availability of planes, men, bombs, gas, ammo, wind velocities, weather forecast, air speeds, radio frequencies, code words, special signals, landmarks on land and ocean, star fixes, distress frequencies, assembly points, starting time, disposition of enemy flak, location of enemy searchlights, latest espionage reports on troop concentration, factory production, shipping reports.

How many man-hours?

How many pencils?

How many quiet, forgotten men?

The B–29 was known as the "three billion dollar gamble." It was supposed to be the battleship of the skies, 65 tons of plane with a range of 3,500 miles, a four-ton bombload, 350 mph speed. Besides all this it had a pressurized cabin, power turrets and a central fire-control system. We had too few of them to use in Europe before that war ended. We used them first in the Pacific, out of China, in June 1944 but they were uneconomical. It took a dozen ferry trips over the Hump to supply enough fuel to fly a single mission to Japan.

Before the B–29's, the people of the islands of Japan had a song they sang:

Why should we be afraid of air raids?
The big sky is protected with iron defenses.
For young and old, it is time to stand up;
We are loaded with the honor of defending the homeland;
Come on, enemy planes! Come on many times!

After the B–29 raid of March 9, 1945, the Japanese people switched from their song to slogans;

ONE HUNDRED MILLION PEOPLE DIE IN HONOR.
BETTER TO DIE THAN SEEK IGNOMINIOUS SAFETY.

Flying out of the Marianas, the 20th Air Force of B–29's found itself faced with a serious morale problem. By the end of February 1945 they had lost 75 B–29's, and one wing alone had 800 casualties. But even more galling were the small results that went with the high losses. The Japanese filled the sky with flak and fighters, forcing us to do pinpoint bombing from extremely high altitudes. Results were most disappointing.

Then came the raid of March 9.

The air was sticky with sweat in the war rooms of the 500th Group in Saipan, the narrow, wooden benches crowded with the 5,000 crewmen waiting for the word.

The walls were covered with maps, charts, photographs, a wooden stage filled with briefing officers. Everyone wore khaki shorts, open shirts, and the silence was forced.

Then came the parade of briefing officers on Intelligence, weather, Bombing, Navigation, Engineering, Radar, Communications.

It would be a total raid, flown mostly at 5,000 feet instead of 30,000, darkness instead of daylight, singly instead of formation, and incendiaries instead of regular bombs. Target: Tokyo.

"One more thing . . ." The airmen held their breaths, "No guns and no ammunition will be carried. Get that? No guns, no ammunition. First of all, if we carried guns, it is likely we'd fire at each other. Second, we will carry all our weight in bombs and gas. Third, Intelligence reports indicate there will be no night-fighters of any account. Therefore, no guns, no ammunition."

Two sergeants named Baden and Spachtaholtz, quiet-voiced and quick-speaking, tested their signals, then visually checked every plane for lights, bomb bays, engine fire, directed them into position, maintaining flow without jam, seeing two planes taking off on parallel strips every fifty seconds.

Two sergeants controlling 162 planes, two hundred million dollars' worth of equipment. Across the bay at Tinian, another 110 B–29's joined the mission, and 54 more from Guam.

At 1:21 A.M., the first arriving word at the Mission Control room: "This blaze will haunt me forever. It's the most terrifying sight in the world, and, God forgive me, it's the best."

That single incendiary raid literally leveled sixteen square miles of the most densely populated place in the world. The individual fires had joined each other to form an inferno. Our tail gunners could see that city burning from 150 miles away. It had killed more than 83,000 people, left a million more homeless. We had lost only fourteen planes at sea out of our 334 on the mission, and we had rescued five of the downed crews.

The enormity of its success was exceeded only by its significance.

We had discovered our ultimate pattern of air war.

Within several months, our incessant fire-bomb raids by B–29's destroyed the productive capacity of five major

417

cities. By mid-July our B–29's were bombing day and night without aerial opposition—burning out 58 cities in 37 weeks.

Then came the clincher.

There were two bombs: one called "Little Boy," and a slightly larger one called "Fat Boy." They belonged to the 509th Composite Group.

There were seven B–29's in that Group and all they seemed to do was to fly practice missions. Noboby knew everything about "Little Boy" or "Fat Boy" except the pilot, bombardier and an ordnance man on one of the B–29's, the *Enola Gay.*

At 0245 hours August 6, 1945, three B–29's took off from tiny Tinian. The trip was uneventful. On the *Enola Gay,* Pfc. Richard Nelson was reading a novel about boxing called *Watch Out for Willie Carter.* Flight engineer S/Sgt. Wyatt Duzenbury, of Lansing, Mich., kept his eyes, as usual, on his gauges. Radar operator Sgt. Joe Steiborik of Texas kept looking for cloud formations. And tail gunner S/Sgt. George Caron threw six apples the length of the tunnel, hoping to hit a sleeping lieutenant who had come along as a special observer.

The *Enola Gay* had the standard set of good-luck charms: three pairs of silk panties, six prophylactic kits, one Good Conduct ribbon, a ski cap, and one shellac-covered lipstick kiss printed on the nose, signed "Dottie," with the note, "Omaha, one time." She was one of the more memorable girls who worked at Omaha Air Base.

They arrived on target at 0815 hours.

"I'd be the biggest ass in the Air Force if I missed the target," said the navigator, as he squeezed the button.

"Little Boy" took 47 seconds to drop and hit.

Target was Hiroshima.

Yeoman Second Class Robert Schwartz later quoted the electronics officer of the *Enola Gay* as describing the blast by saying, "Jesus Christ, if people knew what we were doing we could have sold tickets for $100,000."

There had been an alert earlier in the morning in this city of 343,000 people. It was Monday morning and everybody had rushed to their shelters until the all-clear came. Now everybody was back at work again. The day was mild, the wind hardly perceptible, the sky almost completely clear.

418

And then somebody saw this single plane high in the sky.

"Suddenly a glaring whitish pinkish light appeared in the sky accompanied by an unnatural tremor which was followed almost immediately by a wave of suffocating heat and a wind which swept away everything in its path," a Japanese civilian told Red Cross representative Marcel Junod afterward.

"Within a few seconds, the thousands of people in the streets and the gardens in the center of the town were scorched by a wave of searing heat. Many were killed instantly, others lay writhing on the ground screaming in agony from the intolerable pain of their burns. Everything standing up right in the way of the blast—walls, houses, factories and other buildings—was annihilated and the debris spun around in a whirlwind and was carried up in the air."

That single atomic bomb had killed some 78,000 people, injured 37,000 more, some 10,000 others were never found.

When the Japanese still refused to surrender, we dropped another bomb on Nagasaki three days later.

And, when the Japanese seemed to stall in their final surrender negotiations, we sent a thousand B–29's over Japan in a single raid.

Military leaders in Japan urged the Emperor to fight one last battle for Japan itself. They still had a million men under arms in the home islands, still had more than 5,000 kamikaze planes, still had thousands of tons of ammunition.

But the Emperor refused.

In the first broadcast he had ever made to the Japanese people, Emperor Hirohito told them, "A continuation of the war will result in ultimate collapse and obliteration of the Japanese nation."

Surrender was unconditional. Formal ceremonies took place aboard the battleship *Missouri* in Tokyo Bay on September 2, 1945. The signing started at three minutes after nine on this Sunday morning—exactly three years, eight months and one week after Pearl Harbor.

It was a ten-foot table covered with gold-trimmed green cloth. Aside from all the generals and admirals and foreign dignitaries, there were all the *Missouri* sailors and

Marines. S/Sgt. Bob Price remembered that the Japanese uniforms were made of "a cheap, sleazy green cotton," and that their leather boots looked "artificial." He felt that they had gotten all dressed up to impress us and that it didn't quite come off. "Or then, again," said Price, "perhaps there is something in his military code which tells a man what to wear to a surrender." He also noted how they brought their own lunches, wrapped in white paper, as if they surely didn't expect to be fed. To Price, they looked "strange and lonely."

One of the arriving Japanese pilots raced back to his plane to get three wilted bouquets—roses, pinks and larkspurs. An American interpreter asked him why the flowers, and the pilot answered in perfect English, "Just because."

Sgt. Dale Kramer recorded the reaction of a GI who was operating the broadcasting unit. When he saw the fat leather folders of documents on the green table, the GI said, "Brother, I hope those are my discharge papers."

The signing was completed at 0917 hours, and General Douglas MacArthur spoke into his battery of five microphones:

"Let us pray that peace be now restored to the world, and that God will preserve it always. These proceedings are closed."

Up in the air over Tokyo, during one of those final fiery raids, was a B–29 tail gunner, a sergeant named Ben Kuroki, of Hershey, Nebr. He was an American of Japanese ancestry and it had been a prolonged struggle to persuade people that he should be judged by his spirit and not by his skin and that he had a right to fight for his country. He had flown 58 missions, all over Europe and Japan. And during that Tokyo raid, he remembered wondering about the kind of people the bombs were killing. People who looked like him, maybe some who even thought like him. Besides the Japanese warmongers and fascists, there must be many down there who neither hated nor wanted, but simply existed. The big mass of people were shoved around by fear. And there must be some, too, who had his hate of fascism, his love of democracy. All of them, the good and the bad and the innocent—under the bombs.

He shivered slightly.

"If only all these missions, all the killing of so many people, if only it all adds up to something . . ."

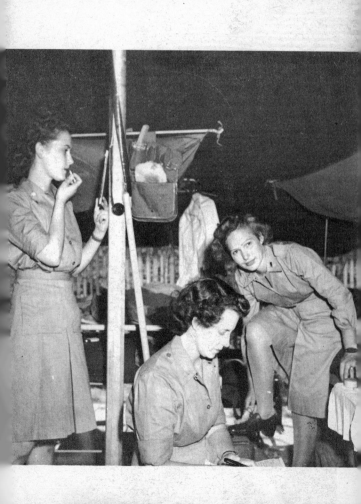

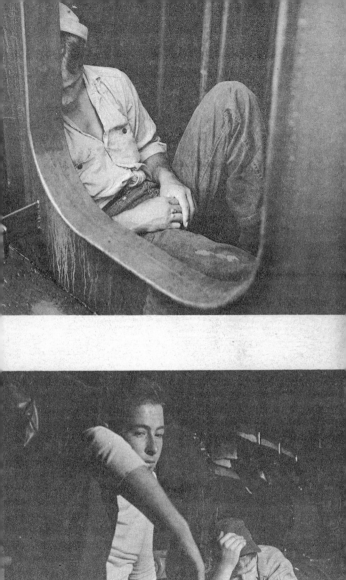

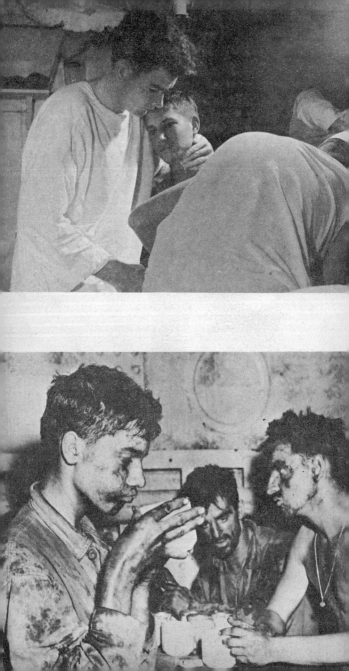

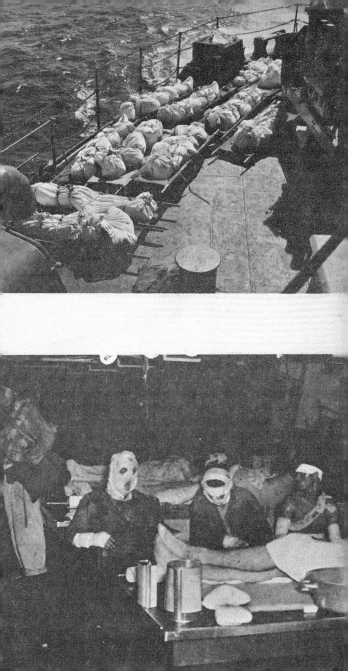

64330

EPILOGUE

Letter to America

*The world must build a new house, America, a
house big enough for all the peoples to live in
(For we on the beaches of Africa are waiting now to
splinter the old house, crash in its weak rafters,
rip up its rotten floor boards, open it up to the
sky. . . .*

—T/Sgt. Milton Lehman

Step into the Signature Room, sign the final discharge
papers, get some back pay, a handshake, a discharge button, and suddenly you are a civilian.

Suddenly.

Perhaps too suddenly. The bridge was too long and
where were the words?

Your girl was warm, but could you ask her how warm
she was the four years you were away?

Your 4-F friends were sympathetic, but how could you
share their soft, settled look?

Your family was considerate, but what could you tell
your mother, after you heard yourself say at the dinner
table, "Pass the fuckin' butter."

The frame was waiting for you to fit into it.

But how sure were you of anything anymore? Did you
still want the same girl? The same job? The same future?

Where to? What next?

When he passed by Bub Wolfe's drugstore, a man spotted him and came walking over fast, his face wide-open in

463

a smile, his hand outstretched. "Sure glad to see you again, Ben," he said. "We've been reading about you in the newspapers and magazines and been hearing you on the radio . . . We folks are sure proud of you, Ben."

The words were warm and friendly, but they made him feel awkward. He wanted to say something clever, or else start laughing to change the subject, but instead he heard himself saying, "I just did my job."

That happened all day long, people stopping him on the street, pumping his hand, slapping his back, smiling at him, telling him what a big hero he was, and how he really had put Hershey, Nebr., on the map. Then there were the kids. Wherever he went, they stopped whatever they were doing to stare at him, counting aloud all his ribbons and battle stars, and arguing among themselves which was the Distinguished Flying Cross and which was the Pacific Theater Ribbon. One kid walked up to him and shyly asked, "Are you *really* Ben Kuroki?" When Ben smiled and said yes, the kid's mouth just fell open and all he could say was, "Gee . . ."

This was his hometown, these were his neighbors. Most of the memories of his twenty-seven years were tied up with them. This man had got him his first permit to trap beaver, that woman was one of his classmates, this little girl was the daughter of his best friend, that man used to work on their farm. He knew them all. Never had there been a single instance, a single word, to let him know that his skin was yellow and theirs white.

Until Pearl Harbor Day. He had gone to that pool hall across the street to pick up a case of beer and some farmer had looked straight at him, and said in a loud voice, "Well, I guess the Japs in this town are really celebrating tonight."

How sharply they still stuck in his mind: the words, the man, the room. And he remembered how he had seemed to freeze, sort of a physical-mental paralysis. He couldn't move, couldn't say anything, couldn't even think. Everything was just a big white blot. Then, somehow, he was walking in the street, walking quickly without knowing where, filled with a hot rush of anger, thinking of the million things he could have said and done. Why hadn't he socked the guy? Why didn't he tell everybody that he and his brother Fred had already decided to enlist in the Army the next morning?

That was four years ago, and yet it still hurt to think of it, even though it was such a small slap compared to all the things that had happened to him in the Army: "Are you Chinese? No? Filipino? No? What? A Jap? Then what in the hell are you doing in the American Army? We don't need your kind."

But everything was all right now. He had proved himself. And this was Hershey, his home. These were his friends. In Hershey, he knew that people were judged as individuals, not by who their father was, or the color of their skin, or the church they prayed in.

This was Hershey, a tiny hunk of American democracy sitting on both sides of U.S. Highway 30, only twelve miles west of North Platte, but you have to slow down, or you might miss it. This was Hershey—sugar beets, corn, potatoes, cattle, and 487 people. And when Farmer Ben Lind hurt his leg and couldn't shuck his corn, somebody spread the news on the party line. That afternoon, Lind's farm was filled with neighbors shucking his corn, neighbors with all kinds of accents—Swedish, German, Italian, Irish, Japanese. But they were all friends and neighbors, all Americans. And when the federal government clamped down on the bank accounts of Americans of Japanese ancestry, the Kurokis had a sudden rush of neighbors dropping in, to offer what help they could.

These memories kept him going when the Army repeatedly turned down his requests for combat; when he found himself doing KP four times as often as anybody else; when he stopped taking passes to town because there was always some drunk who spotted him and started yelling; when he discovered that an FBI agent was trailing him all the time, even after he had been checked and double-checked; and when he cried himself to sleep because he was so lonely for somebody to talk to.

Thinking of these things, Ben found himself automatically walking toward the school. It looked the same, except maybe a little smaller. Across the street, the cows were still mooing and chewing in the field next to the church.

Soon he was inside, walking into the auditorium, hunting up his old desk to look for some scratched initials. All that fun that he, Bill Diamond and Gordie Jorgenson used to have in this room, throwing spitballs and secretly chewing tobacco. And that class play they were all in. He was a French butler, with a mustache and a goatee that kept falling off, Bill Diamond was dressed up like a girl, and Gordie had the leading role because he was the handsomest. Gordie was dead now.

There was his graduation picture, the whole class of fourteen students. How dressed-up and serious he looked. He must have known that the best fun was finished.

When Ben turned around, there was a thin, tall, graying teacher coming quickly over to introduce herself. "You must be Ben Kuroki," she said. "You don't know me, but of course I know all about you. I taught most of your younger brothers and sisters. Are you going to see the principal now?"

The new principal was a solidly built, serious young man, who explained that he also taught several subjects, as well as being athletic coach and the owner of the grocery store. He had talked to a lot of students, and he knew how much they admired Ben, so would Ben please tell them some of his experiences? He could fill the auditorium in five minutes. Ben smiled, nodded. "Okay," he said.

He looked at their faces. Their ages ranged from the small grade-school kids to the fuzzy-faced adolescents to the slightly swaggering seniors. War to them was still heroic and romantic, like in the movies. What should he tell them?

First he told them what he knew they wanted to hear. He told them about some of the raids he was on: Bizerte, Naples, Messina, Rome. Wilhelmshaven, Ploesti. He told what thick flak looked like, and how some of it once tore through his plane's tail and almost killed him; how he saw planes explode in midair, disappearing completely; what it was like in that night raid over Tokyo when his B–29 was bathed in searchlights for five full minutes; how it felt to sweat out every day's raid, coming back to stare at an empty bunk that belonged to a buddy who was alive the night before.

He told them about all the red tape he had to cut, that he had to get special permission from the Secretary of War himself before he could become a tail gunner. And when he told why he tried so hard to get into combat, his voice was low, full of feeling, as if he were giving out his deepest secret.

It was because there were different kinds of Americans in his Liberator crew—Jewish, Polish, German, Italian, and even a full-blooded Indian. That, to him, was Democracy with a capital "D." He was fighting for that.

Later that afternoon, he dropped in at Bub Wolfe's place. Bub was always cracking jokes, and this time a

466

whole bunch of Ben's old buddies were there. They'd all grown up together, from hide-and-seek to basketball to war.

"Why don't you come down to the Legion meeting with us now?" asked Gordie's younger brother, Virge. "All the boys you know will be there. Plenty of beer, too."

Sure, he'd go, he said. He planned to join several veterans' organizations before he made up his mind which was his.

The Legion Hall was on the top floor of a two-story building. It was a big room that badly needed cleaning. Next to the door was a small, pot-bellied stove, already getting red from too much heat. In back of the desk was a huge American flag, and on the wall, right next to it, was a rifle complete with bayonet, World War I style. In the center of the room, were three full cases of beer.

Sitting behind the desk was the post commander, young enough to be the son of either of the two men who flanked him.

"The old Legionnaires gave him the job just to prove that they really intend to hand over the Legion to us World War II veterans," said Virge. "Those old boys deserve a lot of credit for keeping the Legion going until we got back. It almost died out, a lot of times."

On the post commander's left was a big, heavy man, the only one in the room wearing a Legion cap. On his right was a thin man with a small face. The other older men sat next to each other in small clusters, most of them tired-looking farmers, not talking much. When the room was almost full, the thin man whispered something to the post commander, who then loudly called the meeting to order. The big, heavy man started reading the roll call. Most of the names called weren't present. Virge explained it. "They're still in the Army. Their friends and folks signed up for them. Some of them won't even know they're in the Legion until they get back."

Next on the agenda was the treasurer's report. He was the thin man behind the desk, telling that they had paid so much for the band, and so much for that damn government tax, and that left them only twenty dollars net profit on the last dance they had. While he was talking, four older men came in, walking a little unsteadily, greeting all their friends in too-loud voices. The older members smiled nervously.

The trio behind the desk held a quick powwow and decided it was time to induct the new members. The post commander finally persuaded one of the older men to act as sergeant-at-arms and somebody else got the Legion flag, which was embroidered with "Paul R. Martin Post 279." Then the acting sergeant coughed and said, "You boys fall in here."

Being one of the few still in uniform, Ben felt awkward, but then, so did the others. They shuffled around slowly, looking sheepishly at each other. The commander very quickly read the Legion Laws and Oath. It was too fast for Ben to absorb all of it, but he caught such phrases as, "justice and equality," "democracy for all," and "without prejudice of race, color or creed."

It was done. He was a member. The commander was still shaking hands with each of them and the treasurer was collecting the two-dollar initiation fee and selling Legion emblems.

The commander mentioned the matter of getting a memorial plaque in honor of their war dead. He read different descriptions from a fancy folder, giving each price.

"They're pretty expensive," said the treasurer. "I'll bet some goddamned Jew owns all those companies. They own everything else in this country."

A man near Ben chimed in. "Yeah, those Jews can't think of anything else but making money." There was some more of the same.

Ben froze. He wanted to ask them if they had forgotten so quickly the words in that Legion Oath, the ones about equality and democracy. He wanted to plead with them to remember that, if they let intolerance sneak inside of them now, they would never again be able to treat people as individuals, but only as colors and religions and creeds. Then there would be no more of that wonderful democracy in Hershey.

He wanted to say, "Don't make me feel that I've fought for nothing."

But his tongue was paralyzed, like so many times before, when people had called him names. And soon it was too late. The meeting was over.

The street was dark and empty and cold and he suddenly felt lonely. In the car, driving home, he remembered something the principal had told him, after his speech:

"Now, Ben, wouldn't it be wonderful if the boys coming home could really practice the kind of democracy they were supposed to have fought for?"

468

*   *   *

It happened in December 1944: a small story in *The Stars and Stripes* told how the Hood River (Ore.) American Legion Post had wiped off the names of sixteen Nisei soldiers from their Honor Roll on the side of their courthouse.

Sagie Nishioka, who got his forty-second blood transfusion in an Army hospital, wrote a letter, which the Rev. W. Sherman Burgoyne read from his Hood River pulpit, saying he had already forgiven the misguided people who had broken into his house and smashed or "borrowed" his fine furniture. His one wish now was that some day he would be able to come back and work in his pear orchard.

While Burgoyne read the letter aloud, the stores in Hood River all had signs in their windows reading, "NO JAP TRADE."

The tension reached a crucial tightness in January 1945, when the first three Nisei returned. Ray Sato, Min Asai and Sat Noji walked down Main Street and saw people look through them, as if they were ghosts. In front of the poolroom, a few of the regulars stared at them and spat. And when Ray saw an old friend, and rushed over with his hand outstretched, the old friend gave him a glassy look and walked right by. And the kids jeered, "Japs . . . Japs . . . Japs . . ," Nisei who walked downtown said they felt they had signs on their backs, "Shoot Here." When Mrs. Avon Sutton waved hello to Edna Abe on Main Street, Edna rushed over, crying, "Mrs. Sutton, you're the only friend in town who has said hello to me." When Kikue Tabara tried to sell her asparagus crop, the produce man said nothing doing, unless she got a white person to sell it. He didn't want any of his friends to know he was buying Jap goods, he said, Kikue's husband was overseas at that time.

Then, when Bob Kageyana went into the barbershop for a haircut, the barber fidgeted for ten minutes, neither waiting on him nor kicking him out. When Bob finally asked him about it, the barber muttered, "But I've got a son in the Army . . ."

"Well, what do you think this is, a Boy Scout uniform?"

Then, suddenly, strange things happened. The owner of one of the movie theaters stopped a Nisei on the street to say how welcome Japanese-Americans would be in his place. Also, several storekeepers, hats in hand, visited their old Japanese friends to tell them how much they missed them at their stores.

They weren't kidding.

Ever since the four hundred Nisei had come out of their concentration camps back to the Valley, these town merchants had watched the evacuees spending all their money in nearby towns. They needed all kinds of equipment to replace everything that had been broken and stolen and lost while they were away. They weren't buying in Hood River because the signs were still up.

So, one day, the signs came down, all of them.

A lot of town organizations, like the Boosters Club and Veterans of Foreign Wars, began to send invitations to various Nisei to come back again into community life.

Somehow, though, the Nisei weren't rushing back. It took time for their hurt to heal, and they had been hurt so much. All those signs, blank looks, boycotts, threats, hate. It would take time for Ray Yasui to rub away the look on his five-year-old daughter's face when she came back from the grocery store whimpering, "Daddy, they don't like us in there, do they?"

*   *   *

An old-timer, a toothpick-chewing, big, fat man with white hair, answered your question:

"The veterans? Heck, boy, they don't hang around here. They're workin'. Every veteran in this town that wants a job has got one."

Across the railroad tracks, down Main Street, past the post office, right next to a barbershop, was a small store window with a sign, "Peoria Plan."

Peoria was different from other American cities, because Peoria had a plan for its veterans; one so simple that no other city had tried it before. The crux of it was something they called "Human Engineering."

V. D. McClellan was a former Carpenter's Mate Second Class, and before that he was a job specialist with the United States Employment Service.

"With me, there is no such thing as first come, first served," said the brisk-talking, balding McClellan. He shuffled a big pile of file cards. "See these? They're all employers who've been begging me to send them veterans for different jobs. But I can't do it. I only send men to jobs they're fitted for."

470

When he does have a job he can fill—whether it's a truck driver or baseball umpire, or a radio-promotion man —he doesn't send a dozen applicants; he sends one. And the one generally sticks, generally pleases.

If the veterans need any psychiatric help, they're sent to Dr. Irving Turow.

"But the general picture is bright," added Turow. "So many psychiatrists thought that our mental hospitals would be swamped with war casualties. I'm happy to say we were wrong."

Of the 5,000 veterans treated in one year, there was a big group who wanted neither jobs nor psychotherapy. They wanted advice on GI insurance, disability payments, filing claims, going to college, or starting a business. Their man was a tall, graying veteran of both wars, Jacob Haberle. It was Haberle who made most of the early contacts with Peoria's organizations, businesses, prominent people. His file had 300 names, representing at least 60 different businesses and professions, all voluntarily pledging their time, money and advice to the plan. Besides Haberle, Turow and McClellan, there was Director Jack Brennan. He had the job of smoothing the quirks and keeping out the politicians. When the governor of Illinois handed the Plan $50,000 for two years, there were no strings attached. The Community Chest supplied the rest; and former Industrial Consultant Brennan had a free hand and a lot of worries.

"But you know what my biggest worry is?" continued Brennan. "I'm worried about the eleven thousand Peoria vets who haven't come here yet. What's going to happen when all the veterans graduate from college, and the 52-20 payments stop, and the job market tightens up? What are we going to do if we have a serious depression then; is there anybody in America today who is making plans for that day?"

* * *

In a well-decorated Hollywood living room, several friends were having their after-dinner smoke.

"Now, take those veterans in the 52-20 Clubs. I tell you, the government is making bums out of our boys. Why should those boys work? They're living off the fat of the land . . ."

471

They were waiting out in the rain, the mob of them, waiting for the doors to open. Then they filed in quickly, filling up the long lines without too much noise, as if they had been doing it for a long time now. They simply stood in line, shuffling slowly toward the clerk's windows. There was no laughter and not much talk. If you looked at their faces, you could feel some of the shame in their silence. In this huge Unemployment Insurance office in Los Angeles, only a few of the veterans knew the answers. The rest talked in question marks.

One short, almost bald man, who didn't want to give his name, said he used to be a rug salesman in Detroit. War made him a radar specialist, and the Navy discharged him with a back disability.

"No more rug handling," warned the doctor. "Do something else."

He just couldn't get a job. He still had some pride left, he said, "Not much, but some."

It was his turn next at the window, and the woman asked him automatically if he'd been available for work the past seven days. He just nodded. When she handed him his check, he stuck it into his pocket and, without looking at anybody, headed for the door.

He was a big, heavy guy, this Leo Zale—formerly employed as a rifleman. Before that, he had been a crane operator in a shipyard, a jackhammer-man in a gold mine. "Even tried to get a job as a painter's helper, but they tell me I haven't got enough experience. Well, where in hell am I supposed to get experience?"

He talked loudly, his voice full of bitterness, about the sign in the harbor, "WELCOME HOME, BOYS—JOB WELL DONE"; about how he slept on the beach for the first five days after his discharge because no one had a room for him. "You can write that in your little notebook."

Walking up and down the lines, you only saw the tiredness and the bitterness. Inside the offices, all was sweetness and light. The small, round man who didn't want to be quoted, you understand, said that everything was fine and dandy. Things were really picking up, yessiree. Some 9,000 veterans were coming here every week for their checks now, while once there had been 16,000. Matter of fact, the colored boys made up half that load, now. You know what they say about those colored boys—last ones hired, first ones fired. Just can't find jobs for them. No, sirree. Same with the Mexican and the Filipino and the

472

Japanese boys. Yes, sir, if it weren't for them, our office would have a lot better record.

One loudmouth was telling his uninterested neighbors on the line that he was opening a big store in Hollywood next week. A little man with an old face asked him why the hell he was standing here on line, if he had so much dough. The big, handsome, blond guy slapped the little guy on the back, "Why not, bud? It's free, isn't it?"

Behind the big desk, the man said that almost 80,000 veterans had filed initial claims at this office alone, but that there were fewer than twenty-five "exhaustions" a week—that is, 25 vets who had received all 52 payments.

*   *   *

No question about it, said the vice-president of the University of Missouri. Veterans here are a healthy influence on education. They work harder, make their teachers work harder and raise standards all over the place.

It was too bad that the country's colleges weren't really prepared for the veterans. But when the university bought 165 government trailers, it was a gamble. Who could be sure that veterans would even live in trailers? And nobody ever thought that the housing situation in town would get so terrible. Nobody even imagined . . .

"Now it's too late to get any more trailers, and there are almost nine hundred married veterans on the waiting list. The state just gave them six million dollars to build permanent brick apartments, but materials are hard to find. Temporary barracks are being put up, but the vets will still be a little crowded—144 to a big barrack. It is too bad we couldn't see what was coming and plan for it. Because there's no question about it, the best is none too good for our veterans . . ."

Big shiny, private trailers parked so close to small, warped ones that their radio programs seemed to merge. A man mows a pitifully small lawn, only three steps each way. Flowers and vines and curtains try to color some of the drabness. The bottom covering of one trailer is so torn that you can see water dripping down from the icebox into a smelly, stagnant puddle, crowded with flies. Mothers yell for their kids. The stink of the garbage shed, overflowing cans, more flies. A dirty boy carries a big pail of water to his trailer.

In the center of a camp, stands a white wooden house badly in need of a paint job. Here are the toilets, showers, washing machines. The washing machines are all broken, the women's showers scummy dirty, and there are quick, crawling roaches everywhere—in the toilet, under a sign saying, "Remember, this is your HOME. Keep it clean."

"They've just tarred our trailer roof for the eighth time to try to stop it from leaking," said a bright-faced woman named Marian. "Sometimes, we wake up in the morning and there is an inch of water on the floor. The main reason we're so worried is that Sandy is susceptible to pneumonia; she's already had it three times. But then, one of the maintenance men told me that all those government trailer roofs are rotten. You can ask Mr. Ashlock."

Thin, sad-looking Norman Ashlock, sitting in his corner office in Jesse Hall, with maps of the three trailer camps, a pin for each trailer. Behind each pin are people, like the Robert Sconce family. The stove broke down in the winter, when it was so cold they hardly had enough covers for the baby. The trailer roof sagged so in the corner, that Bob bumped his head every time he stood up. And 17 other specific complaints.

When they saw Mr. Ashlock, he referred them to Mr. Johnson of the Veterans Administration, who referred them to Mr. Brady, vice-president of the university, who referred them back to Mr. Ashlock. And when Ashlock finally came around to investigate, he walked inside the trailer and stood up and bumped his head.

"Mr. Ashlock, what do you do about these leaky roofs?"

"We keep tarring them."

"But it doesn't seem to be working."

"You've got me," he said, shrugging his shoulders and smiling resignedly. "I don't know what we can do. They are all old trailers, you know. One thing about trailers, there's not much room to dodge leaks, is there?"

And what about the dripping iceboxes, scummy showers, broken washing machines, roaches?

"That's what we hire maintenance men and janitors for. That's their job. Besides, you seem to forget that those veterans are happy to be in those trailers, in the first place. A lot of vets don't have any place at all to live."

The beautiful campus here, with the ivy-covered columns and greenery, is quiet. Lots of people, but not much noise. No rah-rah college spirit. The faces are older, more serious.

At Gabler's, the jukebox is still screaming, but the faces are only those of the outnumbered teen-age freshmen, their razzmatazz slightly subdued. Most veterans take their dates elsewhere, some place where they can get beer and quiet. They go big for plays and concerts, too. This year, for the first time, there are going to be repeat performances of every concert.

For married veterans, who have to pinch pennies, social life is made up of an occasional bridge game, a rare movie, long walks in the moonlight.

"If we only had some privacy," said one dark-haired woman.

"I like my neighbors, but we all wish we weren't so close together, so cramped. I've almost forgotten what it feels like to walk into my own bathroom, to have it all for myself. As soon as my husband graduates, we're going back to our apartment and I'm going to parade around naked, all day, just to feel the sheer luxury of privacy."

For the wives of veterans, there's only the monotony of conversation, waiting for their husbands to come home. And when the men get through with classes, they've got homework and studying to do.

"When I went to college before the war, I went to have a good time," said ex-Marine Randall Mitchell. "Now I want to learn something."

They're not kids now; they've been in a war.

"Sure, my wife and I live on ninety a month, sometimes," said Norman Holman. "But that's when we don't do anything. I mean things like shows and ice-cream parlors. That also means no clothes. I'm still wearing my Army stuff. What's more, my brother brings us meat and vegetables from his farm every once in a while. But even then . . ."

The university takes care of maintenance, subtracts costs from rent, hands the rest over to the Federal Public Housing Authority. Rent, until recently, was $15 a month. The university announced that it just covered costs. Then, the FPHA raised rents at M.U. (five dollars more if you had other income, three dollars if you hadn't).

But why? Why should they pay $15 a month for a better trailer, with running water, down in Arkansas, and $25 for one in Minnesota? Why shouldn't all veterans, who were given the same $65 or $90 a month, be charged the same rent for the same trailers? And why should the government make a profit on this money? It didn't seem fair; it wasn't.

The veteran who couldn't get a trailer, the married veteran who was No. 700 on the waiting list, had to try to find an apartment or a room in a cellar that sometimes cost as high as $65. Some bought trailers with their savings, hoping to sell them after graduation. For a single vet it was a question of finding a bed anywhere. If it cost too much, he didn't go to college.

A tall, thin man said he'd spent $1,100 of his own money since he'd come to college. He considered himself lucky, he said, because he had the money to spend. He had been a lieutenant. "But what about the poor Joe who was an enlisted man, who wasn't able to save as much as I was?" he wondered.

"My question is," he said, "is a college education worth all this?"

The hell with snap courses.

That was their attitude. They said: "I'm interested in what I can get out of this course, what I can really learn. And I want a prof who teaches, not preaches. I've had enough indoctrination. I'm not the schoolboy I used to be. I'm not just going to copy down every word he says. If I disagree, I'm going to question; if I don't understand, I'm going to find out why."

It's a big problem, said David March, political science teacher, also a veteran. Teachers had to change their whole approach. They were no longer teaching merely seventeen-year-olds; mostly they taught mature men.

To teach these men, Missouri was still hiring a new crop of young, high school teachers, teachers who still emphasized the conjunctive adverb instead of the thought, who asked test questions on dates instead of history. Older teachers were hard to find.

"I'm getting out of here. What's the point of going to college when I get some dumb, young punk of a teacher who isn't any older than I am and doesn't know much more? Everything he's taught me, I could have got out of a textbook. He practically reads the thing. And we've got two hundred and fifty guys in our class."

His friend was listening quietly, then added: "It's true, what a guy learns in college depends largely on himself;
476

out in college they're supposed to make it easier, not tougher."

Arthur Ferrer shook his head. No matter what anybody said, he was grateful and happy to be there. College had always been a dream of his. If it weren't for the Army, he'd never have been there. He had never graduated from high school, and had had to pass an entrance exam to get in. What he couldn't get out of teachers, he'd get out of books. Maybe the Army gave him a rheumatic heart, but it gave him a chance for a college education. No, sir, he just didn't have anything to bitch about.

"These veterans are all so important," said one professor, "because they're going to run the world, and if they don't run it well, we're just not going to have a world.

"At a time when our colleges should offer the best teachers and the best education, they're the most inadequate. We still haven't made the decision whether we should fully educate five hundred, or half-educate a thousand. I just hope we make that decision before it's too late."

* * *

"This place isn't as nice as the one we used to live in before I went into the Army," said Joe Wadrzyk, a short, heavyset, slow-talking man. "We used to live in a five-room house, all by ourselves," he said, wiping his glasses. "But that used to cost us thirty-five dollars a month. That's a lot of money, I guess." He took a quick look around the small living room. "We only pay twenty dollars a month for this place.

"I got my first paycheck this week," he said, "and do you know what I got? I got $39.90. And by the time they sliced off the dough for taxes and insurance, I had thirty-four bucks left to take home. Can you imagine that? Thirty-four bucks a week, only fourteen more than when I started as a messenger-boy for General Motors, twenty-two years ago. Isn't that a laugh? It's like starting all over again now."

Joe's wife unconsciously folded and unfolded her hands. "Thirty-four dollars a week used to be good money, Joe," she said cheerfully. "When we got married five years ago, it was wonderful money."

She relisted everything they had bought with his old salary—all the new furniture, the clothes, the car.

"But what can you buy with it now?" asked Joe. "It

477

goes like that," and he snapped his fingers. "Before the war, we'd go shopping on a Saturday, and we'd buy all the groceries we needed for a whole week for only five bucks," he said. "Now it costs us at least fifteen a week for food alone, sometimes twenty." Then he picked up the paper and looked at the headlines. "And if you read all the papers," he said, "you'd think that all us workers are just a bunch of Reds if we go out on strike to try to get thirty percent more wages. Me, I'm a registered Democrat, and twelve bucks more a week isn't gonna make me a millionaire."

There was no gravy job waiting for Joe when he came back to General Motors. Instead of his old job, assembling 250 window regulators an hour, he was made a bender operator.

"But that was O.K. with me," he added. "I didn't want to be an assembler anymore. It gets damn monotonous doing the same job day after day after day for so many years."

What Joe did object to, though, was getting ten cents an hour less on this job. Ten cents an hour means eighty cents a day, four dollars less a week. That would pay for most of his monthly gas and electric bill, or for the telephone, or for the gasoline every week, or for one-third of the interest on his insurance.

They were both quiet, thinking about that, and then Joe spoke, sounding bitter:

"Do you know how much money we've got saved up in the bank now?" he asked. He stretched out his words slowly. "We don't even have enough money to buy me a new suit. We just don't have a goddam."

Then it was in a strained, hard voice that Joe said, "Now, get this straight. I don't want to go out on strike. I'm not gonna make any money while I'm striking. But if the company won't give us any more money, then the strike is the only weapon we've got left to use.

"I'm not asking for the moon," said Joe. "I just want to make a decent living."

*   *   *

"It isn't as if there aren't any empty apartments in this town," said an Air Corps veteran who still wore his uniform. "I was talkin' to a real-estate friend of mine and he told me there's supposed to be a twenty-five percent turnover of apartments in this town every year, war or no
478

war," he said, beginning to get angry. "It's just that a lot of sonofabitch superintendents won't rent you an apartment, unless you slip them a couple of hundred bucks first. I know a guy who shelled out five hundred for his place. And the landlords just don't seem to pay any attention to what's going on."

"Look, we just got married a couple of months ago, and my wife has to sleep at the YWCA and me at the YMCA. What kind of marriage is that, anyway?

"Listen, mister, I don't want sympathy. I just want a place to live."

"My son, Sammy, doesn't want to come home. He lost both legs at Anzio, and he says he won't come home until we move to some other neighborhood. You see, he was born and raised in this neighborhood and everybody knows him and he just doesn't want any pity . . ."

"It's the same old story," said the corporal with the battle stars. "You fight a goddam war and you finally come home and everybody slaps your back and tells you what a wonderful job you did and all that shit, but when it comes to really doing something, then nobody's home. Nobody seems to know from nothing. All you get is words."

From there, the talk shifted to solutions. Nobody seemed to be very happy about the idea of living in prefabricated houses in Flushing, even if it was temporary. It was too much like the old Army barracks all over again, they said. Oh, they'd live there all right, they'd live anywhere, but it just wasn't the kind of thing they used to dream about in those water-filled foxholes. The same went for the plan of converting substandard flats into something livable by installing toilets and hot water. One quiet little man said that, the way he understood it, the reason for the big delay in building was that construction materials were expensive now, and all the builders were waiting until costs went down.

"That's another reason why it's difficult to get apartments," said one man in a low voice. "A lot of landlords don't advertise their apartments because they're afraid that colored people will try to rent them, and I think there's some kind of law now that you can't refuse an apartment to a man just because he's colored."

"All we've got is six hundred apartments," said the interviewer. "I can't understand why the state and the city didn't plan this a long time ago. They knew it was coming."

*   *   *

Nobody thought Pfc. Franklyn Paul Sandholm coul
live.

He had a big hole in his belly, where a large chunk of
50-pound frag bomb had ripped through, cutting his blad
der and small intestines, tearing through his rectum. An
other fragment sheared away part of his arm.

That was ten minutes to ten, Sunday morning, Decem
ber 9, 1943, in the outskirts of San Pietro, where Pfc. Sand
holm and eight buddies were surveying advance position
for the guns of A Battery, 131st Field Artillery, and 1
ME–109's had suddenly swooped out of the clouds an
plastered the whole area, killing one out of the eight
wounding seven.

But today, after passing through one painful crisis afte
another on the operating table, absorbing bottles and bot
tles of slow-dripping blood plasma and spending fifty-fiv
days in bed, urinating through a tube, Sandholm wa
home again.

When you're stretched out on a hospital bed for week
and you can't move, what do you daydream about?

"You can always get a job as rural mail-carrier, an
Dad still wants us to live on the farm. Darling, you know
you can still do a lot of things you like to do on the farm
You can still drive the tractor." That Chicago kid in th
next bed would think he was crazy, if he told him he'
been daydreaming about a tractor. Yet, he had. Often
Anybody back home in Red Oak, Ia., would understan
the way he felt about it. The tractor was a symbol of hi
whole life. He had taken it apart and put it together s
many times, he knew every screw in it. Driving it all da
long in the fields, it was almost as if it were part of hi
own body. Chicago wouldn't understand that. Just as *h*
could never understand how several hundred people coul
live in one big house for years and still not be neighborly

There were 5,476 people in Red Oak, and he kne
every one of them. He could picture them right now, si
ting on their porches, swaying slowly back and forth i
their rocking chairs. And he could see them smiling an
waving at him, while he walked down the street. Some
body once told him you could measure a man's life by hi
real friends. How many real friends did Chicago have?

But not all his friends were coming back. That one day
when Company M got swallowed up at Faïd Pass. Go

480

Almighty, Company M was Red Oak. All the baseball teams and the drugstore cowboys and the whole high-school graduating class. He still had that newspaper clipping that said if New York City had lost a proportionate amount of men in a single action, it would have totaled 20,000. But even then, the shock wouldn't be so bad in New York; it would be just a list of names. In Red Oak, every name meant a certain house on a certain street. It was such a small town . . .

* * *

He walked slowly out of the farmhouse.

Before he knew it, he had his overalls on, and had gone into the barn and said hello to May and Nellie. He had raised them since they were colts, and they recognized his voice and whinnied at him. Then Rover smelled him and jumped at him and licked him all over. Rover was sixteen years old. That's pretty old for a dog. He had thought he'd be dead.

And then he went out in the field and saw the tractor . . .

At the desk near the door, right next to a USO sign, the thin girl in the bright dress smiled when she said, "It's kinda dead around here now. You should have come yesterday. We had a big dance yesterday." She told how good the band was, and how big the crowd was, and that there were almost as many veterans around as there were soldiers.

"That's because these boys here in Washington just don't have too many other places to get together," she said. "This isn't the Old South, but it's still a long way from New York City, and a Negro is still a Negro.

"Look at him," said the girl at the desk. "That's Chester Whiteside. He's been out of the Army since August and he still comes here pretty regularly. He's lonely."

"A few days ago, I bumped into one of those seven guys in my platoon—three of those seven got Silver Stars," said Chester. "This one guy had all kinds of ribbons, but he was bitter as hell. He said he'd just come back from the South, and it didn't seem to make any difference if you fought or you didn't fight; you were still only a black boy.

"Myrtle and I are going to Liberia," said Chester

481

quietly. "We're going as soon as we can, as soon as I can finish this mortician's course." He smiled faintly. "I'll be the only mortician in Liberia.

"I'm so glad we're going," he said. "It would have been different, if I found America different. I didn't expect any revolutionary changes in the attitude toward Negroes. All I wanted was a sign in the wind, just the smallest sign that things were getting better instead of worse. If Congress had only passed an anti-lynch law or a permanent FEPC or something, anything . . .

"Maybe Myrtle and I are doing the wrong thing," he continued, rubbing his hands nervously. "Maybe we should stay here and stick it out, and maybe, God knows, our kids might some day be treated like first-class Americans, instead of third-class dirt.

"But I guess we're selfish; we don't want to wait that long. In fact, we'll probably give up our American citizenship and become French citizens, like a lot of my friends are doing.

"You see," he said quietly, stretching out his words, "it isn't a question whether Myrtle and I are American citizens, or French citizens; it's whether or not we're human beings."

*   *   *

This was the perfectly planned town of Richland, Wash., 15,000 people living in one of the three homes of American atomic energy—no slums, no crime, no poor, no shortages. Everything reborn, brand-new, off an architect's drawing board. The Town of Tomorrow.

The thing that hurt him most, said Lester Fishback when he came home from the Pacific, was when he got off the bus. He didn't know where he was. It was just completely different. Everything. He was so lost, he had to ask an MP to help him find his old farm. Then when he got there, he was sorry he came. The grapes and asparagus were all dried up, just as if somebody had walked off and left them, and there was this huge powerline over the place where the house was. All of it dry and dead.

But it had to be done. Didn't he say he was in the Pacific? If it wasn't for the atomic bomb, he might be dead somewhere in Japan right now. Wasn't that true?

"Yeah," he said, nodding his head slowly. "I guess that's true.

"Hell, you can't blame the vets here for being bitter. Christ, how would you feel if you gave up the best years of your life and then came here to work for a guy who was making twice as much money as you, even though he wasn't any older or any smarter than you. Guys who came here to get out of the war and sit on their fannies on these push jobs. You know what any vet thinks of those guys."

To change the subject, what about the atomic bomb? He was in contact with more veterans than anybody else, what did they think about it? How much had it changed their lives, their plans, their thoughts?

"Well, to be honest with you, most of the guys don't think much about it anymore. At first, they were all scared to death to talk about it on account of the security. Now, they're just tired of talking about it. It's just another job. They're bored."

Not Emmett Elliott, though. Emmett was a fireman on the No. 2 truck.

"No. 2 only goes out on the big fires." He grinned. "Frankly, I haven't been on a fire yet. This town's so new and clean, there just aren't any fires."

"It's a hell of a lot better than sawing grass," said the young man from Moberly, Mo. Still, he was also qualified as an electrical repairman, a diesel operator, a railroad construction worker. But he knew lots of skilled veterans who were doing unskilled jobs because they didn't have the seniority. But none of them could kick much; they were all getting higher wages than most skilled workers outside Richmond.

"Now look at me, I'm happy. I almost couldn't be happier."

He had come here immediately after his Army discharge, because his wife was working here. Together, they had got a new Type-A house, with two bedrooms, three rooms downstairs, two rooms upstairs, all for $47 a month. And he had fine, friendly neighbors, too.

Did they ever talk much about atomic energy?

"Not anymore. But I'll tell you this. Everybody's sure a lot happier since we're converting to peacetime stuff. A lot of folks didn't feel just right about making bombs when there wasn't any war going on."

Sitting in the spectator seats, watching the bowling, the young man in the old combat jacket blurted out a quick answer to a pointed question:

"Confidentially, I'm getting the hell out of this town as

soon as I can. They say it's a model city—well, it's too damn model for me."

To him, it was a small town with a small mind. He couldn't get over it: people working on the most important single thing in the world, and most of them didn't know what in the hell it was all about. Even worse, most of them didn't care. Just another job. Good money, cheap rent, stocked stores, comfortable homes. They couldn't see ahead of their noses, or they didn't want to see. He knew lots of guys who came here and got fed up and pulled out.

What bothered him most was the mentality of the town, so similar to the small town he came from, and he thought it would be so different.

"Here's what I mean. Sure, the bomb shortened the war and saved my life, but some day soon it might kill me . . . I tell you, it's just as if they don't want to think about it, as if they're pushing it away from their minds . . ."

His voice lowered. "Do you know another reason I want to get away from here?" Unconsciously, he cracked his knuckles. "I'm scared," he said. "The whole thing scares the pants off me."

*   *   *

His name was Epthemios Papadopoulos, he said, but everybody called him Kelly. Even in the Army, they used to call him Kelly. Where the hell they got Kelly from, he didn't know.

He was a slim, dark young man with a big "W" on his sweater, and he looked too young to be a bartender.

Not only was he the bartender, he explained, but he was the manager of the whole clubhouse, had all the responsibility for the money, the ordering and everything. "I even sweep up the place."

His face was serious now. "The way I look at it, you can always have your fun. But when a rainy day comes along, you don't want to be caught with your pants down. So when opportunity knocked on my door, I grabbed it."

He was gesturing with his right hand. Suddenly he stared at it, straightened it, and tried to hold it out steady, trying not to show the strain on his face. But his whole hand kept shaking visibly, and finally he put it down quickly. He tried to smile. "It used to be a lot worse. This job's been good for me."

The Army had kept him in the hospital for a long time

484

efore they discharged him. Then he was O.K. for a
while, until he started school. He'd get into a nervous
sweat, waiting for the teachers to call on him, trying to do
his homework, wondering what good it was. Too much
pressure built up inside of him and he got sick again. Finally, he quit.

"So there I was, free as a bird. But I didn't know what
the hell to do with myself. That's when I got this bright
idea."

The bright idea was to hitchhike around the country.
Plan out a route with stop-offs at the different places his
buddies lived, then start moving again.

He looked toward the door. A few more customers
were coming in. Epthemios went on talking. "And like I
said, this town is good for me. I'm not so nervous like I
used to be. So I guess I'll stick here for a while."

He carefully examined his fingers.

"—until I get sick again."

He carefully examined his fingers, again. "Then I'm
pulling out. I can't stand it when people start feeling sorry
for me."

*　　*　　*

"This is for me," said the young cab driver, smiling and
stretching in front of Chicago's Wrigley Building. "Nobody telling me what to do. So you can put me down in
your notebook that Tony DeSalvo, formerly of the United
States Army, is now a very happy guy."

*　　*　　*

A beardless young man, wearing a yellow sweater and a
porkpie hat, was staring at a huge poster inside the Army
Recruiting Information room. Splashed all over it were
pictures of soldiers having fun in different parts of the
world. Then, in big type, the message: "ENLIST NOW . . .
VACATION, TRAVEL, SECURITY, EDUCATION, CAREER, GOOD
PAY, LIBERAL RETIREMENT BENEFITS . . . THE BEST JOB
IN THE WORLD."

Sitting on the sidelines, watching everything wistfully,
Felix Bezubek told how much he wanted to reenlist. "If I
was single, I'd jump at it," he said. "I'd be right there on
that line with those guys. Honest to God, I would," he
said, slapping his knee.

"And why not?" he went on. "You don't have to worry any more about somebody else's cousin taking your job; you know that your wife is gonna get a paycheck every month, rain or shine, and no matter what they say, it's a good, healthy life." He smiled weakly. "But my wife doesn't see it that way. She says she waited three years for me to get out of the Army, and now she wants me to stay out. You can't really blame her. She was pretty lucky. But then, I guess all women are like that."

Things were picking up, said the recruiting sergeant. They had been getting more than 400 a day for the past week. Mostly veterans and young guys.

"Why am I reenlisting? Why do you think?" exploded Larry Gilchrist, who was still wearing his uniform and a Pacific Theater Ribbon. "Because I can't eat promises and my wife can't and my kids can't, that's why. I've tried the civilian life for three months now and you can have it. When you've got a family, you need a job that pays enough for you all to live on. And I couldn't find it, that's all."

A big, heavy Negro came into the room, looked around for a seat and finally sat down next to two Puerto Ricans. He was thirty-nine-year-old William Blackwell, he said, and if he couldn't be a mechanic in civilian life, then he'd be one in the Army. "Because I'd feel kinda wasted, starting all over again as a porter for twenty-five dollars a week."

James Pegram said he used to be with the 870th AAA Battalion on Okinawa. "Hell, I remember when I was sweating out discharge. All I wanted was to get away from the brass hats and the red tape and the regimentation and the chicken and be a civilian again."

He paused. "So now I'm a civilian. So what. I used to think the discharge button would mean something, but it don't mean a damn thing. Everybody's got one. There's lots of places where you can buy a button for a buck and nobody asks any questions. I couldn't find a job, couldn't find a place to live— What's the good of that button? So now I'm thinkin' that maybe the Army wasn't so bad, after all."

*   *   *

"We have chicken-stealers and hog-stealers! Horse-stealers and auto-stealers! But the lowest, dirtiest of all are our election-stealers . . ."

"To the GI Patriots, Athens, Tennessee: 'Thank you indeed for restoring the faith in America which so many of us had lost. Keep pitching and firing when necessary . . .'"

"YOU CHOSE THE EVIL WAY . . ."

"We don't expect any bullets to fly up here in Brooklyn, but the political machine here is a tight-fisted organization in full control of everything, and we will only win if all the veterans turn out and give us a hand . . .'"

"I congratulate you in the memory of my son, who lies buried in the South Pacific . . ."

"We have returned from the war to find our home-grown Hitlers . . . Most of us didn't care . . . A few of us griped and let it go at that . . . You and your friends are apparently the first ones who had the guts to do something about it."

"It was like Nazi Germany here," said thirty-seven-year-old, graying, Navy veteran Ralph Duggan. "Cantrell's deputies were nothing but a lot of swaggering, strutting storm-troopers, drunk most of the time, beating up our citizens for the slightest reason. Know what they did? In elections, they just kicked out the poll-watchers or else they took the ballot boxes to be counted in the privacy of Cantrell's bank. They even used guns and blackjacks, back in 1940, to prevent 400 people from voting."

For three years, lawyer Duggan pushed the case until the Circuit Court jury brought in a Guilty verdict against three Cantrell deputies. But the judge simply fined the deputies one cent each, told them to be good boys, and let them go free. The U.S. Supreme Court wouldn't rule on it, said it was a state matter. As for the State Supreme Court, everybody knew it was packed with Crump-picked men. So, legally, they were licked.

"It wasn't really a town anymore," declared former GI Jim Buttram. "It was a jail."

Buttram thought about it often. Here he was, a rifleman who had fought all through Tunisia, Sicily and Normandy, getting wounded twice, fighting for a world concept of democracy, and there wasn't even any democracy in his own hometown. It didn't make sense.

Buttram and his friends started a nonpartisan Veterans League, collected $8,000 by calling people in the telephone book. Eight thousand dollars for newspaper and radio advertising, for loudspeakers, for handbills thrown from Piper Cubs, for gasoline to go from precinct to precinct. The old-fashioned campaign of buttonholing, doorbell-ringing. And always, in every speech, every handbook, every radio program, they repeated over and over again, "YOUR VOTE WILL BE COUNTED AS CAST."

They hammered like that every day and the town buzzed with it. At first, Cantrell tried to laugh it off, then got annoyed. Finally, he got mad enough to make his first big mistake. He hired radio time to answer the charges. He denied everything, even the most obvious corruption.

"The charge of open gambling and selling whiskey over the bar is absolutely false; the allegation that GI's have been arrested and their poll-tax receipts taken away from them, does not contain a word of truth . . . For the past ten years, McMinn County elections have been cleaner than they have been in the history of the county . . ."

The whole town listened. To them, it was funnier than Fibber McGee. Who did he think he was kidding? For hours after each Cantrell broadcast, the party lines were full of the laughter of the town.

With their laughter came more hope:

"You know what, Tom, those boys may do it. Did you hear about how they cut down Cantrell's list of absentee voters from 1,200 to 400? They just cut out the names of all those people who were dead and buried. These boys are mad, and they're not scared. Maybe . . ."

The "terrible thing" started early on election morning. While long lines of people waited to vote outside the Third Precinct polling place at Etowah, the next GI election-watcher, named Evans, said to the election judge, "I'd like to look inside that ballot box first, if you don't mind." The judge smiled, "Oh, you would, would you?"

Two minutes later, several deputies dragged a badly beaten Evans to jail. The judge appointed a Cantrell man to take his place.

But the real trouble started that afternoon, on Athens' North Jackson Street. Tom Gillespie came to vote in the waterworks building of the Eleventh Precinct, the same place he had been voting for years. Cantrell Deputy Windy Wise held Gillespie's thin ballot to the light, saw whom he was voting for, and said, "Get the hell outa here . . ."

When old Gillespie protested, Windy slugged him with his brass knuckles. Gillespie staggered, started running, and Windy yelled to the other deputies, "Grab that nigger . . ." Then he pulled out his gun and shot Gillespie in the back.

Shortly afterwards, at the same polling place, Mrs. Vestal and a group of parents and teachers, told election judge Karl Neil that they wanted to stay and watch the ballot-counting. Mrs. Vestal's son, Ed, had to stand still and listen to Neil tell his mother to get out and stay out—there was a gun sticking in Ed's back.

Later, though, gun or no gun, Vestal and Charles Scott, Jr., both objected when Karl Neil placed two deputies so as to hide the ballot box. Neil just laughed at them.

Suddenly, there was a crash of breaking glass, and women screamed. A crowd of several hundred people tensed while they watched Scott and Vestal stumbling forward in the street, their faces covered with blood.

Instinctively, the crowd surged forward, curving to absorb Scott and Vestal, pushing toward the broken glass window. But fifteen deputies quickly formed a semicircle in front of the building, pointing their guns at the crowd to keep them back.

"Oh, my God, here it comes," a woman screeched.

Within minutes, the ballot box had been dumped into one of the waiting cars. The deputies then piled in, and the cars drove back to the jail, leaving behind a noisy, confused crowd.

Almost at the same time, in a restaurant in the Twelfth Precinct on North White Street, election-watcher Bill Hairell asked a young girl how old she was. "I'm seventeen."

"Well, you're under age, you can't vote . . ."

Deputy Minus Wilburn scowled. "Hell she can't." When they carried Bill to jail, his skull had been split wide open by Wilburn's blackjack, and his face was all bloody where it had been kicked.

It was a different street scene on West Washington Street, in front of the Ess-and-Kay Tire Company garage, where the Kennedy boys had beaten three insulting deputies while a big crowd watched, cheered and jeered:

"You boys ain't so tough once you lose your guns . . ."

Four more deputies wandered by, and the three Kennedy boys grabbed them, too, this time some of the crowd joining in to black a few eyes, rip some clothes. This time, the crowd cheered when seven deputies, minus their badges, guns and pants, were forced into several cars to be let out at the city limits. But there were still amost two hundred other Cantrell deputies scattered around the county.

Another sweating deputy was sitting and counting votes in the Niota schoolhouse, while several hundred citizens solemnly looked on. Earlier, Cantrell's deputies had tried to clear the polling place of watchers, but the people simply swarmed in and overwhelmed the deputies. Then somebody read aloud the part from State Election Code 2087, permitting any citizen to watch the ballot counting.

Elsewhere in Athens, a citizen read aloud the section from the Declaration of Rights in the Tennessee Constitution, "that government, being instituted for the common benefit, the doctrine of nonresistance against arbitrary power and oppression is absurd, slavish and destructive of the good and happiness of mankind."

That was the thinking that night of the big crowd of angry, loud-talking people who marched down to the jail, where they stopped and waited, while one of them shouted out in the darkness, "Bring out those ballot boxes. . . ."

From inside the jail, a deputy laughed. "Why don't you call the law . . . ?" The answer came back quickly, cutting the laughter short, "There is no law in McMinn County."

It was a long, stretched-out silence that lasted several seconds and then a deputy yelled, "Aw, go to hell . . ."

Just then, somebody inside the jail fired at the crowd, hitting an ex-Marine named Gunter in the leg. The crowd scattered. From behind a hedge across the street, somebody fired at the jail. The Battle of Athens had started at ten minutes after nine.

"Come on, get guns . . . Get some guns."

They came from everywhere. Farmers with old shotguns that hadn't been fired in years, vets with 45's and rifles, kids with BB-guns. Other men had broken into the armory for more arms and ammunition. A machine gun sat on top of the movie theater overlooking the jail. Another 30-caliber was parked behind the hedge near the post office across the street.

"At first, I thought it was just a lot of firecrackers going off," remembered Mrs. Wilson, who lived in the white house facing the jail. "But these boys came in with rifles and told us we better lie down on the floor. They were firing from the kitchen window, and we could hear the bullets hitting the drainpipe, and the plaster falling down. One bullet hit the faucet, and turned on the water full

490

force. It even scared the boys who were shooting. My four kids were all crying so, I took them down to the Southern Soda Shop. Everybody there was scared, too."

It was like a Wild West show, with a mob of people milling in the side streets, a few of them ducking the ricochets to come and get a peek now and then, racing away when the machine guns opened up. Chuck Redfern had the town's grandstand seat. Chuck was reporting the battle all night long over WLAR and the window of the radio station overlooked the whole scene. To get personal quotes, Chuck would occasionally race downstairs and talk to some of the men doing the shooting. One young vet told him, "I ain't had so much fun since Guadalcanal." An older man said, more seriously, "We're gonna have a brighter tomorrow."

Finally, somebody informed Chuck, "We're gonna dynamite the jail . . . Tell that over WLAR . . ."

It was past two that morning when word of the dynamiting went through the crowd, and a woman started screaming on Gettys Street, "Don't do it . . . I've got a boy in that jail . . ." Another woman crept behind a nearby hedge and yelled, at the top of her lungs, to her husband inside the jail, "Don't be a fool, Bill . . . Come on out . . . You want to get killed . . . ?"

The rest of the crowd cheered at the news, except for some old people who were praying aloud, *"Our Father who art in heaven . . ."*

An ex-GI, who knew how, wiggled close and threw a single stick of dynamite, purposely short. After a long interval, with a second warning to the deputies inside, the second charge, two sticks, landed closer. The next one, three sticks, still closer, and Chuck Redfern watched the blast bounce the needle off his recording machine and told the radio audience, "It won't be long now."

The concussion of the last charge rocked the building. Before the smoke cleared away, the deputies were yelling hysterically, "O.K. . . . We's giving up . . . We's coming out . . ."

"They were scared crazy," said one of the veterans who went into the jail with the first bunch. "They were crawling around on the floor, some of them crying, some of them saying their prayers. One of them grabbed me around the knees and begged me to save him. They all thought we were going to kill them right away . . ."

They had good reason to think so. Outside, some two

dozen new cars, belonging to the deputies, were being hacked, overturned, burned.

Cantrell, Mansfield, the two State Highway Patrolmen, and many of the others had managed to sneak away, leaving about thirty-five deputies in the jail. When the thirty-five were marched out single-file, their hands stuck high in the air, the crowd yelled, "String 'em up . . ."

"Kill the bastards . . ."

"Turn 'em loose and let's see how fast they can run . . ."

Quickly, the hysteria, the car burning, and the mounting excitement of deep-rooted hate was turning the crowd into a mob, a mob ready to do anything.

"I want your attention . . . I want your attention . . . Listen to me . . ."

It was Ralph Duggan, standing on top of a car, yelling as loudly as he could. Slowly, the crowd quieted.

"We've won our victory . . . The votes will be counted as cast . . . There won't be any more gangster rule in Athens. . . . But we're not murderers . . . If we treat these thugs the way they treated us, then we're as bad as they are . . . I ask you go to home peacefully . . . Remember . . . The whole country is watching what we're doing here tonight . . ."

The tension of tight silence broke. Slowly, reluctantly, the crowd started breaking up. But there was still a small knot of people around the much-hated Minus Wilburn, and by the time Duggan got there, somebody had slashed Wilburn's neck. Duggan used finger pressure to stop him from bleeding to death.

By this time, Cantrell's Election Commissioner, George Woods, had called from Chattanooga, promising to come into Athens and sign the election certificates, if they would protect him. Frank Cantrell called soon afterwards, from Etowah, to concede the election for his brother Paul, who was hiding in a church basement, somewhere in Athens.

492

Meanwhile, the six tampered-with ballot boxes had been thrown out; the other six had shown the GI's elected overwhelmingly by more than 2 to 1.

Sunday morning was a warm, clear day, and the men had put away their guns and were pushing baby carriages. And when people went to church that morning, they walked right by the jail, instead of detouring like they usually did. The next day, the paper commented, "The people went to church thankful that the gangsters had gone, thankful that nobody had been killed, thankful that the voice of the people could again be heard."

The mail came in from all over the country, and Jim Buttram got most of it. The letters were full of warm praise and patriotic fervor and strong backslapping, but none of it meant as much to Buttram as a much-folded piece of paper that he always carried in his wallet. Datelined 5th Service Command Separation Center, Buttram had underlined these words, "If you see intolerance and hate, speak out against them . . . Make your individual voices heard, not for selfish things, but for honor and decency among men, for the rights of all people. Remember, too, that *no* American can afford to be disinterested in any part of his Government whether it is county, city, state or nation . . ."

* * *

The man stuck his head into the classroom, and said that he was sorry to interrupt again, but the photographer wanted three more students for another picture in the Sloan Room. The teacher stared at him, then shrugged his shoulders and wearily motioned to several students near the door. Two of them picked up their crutches and slowly maneuvered themselves out of the room. The third got to his feet and walked out, stiff-legged, the wood bumping against the floor, making a lot of noise.

"Why do they have to take all these pictures, anyway?" a student whispered loudly. "Just to show that some more people without legs are going to school? Why don't they leave us alone?"

An older man, in a heavy sweater, sitting next to him, just smirked and said in a low, bitter voice, "Jeezus, fella, they've got to take pictures. They want to show us looking happy, so that the public will know how wonderful America is treating its disabled war heroes."

493

Some of the men in the nearby seats listened and snickered. When class was over, they all went outside for a smoke, and some of the men were still talking about the pictures.

"Why do they always take all the pictures in that fancy, upholstered Sloan Room?" one of them asked. "Sometimes, they oughta take a few in our dumpy little classroom. People ought to see how badly it needs a paint job and some good lighting."

Somebody then remembered how a photographer posed some amputees dancing at a hospital party. "They danced just long enough for the photographer to take his shot, and then they hurried back to their crutches. But the photographer wasn't interested in that; he'd got his phony picture."

The ten minutes were up, and then men tossed their cigarette butts into the slushy snow and filed back into class. Their teacher was waiting for them. He was a young, serious-faced naval officer, who was teaching them Veteran Counseling. Their project that day, he said, was to have two students act out a practice interview. One student was to be the counselor, and the other, a maladjusted veteran.

Quickly, the two men took their places on the platform in front of the class. A few of the students started ribbing the actors, but the ribbing stopped as soon as the student acting as the maladjusted veteran said, "I think I've been ill-advised. They sent me here to the American University to learn how to become a veterans' counselor. Now I'm not sure I want to be one."

The room was hushed when the counselor asked him why he felt that way.

"Well, they've got all these men who come and tell us that we'll never make much money and how we'll have to work eighteen hours a day. Well, this is a tough course. We're learning a year's work in twelve weeks, and we hardly get enough money allowance to live on. I got a wife, and at least when I graduate, I want to make a decent living. And I don't want to work eighteen hours a day; I want to work only eight."

Spontaneously, the whole classroom of thirty-five students started clapping. A few even thumped on the floor with their crutches, and one student excitedly banged his wooden hand on the side of his chair. Their applause stopped only when the acting counselor asked something else. He was asking why the veteran came to the American University in the first place.

"Nobody told me all these things before I got here," said the veteran. "But anyway, I came because I'm disabled, and I wanted to help other disabled veterans."

"So he came to the disabled American University," somebody said loudly, in the rear of the room. The whole class again broke into a roar, and the young teacher nervously tried to get them back into order again.

The students were still in a high flush of excitement when they went to their English class, a half hour later. As soon as they sat down, though, their excitement seemed to fade quickly. There was no horseplay here. Dr. Don Wolfe was one of their favorite teachers; they had raised a stink when the school had tried to transfer him into another section.

Wolfe was telling them how continually amazed he was at the quality of their writing, and that he was going to read from some of their themes.

He read in a sensitive voice, as if everything he read had happened to him.

"They belonged, and I was an outsider," he began from one of them. "How I ached for home. I walked the streets with that throbbing ache inside of me. How I hated anybody who had security . . ."

There was no applause, no comment. The class was quiet.

The next excerpt was about a soldier who had lost his right hand, telling in painful detail how he learned to tie his pajama strings and his shoelaces, and how he shaved himself, and how long it took him to learn to write left-handed, so he could write a love letter himself, instead of dictating it to the Red Cross girl.

Following that, there was a series of combat stories, one of which ended with, "And nobody knows any other human being well enough to call him a coward."

Talking things over after class, Dr. Wolfe kept thumbing through the piles of themes. "I've got the whole war right here on my desk," he said. "They've scraped their souls and poured themselves out, things they probably never told anybody before."

Thumbing through the papers again, he picked out one entitled "A Tough Battle: A New Life," by Irving Peltz. "This man lost an arm, a leg and an eye at Anzio," Wolfe said.

At the bottom of page 5, Wolfe read:

"I wanted to prove to myself and to everybody else that,

even though I was disabled, I could still do anything that anyone else could. My biggest obstacle was people. Yes, I said people! They practically broke down everything that I was trying to accomplish. I'd walk down the street and almost everybody would stop and stare. On the train, bus or trolley, it was always the same. In restaurants, they'd look up from their food. Damn them all! Can't they leave a wounded veteran alone? Haven't they got any sense? Don't they realize they make me feel like a freak? Why the hell can't they mind their own business?"

There was little noise or movement in the big room where the seven Congressmen had been sitting for days, listening to a long line of witnesses tell what they knew about artificial limbs. It was the Labor Subcommittee on Aid to the Physically Hadicapped. Peltz was on the witness stand.

"I got the limb," he was saying, "and it was like a two-ton truck. It kept irritating my stump, kept holding me back from getting well. As for the arm, it's of no use. The only reason I wear it is because it balances me in walking, because I have a leg off, too. Nine out of ten amputees don't wear it at all. And the glass eye they gave me wasn't even a good fit. We've known about the need for better artificial limbs since World War I, but it seems to me that nobody has considered it important enough to do anything about it."

"Here's a couple more," said Dr. Wolfe. "They're both by a boy named John Regan. He lost his leg at Normandy. In the middle of one of them, he wrote this:

" 'My leg is torn to shreds from my knee to my hip. A bone sticks through this mess, pointing upward; I try to push it down, but the pain is too great. I notice a colorless fluid flowing out; it reminds me of chicken broth. There is also an aroma coming from the wound, like that of a freshly roasted piece of beef. I try to stop the blood, but without success. I become aware of the intense pain now. I am sweating and I am awfully thirsty. I start to rave out loud . . . Oh, God, help us . . . Our Father who art in heaven . . . Oh, please, God, help . . .' "

Regan's second theme was shorter, It started:

"As I look around the room in this third-rate boarding house, there alongside the bureau is this *thing* . . . a leather cup, straps and buckles dropping from it. Below this cup, the flesh-colored part and cap, and on its foot, a brown sock and an oxblood shoe. I've called this wooden leg a lot of things . . . Oh, what the hell, a leg isn't everything. You've got to keep on living."

As soon as Representative Kelly introduced him, Regan showed the Committee just how his leg worked, with all the belts and straps. He told them how tough it was to sit down, that it was outmoded a hundred percent, because it was the same leg that amputees got twenty-five years ago. Then he told how it weighed thirteen pounds, and he never wore it anymore because it was too heavy. "It seems I wear it under the same strain as if I were running with two legs," he said.

"I realize I have a very bad amputation," he continued. "I realize that I'm very lucky to be alive, but I feel that something should be done to make these legs lighter. All I ask for is a limb I can get around on comfortably. If the government and private companies can build a B–29, surely they can do this job. Remember, there are 16,000 amputees coming out of this war."

When Representative Kelly thanked Regan and all the others for coming, a veteran named Robert Rogers jumped up and said, "We thank you for listening. Most people are scared to listen and say, 'Jesus Christ, let the Army look after you.' Of course they do nothing about it. We certainly thank you for listening."

Outside the small red buildings of American University, the sidewalk was dangerously icy. Some of the students were slowly crossing the slushy street, but most of them were still eating in the small luncheonette.

Several of the men were talking about a story in the newspapers, telling how the government had indicted forty-five manufacturing firms of artificial limbs for agreeing on "identical and noncompetitive prices," forcing amputees to pay several hundred dollars for a limb. The story also mentioned that the government had decided to spend a million dollars that year for prosthetic research.

A short, chunky man said it was about time, but that he wouldn't believe it until it really happened. Another student said that's the way it was, that nobody ever got anything unless he yelled for it. He mentioned the Grievance Committee they had formed, to get heat for their cold classrooms, and the books that the Veterans Administration had paid for, long ago. They had also bitched about the constant changing of teachers. Like the one teacher who had wandered in, slightly bewildered. He told the class that he had just received this assignment the day before, and what would they like him to teach them?

"I wish somebody would get up and yell about the allowance they give us, and ask how we're supposed to live on it. If some of those fat Congressmen would come and take a look at the rathole my wife and I live in, and if they tried eating here in Washington on ninety cents a day —maybe then they'd get busy and do something," he said.

A tall man with one arm just laughed. "What the hell do you expect?" he asked. "V-J Day was a long time ago, and people don't want to hear anything more about the war. As for cripples, nobody likes to hear about cripples. It bothers people."

There was a long pause, and nobody seemed to know what to say after that, so they started getting up, paid their checks and walked out.

The cashier watched them leave, and shook his head. "They don't kid around much anymore," he said, "I've seen five classes so far, and it's always been the same thing. When they first come here, they're all excited about the lucky break, and they're always tripping each other with their wooden legs and then busting out laughing. I remember once they told me about this one guy who fell asleep at a party, and the guys got all the girls to write their names and telephone numbers in lipstick on his wooden leg. When he woke up and saw the lipstick, he wiped it off; later he was sorry, because he wanted a date."

He rearranged the chewing gum. "But that doesn't last long," he said. "They get nervous after a while, and they don't laugh much. It takes three months sometimes before they get their first check, and some of them go around half-starved all the time."

A customer walked up, paid his check, picked up a toothpick, and left. The cashier was still thinking. "I've been wondering," he said slowly. "They must be awful bitter about the world."

*   *   *

Young Ray Clutts stood outside of his small wooden house, cracked his big mule whip and laughed. "Happy? Sure, I'm happy. I'm home, ain't I?"

Home is Coulterville, Ill., a coal-mining town, population: 1,284.

"The point is," said Clutts, "we coal miners don't expect to be as rich as Rockefeller or as poor as Job's turkey. All we want is a comfortable place to live and a chance to do an honest day's work for a decent living wage. And that's what we finally got here. If those newspapers and politicians want another war, let them do the fighting next time."

He didn't like cities, didn't like traveling. What he wanted, he had.

"Come to think of it, mister, there is one more thing I want in my lifetime. Only one thing. No more wars . . ."